A Guide to Critical Legal Studies

A Guide to
Critical Legal Studies

Mark Kelman

Harvard University Press
Cambridge, Massachusetts
and London, England

Library of Congress Cataloging-in-Publication Data
Kelman, Mark.
  A guide to critical legal studies.

  Includes bibliographies and index.
  1. Law—Philosophy. 2. Sociological jurisprudence.
I. Title.
K230.K43G85   1987   340′.1   87-8504
ISBN 0-674-36755-3 (alk. paper) (cloth)
ISBN 0-674-36756-1 (paper)

Acknowledgments

Since this book was inspired by the work of participants in the Conference on Critical Legal Studies, I owe an incalculable debt to all those participants. Although the book focuses specifically on only a tiny fraction of the scholarly works produced by people associated with Critical Legal Studies, I have no doubt that both my own ideas and the views of those whose writing I discuss were forged collaboratively. The book owes whatever force it has not just to the academics who have written in the Critical tradition but also to the students and practitioners who have attended our meetings and, ultimately, to the people whose collective efforts to transform our polity give us the confidence that we do not live in an immutably bleak or unjust social world.

There are more particular debts as well. My colleagues Jerry Lopez, Bill Simon, Bob Gordon, and Tom Grey made innumerable helpful comments on the manuscript, and other colleagues, notably Tom Heller, Bob Rabin, and Paul Brest, helped me to develop ideas in the book.

Over the years, I have learned a great deal in discussions with Tom Heller and Duncan Kennedy, the participants in the Critical Legal Studies movement with whom I have had the greatest chance to spend time and whose concerns have been most similar to mine. Each has been both a source of insight and a supportive friend.

Many of the ideas presented in this book were developed in a course I taught twice at Stanford on Critical Legal Studies, and I am grateful to the students in those classes, whose comments and questions aided me significantly. In particular, Stacey Hawver, Jennifer Wright, Martin Wald, and Palma Strand stand out for their help. My colleague Bob Gordon attended the class the first year, and his participation was invaluable, both for me and for the students.

Many people helped considerably in translating an outline into a book. Susan Lubeck and John Whitelaw did terrific work as research assistants.

Mary Peabody and Jean Castle typed early drafts. Roberta Pottorff did a great job updating the manuscript, coping with footnotes, and keeping everything organized. It would be a lovely world indeed if every author had the chance to work with someone who is as fine a secretary, and as fine a person, as Roberta. Lindsay Waters, my editor at Harvard University Press, has been a great encouragement.

My greatest debt as an academic belongs to Mort Horwitz, who taught torts in my first semester at law school, a time when I wondered daily whether my pursuits were especially worthwhile. His passionate engagement as a teacher and scholar continues to inspire me with the conviction that my scholarly work and classroom efforts can really matter. Although our precise interests and specific beliefs have diverged somewhat over the years, I hope he realizes the central role he plays in my career.

Finally, Ann and Nick have been far more important to me than this book, or any imaginable book, could ever be.

Contents

Introduction

The invitation to the first annual Conference on Critical Legal Studies in 1977 gave little hint as to what the organizers thought "critical legal studies" (CLS) was or might become.[1] In a sense I suppose this was perfectly natural, since only those organizers long associated with the empiricist, generally politically reformist Law and Society movement[2] had done much of their work yet. It seems that the organizers were simply seeking to *locate* those people working either at law schools or in closely related academic settings (legal sociology, legal anthropology) with a certain vaguely perceived, general political or cultural predisposition and a relatively better defined relationship to ordinary legal academic life. At the general level they sought something akin to New Leftists, in an obviously inexact sense: people on the left at least relatively skeptical of the State Socialist regimes (although many were undoubtedly more or less sympathetic with revolutionaries arguably seeking to establish such regimes), egalitarian, in a more far-reaching sense than those committed to tax-and-transfer-based income redistribution, culturally radical, or at least unsympathetic to the furious New Right assaults on permissiveness. In terms of the cultural politics of the law schools, the people the organizers were seeking were those appalled by the routine Socratic discussions of appellate court decisions, repelled by their sterility and thorough disconnection from actual social life (their mainstream fellow teachers seemed barely to care or notice whether either arguments or case results had any impact on actual practice); repelled by the supposition that neutral and apolitical *legal* reasoning could resolve charged controversies; impatient with the idea that people freed by Rigor from a stereotypically feminized or infantilized preprofessional sentimentality must ultimately share some sober centrist ideals; put off by the hierarchical classroom style in which phony priests first crush and then bless each new group of initiates.

By the time I began this book in the fall of 1984, there had been nine large national meetings of this once tiny Conference; innumerable "summer camps" and workshops where newcomers and founders alike argue obsessively over the usual issues that have puzzled those on the academic left since the cruder Marxisms have gone out of vogue; a popular book, *The Politics of Law*,[3] published collaboratively with the National Lawyers Guild, the best-known organization of left practitioners; an increasingly lengthy underground bibliography of CLS work that would soon be only as "underground" as anything else published in the *Yale Law Journal*;[4] and a hefty symposium on the movement in the *Stanford Law Review*.[5] Yet it was still a fair question whether anyone knew what "critical legal studies" meant.

In this book I present a summary and a self-critical assessment of certain recurring themes in CLS writing on law and legal discourse that have emerged in the early years of the movement. Mine will be a rather "academic" account of what I perceive to be the most basic claims, largely about the structure and meaning of standard legal discourse, made repeatedly by certain early participants in the Conference, but I by no means suggest that I can capture the essence of all the work that has been done by people who have identified themselves with this organization (come to meetings, put themselves on a mailing list, engaged heavily in the incestuous mutual citation practices toward which "schools" of academic lawyers tend), much less identify the essence of what a "critical theory" of law might be in a more general sense. Many people associated with the movement would surely disagree with the substantive ideas I attribute to Critics generally and even with my view of the meaning of the particular works I identify as central or definitive.

Nor do I claim that anyone in particular imagined, recognized, or would now agree that his or her work was a piece of the structured jigsaw puzzle I have now assembled; it may simply be instructive to read what I see as the key early CLS works with this account in mind.

The essential picture I propose is that of a movement attempting to identify the crucial structural characteristics of mainstream legal thought as examples of something called "liberalism." While some CLS writers try to define what they mean by liberalism at considerable length (the first part of Roberto Unger's *Knowledge and Politics*[6] is arguably an extremely extended definition of liberalism from the perspective of a "total critic"), more often "liberalism" is little more than a very loose term for the dominant postfeudal beliefs held across all but the left and right fringes of the political spectrum. There is little regard for the distinctions that often preoccupy people who hardly consider themselves allies, much less indistinguishable; for example, people who think of themselves as deontological rights theorists and those who are openly utilitarian are linked; anarchic libertarians and New Deal apologists are treated as forming a school because, CLS proponents believe, they share certain fundamental attitudes and rhetorical styles that overwhelm their undeniably real differences.

The descriptive portrait of mainstream liberal thought that I present is a picture of a system of thought that is simultaneously beset by internal *contradiction* (not by "competing concerns" artfully balanced until a wise equilibrium is reached, but by irreducible, irremediable, irresolvable conflict) and by systematic *repression* of the presence of these contradictions. I will argue that a standard four-part critical method has been used again and again, whether consciously or not.

First, the Critics attempted to identify a contradiction in liberal legal thought, a set of paired rhetorical arguments that both resolve cases in opposite, incompatible ways and correspond to distinct visions of human nature and human fulfillment. Chapters 1 through 3 of this book give a detailed review of three central contradictions in liberal thought that have been identified in the CLS writing: (1) the contradiction between a commitment to mechanically applicable rules as the appropriate form for resolving disputes (thought to be associated in complex ways with the political tradition of self-reliance and individualism) and a commitment to situation-sensitive, ad hoc standards (thought to correspond to a commitment to sharing and altruism); (2) the contradiction between a commitment to the traditional liberal notion that values or desires are arbitrary, subjective, individual, and individuating while facts or reason are objective and universal *and* a commitment to the ideal that we can "know" social and ethical truths objectively (through objective knowledge of true human nature) or to the hope that one can transcend the usual distinction between subjective and objective in seeking moral truth; and (3) the contradiction between a commitment to an intentionalistic discourse, in which human action is seen as the product of a self-determining individual will, and determinist discourse, in which the activity of nominal subjects merits neither respect nor condemnation because it is simply deemed the expected outcome of existing structures.

Second, the Critics tried to demonstrate that each of the contradictions is utterly pervasive in legal controversy, even in cases where practice is so settled that we nearly invariably forget that the repressed contradictory impulse *could* govern the decision at issue. These impulses are ready to destabilize settled practice should we ever be forced to articulate or ground that practice. There are, in short, no easy cases, though there may be ones whose outcomes are perfectly predictable.

Third, Critics have attempted to show that mainstream thought invariably treats one term in each set of contradictory impulses as *privileged* in three distinct senses. The privileged term is presumptively entitled as a normative matter to govern disputes; it is simply assumed, as a descriptive matter, to govern the bulk of situations; and most subtly, but perhaps most significantly, departures from the purportedly dominant norm, even if they are obviously frequent, are treated as *exceptional,* in need of special justification, a bit chaotic. In essence, my argument is that liberal legal discourse most strongly purports to be committed to and to exceptionalize departures from both individualism and the Rule of Law. It is also committed to the idea that subjective value choices are the only arbiter of the good, at least in the abstract sense that the general theory of law and the state is one in which the state seeks not to further particular life plans but to facilitate people's fulfilling diverse plans (although it would be misleading to believe that all liberal thinkers *presume* that the correct answer to a legal problem is the one consistent with the notion that values are subjective, in the same way they presume that the rule form should govern). Liberalism also privileges an intentionalist discourse that both presumes to be able to explain why we can legitimately reward and blame in the vast bulk of cases and purports to provide a reasonable description of the so-called private world (that governed by contract rather than state action beyond enforcement of contract), which is presumptively deemed to reflect the uncoerced intentions of individuals. Finally, liberalism privileges an uncritical respect for the announced choices of subjects—uncritical both in the sense that the subject is viewed as unambivalent enough that we need not scrutinize particular choices for consistency with a broader life plan and in the sense that pure paternalism, the possibility that the subject has simply chosen badly, is ruled out.

Fourth, the Critics note that, closely examined, the "privileged" impulses describe the program of a remarkably right-wing, quasilibertarian order. I draw several implications from this recognition, though I believe that in this regard I differ considerably from many, if not all, of the CLS authors whose work I shall be discussing. One purely descriptive implication that I have long drawn affects my own agenda in my own critical writing and is undoubtedly an important bias for the reader to note in dealing with my interpretation of CLS: I believe that liberalism is culturally and intellectually self-confident only in its right-wing libertarian form, because libertarianism is in one sense simply the *summary* of the privileged positions in liberal thought. My strong belief is that people who call themselves liberals can most comfortably explain their attachment to a society based on the privileged poles I have just noted, but that they are remarkably inarticulate and uncomfortable explaining their often powerful nonlibertarian impulses. One way for left-liberal law teachers to test this proposition, (which I don't doubt they will instinctively bristle at) is to ask themselves whether they find it easiest to bully students in their Socratic mode when playing either libertarian or right-wing legal economist, and not in advocating their own left-liberal beliefs. Thus, I do not believe that I, or other CLS practitioners, have by any means been attacking straw men, even when the positions we analyze, in their purest forms, are not the mainstream positions but somewhat more extreme ones. Another implication I draw is that one of the foremost, if unintentional, political accomplishments of CLS has been to arm left liberals against more politically conservative ones; by resuscitating the unprivileged positions, by noting the degree to which they remain pervasive in the face of complex efforts to repress their presence, CLS adherents may demonstrate that the left liberal's instincts are better grounded in the cultural tradition of liberalism in which they operate than they sometimes seem aware of themselves. (I say this knowing full well that many CLS spokespersons, most notably Duncan Kennedy, focus nearly all their explicit attacks on left liberals, not right-wing libertarians.)[7] I actually believe that the avowedly left-of-liberal CLS lawyers may often best serve decidedly liberal programs for a perfectly coherent reason: CLS adherents find themselves in roughly the same relationship to their *actual* political beliefs as left liberals are to theirs. That is, they have all learned to argue confidently for a position one step to the right of their actual position. CLS proponents have, in a sense, developed a coherent and self-confident left-liberal discourse that the left liberals have not yet devised, just as the left liberal is able to argue coherently only for a formally egalitarian individualistic liberalism, tempered by a far clearer vision than that of his conservative brethren of the massive interventions needed to equalize opportunity and the need to reconcile essentially contradictory pulls toward either meritocracy or equal opportunity on the one hand and nonintervention on the other. Arguments for their *actual* vision seem far vaguer and more unfocused, more apt to be captured in moments of thick description, or in stories that could as easily be fiction as description, than in general theory. Commitments to "community," "unalienated related-ness," "abolition of illegitimate hierarchy," and so on, could scarcely be animated by those vague, contentless slogans. Unger argued in his summary of critical legal theory[8] that the substantive CLS program was a "super-liberal" one, that it bore roughly the same relationship to the welfare state that the welfare state bore to laissez-faire capitalism. I am far more certain that its justifying rhetoric bears that relationship than that its ultimate world vision does.

I continue my account of liberal legal ideology in Chapter 4 with a description of the relationship between CLS and the Law and Economics movement that has been so prominent in American law schools over the past decade. I hope to show both how Law and Economics has implicitly adopted a theory of the state and legality fundamentally consistent with the views I have described as the privileged liberal positions, suppressing any recognition of internal contradiction. I shall then trace some of the critiques of the central normative propositions in law and economics that have been made by the CLS authors. In Chapter 5 I reiterate some of the attacks CLS authors have made on the politically conservative institutional biases of Law and Economics scholars (for example their suppositions about the beneficence of private property or competitive markets). This chapter, which largely traces relatively technical disputes within the economics tradition, is, in a sense, the most peripheral to my overall account of the unique Critical posture, though I think that in the political context of American legal education in the 1970s and 1980s little Critical work has been more clearly significant.

I conclude my account of the Critical picture of liberal ideology with a relatively fragmentary discussion of the Legal Process school (Chapter 6), with a discussion of the proposition that the fundamental political choices we must make are ones involving the allocation of decision-making authority, whether between courts and legislatures or between central and local government. Critical Legal Studies insights will be applied to show that both the typical adulation of traditional democratic institutions and the suspicion of both uncontrolled and inadequately activist courts are more troublesome within the liberal tradition than the process-fixated theorists suggest. I shall also review the rather sketchy CLS attacks on the traditional picture of both the virtues of federalism and the relationship of substantive federalist concerns to federal court issues.

I shall then discuss history. First I shall detail the Critics' efforts to identify and critique the way their mainstream colleagues use history in solidifying their normative positions: ways in which the mainstream legalists alternatively attempt to use history to derive current practice by reference to the supposed command of some privileged, Golden Age historical figures (like the Founding Fathers), ignore history utterly by asserting the possibility of an uncontingent ahistorical legalism, or derive concrete results by "getting on history's bandwagon," by attempting to discover the teleological laws of progressive motion, which the prudent observer can help accelerate by recognizing (Chapter 7). I shall then attempt, in a more cursory fashion, to criticize some of the early CLS histories (particularly those that attempted to distinguish feudal from liberal capitalist societies), using the insights the Critics themselves gained in dealing with the work of more mainstream legal historians.

Finally, in Chapters 8 and 9 I explore developing Critical views on the "role of law." CLS writers have distanced themselves from traditional social-functionalist thought by questioning the supposition that societies are united, not divided, by questioning the extent to which particular legal responses are necessary to advance any identified interest, by emphasizing the degree to which the legal system should be seen as relatively autonomous. But they have gone even further than that in transforming the terms of a debate over the role of law, a debate that invariably assumes that what is at issue is the degree to which some superstructural, peripheral law does or does not impede or advance some basic, separate society's needs or wants. CLS theorists have devoted a great deal of their efforts to demonstrating that law and society are inseparable or interpenetrating and arguing that traditional pictures of the relationship between law and society that ignore that point almost invariably make law seem both more important than it is (in supposing that particular structures require particular rules) and less important than it is (in ignoring its basic constitutive nature).

I shall also describe in more detail CLS work that sees law as a major rhetorical apparatus used to justify the (occasional) exercises of explicit state force that always lurk behind routine assignments of hierarchical position and prerogative. In this regard I suppose that what I will be discussing is something akin to "legitimation," though my claim is that the CLS movement has basically adopted a more down-to-earth view of the role of legal rhetoric in influencing thought than have most who would describe themselves as legitimation theorists. Most important, I shall claim that legal rhetoric often obscures the presence of the contradictions I have been referring to and that a whole panoply of legal rhetorical devices frequently makes it difficult to think certain thoughts—

thoughts, I shall argue, that depart from a rather complacent world view in which our ends are met as best they can unless we distort the beneficent workings of the private world through collectivist utopian meddling.

It is important to emphasize that this account of the Critical Legal Studies movement is by no means the only conceivable one. It might be helpful, then, to describe briefly what this book is *not,* to mention just a few of the possible narrative points of view that readers reasonably familiar with CLS might wrongly expect me to present.

To take but one example, it is not immediately apparent why one would choose to recount the history of Critical Legal Studies as *intellectual* history at all, rather than, say, institutional or local political history. To the limited degree that people outside the law schools have heard of Critical Legal Studies, it is almost surely because a startling degree of mass media attention has been paid to the battle at the Harvard Law School between its large CLS faction and the "others."[9] This heated battle has almost certainly *not* been largely about either grandiose academic claims (for example the degree to which Kennedy, a CLS proponent, is correct to assert that the history of legal discourse is the history of shifting efforts to paper over or suppress a painful "fundamental contradiction" in our attitudes about the self in a world of others we both need and fear)[10] or more particular controversies between CLS revisionists and their mainstream colleagues (such as whether Karl Klare is correct that the Supreme Court suppressed interpretations of the Wagner Act that emphasized worker control and antihierarchical role leveling).[11] I leave it to others to try to detail (or debate) what the "real" source of this intense conflict has been,[12] whether conspiratorial political ambitions by Critics, paranoia and intolerance on the right, or the academic equivalent of table manners.

I should note, though, that a difficulty with the rather dry, academic perspective I offer on CLS, one that ignores intrainstitutional conflicts, is that it does a very poor job accounting for the wrath and fury the opponents feel for the movement, particularly since few of these opponents have ever seriously addressed any CLS work at all. People who are generally ideologically predisposed to tolerance and pluralistic diversity have urged the law schools to start purging the CLS faction without ever having offered a word of substantive critique. Paul Carrington, the dean of the Duke Law School, who has never attacked in print any particular CLS work, wrote the following, purportedly in reference to ideas expressed by Unger in his article on the CLS movement:

> Some of our colleagues may be heard to say, law is a mere deception by which the powerful weaken the resistance of the powerless . . .
>
> The professionalism and intellectual courage of lawyers does not require rejection of Legal Realism and its lesson that who decides also matters. What it cannot abide is the embrace of nihilism and its lesson that who decides is everything, and principle nothing but cosmetic . . . In an honest effort to proclaim a need for revolution, nihilist teachers are more likely to train crooks than radicals. [Thus] . . . the nihilist . . . has an ethical duty to depart the law school.
>
> This is a hard dictum within a university whose traditions favor the inclusion in house of all honestly held ideas, beliefs, and values. When, however, the University accepted responsibility for training professionals, it also accepted a duty to constrain teaching that knowingly dispirits students.[13]

One could also, conceivably, tell the story of CLS in a way that ignores both the bulk of its actual law-focused academic contributions and its institutional role at the law schools. Critical *legal* theory might simply be seen as yet one rather minor outpost of critical theory more generally. The predominant task would be to try to place the Conference in a *broader* perspective, to see the work as adopting certain characteristic positions that are expressed in the debates that rage in left academic circles on Neomarxism, structuralist Marxism, post-structuralism, the Frankfurt school, and so on.[14] Certainly, many of the issues that were grist for these debates have a "legal" slant to them: Is what is so charmingly called the state apparatus wholly superstructural or at least semi-autonomous from the base, from (production-based) class relations? How significant is explicit force compared to cultural hegemony, compared to the "legitimacy" of existing power relationships in containing challenges to existing institutions of power? How deeply involved is the state in the force venture? the legitimation venture? Even the less obviously "legal" philosophical agenda of those who "do" social theory, which can perhaps best be summed up as hinging on the appropriate attitude to take toward the liberal's nomadic, amoral Cartesian subject, has clearly had an influence on CLS. Many writers in CLS have simply rehashed these debates for new audiences, and some have arguably integrated these works successfully into their writing about law.

It is undoubtedly true that many of the concerns about the significance of legitimating ideologies and the utility of delegitimation as a political weapon that have animated Western radicals to question their traditional orthodoxies have been of interest to the people who worked within the Conference.[15] Indeed, traditional leftist lawyers and legal academics often condemn CLS adherents as hopeless idealists, preoccupied with the empty words and sham ideas that those exercising authority use to explain their conduct.[16] In part, this attack simply replicates an apparently wholly theoretical debate common on the left between those who believe that law (and culture more generally) are superstructural and those who believe it to be central. In part, though, it is actually a stand-in for a battle over class and cultural style. The CLS focus on case law and ideology is seen by many traditional leftists as reflective of a distasteful desire among elite school law professors to "stay clean" in the libraries, to avoid either dirty academic work (gathering data about how the law actually functions on the shop floor or in the Legal Aid office) or the even dirtier organizing work with those who are privileged in traditional Marxist thought as our political saviors, the proletariat. Revisionist leftists, though, within or outside CLS, have all learned to take ideology quite seriously (and legal rhetoric would certainly qualify as significant ideology), so perhaps CLS is indeed just revisionist Marxism writ small.[17]

Once again, a focus on Western Marxism, in which CLS appears as a minor instance, may be quite appropriate, and I am slightly bothered that I must virtually ignore the ways in which CLS is derivative of other social theory. It would probably be disingenuous, though, to say that I am *deeply* bothered by having to ignore connections to more general social theory, even though I would welcome more work on the connections between CLS and other revisionist work. I actually believe that most efforts by leftist lawyers to rework social theory have failed to engage adequately the *details* of legal argument or practice, and that what is most interesting and innovative in CLS is not the restatement of generalizations about legitimation or the relative autonomy of law but the more detailed, focused accounts of what lawyers and the law influenced do and say. Still, the CLS theorists do, after all, face the same day-to-day political questions that face everyone on the left in the advanced capitalist countries, and my account might make their work seem more internal to the legal academy than it might actually be.

But there is yet one more significant picture that presents the work as wholly internal to the world of legal academics, a continuation of a struggle that has overtly dominated American academic legal discussion in this century. CLS might well seem to be the latest revival of an anti-Formalist, Legal Realist movement at law schools that have historically vacillated between "conceptualists" believing in both the autonomy and scientific purity of judicial legal discourse and policy-oriented scholars who felt that legal discourse was just economics, psychology, or politics applied to disputes processed by courts, agencies that (more or less) wield only certain forms of state power.[18]

It is actually quite difficult to define anything one calls conceptualism or Formalism in a way that does not covertly disparage its adherents, make them sound like a rather compulsive and self-deluding bunch.[19] Traditional Realist definitions of what is usually dubbed the "arid Formalist" conception of legal argument focus on the alleged tendency of Formalists to decide cases based on imagined transcendental qualities or intelligible essences of the concepts or words we must define in framing a dispute. Thus, in trying to decide whether a defendant ought to be subject to a court's jurisdiction, the Realist's ideal-typical Formalist asks whether the defendant is somehow metaphysically "present," or subject to the court's "power."[20] In trying to decide whether a promise (covenant) from a landholder to his neighbors runs to (binds) subsequent purchasers of the land, the Formalist asks whether the promise "touches and concerns" the land.[21] Realist critics claim that none of these questions can be answered without making strictly consequentialist calculations. In the first case, one must tote up the gains in convenience to plaintiffs versus the inconvenience and prejudice to defendants;[22] in the second, one must try to save the often prohibitive costs of renegotiating desirable contracts while not imposing unwanted contracts on people.[23]

Of course no Formalist ever really views herself or himself as ruminating on the abstract meaning of words and concepts. The Formalist believes that the Realist is far too ad hoc—both that all high-order controversies can be deduced by reference to the demands of a rather short list of principles, and that the working rules or operating procedures of the legal system should themselves be easily mechanically applied to raw facts without the need to rely on a great deal of subtle judgment, with only open-textured standards to guide the decision maker (for example a decision rule to enforce only "reasonable" contracts). But the Formalist is not likely to believe that the short list of principles is contentless or abstract, little more than a verbal game. At least in the modern context, no one at the law schools ever calls himself a conceptualist or Formalist (much less an arid one), though the term is frequently bandied about as a derisive description.

For instance George Fletcher, a prominent criminal law theorist and comparativist, essays to solve the long-standing dilemma of which "impossible attempts" (acts complete in temporal terms that have still not caused legislatively proscribed harm) ought to be punishable by speculating on what it *means* to attempt to do something.[24] While I have criticized his venture as hopelessly formalistic, both undirected toward meeting any reasonable policy goals and indeterminate (a standard Realist critique),[25] he undoubtedly sees it as an utterly substantive effort to realize the program of Legalism, of not punishing people unless their acts are at odds with a reasonably precisely defined set of proscriptions. Similarly, a number of people associated with CLS condemned the Law and Economics movement as a latter-day formalism,[26] committed to deriving concrete and uncontroversial results to disputes by reference to the dictates of a single abstraction, efficiency or wealth maximization. The Critics, of course, once more in the standard Realist tradition, believe that even if one were priggish enough to have a one-principled world view, ruminating on the dictates of efficiency would get you nowhere, for its dictates are utterly indeterminate and manipulable. Still, it strikes me as difficult to maintain the belief that Law and Economics is susceptible to the easiest attack on Formalists; it would be folly to claim that they are nonconsequentialist.

CLS has often been seen as the latest attempt at deconstructive Realist critique, and it is plausible to view its emphasis on the indeterminacy of case results and the manipulability of precedent as a continuation of the Realist project. I believe it will be clearer by the book's end why this would be a serious misinterpretation of CLS, but let me give a condensed account here.

First, the Realists seem to me to be fixated on the indeterminacy of language, on the difficulties any rule maker would have in restraining the discretion of those who apply her rules simply by abstract verbal directive. Realists are obsessed with referential vagueness and the need to import a knowledge of the rule makers' purpose into interpreting linguistic directives: every post-Realist law student ought to know that when the town council declares that there shall be no vehicles in the park, it becomes no easier to tell whether it meant to bar wheelchairs, bikes, or a statue of a general in his jeep if we simply think harder about what the word *vehicle* means. (Naturally, the linguistic indeterminacy critique is apposite whether the rule maker is a legislature or a constitutional draftsman whose work a court seeks to interpret, or a judge whose product will serve as precedent for future judicial work.) While most CLS adherents often rehearse the story of language indeterminacy and seem to believe (incorrectly, I think) that it is quite important to their work,[27] there is a CLS vision of legal indeterminacy that is quite distinct from the Realist one. This stronger CLS claim is that the legal system is invariably simultaneously *philosophically committed* to mirror-image contradictory norms, each of which dictates the opposite result in any case (no matter how "easy" the case first appears). While settled *practice* is not unattainable, the CLS claim is that settled *justificatory schemes* are in fact unattainable. Efforts at norm legitimation are radically indeterminate not because the source of authority *cannot* speak clearly (though, rather incidentally, she often cannot) but because if pressed, she would not want to.

Second, the "purposive" readings of language that the Realists assert can solve the problem of referential ambiguity assume that such readings will be both far more determinate and less politically charged than the CLS adherents believe. The Realist may be right to laugh at the caricatured Formalist who asks whether a covenant touches and concerns the land; it is hard to see that the purported question does more than restate the underlying issue the question is supposed to help answer: whether the covenant ought to bind successors. But the standard Realist policy inquiries may be just as open ended as the linguistic inquiry: a good deal of CLS effort has gone into showing that the most prominent consequentialist movement at today's law schools, the Law and Economics movement, does not deliver redemption from formalist indeterminacy.[28] When a legal economist tells us that covenants should run when they would have been negotiated in the absence of transaction costs, he may not have done much more than restate a problem either.

Finally, at least one other intellectual history seems to me plausible, though unlike the other conceivable stories, I suspect it would be fragmented, even if related carefully.

Debates in the world of literary criticism have undoubtedly had some influence on many people writing CLS works; it is attractive to those who want to argue that practice is rarely constrained, whether by laws of nature or fidelity to the commands of tradition or rules, to draw on those who find all texts (including legal texts) open, manipulable, multi-faceted. Schools of literary criticism that emphasize the subjectivity of the interpreter and deny even the presence of stable interpretive communities that can give a listener's meaning to texts even if a speaker's intention remains in significant ways elusive are easily echoed by those whose task is to deny the possibility of *any* apolitical, technical action, even by judges who may see themselves as politically charged in private life but technocratic and neutral in their interpreter's role. This lit. crit. tradition has been central to debates between CLS constitutionalists and anti-CLS left centrists at Yale (including Bruce Ackerman, now of Columbia) who want to recapture at least one branch of fancy literary theory to argue for the possibility of reaching legal principles roughly consonant with the ideals of the Kennedy administration through careful reading of our cultural tradition. But the debate ultimately seems far too thin to me to capture much of what is new and interesting in CLS writing. To use the dialogue form that has become nearly mandatory in New Haven: an interpretive community exists, according to Owen Fiss of Yale, that can come to significant consensus even if it cannot reach absolute agreement on all aspects of the meaning of texts. The search for "objective truth" is misguided; consensus within a viable community is all we mean by the truth of ethical propositions, just as it is all we mean when we say that a reading of a literary text is a true or sensible one.[29] According to Paul Brest (who is sympathetic, in this regard, to CLS), even if such a unified community did exist, which it doesn't, and even if everyone in it didn't carry within him contradictory maxims and ideals that are available to resolve every controversy, the "community" would consist of a bunch of stuffy old privileged white males, whose opinions would scarcely be worth tossing onto a trash heap.[30] This argument is not altogether unimportant, but it is fundamentally too short to form the basis of a book.

CHAPTER ONE

Rules and Standards

Duncan Kennedy's "Form and Substance in Private Law Adjudication"[1] remains one of the central works in the critical legal studies literature. In this chapter I shall reiterate, extend, and criticize the basic substantive claims of this article, as well as the two other central pieces in the CLS literature that focus on the choice between rules and standards, "PINS Jurisdiction, the Vagueness Doctrine, and the Rule of Law" by Al Katz and Lee Teitelbaum,[2] and "Legality, Bureaucracy, and Class in the Welfare System" by Bill Simon.[3]

The basic claims I will address are:

1. Actors in this legal system feel impelled to constrain decision makers to judge particular cases mechanically by applying simple rules to a limited number of readily ascertainable facts, even though the use of nondiscretionary decision-making procedures will inexorably lead on at least some occasions to results the policy maker did not intend. The point is familiar[4] to anyone who has been through a semester of law school and can even be illustrated to a nonlawyer quite readily. For example, if the purpose of establishing a voting age is to screen out immature or imprudent voters, directing the voting registrar to allow only those older than eighteen to vote will screen out some who are mature and entitle some who are immature, but at the same time it will reduce occasions for the registrar to exercise arbitrary power and discretion. At the same time, all actors in our system are deeply committed to a jurisprudence of informal standards, of highly general policy commands, permitting ad hoc situation-sensitive decisions in particular cases with little precedential value. Because all actors are simultaneously committed to both positions, and because the arguments for one are ultimately counterbalanced by opposing ones, we should, as a purely predictive matter, expect instability, oscillation, and unsettled conclusions on every significant issue along the purely *formal* dimension—that is, along this

dimension of whether to cope with any issue by imprecise rule or by imperfectly administrable standard. This is not to say that we could not posit hypothetical rules that are *excessively* inapt or posit standards that are *excessively* nonadministrable, as some imply when they attack claims that the choice of form poses a contradiction rather than a soluble problem of balancing. It *is* to say, though, that there will remain in any legal dispute a logically or empirically unanswerable formal problem, that granting substantially greater discretion or limiting discretion through significantly greater rule boundedness in the formation of the prevailing legal command is always perfectly plausible.

2. The contradictory impulse to resolve particular doctrinal disputes with a rule or with a standard is accompanied, if not necessarily created or sustained, by a list of counterpoised functional arguments for rules and for standards at an abstract and general level. Most of the arguments the CLS proponents identify for each position are perfectly familiar ones within the legal culture. Some of the arguments, particularly those against both the *possibility* and the *normative desirability* of a rule-governed system, have tended to be repressed to a far greater extent in the dominant discourse so that the CLS arguments in this regard appear more novel or at least more forceful and focused. One should expect that those on the political left like the CLS writers would contribute most heavily to the pro-standards position, if one believes that the pro-rules position is ideologically *privileged* in liberalism, an ideology that obviously puts great stress on its ability both to contain the great potential abuses of state power through the Rule of Law and to avoid harmful interactions between private parties simply by inducing rule obedience.

3. The most original claim that Kennedy in particular has made is that the deep ambivalence over the choice of form is intimately connected to an even deeper ambivalence over substantive political visions. The rule form is said to express the substantive ideals of those committed to self-reliance and individualism (egotism constrained by a respect for the rights of others). The willingness to resort to the standard form is said to correspond to the embrace of substantive altruism (a belief that one's own ends are not normatively prior to others', although the altruist's commitment to the welfare of others is differentiable from the saint's self-abnegation in that the altruist's care is not universal or nonparticularized but may depend on factors such as his proximity to the people he cares to share with or his sentiments about how blameworthy they are in being distressed). The conception of the self at war over a

simultaneous commitment to both self-reliance and altruism is thought to be symptomatic of something even deeper than abstract political theoretical commitment. By the time he wrote the most-often cited of all passages on critical legal studies, in his structuralist analysis of Blackstone's *Commentaries,* Kennedy believed that the ambivalence was reflective of a "fundamental contradiction" between the desires to fuse with others yet remain separate from them, to assert one's existential independence and authenticity while recognizing that one is socially formed and framed, to recognize that all that is noble and desired (love and community) as well as that which is utterly debased and feared (conformism, role-constrained uncreativity, the rejection of those who matter to us) is a product of the existence of an intense social life.[5]

The connection between form and substance has never been said to be one of either logical entailment or material necessity. In some ways it is difficult to interpret the critical articles to make any claim at all about the nature of the connection other than that it *exists.* My argument is that to the extent Kennedy's point is interpreted (wrongly, but frequently)[6] as an empirical prediction (for example that rule orientation in particular controversies will inevitably be the program of political individualists), it will often be simply wrong, other times simply irrelevant. To the extent, though, that there is supposed to be a *cultural connection* between a fuzzy ideal of a world of rule-grounded persons (rather than an unbending commitment to the use of rules in all cases) and both political individualism and a personal or philosophical commitment to the privacy of some asocial self, I believe that this insight of "Form and Substance" remains invaluable.

The Omnipresent Problem of Form

In every dispute about the appropriate resolution of a legal controversy, rulelike solutions, standard-based solutions, and intermediate positions will uncomfortably coexist, none fully dominating either day-to-day practice or *a fortiori* justificatory rhetoric.

CLS adherents have been adept at reminding legal academics of the number of important controversies that can obviously be seen as instances of an irresolvable rules-standards conflict. More interesting, perhaps, their recognition of the centrality and pervasiveness of the rules-standards conflict has led them to see the tension as covertly present in innumerable disputes where that dimension has generally gone unseen.

The Critical Claim in the Contract Area

Kennedy's article focuses primarily on contract law, and it is particularly helpful to see the bulk of issues in contracts as occasions to work through this painful dilemma.

Assume that we are trying to decide *when* a contract is formed. There is a readily available rule position, a position easily and mechanically applied to concrete factual settings: no one has taken on any obligations to anyone else until there has been an offer and an overtly communicated acceptance (either reciprocal promise or full performance) whose terms precisely mirror those of the offer.[7] There is an equally readily available position that is quite open ended, standardlike: once a party begins to negotiate with another party, she has taken on an obligation of good faith dealing[8] and must compensate a party damaged by the failure to act in good faith. It is never readily mechanically determinable when someone has breached the obligation to act in good faith, but if the *purpose* of dividing the world into unbound contractual strangers and those with contractual duties is to prevent parties from appropriating benefits from another with whom they deal without taking on some reciprocal obligations, the rule, which treats even people who have taken many steps in the course of negotiation as legal strangers until they have formally consummated a quite exacting relationship, may seem suspect. Naturally, too, there are characteristic intermediate positions. On the more rulelike side, one can assume people to be bound once there has been a formal, if "not too seriously" incomplete contract, a fairly clear commitment to reciprocity on *some* terms. The Uniform Commercial Code (UCC) treats trading partners as bound even when critical terms (including price) are unspecified, as long as terms can be filled in in accordance with more or less vague "reasonable commercial practice" (such as past dealings or a market price).[9] On the more standardlike side, parties may be bound to at least a limited obligation to restore the offeree to the *status quo ante* on the basis of "promissory estoppel" of an offeror, coupled with the "reasonable reliance" of the offeree on the offeror's expressed intention to reward his efforts on the offeror's behalf. The paradigmatic cases are ones in which a donor pledges money to a charity and the charity seeks to enforce the pledge, though no exacting reciprocal dealing has occurred, or ones in which an offeree partly performs a task when the offeror has stated that he will owe something to the offeree only when performance is complete.[10] When is partial performance sufficient to ground obligation? When was the offeree's reliance on the offeror's intention reasonable? Obviously these are more open-ended questions than the rule advocate would want asked, though they may be a touch less open ended than questions about whether a party has bargained in good faith, since they sometimes focus on a partly mechanically ascertainable and linked set of *acts,* those not just taken to the offeree's detriment in reliance on a promise but explicitly described in the contract offer. (While the steps the offeree may have taken when an offeror has breached the more standardlike good faith bargaining duty may be classified as partial performance under certain interpretations of a course of conduct needed to perform, it will never be *obvious* or readily discernible that this is the case.)

Assume that we are trying to decide which contracts are enforceable. Again, the rulelike answer is that all contracts are enforceable that are even arguably bilateral; that is, wherever each party has received *something,* even the most nominal consideration, for his performance, the court will not inquire into the substantive fairness of the bargain.[11] Again, too, there is a standardlike answer at the other pole of concrete administrability: courts should never enforce bargains that are substantively unconscionable,[12] where the disproportion between the value of what one party received and what she gave is so great as to negate our sense that the underlying social purpose of contract (to facilitate *mutually beneficial* exchange) has been met. Obviously, applying a standard of substantive unconscionability involves far more discretion than applying a rule that nominal consideration suffices to validate a contract. Of course, once more, there is a variety of intermediate positions. Courts may attempt to identify prototypical descriptions, more or less mechanically applicable to actual facts, in which nonmutuality is presumed and negate those, and only those, presumably nonbeneficial contracts. Contracts are void that are made with parties who lack formal contractual capacity (infants are readily mechanically identified, the insane a bit less so). Contracts may be voided when made under conditions (duress, fraud) that are probably less clearly identifiable than those committed to strict rule-bound legalism would prefer, but that may well have been confined enough in practice to be considered relatively rulelike. On the standardlike side, contracts may be negated if the parties are said to have had "unequal bargaining power"; the concept may well be empty, since it by no means negates all contracts where the seller has what economists describe as market power,[13] or it may serve as a simple cover for an inquiry into substantive unconscionability, but it has historically been considered a somewhat less open-ended standard by its proponents.[14]

In both these classes of cases two important points must be emphasized. First, the legal system simultaneously embraces doctrines that allow any particular case to be decided as if either the rulelike decision mode or the standardlike one were in force. Day-to-day practice may well vary in a predictable fashion both over time and across different actors with different political perspectives (right-wing late nineteenth-century judges were less likely to reject a contract as unconscionable than a postwar liberal reformer like Skelly Wright), but no polar position has such killer force as to negate utterly its opposite, to make it go away.

Second, the rulelike position is privileged in both cases, experienced as the starting-point "free contract regime position" from which other positions represent *departures*. Liberal writers have taken two strategies, both of which I shall detail and criticize at some length. I shall detail the positions to remind readers how powerful the urge is to privilege the rule pole; I shall criticize them in order to preserve the Critical claim that no noncontradictory commitment to that pole is ultimately rationally stable or sustainable.

Members of the right-wing mainstream (whether libertarians or economists) have been more straightforward. They spend enormous time and energy attempting to show that the departures are unusual, consistent, and justified by the same principles that justify the rule, that they are both exceptional and reasonably carefully confined. Nineteenth-century Formalists thought that contracts should be enforced because the parties so willed; the narrow limits on enforcement were thought to flow directly from the same idea (parties who acted under duress were will-less).[15] Modern legal economists believe that contracts are enforced to maximize wealth (largely by giving information to parties about when breach is efficient and permitting risk allocation and planning);[16] contracts may not be enforceable when exchange was uninformed (and hence not inexorably beneficial),[17] unless the asymmetry of information resulted from the sort of worthwhile search that must be rewarded to maximize wealth.[18]

The more politically centrist writers, like Melvin Eisenberg, openly acknowledge an ad hoc breakdown of the privileged nominal consideration "bargain" principle, the development of a contradictory paradigm, but covertly defend its privileged status either by pure fiat or by the rhetorical technique of using only extreme cases when (nervously) justifying departures that can be justified far less extremely. For instance, despite the fact that price dispersion for homogeneous goods is almost undeniably the *norm* in consumer markets,[19] Eisenberg defends the principle that sellers oughtn't exploit price-ignorant consumers by reference to stories of stores that sell to ignorant tourists passing through town, never to be dealt with again, and high-pressure door-to-door salesmen.[20]

The Critics here, perhaps more than anywhere else, simply following in the footsteps of left-leaning Realist forebears like Robert Hale,[21] have shown that these attempts at confinement will never fully succeed. In *every* contract, for instance, it is an open question both whether the more informed party ought to have shared more of his information with his trading partner (that is, a question of "fraud" arises, in some sense, in every case) and whether the contract would have been made had each party had other physically imaginable though socially unavailable options accessible to him (that is, a question of "duress" arises in every case).

Attempts to evade the sense that the fraud issue is omnipresent, for example by positing that we can determine when a contracting party must be given the incentive of getting a good bargain by possessing unshared information in order to acquire that information,[22] are both utterly indeterminate in resolving actual cases and politically grounded in a controversial hypothesis that the law should predominantly aim to maximize wealth. City slicker X knows that the market price of bumpkin Y's antique rockers has skyrocketed back in town, unbeknownst to Y; must he share that information? The traditional answer is a resounding no, but applying this answer to the purported efficiency policies is, to put it mildly, difficult. To argue that this must be the answer to *induce* X to obtain the information is folly, unless we know much more about the *marginal* costs of acquiring the information than we would know simply by answering Anthony Kronman's question of whether the information was deliberately acquired (and hence, apparently, induced by a property right) or casually acquired (presumably at zero marginal cost). To argue that in the absence of X's ability to cash in handsomely on his superior information, substantially fewer parties will go off to the country to bring rockers back is to speculate in a quite extraordinary fashion that entrepreneurs are not willing to work at anything but supercompetitive profits, a claim hard to square with the existence of competitive equilibria. In fact a perfectly plausible claim, at the ludicrously general level at which these arguments are invariably made, can be asserted that buyers will waste resources seeking the rents they can gain from ignorant sellers unless they must disclose all information they obtained cheaply. It is impossible to see that any of the arguments that connect the radical limitation of a fraud defense to the need for property rights in superior information have rigorously demonstrated what precise level of return to superior information is needed to induce its efficient production, given that increasing the return to its creator or discoverer comes at the expense of others who would make use of it. To take a ready analogy from the copyright field, only a charlatan would claim to know how much more literary production we would get if novelists had to be paid by parodists of their work, or how much parody we would lose, or how to evaluate these gains and losses objectively.

Moreover, unstated ethical-distributive and efficiency arguments are suggested if parties receive an unqualified right to withhold even information they have "worked" to gather without regard to the capabilities the party from whom it is withheld has of gathering it or the consequences of the lack of information. In distributive terms, there is no efficiency theory that tells us whom the information holder ought to bargain with without disclosure if he can be induced to produce a certain level of information by exploiting only a subset of potential ignoramuses. In traditional efficiency terms, an unqualified nondisclosure rule will inexorably result in at least some deals being made in which the ignorant party would have compensated the informed one to disclose, but these deals will not be made because the informed party cannot readily ascertain which ignorant parties would benefit most from disclosure.

Attempts to evade the sense that the duress issue is omnipresent, for example by trying to distinguish illegitimate threats from legitimate offers, founder in their obvious inability to ground a politically uncharged theory of each party's initial entitlements. Thus, to take the most sophisticated effort to distinguish duress-based contracts from "free" ones, the libertarian philosopher Robert Nozick has argued that a contract is free when the promisor has accepted an offer, unfree when he has responded to a threat.[23] An offer is a proposition the promisor would choose to receive whether he accepts it or not, a threat a proposition the promisor would sooner never have heard. In the cases Nozick believes are easy the argument goes like this: X, the knife wielder, says to Y, "Your money or your life." Since Y could easily have forgone this suggestion altogether, the statement is a threat and the transfer of the money a result not of free contract but of duress. In contrast, if Y is starving to death and X says, "I'll sell you food for ten times the market price," Y would at least want to consider the proposition; hence, acceptance is the acceptance of an offer, and the contract is morally legitimate.

The argument is hopelessly confused. Nozick acknowledges how difficult it is to apply to "hard cases," but he fails to see that all cases are hard. X, secure on his boat, tells man overboard Y, "Pay me $10,000, or I'll let you drown." Nozick notes that one cannot tell whether this is a threat or an offer unless one knows if X has the right to let Y drown: if he has such a right, Y would want to hear X's proposition. Of course, though, if certain forms of violence are acceptable, then the proposition "Give me your money or I'll (exercise my right to) shoot" is an interesting one for the recipient. But "pay me ten times the market price for food or I'll (impermissibly) let you starve" is clearly a threat if allowing someone to starve is not a privileged act.

One can try to rescue this argument by coming up with a prepolitical definition of rights, but this seems utterly unavailing, both because no definition will imbed universally acceptable propositions about the ideal form of human organization and, more important for our purposes, because no definition will provide the rulelike clarity that a *contained* definition of duress demands. The best efforts of libertarians have centered on our purported capacity to distinguish cases where we have a duty not to harm from cases where we have no duty to help.[24] X has a presumed privilege to socially unrestrained action in situations in which the world would be no worse for Y if X simply dropped out of the picture; X is presumed to take on a socially imposed duty to change his ways if his conduct worsens the position Y is in.

This attempt to limit the category of wrongful action will fail: it is both logically incoherent (impossible to apply to cases) and morally unappealing. It is logically incoherent in two ways. First, if it were supposed to guide us in the bulk of cases, neither of two opposing parties in a typical interactive harm situation could have a right or entitlement. Where the polluter spews forth pollution and the people downstream desire clean water, each is the but-for cause of harm to the other.[25] Polluters cannot have a right to pollute (use the water as they wish) because the users would be better off had the polluter never existed. Conversely, though, the users cannot have a right to clean water (a right to enjoin the pollution) because if the users dropped out of the picture, life would be better, cheaper, and simpler for the polluter. One can seemingly avoid this problem only by shifting away from framing the harm versus failure-to-benefit distinction by imagining the party whose behavior we question absent from the scene and shifting instead toward a focus on causation. But unless we embrace premodern views of objective causation, as Richard Epstein has,[26] where the most concrete physical source of a harm is always thought blameworthy, this will be completely unavailing. Epstein uses a psychologically primitive analogy: since we all "know" that the person whose nose blocks the assailant's punch is not really the but-for cause of the assault, even though there would have been no injury had his nose not been there, how can the equally passive downstream water user be the cause? But of course we don't know that the "victim" is blameless in the assault case except by assuming that his desire to put his nose in the way of the punch is socially legitimate, and we certainly don't know that a desire for a swimmable river trumps a desire for cheaper manufactured goods, just because those who want a swimmable river may seem to sit back more passively when they cry foul. Even those who (mysteriously) find Epstein's argument initially appealing may lose their enthusiasm when they realize that he endorses (and must endorse) distinctions like the following: it is tortious for a party to direct or shine light on another party's property in a fashion that diminishes the value of the property, but unexceptionable to block one party's access to valued light by building a tall building.[27]

Second, the attempt to limit the category of wrongful action is also illogical in that the "thought experiment" that is implicitly suggested by asking that we focus on whether X's present conduct makes the world worse for Y than it would be if X were wiped out is uncontrollably manipulable: Y calls Dr. X in the middle of the night for emergency care and X refuses. The world may seem to be no worse for Y if we wipe out X, and hence, according to this view, X has no duty (and there is thus no duress if X charges a staggering sum to reverse his initial decision). If, though, one extends the thought experiment over time, one realizes that had X not held himself out as a doctor in that town, another one might well have come along.

Even if this duress-confining procedure were logically coherent, it would seem morally suspect. In cases where we have clear, legally mandated duties (for example those of parents to children), grounding these duties in bogus empirical assumptions that the *existence* of parents precludes others from giving care and thereby affirmatively harms the child only preserves an illusion that duties inexorably prevent only "active" harm. The fact that no parent could plausibly claim to be less culpable for starving a child no one else was aware of (and therefore prevented from helping by a false assumption that the parents would render care) is sufficient to indicate that this is surely a disingenuous account of the duty.

The rules-standards dilemma pervades not just the problem of contract formation and contract acceptability in which it has probably been most recognized but innumerable other issues in contract law. Here are just a few examples drawn in part from Clare Dalton's essay on contract doctrine:[28] Do we insist on performance once a formal contract is formed, having established no duties at all until that mechanically perceivable, magic moment, or do we allow a series of excuses to negate duty (mistake, impossibility, changed circumstances)? All a bit vague and standardlike compared to an ironclad insistence on performance, but the excuses themselves can certainly be defined in more or less precise ways. Do we disallow midterm modifications in terms because the burdened party would receive no formal consideration for his promise to do more (since he is in theory entitled to full performance on the original terms) or inquire more fully and fact sensitively into whether the revised contract involves unfair overreaching by the originally bound party? Should the Statute of Frauds bar all oral contracts of certain types or only those where there is an actual evidentiary controversy about whether the contract existed or real question about whether the party now seeking relief had adequately reflected on the contract?

Latent and Patent Problems of Form in Substantive Criminal Law

As I've noted in regard to contract law, the legally enforceable obligations that private citizens owe to one another may be described precisely or vaguely; proponents of precision will generally note that they are limiting the power of the state in stripping those judging private disputes of discretion as well as confining the substantive demands each individual faces from his fellows to demands he can readily, at a minimum, know in advance and plan for, perhaps avoid. Generally, in referring to public law, particularly criminal law, we tend to view the battle as a two-sided one between, on the one hand, restraining state discretion in an area where the consequences of misused discretion—the deprivation of physical liberty—are most severe and, on the other hand, reaching substantively correct judgments in complex cases, both where we are defining wrongdoing and where we are grading the severity of admitted wrongs.

Again, there are some obvious instances of a rules-standards conflict in criminal law, though even the most obvious cases are somewhat obscured by the hyperprivileged status of rules in the criminal area, the bloated tributes to the special importance of the Rule of Law in the field that all mainstream substantive criminal law text writers and comentators seem impelled to rehearse. To listen to the most renowned mainstream commentators on the criminal law—people with such otherwise diverse points of view as Herbert Packer,[29] Jerome Hall,[30] and George Fletcher[31]—one might forget for a moment that the rules-standards battle is constantly raging both openly and covertly in substantive criminal law.

An issue that we face in criminal jurisprudence is how to distinguish mere thought crimes, or plans to commit crimes, from punishable attempts. If we punish only when harm is consummated, some parties will go unpunished merely because they are "lucky" enough to be unsuccessful or thwarted, though they are as blameworthy or in need of incapacitation or reform as successful criminals, and even though we may want to deter others from taking actions that pose a high risk of harm. If we punish acts insufficiently proximate to harm, we both ignore the possibility that a person might have voluntarily desisted, thus wrongly conclusively presuming that he is distinguishable only in terms of luck from those who consummate harms, and threaten to intrude on what amounts to a harmless fantasy.

It ought to be reasonably obvious that the long-standing controversy in differentiating unpunishable preparation for crime from punishable attempts is just another instance of the usual battle over the appropriate form of legal doctrine. There is a rulelike solution (the defendant is simply preparing until he has taken the easily ascertained *last possible step* in his control to cause the proscribed harm);[32] a standardlike one (the defendant is preparing only until he has taken the harder-to-define *substantial* step that strongly corroborates his intent to commit the crime);[33] and various intermediate positions that are more rulelike (only if the acts of the defendant unequivocally bespeak an intention to consummate the harm, without regard to extrinsic evidence of intention, can the defendant be convicted)[34] or more standardlike (the defendant is guilty of an attempt if his acts are proximate to the harm, or if we believe that he would have committed the harm but for an unforeseen interruption).[35] The rulelike solutions seem obviously underinclusive if we hope to identify persons who have not just thought dangerous thoughts but actually done deeds that reveal a disposition to do much more than dream; the fact that the police interrupt a temporally drawn-out scheme before the defendant has consummated his plan hardly speaks to the defendant's substantive innocence. The standardlike solutions, though, seem clearly subject to prejudicial or random enforcement. The fact finder's judgment about whether the defendant's acts clearly demonstrate the firm disposition to do wrong may be inescapably tied to judgments about the defendant as a whole person and not just his inevitably ambiguous acts.

Similarly, it ought to be reasonably obvious that the historically oscillating decisions about whether or not to merge a conspiracy conviction into the conviction for the object crime of the conspiracy can readily be understood as typical of rules-standards conflicts. Two rules positions— that defendants should *never* be sentenced separately for the conspiracy[36] and that defendants should *always* be sentenced for both the conspiracy and the object crime[37]—alternate uncomfortably with a position that states the doctrine in the usual situationally sensitive standards form (tag defendants'· sentences when and only when the conspiracy poses risks *beyond* the risk of consummating the particular harm that was the object of the initial conspiratorial agreement).[38] The standards form assumes that the fact-finder can judge whether the agreement was ongoing, multifaceted, and established like a criminal organization, though this is rarely a mechanically applicable, straightforward issue of the sort that constrains prejudiced or arbitrary judgment. The rules forms are inapt in terms of the purposes ascribed to conspiracy rules: the rule always to tag sentences is based on a supposition, sure to be untrue on some occasions, that all criminal agreements establish multifaceted criminal organizations; the rule never to tag is incompatible with our other practices that assume that organizations pose special dangers.

Likewise, it is hard to look at the Supreme Court's attempts over the past decade to elucidate the occasions when the death penalty may be applied constitutionally as anything more than a particularly dramatic lesson in the instability of both the rule and the standard form, with each pole rapidly and completely undercutting the other.[39] The Court eliminates a death penalty grounded in unguided jury discretion,[40] forcing the legislatures to write statutes establishing ostensibly rulelike aggravating circumstances that define capital murder[41] as long as they are not applied in a rigid, rulelike, mandatory, nondiscretionary fashion,[42] until there is a requirement, vaguely guided by statutes that now seem to have only vague exemplary power,[43] that the jury hear of practically everything that may mitigate punishment, once they are satisfied that an aggravated form of murder has been committed. Rules will surely be imprecise, for it is obviously impossible to capture categorically all meaningful distinctions between killers; standards will be enforced in an arbitrary way, perhaps even a racist one.[44]

My sense is that most mainstream lawyers will quickly acknowledge the degree to which these rules-standards problems prevail in these areas of the criminal law, despite our ostensibly strong ideological commitment to rule boundedness. I suspect too that most mainstream lawyers will acknowledge that the constitutional injunction against vague statutes is hardly applied to all statutes with language that is anything but mechanically or uncontroversially applied to facts, and that the void-for-vagueness doctrine itself is anything but rulelike.[45]

What is perhaps even more interesting is that innumerable covert battles between rules and standards are simply never interpreted that way, in part because the rules pole is believed to be so privileged in criminal jurisprudence that non-CLS commentators invariably seem to ignore the pervasiveness of the dilemma.

Most interesting, the battle between the tendency of certain courts and legislatures to hold defendants strictly liable for causing certain harms[46] and the absolutely uniform ideological hostility to this practice by academic commentators[47] and reformist legislatures[48] has simply never been seen, outside of CLS writing, as a simple rules-standards battle. Still, the interpretation ultimately seems unexceptionable. Say that a legislature is trying to decide on the appropriate *form* of command to fact-finders who will ascertain when a bar owner whose employees sell liquor to the underaged is blameworthy for supervising inadequately. One possible rules form is associated with strict liability: one could, hypothetically, tell decision makers that the third time a defendant's establishment sells to the underaged, he is conclusively presumed to have been too careless.[49] The standards form is associated with a general definition of negligence: wherever the defendant has made an illicit sale and taken *unreasonable* risks that the persons he sells to may be underage, he is guilty. A third possibility is to *define* negligence in a relatively rulelike fashion: for instance, if defendant has sold to a minor, and has not established a system under which ten strangers with fake IDs have tested his employees in the last month, he is culpable. Each position has characteristic formal flaws. Conclusive presumptions will surely be inaccurate in certain cases: there may well be a defendant who was simply unlucky. The rulelike negligence standard may also be unduly bureaucratic, overcentralized, and irrational, forcing people to adopt ineffective, overpriced systems just to stay out of trouble,[50] or inaccurate in the same way as strict liability (if fact-finders convict people who have actually been as careful as those who have adopted the suggested system). An open-ended negligence standard, though, allows prejudice and discretion and may well permit conviction not only for no reason (defendant happens to be unlucky) but for *bad* reasons (defendant happens to be unpopular). The fact that strict liability has been universally condemned in postwar mainstream legal writing without any mention of the possibility that the debate is just another replay of the rules-standards problem is really a tribute to the power to gain new insights by recognizing the degree to which legal discourse is often simply a recurring restatement of a small number of contradictory postures.

One would see any number of other doctrinal issues in the criminal law afresh if one focused on the centrality of the form problem. For example, a longstanding question in criminal law is how to grade the imperfect self-defender's crime. A defendant kills intentionally, unreasonably believing the victim to have posed a threat against which he was entitled to defend himself.[51] Ought he to be characterized as a (relatively nonculpable) negligent killer or as something more culpable? The dispute may be profitably seen as a battle between those committed to the rule-obsessed legalist notion that levels of culpability must, because they are formal definitional elements of an offense, be accurately captured by a limited number of mechanically applicable descriptions of mental states (acting with purpose, with knowledge, recklessly, or negligently)[52] and those who have no such unbending legalist commitment. The "nonlegalists" are obviously more willing to let the factfinder recognize that the imperfect self-defender may be neither much like the typical negligent killer (who kills without any awareness that anyone will be harmed) nor like the typical intentional killer (who can explain his decision to kill, insofar as any decision can be explained, only by reference to incidents, beliefs, and fears temporally removed from the homicidal act), though he is surely neither knowing nor reckless, the two intermediate categories the rules advocate can comprehend.

For a second example, a defendant makes a mistake about "legal facts" germane to the issue of whether he is violating a governing statute of which he is at least nominally aware.[53] The question of which such mistakes are exculpatory is illuminated once one sees that a rules-standards dilemma is once more covertly present. Defendant knows it is illegal to commit bigamy but is unaware that he is still married (a legal fact germane to the question of whether he is violating the general governing norm against bigamy). He may not realize that he is still married (a legal conclusion) because of what would uniformly be deemed a potentially exculpatory factual mistake (for example, he received a forged divorce decree, a situation we describe as involving a factual error because drawing a legal conclusion would be easy and uncontroversial once one knew the particulars of the situation). Or he may make two different types of "legal factual" mistakes: in one sort of case he is unaware that he has a common law spouse because he is unaware of the existence of common law marriage, or he is unaware of the invalidity of an out-of-state divorce; in the other sort he believes that physical separation from his wife constitutes a valid divorce. Rule advocates will feel impelled to treat these two cases identically at a doctrinal level; if they are to be differentiated, it can be done only on a factual basis, such as whether one belief was more reasonable than the other. Standards advocates may recognize that the second mistake "slides toward" the traditionally nonexculpatory pure mistake of law, that it is in some inevitably vague sense hard to say what it means to know the law against bigamy but not understand the difficulty and solemnity of divorce. To take this position, one must recognize that one cannot determine culpability by making a series of discrete and seemingly technical rule-bound inquiries, for there are only two available rules to guide us. The first is, "Mistakes as to governing statutes are nonexculpatory (if defendant seemingly "knows" the statute). The second is, "Mistakes as to germane legal facts may be exculpatory." Since defendant's mistake is legal-factual, the rule advocate is bound to acquit if the error is nonculpable. Instead, one must make a nonmechanical judgment about the degree to which defendant's conduct actually undermines "statutory schemes," must recognize that the distinction between knowing a statute and knowing how it applies to particular situations is inexorably blurred.

For a third example, let us assume that one is in a jurisdiction where a rape defendant's subjectively held belief in a victim's consent to intercourse is nonexculpatory unless the belief is reasonable.[54] Assume too that we want to figure out whether a parallel negligent mistake of fact should inculpate when the rape is interrupted, when defendant is charged with attempted rape or assault with intent to commit rape.[55] Once aware of the pervasiveness of the rules-standards problem, one is prone to rethink completely an issue that is generally answered mechanically and formally. The real substantive worry is that since rape occurs over time, we may be reluctant to assume that a defendant who has not had all the opportunities that would ordinarily arise to learn of the victim's nonconsent would have proceeded to have unconsented-to intercourse. Those comfortable with standards might simply ask the fact-finders to convict only when they believed on the facts that they were sure beyond a reasonable doubt that rape would have occurred; one can readily imagine a situation, for instance, where the victim was bound and gagged and could not possibly have manifested further nonconsent had the attack not been interrupted by a third party. Those committed to rules might either demand that defendants in those circumstances *always* be exculpated (since abandonment was always possible) or inculpated (since abandonment should never be presumed) rather than allow jury discretion. The rules-standards dilemma is the inescapable one; the traditional way of dealing with the case (arguing that a subjectively unaware defendant *intends* not rape but consented-to intercourse) depends on an undefended assertion that it is somehow verbally impermissible to use an objective, *ex post,* rather than subjective, *ex ante* naming scheme in describing the objects of intention: since the defendant intends to commit deeds that outside observers would call rape, *ex post,* it is a silly formalist dodge to say that he clearly lacks the specific intent that attempts require.[56]

The list could readily be extended. It is not possible in fact to conceive of a legal dispute in which the choice of form is not implicated. What is more important, or more controversial at any rate, is that in each case there are no clear reasons to prefer one formal resolution to the other. It is indeed the case that one can imagine rules that have too many of the flaws ordinarily associated with rules or a standard that is excessively vague and nonadministrable, but when one actually gets down to disputes between "good" versions of rules and "good" standards, the formal arguments hardly seem resolvable. Moreover, the question of form remains "close," but not because the reasonable solutions are formally close: by eliminating very bad standards we do not reach formal solutions that are barely distinguishable but rather ones that still seem quite *opposed* to one another.

Let me illustrate this last point a bit further. Most mainstream scholars would assert that while there are certainly advantages to the use of standards in legal settings, by and large a good functionalist analyst "knows" that the costs of vagueness are so high in the criminal area that rules ought generally to be preferred. Any such grandiose assertion, though, is clearly sloppy and inapt: if nothing else, our commitment to premising punishment on the discovery of factually inaccessible mental states instead of just ascertainable acts demonstrates the difficulty of generally committing oneself to the rule form. It is surely true that one can imagine rules that are unduly inapt (for example, if one conclusively presumed that everyone who killed someone in an auto accident intended to kill) or standards that are unduly unadministrable (for example, if the entire criminal code consisted of the sentence, "People should be punished in proportion to the evil of their deeds"); but in any real substantive dispute a rulelike and a substantially more standardlike position could readily be offered to do equal battle (a well-tailored conclusive presumption is never conclusively better or worse than a well-guided discretionary standard). Still, though, the well-tailored rule and the standard will not closely resemble each other. For instance, the Model Penal Code standards defining attempt or conspiracies where cumulative punishment is apt are by no means fraternal twins with the available rules. Likewise, even if we eliminated truly unreasonable versions of strict criminal liability (conclusive presumptions of negligence in situations where nonnegligent harm causing was in fact *common*), the *reasonable* versions would still differ greatly from an open-ended negligence standard, and formal critiques of each position would remain to be made. It is true too that the extreme standards and extreme rules sometimes converge in the sense that open-ended standards are made more rulelike by the use of exemplars and in the sense that rules are tempered to become more standardlike by limiting their jurisdictional coverage or scope; but the convergence I believe I have demonstrated in dealing with real doctrine is not toward *a* point but toward at least two distinct and distant points. If mainstream lawyers are to make a convincing case that the Critics are wrong to see formal *contradiction,* rather than a list of policy concerns to be balanced to arrive at a rational and sensible solution, they must demonstrate some fairly general tendency for formal disputes to converge toward a single balanced solution, must counter the tendency, which I believe I have demonstrated in my examples, for irreducible formal conflict to persist. Perhaps my claim will be even more plausible as I extend the analysis of the problem of form to include examples from both public and private law outside the areas of contracts and criminal law.

Examples from Public Law outside the Criminal Area

Simon's article on the welfare rights movement[57] shows quite vividly the perceptions one can gain by analyzing an issue as an instance of a rules-standards conflict. Broadly speaking, welfare reformers in the late 1960s and 1970s implemented changes in the public assistance system so that it is now largely administered through two sorts of rules: *substantive* rules describing eligibility requirements in terms easily applied and *procedural* rules demanding formal proof and records that one meets these mechanical eligibility requirements. Though the two forms of rules are not intrinsically or logically inseparable, if one couples a commitment to eligibility rules with a desire to easily supervise those charged with the duty to enforce these rules to ensure that they are complying, procedural rigidity indeed seems a natural correlate. The pro-rules vision is contrasted with the traditional professional social work vision in which caseworkers have authority both to make situationally sensitive grants and to judge recipient credibility on a case-by-case basis.[58]

As Simon notes, the nightmare vision in the standards-based system was the welfare worker as intrusive despot, disciplining recipients for departures (particularly sexual departures) from stuffy caseworker norms; the nightmare vision of the "reformed" rule-bound system is the Kafkaesque bureaucrat sending the would-be recipient from line to line, ultimately to have her request for funds denied because she lacks some utterly meaningless, unattainable slip of paper. The welfare recipient without rights, without formal entitlements may feel that she has nothing to call her own; the welfare recipient with nothing but entitlements may never sense that anyone cares for her at all.

Part of Simon's achievement is to see what CLS adherents understand will always occur in situations of rules-standards tensions and to see it, once more, in an area where controversy had seemingly died. Neither position can ultimately dominate the other; legalist ideology (which at first was associated with welfare reform lawyers, later with welfare cost cutters) excessively privileges the rules position, simply suppressing the costs of legalism. Simon also sees previously unobserved consequences of the move toward rules in this area that may prove especially interesting; in the rule-bound system one would expect casework to be proletarianized, turned from a professional to a clerical skill. This in turn poses both new divisions or hostilities between worker and client and different opportunities for longer-term political unity between recipients and workers.

At a more general level, of course, the usual battles we confront over regulatory bureaucratization is in large part a parallel rules-standards battle: must the Occupational Safety and Health Administration (OSHA) tell everyone precisely how many feet wide scaffolding must be or just proscribe "unreasonable" safety hazards? The rule will surely ignore relevant distinctions between work settings (distinctions, for example, in the capacity of employees to avoid harm in other ways), but the standard might well be unenforceable or subject to abusive discretion. Moreover, to the extent that substantive compliance depends on easily verifiable complaints—which it arguably will if all enforcement is centralized—the standards may be paper tigers. Only in a setting in which beneficiaries of regulation have sufficient independent power to reverse unsafe conditions without relying on state intervention will the state feel utterly free to set up a standard against unreasonable danger without fear that victims have not really been additionally empowered. (The Swedish occupational safety act, which is frequently enforced through far vaguer regulations, is enforced in a setting of relatively strong union power, where the additional chip of state certification of the reasonableness of taking private action against unsafe conditions is exactly that, just another chip.)[59]

Similar questions can be posed in most of the regulatory areas: how flexible ought the Environmental Protection Agency (EPA) to be in limiting effluent discharge? how sensitive to marginal variations in containment cost for different sources?[60] Should antitrust regulators adopt per se rules on such practices as horizontal mergers, price discrimination, or resale price maintenance, or make case-by-case determinations of the effect of each potentially regulated practice?[61] Should we categorically prohibit defensive tactics against corporate takeovers or analyze each takeover to see whether it would serve the efficiency-increasing purposes attributed to beneficial takeovers?[62] Simon's insight that substantive bureaucratization will generally be coupled with procedural bureaucratization because of the impulse to control front-line discretion by centralized, hierarchical management means that we can expect "victims" of rule-bound regulation to complain not only of substantively unjust restrictions but of excessive record keeping and compliance costs; but it is of course plausible that in some regulatory fields a move away from per se rules would mandate that actors present far *more* extensive documentation, not just documentation of *what* they were doing but *why* they were doing it. (For instance, if the Federal Trade Commission were to rule on the acceptability of proposed mergers, record-keeping and information-reporting requirements would be *less* extensive if one simply had to report the market share of the would-be merged companies and defend one's market definition than if one had to argue more extensively that no damage would be done to the capacity of others to enter the market in the future, or argue that there had been no shift in the possibility of oligopolistic collusion.)

Similarly, the rules-standards dilemma has been pervasive in tax law

as well. It is always questionable whether Congress can actually differentiate favored from unfavored transactions in a rulelike fashion, particularly given the fact that taxpayers learn the Internal Revenue Code
and then plan their transactions so as to meet the objective requirements
that a rule promising favorable treatment demands.[63] Take a typical
substantive problem: we believe that taxpayers who receive benefits in
kind may not value them as highly as their market price, but it is also
plausible that in-kind benefits are (or worse, have become since the
Code has been enacted) a bargained-for substitute for cash if in-kind
receipts are not taxed at market value. Take a typical relatively rulelike
solution: §119 of the Code provides that when an employee is required
to live on the employer's premises as a condition of employment, the
value of lodging is excludable. But of course it is perfectly plausible that
someone who wouldn't at all mind living on the employer's premises
will bargain to *appear* contractually bound to do so. A "standard" that
excluded the value of lodging only when there was reason to believe
the taxpayer significantly disvalued it might better cope with the case.

The battle has been joined by the courts, which announce perfectly
counterbalanced, perfectly contradictory paeans to both the rule and
the standard position. On the one hand, a taxpayer is allowed to minimize taxes (as Learned Hand said in Gregory v. Helvering, "Anyone
may so arrange his affairs that his taxes shall be as low as possible").[64]
On the other hand, the courts and Internal Revenue Service (IRS) retain
the power to recharacterize all transactions either where the purpose of
the transaction is solely to lower taxes (unless Congress clearly approves
that purpose, as it does, for instance, in encouraging people to purchase
lower-yield tax-exempt municipal bonds) or, more commonly, where
the sole motive the taxpayer had for *characterizing* the transaction in
the form she did, rather than a form that would have identical business
consequences, was to minimize taxes. As Judge Hand also said, dissenting, in *Gilbert*,[65] "If . . . the taxpayer enters into a transaction that
does not appreciably affect his beneficial interest except to reduce his
taxes, the law will disregard it." Not all of the "abusive" tax shelters
we hear about involve using the rules counterpurposively—the bulk may
well involve simple deceit, particularly overstating the value of depreciable property by ostensibly purchasing for a high face-value note the
"buyer" will never actually pay—but it is surely also the case that some
of what we call "shelter abuse" is rather like working the rules too hard,
walking the line carefully but counterpurposively.

The battle occurs not just in the domain of abstract judicial statements on whether a taxpayer's duty is to comply not just with the words but the spirit of the Code; it also occurs when reformers try to ascertain how best to eliminate what is widely perceived as wholesale tax shelter abuse. One should expect a reform response consistent with the standards form: let the IRS knock out, on a case-by-case basis, deductions that would seem to be permitted until we look more closely at the reasons behind the deduction. At the same time, we should expect rule-bound responses (such as §465 of the Code, which limits the depreciable basis of nonrealty to the amount at risk, even though were all nonrecourse loans properly valued, the limitation would be hard to fathom). One should expect this oscillation to occur wherever the possibility of abuse is perceived. Can the IRS judge case-by-case when §125 "cafeteria plans," which in essence insure employees who make certain favored expenditures (medical, legal, educational), become cash-compensation substitutes because funds are received whether spent in the favored way or not, or must any plan with any cash options ultimately be rejected as a cash substitute? The interest from municipal bonds is tax exempt in order to aid local government. What formal governance structure will best preclude private parties from receiving the subsidy intended for local governments by issuing corporate bonds through municipalities: a hard-to-administer set of "standards" that attempt to describe when a project is inadequately "public" or when more clearly private Industrial Development Bonds are nonetheless acceptable, or rules placing limits on the sort of low-dollar offerings we believe are most likely to be abused? Once more, the list could be practically endless.

Finally, Al Katz and Lee Teitelbaum have traced the degree to which another public law field, juvenile law, has oscillated between rule-bound models (which constrain or attempt to resocialize juveniles only when they violate precise, quasicriminal norms) and standards models (which try to judge in a more open-ended way whether a child is becoming wayward).[66] Once more, Katz and Teitelbaum rehearse the usual sense of irresolvable conflict, but also like Simon, they note an interesting set of consequences that are particularly powerful in the specific area they are studying. To the extent that one of the capacities one wants a juvenile to develop is independent judgment, a juvenile law that lists precisely all the things he may not do hampers development. A rulelike juvenile law thus poses dilemmas of autonomy and socialization. Once more, though, the focus on the centrality of our contradictory *formal* postures enables us both to put a perennial debate in perspective and to gain new insight about its underlying substance.

Examples from Private Law outside of Contracts

While Kennedy's critical article focused largely on contract, disputes in the other common law or private law fields could readily be understood as implicating rules-standards problems.

The most basic issue in tort law, the standard of care we owe to strangers, has historically been answered in the oscillating ways consistent with the basic prediction that neither the rule nor the standard form is stable. There is a paradigmatic rule position: defendant is strictly liable to plaintiff; that is, he is liable wherever he has caused harm (the only vagueness surrounds the tricky causation issue, but since this degree of vagueness ineradicably occurs regardless of the standard of care, strict liability is maximally rulelike). There is a paradigmatic standard position as well: defendant is liable only when negligent—that is, only when his level of care is "unreasonable." (Economists have often argued that the negligence standard might be interpreted in a relatively rulelike fashion.[67] To believe this argument, one must believe several implausible claims: that courts in fact have decided that people are unreasonable when and only when they have failed to take precautions that would have averted more damage than they cost, and that courts can as readily and mechanically decide in actual cases whether the defendant has failed to take precautions that avert harm most cheaply as they can decide that defendant will be deemed the cause of a particular injury.) Naturally, too, there are paradigmatic "intermediate positions": defendants may be strictly liable as long as their product designs are defective[68] or plaintiffs make reasonable uses,[69] or defendants may be presumed negligent if dealing with ultrahazardous activities,[70] or if they violate a statute mandating a certain level of care,[71] or even in the absence of explicit proof, if there is little reason to think that the accident would have occurred but for negligence (res ipsa loquitur).[72]

Naturally, rules-standards issues appear in other aspects of tort law as well. Often proponents of abolishing certain duties argue that the properly delimited version of the "duty" that they want abolished could only be defined so imprecisely that inconsistency, unpredictability, and prejudicial judgment will run rampant. Ought there to be action for inflicting emotional distress? Opponents usually note that courts that have been sympathetic to such a claim inevitably restrict it to situations is which defendant's conduct is "outrageous"; then they complain that an "outrageousness" standard is nonadministrable.[73] Ought we to maintain the historic tort action for criminal conversation? Assume we believe that the *traditional* rigid rule was too harsh in not allowing a defendant to plead that he had been seduced or even lied to about the marital status of the person with whom he had sexual relations. Those who urge abolition of the tort will argue that the *reformed* tort, allowing rather open-ended defenses based on the actor's substantive innocence, is so unadministrable that a new rigid rule of no duty is preferable.[74]

In property law, rules-standards dilemmas are likewise omnipresent. Rules exist that seemingly imply that property cannot be transferred at death except through hyperformal wills;[75] yet many far less formal devices exist to reverse the results that would have been reached if rules were unfailingly rigidly enforced (for example quasicontracts to transfer property at death to those who served the deceased in reliance on a promised bequest;[76] finding irrevocable *inter vivos* transfers even when the donor seems to have retained most significant control).[77] Easements (formal interests permitting a non–fee holder to make some use of land from which the fee holder could otherwise exclude the user) may seemingly be created only by formal written deed in the absence of prescriptive use or implication,[78] but irrevocable licenses with nearly identical effects may be found through promissory estoppel and reasonable reliance.[79] Should the Rule against Perpetuities be remorselessly applied to classes of beneficiaries (that is, as a readily applicable rule)[80] or applied only to those particular beneficiaries whose interests might actually vest remotely?[81]

Often the pervasiveness of the rules-standards dilemma in property law is obscured for a reason that may seem formalistic, historically quirky: the rules position is associated with the traditional common law domain, the standards position with the traditional equity domain.[82] To the extent that we believe that we are dealing with distinct doctrines rather than doctrines that address the same underlying factual disputes, we may not see the dilemma. Historically, many contract disputes were resolved differently in equity and at law, but mainstream commentators have so thoroughly integrated decisions from these dispute-settlement traditions that one would be hard pressed to find a commentator who did not, say, integrate (law-based) decisions that disallow midterm contractual revisions for want of consideration with those (equity-based) ones that allow an implicit recision followed by a new contract. In property, the legal tradition is to use rules to promote full-blown, unfettered alienability of each generation's holding, even when a paternalistic settlor wanted to restrict the grantee's control. Attempts to limit full-scale alienability of property were simply struck down regardless of reasonableness or of the probability that alienability would actually be seriously impaired. The mechanical imposition of the rule against restraints on alienation, the Rule against Perpetuities, or the doctrine of the destructibility of contingent remainders all result in ensuring that someone will hold fully and freely alienable fee property as soon as possible. But the attack on restrictiveness is by no means thoroughgoing. It is an often invisible conflict with the equitable *trust* tradition of spendthrifting (restricting grantee and creditor access to capital)[83] or the *Claflin* doctrine for avoiding premature termination of an income-paying trust,[84] doctrines that permit significant barriers to alienation often invoking vague standards that the restraints be in some fashion reasonable.[85] More frequently these have been seen as utterly separate doctrines, generally taught in law schools in separate courses.

It is not just these technical disputes that mainstream academics, at least sometimes, recognize as involving issues of form but larger substantive issues about the nature of property that invariably covertly invoke the most basic rules-standards dilemma: the degree to which we ascribe to any member of a class the features of all members of a class (the rule position) or the degree to which we never categorize more than the limits of language seem to require us to do. Take the series of disputes that engrossed the Supreme Court for over a decade on the degree to which shopping center owners could exclude nondisruptive political pickets and speakers.[86] In a sense, the dispute can most profitably be seen as an ongoing battle between those who unconsciously argued that the *property ownership* category should be rulelike, general, and abstract rather than situationally sensitive and those who unconsciously argued that the *speech rights* category must be rulelike. On the one hand, proponents of the right to exclude analogize the shopping center owner to the homeowner, thus implicitly analogizing kicking out a picket to throwing a door-to-door missionary out of one's living room, without detailed inquiry into the situational distinctions between the cases.[87] Ownership is ownership; a rule is a rule. On the other hand, proponents of access often seemed to treat the ban on speaking as if it were invariably a total ban on effective communication, with relatively little regard to alternative outlets (at least until they were forced to defend a shrinking core of privileged shopping center speech once the Court's majority had accepted some clear property-owner rights to ban speech).[88] Bans on speaking are bans on speaking; rules are rules. In a sense, any politically charged issue on ownership rights covertly but significantly shares some of this formal dimension: anytime one defends

an owner's right to close or move a particular business, refuse to deal
with a would-be buyer or worker for no reason or for "suspect" reasons,
or make political contributions on the basis of an "analogy" with some
other owner whose discretion to take such actions we want to protect,
one is covertly arguing for the more rulelike form, *against* the possibility
of increasingly situationally sensitive judgment.[89]

General Arguments for Rules and for Standards

In this section I shall explore the abstract arguments for and against
each formal position, emphasizing the traditional list and presenting
additional CLS arguments against the pro-rule position.

Why Rules and Standards Are Both No Good

Rules are bad because they are underinclusive as to purpose, overinclusive as to purpose, or both. Any age of majority (for voting, contract,
sexual consent) obviously is both under- and overinclusive as to purpose;
some people below the age will be as capable and mature as the typical
adult; some above the age will still be immature and incapable. Section
119 of the Internal Revenue Code is likewise both: some people required
to live on an employer's premises don't radically devalue the receipt of
these lodgings; some people who live near but not on the premises or
feel constrained, though not contractually bound, to live on the premises
will value these premises far less than their market price. Rulelike definitions of attempt—which allow the actor to go unpunished until he
has taken the last possible step in his control—or contract norms that
leave a party unbound until there has been a mirror-image acceptance
to his initial offer are predominantly underinclusive, though with some
strain one might see their overinclusive aspects as well,[90] for each fails
to impose legal consequences on parties whom we might substantively
wish faced such consequences. The rulelike lists of aggravating factors
in statutes describing the conditions under which murders are capital
crimes and rules enforcing all contracts in which each party receives
some nominal consideration are predominantly, though not exclusively,
overinclusive in that certain explicit legal consequences would be visited
on more parties than we would want if these rules were remorselessly
applied. Since standards are simply *restatements* of purpose, they cannot,
in theory, be under- or overinclusive as to purpose, though of course

they may be *applied* in a way that fails to meet the decision maker's purposes.

Standards are bad because they are subject to arbitrary and/or prejudiced enforcement.The unguided death penalty standard (which *Furman* ostensibly rejected but to which we have more or less returned) is arguably subject to both sorts of critique: it is probably arbitrarily enforced (in the sense that few claim to discern morally lucid patterns to death sentences) and probably prejudicially enforced (at least in discounting the value of protecting black victims, though probably not in executing disproportionate numbers of black defendants,[91] except when rape was a capital crime).[92] Rules, of course, are designed to permit little discretion; they ensure that people will perceive that they are treated uniformly, even if the dimension along which they have been treated uniformly strikes them as insignificant.

Rules are bad because they enable a person to "walk the line," to use the rules to his own advantage, counterpurposively. Farmers were allowed to deduct feed costs immediately rather than capitalize them over the useful life of the herd, on the theory that it would simplify bookkeeping for financially unsophisticated operators;[93] perfectly financially sophisticated syndicates of physicians formed cattle-feed shelters that used this and other deduction-accelerating rules to reduce unrelated taxable income.[94] A perfectly competent infant enters into a contract knowing he can void it should it prove advantageous to do so; a legally sophisticated buyer enters into an oral forward contract with a legally naive seller, expecting to take delivery if the price of the goods rises but to use the Statute of Frauds to defend against any claim to pay up should the market fall.

Obviously people could not "walk the line" if rules were not overbroad, but this critique of rules is distinct from the first one in two significant ways. First, the only implication of the first critique is that a set of rules applied to a *fixed* social situation will lead to some injustice or counterpurposive results; this critique implies that the social situation will not stay fixed once the rules are in place, but that unjust outcomes will occur more often because people will actively attempt to arrange their affairs so that they are favored by the rules. The rule that allowed farmers to deduct immediately total feed costs was *always* somewhat inapt (since some farmers were undoubtedly financially sophisticated even when the general rule was announced); this critique centers on the fact that it *becomes* more frequently inapt once announced as others (the cattle-feeding tax shelter partnership) pretend to be worthy beneficiaries. Second, "walking the line" is an objectionable social practice in and of itself, a mode of relations to others we might deplore as much as or more than we deplore the fact that bad social decisions occur in random cases.

There is also an aspect of the "walking the line" problem that Simon brought to light in his article on legal ethics,[95] another example of the utility of maintaining one's focus on these recurring dilemmas. Lawyers have learned to make ethical distinctions between taking advantage of what I would call (only for convenience) primary and secondary procedural barriers. No mainstream tax lawyer seems to feel that it is legitimate to misdate a document of purchase or sale so that one will meet, say, a holding-period requirement for paying the (pre-1986) lower capital gains tax, simply because the objective chances of audit are small enough to make the benefit of lower tax payment higher than the expected penalty. The limitation on audit resources (a primary procedural barrier) indeed limits what the state can hope to accomplish if citizens make purely self-interested choices, but mainstream practitioners simply assume that it does not undercut the vitality of the substantive norm— that is, that people are not "meant" to pay a lower rate of tax unless they actually hold property for the holding period. Likewise, though no one may be convicted of murder unless he is proven beyond a reasonable doubt to have killed, no lawyer would tell a client, prospectively, that it is not murder if he kills without leaving proof beyond a reasonable doubt. Holmes's strong positivist injunction that the law is simply a prediction of state action seems clearly excessive from the vantage point of the mainstream.

But *every* mainstream tax lawyer sees it not only as legitimate but as his *job* to give advice to clients about how to structure a deal so as to maximize favorable tax consequences, even when the deal is not one Congress would have wanted to favor. No mainstream tax lawyer would tell a client that it is illegitimate to exclude from income the value of accommodations under §119 if he would have paid market price for those accommodations; quite to the contrary, tax lawyers in fact busily drew up plans for Zero-Based Reimbursement Accounts (ZEBRAs) under §125 (on "cafeteria plans") which gave taxpayers a choice between cash and ostensibly in-kind receipts as long as Congress allowed them to do so. Yet it is perfectly plausible to see the rulelike nature of §119 as precisely parallel to a factual limit on the number of IRS auditors: both are simply concessions to the high administrative expenses of policing. It is a *secondary* enforcement limit, not one where we see constraints (of cost, of competing principle) in the enforcement of existing norms, but one where the definition of the substantive norm itself is somewhat constrained because of costs and competing principle. Claims that the two sorts of limits on enforcement are radically distinct, because only in the case of primary enforcement bars do we really *know* that a norm has been violated, survive little detailed scrutiny. One could readily say that Congress intended only those persons who could be caught, given our auditing resources, to pay ordinary income (not capital gains) taxes on property whose holding period could be readily lied about. In fact we routinely make just such arguments about laws against private consensual nonmarital sex, where we believe that they are *intended* to be dramatically underenforced. Conversely, it is difficult to ascribe any plausible purpose to Congress's enacting §119 that does not relate to the purported devaluation of forced in-kind receipts by taxpayers. The rule form, though, creates opportunities for counterpurposive activity; exploiting these opportunities may well be one of the special and central aspects of lawyering, so much at its very core that to question its ethical status is to turn the mundane and routine into the charged and equivocal.

Standards are bad because they give people no clear warning about the consequences of their behavior. This leads both to the unfairness we associate with surprise and to the inefficiency we would expect when private parties are unable to plan. Knowing whether to expect delivery of goods or the benefit of one's bargain depends both on knowing clearly that one is in a contractual relationship and that its terms will not be scrutinized for substantive fairness. A party will never be sure if he can expect something from someone who arguably bargained in bad faith; a party will never completely know if a judge will consider the terms he dealt on unconscionable. Many of the standard arguments for a rulelike legal code were based on the idea that commercial planning required legal certainty, an argument often (somewhat misleadingly) attributed to Max Weber.[96]

Standards are preferable because their efficiency cost may be low or, alternatively, they may indeed be *more* efficient. It is by no means obvious that, as a source of risk, legal uncertainty is either significant or especially difficult to insure against. To assert that a contractor is nearly as worried about the uncertain legal interpretation of a vague standard as he would be about the potential insolvency of his contracting partner is to engage in mock-empirical fancy. Moreover, parties who expect good faith behavior may well be taken off guard by the imposition of rules, particularly when ongoing relations have typically precluded the intervention of a rule-observing judge or arbitrator.

Rules are good because they make the outcome of any possible litigation so certain, so readily ascertainable in advance by both parties, that the administratively expensive process of litigation will rarely be invoked. Assuming that parties will not ordinarily litigate but settle when they know and agree on which party will ultimately prevail (unless they have dramatically divergent estimates of their relative litigation costs), the idea appears unexceptionable that increasing predictability will lower the use of a costly system.

Rules are bad because they inevitably have gaps and conflicts and are thus less mechanically applicable than they might appear (this is an issue I'll return to). The open invocation of an apparently vague standard, though, may be reasonably predictable in practice because even relatively detailed tacit community norms so converge that application of vague policy sentiments to cases poses little danger of disagreement. Moreover, to the extent that the application of a rule leads to what is routinely perceived as an unjust or harsh result, litigation may actually flourish as courts attempt to limit the force or scope of the initial rule with counterrules, and as people are then forced to litigate the scope of the proliferating counterrules.

Rules are good because they are dynamically stabilizing. If decision makers are willing to put up with disquieting results in particular cases, people will gradually learn to comply with the rules. The first time one invalidates a will because of a formal defect, one may well feel that one is both failing to observe the testator's intention and illegitimately favoring legal heirs over would-be beneficiaries; but over time people will learn to draw their wills correctly, and disputes will diminish.

Rules are bad because they are dynamically *de*stabilizing. First, they may become more inaccurate over time as people "walk the line" and increasingly arrange their affairs so as to benefit from the rule. Second, as results become more visibly unjust, the rule system may grow more complex in order to accommodate exceptions. Third, as it becomes apparent that legal results turn on technical factors, on at best random (and at worst class-biased) access to legal counsel, the pressure to skirt a rule-bound system will grow. If we assume that welfare eligibility comes to turn increasingly on irrelevant documentation, it is possible *not* that people will better document their transactions but that recipients

will simply resist both reasonable and unreasonable bureaucratic requests. As citizens perceive that taxable income is measured not by a
standard (well-offness) but by exacting application of income-measuring
rules manipulated by those with access to counsel, they may resist routine legal demands and simply fail to comply with a self-reporting
system.

Are Rules Possible?

The CLS position has generally been quite skeptical of the very *possibility* of a rule-governed regime. Later on, we shall explore whether it
is possible to claim simultaneously, as CLS writers seem to, that the use
of rules to govern a regime has certain political implications *and* that
such a regime of rules really doesn't exist. But for now I shall focus on
the claim of nonexistence.

CLS adherents do not usually claim that there are no decision-guiding
statements that radically diminish enforcement discretion. While most
CLS writers have undoubtedly emphasized the inherent ambiguity of
language, and the correlate incapacity to restrain discretion through
language,[97] the more coherent CLS position has moved *away* from the
tendency of certain Legal Realists to focus on the limitlessness of interpretations of each verbal command. The prototypical Realist claim about
the impossibility of rules focused on the fact that a seemingly clear
referential word in a statute would cover cases no one would want it to
cover unless the statute were reread purposively. If the local ordinance
proscribes vehicles in the park, does it cover the statue of the general
in his jeep? Can we know without thinking about why the ordinance
was passed, simply by scrutinizing the meaning of the word *vehicle?* My
belief is that the CLS position has partly embraced and significantly
reformulated the Realist position on two aspects of rule ambiguity—
both the claim that language is vague and the claim that when two
conflicting rules often cover the same factual setting, there is no separate
mechanical rule as to which one governs. In addition, the CLS position
has emphasized the degree to which the question of the *extent* to which
governing bodies are committed to *total* rule enforcement is itself invariably ambiguous, so that the real operative rule is rarely clearly
known even when the nominal rule is, on the face of it, unambiguous.
Once more, then, the point is that no significant legal *regime* is rule
grounded even when there appear to be particular rules.

Language Ambiguity

One of the most entertaining sports that the early Legal Realists engaged in was to tweak their treatise-writing, rule-collecting Formalist forebears for announcing that they had discovered legal rules that were, on inspection, utterly vacuous and question begging. Mainstream first-year law teachers still take a certain delight in demonstrating that the hornbook statement of a rule the students have struggled mightly to memorize gets them absolutely nowhere. It is all well and good, say modern mainstream post-Realists, to know that a covenant will bind successors when it "touches and concerns" the land; but if the determination that it touches and concerns the land is indistinguishable from our judgment that it ought to bind successors, we have not really reduced the law-determination process to the desired simple mechanical operation. A contract may be voided when the parties have made a mistake that "goes to the essence of the transaction"; but there are few such readily discernible essences out there in the world. Corporations were subject to a court's jurisdiction, said the Formalists, when and only when they were "present" in the jurisdiction; Realists emphasized the extent to which the determination of "presence" was undifferentiable from the open-ended determination of the wisdom of subjecting them to jurisdiction.

It strikes me that CLS adherents have modified this claim to a significant degree. It *is* possible to establish legal rules, increasingly detailed in covering available cases, that can become mechanically applicable to the vast bulk of actual controversies, but *practice* may well become settled only at the cost of *principled doctrine* becoming chaotic.

Let me give an example. The Supreme Court mandates that state legislatures must list in their capital murder statutes those circumstances that aggravate an ordinary premeditated homicide. The legislature responds by listing, among many other possibilities, that two particularly heinous forms of killing are killing witnesses or otherwise killing to avoid arrest and killing for financial gain.[98]

The point the language-fixated Realists made was that such statutes are inevitably vague on their faces, and, in a sense, it is true that it is not at all clear what actual situations are covered by these categories. It is surely the case that a defendant who murders someone on the morning he is due to testify against him in court has killed a witness, but is it true that the gas station hold-up man has also killed a witness when he decides to wipe out anyone who *might* later identify him? What if he says, "Nobody's going to testify against me," as he shoots? Likewise, a hired killer has clearly killed for financial gain, but is the section also meant to refer to those who kill in the course of ordinary robberies? What about those who kill because they would otherwise be unable to seize desired property?

The most typical CLS position, I believe, is that it is an exaggeration to hold that contexts and situations are *perceived* as so rich that an infinite variety of testing cases will actually arise: courts will soon decide what to do with killers of on-the-scene witnesses and robbing murderers, and practice will be as settled as a rules advocate would desire. The word *witness* will be deemed to apply to certain common situations and not to all others; the delimited "witness" concept will soon be reasonably mechanically applicable, even if the single word was not.[99] The larger problem may be that practice becomes settled only at the risk that it becomes openly arbitrary, that all rules become rules maintained simply for rules' sake. The Realist hope that vague language will be rescued by recourse to settled purpose is turned on its head in the CLS critique: language remains relatively clear, but a knowledge of purpose makes the clarity appear arbitrary. If no one can comprehend *why* it is worse to shoot a witness in a judicial proceeding than to shoot someone who has claimed he will report your criminal conduct to the police, or even someone who *might,* the hope of all rule advocates that their system will be derivable from a relatively short list of governing principles fades completely. The need for a longer list of increasingly fact-specific rules negates two key features of the normatively desired rule system. First, citizens cannot conceivably know their precise obligations if they are not apparent from a knowledge of a short list of clear principles. Second, and more significant, while official discretion may be restrained in particular cases, the sense of arbitrariness and horizontal inequity that is supposedly limited by containing discretion runs wild when meaningless factual distinctions govern outcomes. It may be a *rule* that all defendants whose last names start with the same letter as that of the judge be acquitted or executed, but it hardly mitigates one's sense of facing random and unprincipled treatment.

The process I have described in the context of the death penalty is by no means unique to that setting. It is clearly the case, for instance, that a taxpayer may hold municipal bonds while carrying and deducting interest payments on a home mortgage that is larger than his bond holdings,[100] even though the Code ostensibly disallows interest deductions on borrowings incurred in order to carry municipal bonds. It would be hard to defend the practice either on the basis of the obviously

unconstraining statutory language of §265 *or* policy, but not the least
bit difficult to assure oneself that it definitely *is* the practice. One may
have been able to *predict* many more limitations on recovery for economic loss in tort law or acknowledge that courts traditionally were
more reluctant to give damages for emotional suffering in the absence
of physical injury than in its presence without seeing a cognizable general
principle applicable to innumerable cases covered by one's predictive
rule.[101]

Gaps and Conflicts

Realists were also fond of noting that *competing* rules existed side-by-
side, and that while each appeared to solve a problem without much
room for discretion, the *choice* of governing rule was so unconstrained
that each rule was in fact radically undercut by the presence of its
fratricidal twin. There is a seemingly clear contract rule that one cannot
enforce a promise to adjust the price of performing a contract in midterm
because the would-be obligor has received no consideration for his promise to pay more; yet the same factual situation is covered by a rule only
somewhat less formally realizable that parties may voluntarily rescind
an initial contract (in the absence of duress, fraud, and the like) and
negotiate a new one.[102] The parol evidence rules seemingly precluded
the introduction of any evidence of the parties' subjective intent extrinsic
to the final integrated writing, but supplementary undercutting rules
allow such evidence to be introduced to establish whether the writing
is a final integration, whether it is complete or meant to be read alongside
ancillary agreements, and whether it is defectively formed (for example,
if it is a product of fraud or duress).[103] Most commonly, an equitable
standard exists to counterbalance an overly harsh rule: I have already
mentioned that the informal law of irrevocable licenses exists side by
side with what is obviously, in practical terms, an incomplete formal
law of easements; likewise, informal gifts or irrevocable trusts or contracts to make wills could often be found where formal wills failed.

   Those in the CLS movement have made us aware that we must extend
the argument on gaps and conflicts in two significant ways. First, they
are more prone than the Realists to see the possibility that the invocation
of a clear rule in one area may not be counterbalanced by a conflicting
rule or standard that actors in the system see as arising in the same field,
but as "corrected" in what is generally seen as a separate domain. The
rule-respecting limitation of AFDC (Aid to Families with Dependent
Children) benefits to those with certain formal legal entitlements may

well be unaccompanied by a counterrule within AFDC, but may put pressures on other programs that deal with the poor. If the "factual situation" that the legal system deals with is poverty, it is obviously not enough to know precisely how the transfer-payment bureaucracy operates. The level of available revenue sharing for local housing programs, shifts in tax laws on charitable contributions or depreciation schedules for low-income housing, rules that do or do not require doctors with federal loans to work in poverty areas all represent legal responses to the *facts,* and the sum total of such legal responses is badly comprehended by any rule that purports to describe a poor person's entitlements, even if each and every agency correctly perceives itself as simply applying mechanical rules. The relevant legal *regime,* whether from the vantage point of an individual who would try to state in a simple fashion what he can expect given his circumstances or from the vantage point of a rule-bound state, at least insofar as a key commitment of the rule bound is to treat similar people similarly, is anything but mechanically derivable from a limited set of facts.

Second, CLS writers are more prone to see that complete legal relief depends not simply on the application of a rule but on a vague standard as well. Sometimes this breakdown is quite obvious: in the context of the death penalty, for instance, even defendants who have clearly committed mechanically knowable *aggravated* homicide (by certain means, on certain victims) are still not supposed to be executed if there are (invariably vaguely defined) mitigating factors that outweigh the aggravating ones. At other times the breakdown may be less apparent: in every tort case, no matter how rulelike we are in defining defendant's duty and the standard of care (for example, we might know with certainty both that chemical manufacturers have a duty not to pollute the air and that they are strictly liable for damage), we still have to answer the inevitably vague and open-ended question of what damages are proximately caused by the breach. If the overriding ideological goal of the tort *regime* is to ensure that some initial set of entitlements is protected, that shifts that do not occur through *ex ante* consensual transfer are protected by *ex post* compensation, then the regime will not be fully rulelike as long as it is unclear whether a particular shift in the plaintiff's deserved status was or was not caused by the defendant.[104]

Enforcement Levels

Take what appears to be the most mechanically applicable of rules: no vehicle may go faster than 25 miles per hour on a particular road. The problem with assuming that there is a clear rule governing the traffic-control *regime,* even when there is at its core a linguistically clear rule without apparent conflicting counterrules, is that the rule will by no means be universally enforced. In fact, in many settings the universal enforcement of the rule would be perceived as anarchic and chaotic, disruptive of ordinary local life, not stable, lawful, and facilitative. The "real" governing norm may be some incredibly open-textured set of standards: a particular speeder may be stopped when and only when there has been recent pressure from community residents that too many people are driving fast or pressure that too many people are using their road as a thoroughfare, perhaps because they are allowed to drive fast. A motorist may be stopped not for going faster than 25 but for driving much faster than others around him, or needing to weave to keep his pace, or because the police are suspicious of him and need a pretext to pull him over. A particular speeder may not be picked up simply because enforcement is expensive. Each breakdown of rules has a substantive side (our interests are distinct from those we at first claim) and a procedural one (unnecessary enforcement would be too expensive or too intrusive).

Simon emphasizes this point, a point that surely has its antecedents in the Law and Society movement's focus on differentiating law on the books from the law in action. In his welfare rights piece he notes, for instance, that an explicit strategy of welfare reformers in the 1960s was to put intolerable fiscal pressure on the welfare system by having all eligible beneficiaries vindicate their formal entitlements.[105] But Simon generalizes the point as well, stating that it is obvious that the criminal laws against various forms of consensual sex and drug possession could not be universally enforced without enormous social disruption, both because enforcement procedures would be offensive and because thoroughly criminalizing such widespread behavior would disrupt ordinary life, jailing enormous numbers of people who think of themselves as harmless model citizens. Robert Weisberg notes that the federal courts may have made executions difficult and expensive by providing a complex and costly set of avenues for appeal in part because the execution rate that would result from the imposition of the relatively mechanical capital murder statutes might far exceed even the rate that capital punishment proponents would wish for.[106] Too many killers commit the statutorily categorized aggravated forms of murder to execute them all. Yet in all these cases there is nothing resembling a metarule to describe when enforcement of the rule will occur.

Katz and Teitelbaum used this insight that universal rule enforcement is exceptional to note that a nominally vague statute declaring that a child is in need of supervision when his or her behavior is "dangerous" might be less uncertain in application than a statute nominally far more consistent with strictures of legality.[107] If nearly all teen-agers engage in the sort of conduct a nominally precise PINS (Persons in Need of Supervision) statute describes as the basis for jurisdiction (engaging in premarital sex, using drugs or alcohol, associating with people with criminal records), *and* there is no metarule to describe which of the near-universal class of formal violators will be singled out, teen-agers might feel that they were subject to less arbitrary treatment if they faced a facially vague open declaration that they had to be *very* bad before any state official would take notice.

Are Rules Really Desirable?

Substantive and Procedural Autonomy
In their piece on PINS jurisdiction, Katz and Teitelbaum note that there may be a hidden interplay between the procedure-based autonomy gained from a rule-bound form and the substantive *loss* of autonomy that results when overbroad rules proliferate in order to avoid situationally sensitive judgment.[108] The example they give is quite lucid: a judge may order a child to obey all *reasonable* parental commands. Because the word *reasonable* is open textured, classically vague, the child is placed in the position the rule advocate fears: ultimate judgment will be unpredictable, possibly biased; the child has no clear sense of what she may or may not do. But an effort to *avoid* the loss of autonomy inexorably caused by vagueness will significantly misfire if the judge feels impelled to establish an overbroad rule to reduce his subsequent discretion. If he tells the child to "obey *all* parental commands" (and if he really enforces the order), her substantive autonomy will decline, even though she will know far better when she will be subject to state supervision.

I believe that the problem is reasonably widespread, at least in the criminal law. Assume that we are trying to draw the line between preparation and attempt, discussed earlier. If we fear the vague, situationally sensitive Model Penal Code standard (convict when defendant takes a substantial step that strongly corroborates criminal intent) and adopt a rule (convict only when the defendant has taken the last possible step), there may well be pressure to reduce general civil autonomy by either criminalizing across the board some behavior that might have been treated as an attempt under a situationally sensitive standard or by harshly grading a class of already criminalized behavior that might on some occasions have been viewed as an attempt were we using the vaguer standard. Here are some examples. We fear nighttime break-ins, but we also fear that if we allow fact-finders to determine when a particular person looking in dark windows is attempting to break in (or allow apparently vague statutes proscribing menacing forms of loitering or allow police to stop and frisk when it seems "reasonable"), the decision rules will be applied both unpredictably and prejudicially against people who have done nothing explicitly criminal. An alternative is to establish a general nighttime curfew, an overbroad general limit on substantive freedom, but one that allows little or no discretion. (Or we can register felons; forbid them to own certain tools; allow the police to arrest *anyone* who won't state his identity and intentions, and so on.) Imagine that one common step in an insurance-fraud scheme is to file false police reports. Should we set the penalty for filing false police reports (too) high on the supposition that (some) such filers are en route to fraud, or should we leave it up to fact-finders to determine on a case-by-case basis whether the particular defendant, arrested after he filed the report, was on his way to committing fraud? If we can't convict the slow poisoner of attempted murder until he has administered the last dose, should we treat *everyone* in possession of poison (perhaps unduly) harshly, knowing that *some* are attempted murderers?

The problem as I've put it is obviously even more politically charged in the area of administrative regulation. If OSHA despairs of making elaborate case-by-case judgments that a particular workplace is "reasonably safe," it will issue autonomy-limiting detailed commands on work conditions. We may ban door-to-door sales outright rather than scrutinize each deal for its fairness. The point is certainly not that the rule form in all cases ought instantly to be overturned; the point is simply that the connection between rules and autonomy is far more paradoxical than is ordinarily acknowledged.

Simon explores Katz's substantive-procedural autonomy dilemma in a somewhat different fashion. He notes that in the welfare context, recipients may have gained a certain degree of procedural freedom at the cost of being far more subject to the vagaries of private life; that is, they may have gained what traditional liberals call negative rights (in this case against arbitrary procedure) at the expense of what they traditionally call power. A requirement that a recipient need only produce formal verification of theft before receiving a replacement check may indeed establish a clear-cut nondiscretionary entitlement to replacement checks, and should be expected to give rise to one significant form of autonomy: a diminished sense of subjugation and vulnerability to welfare bureaucrats. But it may well increase a recipient's actual vulnerability: while he waits for the check (and he must wait, since there is no provision for discretionary emergency grants based on the caseworker's judgment), he may starve, feel impelled to steal or peddle drugs, bear all the other burdens that welfare payments are designed to relieve.[109] Obviously, too, in the field of private law, the trade-off is often between procedural clarity and substantive protection: the choice to "free" a party from inquiry into the wisdom of his contracts or to "free" him from obligation until he has explicitly contracted is also obviously a choice to subject him to overreaching and manipulative negotiating tactics.

Sovereigns and Bureaucrats

Simon notes that the rule form makes, but cannot possibly deliver on, two simultaneous promises: that the party whose entitlements are set by rules will feel both that decisions are reached *impersonally* and that they are made by *legitimate* sources of authority.[110] The rule interpreter (for example the caseworker-bureaucrat in the welfare scheme) is not a legitimate authority. He is simply to be a mechanical tool of the legislature, the legitimate sovereign.

Simon expresses the dilemma as follows. On the one hand, if the sovereign remains uninvolved in administration, its will must inevitably be misinterpreted, and recipients will feel that nonauthoritative sources govern their rights. (While Simon emphasizes the indeterminacy of language as the root of bureaucratic misinterpretation, he could well have argued on any of the bases I have detailed.) On the other hand, if the sovereign becomes directly involved in administration (for instance through legislative vetoes of particular administrative acts), those affected by the particular decisions will feel that they have been subject to personal domination, a breakdown of prospective, impersonal governance.

At the same time, Simon notes that one of the key benefits that supposedly derives from rule-bound bureaucratization is that the petty officials one routinely deals with are cut down to size, that they experience themselves as unpowerful, unimportant, not entitled to any great deference because their roles are so technical. But while rules may indeed seemingly create the preconditions for a humble street-level bureaucracy of drones, they simultaneously create the conditions for a grandiose one: low-level bureaucrats in a rule regime may believe that they can appeal directly to the rules (become whistle blowers), go over the heads of superiors whose judgment might never be questioned in a regime of discretionary standards. Obviously Simon would by no means be altogether unhappy with a breakdown in the bureaucratic hierarchy, but if the affirmative claim for rules is that they will inexorably lead to the sort of hierarchy that enables citizens to confront only routine, humble bureaucrats, the claim may well be overstated.

Political Philosophy and the Rules-Standards Debate

Let us now turn to the connection between the rules-standards dilemma and both substantive political theory and existential philosophy.

Individualism and Altruism

The most striking and unusual claim that Kennedy made in "Form and Substance in Private Law Adjudication" was that the fundamental contradictory impulses that led to formal instability, to an inability for any actor or the legal system to maintain an unambivalent commitment to either the rule or the standard pole, were substantive. An actor might experience himself as rehashing arguments about imprecision versus nonadministrability, but the arguments seem so unsettled because they are in fact experienced in part as stand-ins for arguments about individualism and altruism, and all actors face these political theoretical issues with a sense of the most hopeless contradiction.

I want to explain Kennedy's claim, critique it as I believe it is frequently (and understandably) misinterpreted, and then attempt to reconstruct it.

Rules Equals Individualism, Standards Equals Altruism

Kennedy claims that there are two vital competing political paradigms that are at war both among and within us. We believe in the politics of individualism, a political theory that holds that one's own chosen ends are normatively primary, that one is entitled to pursue these ends as long as one respects the rights of others (thus it is not a pure egotism, which would disregard the very existence of others as normatively significant). Simultaneously, we believe in the (less well defined) politics of altruism, a political theory in which there is no normative priority to one's own ends, in which one is bound to seek others' advantage whether they are strictly entitled to one's help or not. One is not bound to treat *anyone's* ends as making equal claims; unlike the saint, the altruist may care more for some particular people (whom he sees, who he believes merit care) than others.[111] Kennedy claims in the article's introduction that the attachment to the rule form is ordinarily associated with individualism, the standard form with altruism,[112] though he clearly disclaims the idea that the connection is functional or invariable.[113]

Kennedy may well have drawn this close connection because he most carefully analyzed the body of law in which the claim probably fits best: contract law. It seems to be the case that most of the formally vaguer positions are associated with exacting greater degrees of solicitude from one contracting party for the other than the stricter rules demand. The standard that one can't enforce an unconscionable contract makes each of us responsible for ensuring that we don't take advantage of improvident fellow contractors, while the rule that a judge will look only for formal consideration, not a substantively fair bargain, allows us to celebrate when we find a chump to contract with. The standard that one must bargain in good faith demands that one watch out for the interests of a trading partner to ensure that he doesn't hurt himself courting one's business; the rule that enables one to skirt obligations until the contract is fully formalized enables one to get what one can from someone eager to please before committing oneself at all. The traditional mechanically applicable parol evidence rule congratulates the successful individualist on memorializing the contract as he desires, even if he gives (unenforceable) verbal assurances that he will do things unmentioned in the text; the more standardlike exception or counterrules demand that the less wary party be taken care of as well as the more wary one.

I believe that the claim of close connection could have been equally well made in the tax area. If we view each taxpayer's efforts to minimize his own taxes as a competitive game played against other taxpayers whose payments will have to rise to meet separately set revenue goals when some taxpayers evade, then the rules form is generally associated with an openly adversarial, each-taxpayer-for-himself attitude that we owe nothing but what some "they" can clearly catch us owing. The standards-oriented positions are that we can best describe what we owe in terms that have a general meaning but are hard to specify—our realized market power (net earnings) reduced by deductions for spending that Congress wishes to encourage—but that we have a duty not to disguise either market power or the real intent and nature of our spending transactions.

Kennedy does not make much of an effort to explain the connection between form and substance. The piece is often read to imply that the connection might be a logical or necessitarian one,[114] but he seems to me to duck this view rather explicitly.[115] While one might imagine that one could not, as a practical matter, express all demands for sharing with the relatively needy in a general fashion, it would be difficult for the necessitarian to explain why many of our clearest altruistic duties are set out as rules (such as those set forth in tax programs that tax the relatively rich and in transfer programs that give money to the relatively poor). Unless there is a way of distinguishing demands for case-by-case situational sharing from more general redistributive demands that do not occur to me, any attempt to explain the parallel as a logical necessity seems to me futile. My guess is that any effort to explain the connection as if it were a prediction of correlation will fail, because, as a matter of prediction, there simply is *no* connection.

Form Matches Substance: A Critique

It strikes me that there are three distinct sorts of critiques of the claim that the rule form is individualistic and the standard form altruistic: first, that it is frequently irrelevant; second, that it is sometimes more or less correct depending on whom one views as the relevant disputants; and third, that it is hopelessly and needlessly ambiguous on the distinction between selfish quasialtruism and genuine selflessness.

The irrelevance claim is quite simple: arguments resting on either the inevitability of bias or the nonadministrability of standards or problems of the over- and underinclusiveness of rules are powerful in their own right and will occur even where no issues of altruism and individualism are implicated. The debate over the amount of discretion permitted fact finders in sentencing defendants to death partakes of all the usual rules-standards indeterminacy, but it seems futile to me to identify pre-*Furman* decision making with altruism (even though, as a matter of fact, the vaguer aspects of post-*Furman* decision making, the open-ended admission of mitigating material, have been those that partake of mercy, a distant kin to altruism). This surely need not be the case: one *could* describe aggravating conditions in loose terms (for example heinous or monstrous crimes)[116] and mitigating conditions in rulelike terms (for example, being a drug addict or an alcoholic, or having been seriously physically abused as a child). The welfare-rights debate is equally hard to see in altruism-individualism terms: those who favor explicit entitlements may well have blinded themselves to many of the flaws of rules, as Simon so trenchantly points out, but they are no less committed to sharing.

The claim could be made that the individualism-altruism split may invariably underlie only *private law* disputes (Kennedy's piece *is* called "Form and Substance in *Private* Law Adjudication"), but even this claim seems only partly justified. The second criticism of Kennedy acknowledges that it is true that one can always construct a vision of the use of rules in private disputes that makes it seem as if the rules advocate is committed to, or at least tolerant of, one of the classic excesses of individualism. It is practically tautologically true that the existence of a rule will permit a party to take advantage of another party even when no one who established the rule would have believed the case fit the rule's purpose. From the rule beneficiary's vantage point, the rule legitimates and facilitates a lack of concern for whether an opponent's valid interests are met, a classic individualist pose. But this focus may be significantly misleading if we are attempting to see how well the rule position matches up to actual individualistic politics.

If, for instance, we focus on the *plaintiff* in a torts case where the issue is what standard of care the defendant owes, both the traditional rule and the traditional standard position correlate neatly with substantive individualism and altruism. The strict liability *rule* (with no standardlike defense of contributory negligence) is seemingly subject to attack because it enables the plaintiff to be excessively individualistic. Assuming he can be fully compensated by tortfeasors, he need show no concern at all about avoiding harms that defendants cause, even if he could more readily and cheaply avert them than the defendant could. Yet one can see that the negligence *standard* demands seemingly excessive altruistic sacrifice by the plaintiff. Why should a person cede her entitlements whenever a defendant can't reasonably avoid harm? This is particularly obvious and dramatic in cases in which courts adopt a Hand formula definition of negligence (defendant is negligent only if the costs of accident prevention would have been lower than the expected damage). Imagine a downstream water user facing a polluter: the negligence standard seems to demand the user share his entitlement to his water whenever it is too expensive for others to let him keep it, while they need not even compensate him for his loss.[117]

But from the *defendant's* point of view—which seems to have been

the vantage point most nineteenth-century writers adopted—the negligence standard seems to fit not the altruists' but the individualists'
program. (In "Form and Substance" itself, in fact, Kennedy notes that
in the heyday of modern individualist legal ideology the negligence
standard came to be dominant; a key rallying cry for classical individualists was that liability without fault was unprincipled).[118] The self-
reliant individual's obligations could come from two sources only: contract and fault. Now, of course, it is perfectly *possible* to construct a
definition of fault that asserts that any diminution of another's initial
property rights without compensation is blameworthy, but it is also
perfectly plausible to do what the classicists did: to define those acts
that gave rise to a duty to compensate in terms of the reasonableness
of the damaging conduct. All of our property rights may diminish in
value as the result of the reasonable conduct of others, but in a Social
Darwinian sense: that's the way the race for the fittest is run. Nonnegligent injury can be and has been treated as an accident, a fact of natural
or prelegal social life.

The same form problem exists if we focus on battles between those
who demand full formal compliance with Wills Acts and those who
demand only substantial compliance, only assurances that we know the
testator's actual intention and that the testator engaged in reasonably
sober reflection. Looked at from the vantage point of the battle between
the heirs-at-law and the named beneficiaries in a formally defective
document, it appears the heirs-at-law are resting on their rights in a
manner ordinarily associated with the most rugged individualism. But
it is not at all clear whether the individualist focusing on the *testator*
would favor full formalism since it subverts the testator's subjective,
individual intention.

Finally, and perhaps most important, because it partly subverts Kennedy's most powerful claim that the ideological core of liberal law, the
law of contracts, shows strong congruence between form and substance,
one should look at statutory consumer-protection legislation. While one
can interpret a whole array of rulelike solutions to the problem of consumer mistakes and ignorance as giving the *consumers* excessive individualistic rights to cancel contracts that were in fact perfectly justly
made, it is surely the case that it was *altruists* trying to enforce in a
practical fashion a duty of *sellers* not to take advantage of buyers who
pressed for the enactment of rules providing for waiting or cancellation
periods on door-to-door sales[119] or nonwaivable implied warranties of
habitability.[120]

The third problem is that the functionalist does not seem to know what to make of the use of standards by subgroups not at all committed to a generalized altruism, even though they are committed to avoiding the appearance of taking advantage of a purely formal edge in particular cases. Merchants in ongoing commercial relationships are probably the most frequent users of standards for resolving claims (both as a result of underlying law, the standard-filled Uniform Commercial Code (UCC), and as a matter of practice, since they so rarely litigate at all).[121] It seems to me problematic to view the selfish desire to maintain a particular profitable long-term relationship even at the cost of short-run legalist gain as a substantively altruistic position. Of course one can easily enough work oneself into a slippery slope definitional nightmare: must we disqualify all altruism that individuals perceive as making them personally happier?[122] But even skirting such grand questions, as Kennedy artfully does in "Form and Substance,"[123] I don't think one can assimilate long-run profit maximizers who ignore the chance for short-run legal victories into the politically altruistic camp without sacrificing all the vitality of the distinction between the camps. This problem is clearly most pronounced in thinking about the attachment of ongoing trading partners to informal dispute settlement guides, but it arguably describes the work-out mechanisms for many egotistical parties bound to a long-term relationship (business partners, stock owners with limited standardlike disciplinary power over corporate directors, concurrent interest holders who must tolerate almost all competing uses unless willing to dissolve their dealings).

Aesthetic Vision of Self-Reliance

Even if particular rule positions have little seeming substantive bite, the rule *form* may always tend to appeal to the *substantive* individualist because its formal virtues match up aesthetically with the virtues he is inclined to admire. In a sense, as with most aesthetic claims, there is little way to prove the connection other than by laying it out and directly assessing its plausibility, but my sense is that one can match up the spirit of rules quite readily with either stereotypical individualism or, to take a second possible form, stereotypical masculinity, while the arguments for standards invoke the spirit of altruism and stereotypical femininity.[124]

The person who lives by the rules does not beg for fairness or a second look at transactions when things go wrong; consequences are accepted, allowed to fall where they may as long as no one has explicitly cheated. The demand for situational altruism is a demand to look back once things haven't worked out for you, to depart from the ceaselessly and mercilessly prospective view that one should be able to take care of oneself or live with one's failure to do so. The self-reliant person wants to know just what is expected of him: even if a lot is expected, he can do it, as long as there are no surprises, as long as he can plan his life anticipating and controlling all obligations that he will ultimately be asked to meet.

Standards assume that factual inequality trumps formal equality, that one has to see whether one's trading partners can *actually* take care of themselves; one can't simply presume that their formal legal capacity is the same as actual capacity. This requires, if nothing else, sensitivity and awareness to others, even to others one hasn't voluntarily chosen to be sensitive to. Moreover, situationally sensitive standards contemplate the necessity of at least occasional paternalism, of overturning the individual's judgment when the individualist demands that sovereignty be limited only for gross categorical defects (like infancy), that to assess positive incompetence is to emasculate, enslave, infantilize (not let go).

The rule form is generally associated with a commitment to theory, general knowledge. Standards are associated with facts, with intuition. In theory, all strictly liable criminal defendants are actually negligent; the generalist claims he can make reasonable conclusive presumptions, more reasonable than any case-by-case judges can make. In fact, the standards advocate says, we may actually better intuit blameworthiness on a case-by-case basis. In theory, rules are dynamically stabilizing and compliance increases over time; in fact, only those with access to legal help may ever learn the rules, and counterpurposive uses of the rules may only grow over time as some seek legal advice to better exploit others. In theory, practice settles once ambiguous language is interpreted and reinterpreted until each case is governed; in fact, systems generate exceptions, practices of nonenforcement, whole new systems to evade the harshness of the now-clear mess.

Rules test cunning; they set up one more test for the self-reliant person to pass: can he play the rules just right? Standards are redistributive; they take a trait that is unevenly distributed (ability to play the rules right) and render it inconsequential.

Rules respect strong, individually chosen distinctions in relations; they demand nothing but allow for care or forgiveness or charity where the donor loves or pities. Standards assert that simply living in a community establishes a relationship of some trust and care, though one can scarcely be said to voluntarily choose to inhabit the same political world with another.

Rules appeal to the aesthetics of precision, to the psychology of denial or skeptical pragmatism (or, alternatively, of blinding ourselves to imprecision and mistakes or believing it is girlishly utopian to hope for perfection); standards appeal to the aesthetics of romantic absolutism, to the psychology of painful involvement in each situation, to the pragmatism that rejects the need for highfalutin generalities.

If you teach in a law school, you should be able to gaze out at your students and guess rather accurately where each one's initial sympathies lie along the formal dimensions on the basis of dress and manner. If you don't think you can, you're simply unobservant, simply a bad workaday anthropologist of your own culture.

It is important to note that once one reconstructs the argument that the rule form is individualistic in its aesthetic form, it is no longer a powerful objection to the CLS argument that adherents believe both that rule-bound regimes are impossible *and* that "rules" represent the working out of an ideological program. The ongoing vitality of the imagery associated with the invocation of the need for a more rulelike solution in any case is a reaffirmation of the substantively individualistic ideological position, even though individualism need not, nor can it possibly, ultimately rest on a rule-bound regime.

Rules, Value Skepticism, and Individualism

In Chapter 2 I shall discuss at length a second key feature of the Critical picture of liberalism: that it privileges the belief that values are arbitrary, individual, and subjective rather than communal or objective. For now I would like to note briefly the relationship between the privileged belief in subjective value and rules, and the connection between the belief in subjective value and individualism. It is a plausible minor thesis in "Form and Substance" that one of the connections between rules and individualism is that the normative case for each depends in great measure on the supposition that values are arbitrary and subjective.

One can see the connection most readily if one imagines the critique of the feasibility of standards that the value skeptic would make. A typical standard ("Don't act *unreasonably*," "Enforce *fair* bargains") requires that the enforcing community (such as a jury) can come to some consensus on the meaning of a value term, that the group can come to share a conception of reasonableness or fairness. But value skeptics deny precisely that capacity: while *reason* (the capacity to describe and understand the external world) is thought to be universal, so that rules, referring only to external events, can be comprehended, *tastes* (including "opinions" about what lives are well lived, which are needed to give content to terms like *just*) are thought to be shared only as a matter of happenstance.

A reliance on standards is premised on the hope of moral dialogue and ultimate consensus, since the standards will remain contentless unless such moral dialogue succeeds in overcoming the skeptical sense that one person's conception of what is just is nothing more than either a whimsical taste or a rhetorical cover for a self-serving program. The value skeptic denies that possibility in his individualism; morality is individual, exogenous, a presocial fact. Rules, though, can still function to avoid the worst clashes of egotists (although, as I shall discuss in the next chapter, the *legitimacy* of the chosen rules would always be an insoluable problem for liberals if value-skeptical beliefs dominated liberal ideology in a noncontradictory fashion). Rules do not depend on ongoing dialogue to gain dimension or content; they can be understood, since they refer to "objects" in the exterior domain of reason, even by someone who shares no sense of community with his fellows. In sum, the case for rules depends in part on the supposition that standards are not feasible because they depend on the possibility of reaching consensus on the good, which is impossible if there is no general good but simply a series of whimsical, individual accounts of it; likewise, a main bulwark of the case for individualism is that collective attempts to run particular lives would be well conceived only if there were some objective good, rather than a series of whimsical, individual varieties of good lives. Thus, rules and individualism are in part linked because the case for each is bolstered by nearly identical value-skeptical arguments.

Rules and the Fundamental Contradiction

In his piece on Blackstone's *Commentaries,* Kennedy makes an observation that has surely become the most widely cited passage in Critical Legal Studies:

> The goal of individual freedom is at the same time dependent on and incompatible with the communal coercive action that is necessary to achieve it. Others . . . are necessary if we are to become persons at all—they provide us with the stuff of ourselves and protect us in crucial ways against destruction . . . But at the same time it forms and protects us, the universe

of others . . . threatens us with annihilation . . . Numberless conformities, large and small abandonments of self to others are the price of what freedom we experience in society.[125]

The role of rules in mediating that Fundamental Contradiction is relatively straightforward: one can deny that one's attitudes about others are painful or contradictory if one believes that one has established categorical bases for dealing with them, for distinguishing benevolent interaction from exploitative attacks. The legalistic liberal response to the Fundamental Contradiction is simple: I will interact with others as long as they respect my rights. The state will police all boundary crossings by private parties. If no boundary has been crossed, we can pretend that the interaction has been painless. Because state officials might, in the ostensible course of policing private boundary crossings, themselves become a source of painful oppression, we limit them both by insisting that they enforce only clear rules and by establishing some separate rights that are relevant only vis à vis the state.[126] Rules are associated with distancing and role playing; the bureaucrat need not listen as long as he does his job, gives you your due. No one can demand anything but compliance with preset rules; conversation and explanation of one's conduct are avoided, for it is easily ascertained whether one has done all he must. One can shut up those who ask for explanation—a rule's a rule, don't complain to me. Ongoing attempts to reassert the coherence and comprehensiveness of doctrine, of whatever web of legal rules purports to describe social relations, are part of a collective effort to pacify and reassure us that we have been delivered from existential tragedy. Rules are the opiate of the masses.

CHAPTER TWO

The Subjectivity of Value

A central theme in what is perhaps *the* seminal early CLS work, Roberto Unger's *Knowledge and Politics,*[1] is that liberal thought (whether "psychological," political, or epistemological) is characterized by an ostensible commitment to a dualistic view of moral and "scientific" knowledge, by the belief that there is a radical distinction between facts and values, between reason and desire.

According to Unger, the characteristic stance within both mainstream culture and sophisticated liberal social theory is that values—beliefs about what is worth pursuing—are seen as nothing more than tastes, the purely arbitrary assertions of individuals. Reason is utterly separate from desire; desire impels, reason simply tries to achieve what desire demands be sought. Desire is not just subjective and individual but *individuating;* that is, we are distinguished from one another by our wants, while reason and perceptions are universal. Of course a strong, reasonably open undercurrent of tension has developed, at least epistemologically, in the claim that reason aspires to universality: not only will supposedly factual observations usually be "biased" by inevitably imperfect, self-interested observers but also, and far more ineradicably, *all* the categories we use to describe supposedly external reality will be purposive, creatures of our own interests in naming. Since we suspect that there are no natural nominal categories, we believe that we name things to serve our ends; thus the "correctness" of our names must inexorably be judged in terms of their capacity to serve ends that cannot themselves conceivably be correct or not. Though Unger does not fully seem to acknowledge this, the commitment to value subjectivity is also *openly* perilous. In ways I shall return to, libertarians must (and do) acknowledge that substantive values infuse initial rights assignment; utilitarians believe that we are *morally bound* to seek to maximize utility, not simply that we might *desire* to do so. But the ready availability of value-skeptical attacks on both distributive and paternalist public policy reflects the magnetic pull of the commitment to the arbitrariness of values. Unger's notion that some "unified" liberalism is ultimately committed to privileging value neutrality is bolstered by the way in which utilitarians justify distributive and paternalist preferences. While a belief in the *propriety* of utility maximization could not itself be justified in a value-skeptical scheme, once one adopts the perspective, more particular arguments tend to reassert the binary opposition between reason and desire. Distributive preferences are not ethical but factual; redistribution of income reassigns money to those who, as a supposed matter of fact, subjectively value it more.[2] Paternalism grows from defects in reason, from defects in the capacity to fulfill ends that are not themselves in theory the focus of our concerns.[3]

Unger did not organize *Knowledge and Politics* as Kennedy did "Form and Substance"—that is, as a study in the existence and repression of contradiction. Unger's belief that it is central to liberal thought to experience a nonpermeable vacuum boundary between reason and desire seems, in many senses, unpersuasive to me, but the position has clearly inspired a great deal of Critical work that does not adopt his supposition of vacuum boundedness. It might be most fruitful to restate or reconceive Unger's insight. Organizing the material on value subjectivity in the same way that I organized the study of Kennedy's insight on the dilemmas we face in choosing the appropriate *form* for legal pronouncements strikes me as useful, though not especially faithful to the text that inspires the discussion. First, we should note the degree to which problems of maintaining an ostensibly privileged commitment to value subjectivity are as significant in law as problems of maintaining the supposedly privileged commitment to rules has been. It is less fruitful to organize a myriad of detailed doctrinal disputes as recurring issues of controversy between one variety or another of "closet" value objectivists and self-confidently preference-neutral liberals than it was to see rules-standards disputes as omnipresent, if occasionally hidden. Still, many of the most significant legal issues do indeed seem to involve the need to acknowledge that the faith in value subjectivity that is so central an article of faith in defending liberal individualism is in actual practice an imperfect faith, one that must frequently be sacrificed in the name of an irreconcilably contradictory opposite faith. Once more, too, there is no persuasive sense either in which subjective and nonsubjective conceptions of value can be harmonized or balanced or in which we can choose, functionally, more and less appropriate *domains* for value subjectivism.

Second, we should note the degree to which the contradictory commitment to both accepting and overcoming value subjectivity in part reflects
a deeper contradictory commitment to distinct visions of dealing with
the problem of acting in role, that it reflects a decidedly different version
of the problem of the self and others in liberal society from the ones
Kennedy or Simon offered in their essays on rules and standards. Finally,
we shall see an implicit Hegelian utopianism or hope for synthesis in
Unger's work that is wholly absent in Kennedy's work, which is implicitly
far more cautionary and tragic, antiutopian in grand theoretic ambition,
though by no means more despairing, resigned, or antiutopian in its
implications for daily practice. In looking at CLS as visionary thought,
recognizing both the grand synthetic and "localist" strands seems crucial.

The Dilemma in Political and Legal Theory

At the broadest level of political theory the commitment to the subjectivity and arbitrariness of preferences implies a commitment to a merely
"facilitative" state, one that does not seek that particular good lives be
led but simply allows persons to achieve their own vision of the good.
In fact, this broad "facilitative" model is almost surely the place in which
the privileging of value subjectivity is most pronounced.

Freedom and Order

The fundamental political problem that is created when one embraces
such an end-neutral vision is the dilemma that one cannot reconcile the
simultaneous demands for both order and the freedom to pursue one's
subjectively chosen ends. If freedom allows one to express unconstrained
subjective desire, it must obviously permit even the expression of pure
egotism (since there is no valid, general substantive limit to restrain
selfish desire). Once one faces the nightmarish possibility that a regime
of unrestricted freedom and self-seeking would be, in essence, the
Hobbesian war of all against all, though, constraining that war through
some sort of centralized order-imposing force becomes a central task;
yet the demands for order and egotistical freedom will simply not mesh
unless, miraculously, either no one ever wants to do anything anyone
else minds or everyone is willing to tolerate *all* offensive conduct.

This extremely broad political dilemma is reflected in far more concrete legal problems. At base the dilemma is how to justify *any* rights
framework, any design for order, in a world in which values are seen

as nothing but subjective whims. If there is nothing but discrete individual desires, why should one desire ever trump another? Why does one person's desire for bodily integrity trump another's desire to batter? Why shouldn't the would-be batterer see oppression, see his freedom unjustly squashed, when the rights bearer has recourse to the state to protect what may be, after all, only his will?

The modern liberal legal economists have simply denied this problem in a way in which the traditional liberal rights theorists could not. In a sense, though Unger never makes any reference to the legal economists, his claim that "liberal thought" fully privileges moral end neutrality can be validated only if one believes, as I do, that the legal economists' position rather than that of the more traditional natural rights theorists represents the inevitable end point for "mature" liberal thought *or* if one believes that in pronouncing their broad paeans to value subjectivity and the unimaginable diversity of good lives libertarians simply blind themselves to the initial rights-assignment issues. (In a sense, I treat it as one extremely powerful form of vindication of Unger's deep understanding of the core of liberal thought that he *anticipates* at the theoretical level the development of the legal economists' position, though Unger was apparently not yet aware of the emerging position when he wrote.)

Take a standard interactive harm case. The upstream manufacturer wants to foul the water used by people living downstream. The legal economists, in their most central organizing insight, the Coase Theorem,[4] see this as nothing but a battle of arbitrary whim. One side wants clean water, the other cheaper manufactured goods. The resolution of this conflict between wills must be seen as either unimportant (and thus nonoppressive) or rationally soluble (technical) with recourse limited to summing up individual wants.

For the Coase Theorem advocate, the conflict may be unimportant in two ways. First, in the absence of transaction costs—that is, impediments to negotiation between the parties to such disputes—allocation will be unaffected (the amount of pollution and the precautionary guards, including nonuse of the water, taken by the people downstream will be the same). Second, though the distribution of income between disputants will be affected in any particular case (if the polluter has the first-line entitlement to pollute, he will be wealthier since either the user will pay him to install pollution-reducing devices or he will get to use the cheaper, polluting process), the assumption is that there is little reason to expect any party to be favored recurrently and nonrandomly in a series of decisions about who has first-line entitlements in interactive harm situations. For example, if the downstream water user "loses" here, he may well be a winner in a decision about whether he has to avoid blocking his neighbor's access to light or a view.[5]

The conflict will be significant only when transaction costs prevent ready reassignment of the initial right; but, say the legal economists, the right can and should still be assigned without recourse to an ungrounded assertion that one desire is morally superior to the other. Instead, the right to preserve a desired end state should either be assigned in the way that better facilitates its transfer (if its transfer is easier when it is initially in one party's hands than the other's) or be assigned to whichever party the central authorities believe would have ended up purchasing the end state had bargaining been possible. In this way, the state simply either facilitates or mimics the social arrangements that private desires would impel, a solution that seemingly never demands any grounded preference assertion by the state official other than the commitment to allow the preference assertions of others to hold sway. Thus, the rights creator's task is simply factual and rational: to determine who, in fact, would have purchased the right to designate the end state or to ascertain in whose hands the right would be more transferable should the parties choose to rearrange an unsatisfactory initial assignment.[6]

As I shall discuss in Chapter 4, the Coase Theorem may well be altogether ungrounded as a descriptive or empirical proposition. For now, the only point I want to make is that one of the attractions of generalized Coasean analysis is that the potentially explosive issue of imbuing substantive preferences in the rights-creation process is skirted. Yet most liberal right theorists find the Coasean description of our practices wholly inadequate. They imply, for instance, in a fashion that has been an easy target for antieconomistic liberals, that women have the right not to be raped only because it is the society's *factual* judgment that they would probably purchase the right from would-be rapists were it first assigned to would-be rapists (thus necessitating costly and unneeded transactions) or that it is transactionally easier for those who want sex to purchase it (though of course that is uniformly illegal too) than for those who don't want it to purchase agreements to desist from those who would otherwise "take" it.[7] But if there is nothing but desire to impel us and nothing to desire but whim, the moralizing liberal rights theorist is left without a cogent basis for his decision that the woman is to be granted the entitlement here. (The other, not markedly coherent libertarian response is that the right should be assigned to the passive party, the one who would not *cause* harm through his desires.[8] Coase, though, was clearly persuasive in arguing that each party hurts the other, that one party cannot fulfill his desire without the other's lot being worsened. A focus on causation is simply an incoherent dodge.)[9]

Unger pays no attention to the efforts of the legal economists to embrace the groundlessness of moralistic rights decisions; he deals instead with the efforts of the traditional moralists to justify a rights framework that does not explicitly invoke end preferences. Unger's arguments are atypically sketchy when he critiques those writers in what he calls the "natural rights" tradition of Locke and Kant who have attempted to justify particular entitlements frameworks. But the thrust of his argument is, I believe, that the natural rights theorists invariably postulate that under certain arrangements and definitions of rights, and only under these arrangements, the attainment of each subjective agent's selfish ends will be maximized. Unger believes that the traditional argument is hopelessly indeterminate because it is utterly ambiguous about whether power (the actual capacity to meet one's ends) is relevant in determining when we have maximized subjective end attainment, or whether the rights theorist worries that a person can't meet his aims only in situations in which he has no right to do so (that is, the state formally precludes or bars a particular form of end seeking). To the extent that power matters at all, the notion that everyone can get as much as he wants without clashing with others' desires becomes manifestly absurd. (Though Unger does not make this claim, the argument I made earlier in discussing omissions implied that not even traditional negative liberal rights can be assigned without one party's ends being sacrificed, given the problem of clashing desires.)

This problem of freedom and order can be seen as legally significant in at least two other critical regards: first, the problem of determining the legal or moral status of obedience to law induced solely by selfish calculation, and second, the problem of restraining the selfishness of state officials.

The obedience problem is easily posed at a general theoretical level. Given the impossibility of complete enforcement or the extreme unlikelihood of setting penalties high enough so that expected penalties (nominal penalties discounted by the probability of enforcement) are as high as the social cost of violation, it will often be the case that it is in an actor's narrow self-interest to violate the law. Efforts to assert that it will almost invariably be selfishly worthwhile to comply when one compares punishment costs with noncompliance costs rest on the empirically implausible rule-utilitarian assumption that each actor believes both that his violations will be known and that they will lead to a more general breakdown in compliance that will ultimately harm him personally. Obviously, a seriously selfish rule utilitarian would have to calculate in each case the probability that his noncompliance would be known and would induce more general noncompliance or make some assumptions about how costly case-by-case information processing would be. It is simply not enough to believe that one could imagine cases in which chaotic breakdowns would occur that would cost the violator more than he initially gained. Yet since there is no "good," no objective morality, obedience must, by hypothesis, be someone's desire if we are to maintain fully the nominally privileged commitment to the subjectivity and arbitrariness of values. The claim that the Critics make is that rule obedience must in fact be covertly deemed a *preferred* desire, not just another whim, and that the ostensible commitment to subjective value once more cannot hold firm.

The degree to which the privileged commitment to value subjectivity must in fact fade here, as it must in the area of assigning entitlements, can be seen by looking at a somewhat more complex and less obvious legal case.

In many jurisdictions defendants can "undo" or decriminalize what would be a punishable attempt if interrupted by external force, by voluntarily renouncing or abandoning that attempt. It is simple hornbook law, though, that an abandonment motivated by fear of adverse legal consequences on the particular occasion is not adequately voluntary to result in the defendant's acquittal.[10] The core case, of course, is the thief who desists from completing a larceny because a policeman comes onto the scene. What is problematic, though, is that our attitudes about selfish compliance are fundamentally ambivalent: one jewel thief desists because the hotel's safe alarm goes off, another because he learns that the hotel has installed a more sophisticated alarm he can't disconnect, a third because he learns that safes have alarms, a fourth because he learns that judges have been sentencing thieves harshly. (I should note that under certain formulations of the line between nonpunishable preparation and attempt, any of these would-be thieves could have done enough to be guilty of an attempt were they not to abandon.) The first abandonment is clearly noncreditable, the second and third arguable, the fourth clearly creditable as a practical matter, since the defendant has simply integrated general deterrence signals in reaching a decision.

Part of the problem in these cases seems factual, the difficulty of drawing general inferences from particular acts: we must believe that the defendant has abandoned the criminal category, that he is not just postponing his crime until a safer occasion; yet all we see and know with certainty is that he has abandoned a particular instance in particular circumstances. But the intractable factual problem runs even deeper: we cannot know whether someone has understood the general impropriety of crime or is simply looking for a safer target because a vital part of the way we claim to *communicate* to citizens that crime is improper is simply to deter them through punishment, to play on the very selfishness we condemn if we see it operating in a particular setting. It is disingenuous to claim that selfishness is perfectly fine as long as it constrains people "generally enough"; if all we really could hope for was that deterrence would work, we'd soon all be looking for safer targets or living in a police state. Yet we seem unable to view the generally deterred citizen in any particular case as anything but a model citizen, the perfect integrator of the signals we send out. The effort to contain egotism, to establish an order consistent with morally contentless egotism, shows its first strain when we recognize that the particularistic egotistical calculator is surely antisocial; its deeper strain is shown when we try to imagine a world of less particular egotistical calculation. When I return in Chapter 5 to discuss the claim made by many Law and Economics advocates that tort rules can be efficient, that selfish calculators restrained by properly designed backdrop rules will never harm one another, we shall see that this tension cannot be made to disappear, that calculated obedience will never be enough.

The problem that we cannot seemingly allow end-neutral freedom full reign while establishing a morally contentless political order that contains the exercise of freedom is posed not only in the assignment of entitlements and in coping with the problem of purely selfish compliance but also in the obviously critical problem of restraining presumably selfish state officials. Those who are allowed to govern will surely have their own subjective ends. What is to prevent the commands of government from being the self-seeking commands of individuals who happen to be governors?

Unger notes that the liberal tradition is rich in efforts to wish away the problem that it postulates a cultural tradition that both requires the establishment of rights and yet can trust no one to do the establishing. Unger speaks of Hobbes's effort to deify the unself-interested sovereign, to hypothesize the problem away with a utopian fantasy of a reigning cultural outsider; of the process-oriented *Rechtstaat* tradition (associated, for instance, with Friederich Hayek)[11] that if one mandates that rules be stated in general enough terms, no self-interested rules can conceivably be established; and of the natural rights vision (which he associates with Locke and Kant) that rights are so obvious and self-defining anyway that there is little discretion for governors. Unger's critiques are rather hasty. He seems to view the Hobbesian position as obviously fanciful, a transparent confession of the impossibility of solving the problem within liberal culture. The Hayekian solution seems legally naive, unable to recognize the manipulability of language that permits us easily to create seemingly universal rules with utterly disparate, narrow impacts. Unger does not give examples, but examples are readily available: for instance, perfectly general prospective tax legislation may in fact aid only particular interests.[12] The Lockean-Kantian solution is wrongheaded, if only because it has never resolved and can never resolve questions about the degree to which people are entitled to guarantees or efforts to facilitate the development of greater substantive autonomy, not just freedom from explicit state restraint.

Unger does not directly address the most common modern Anglo-American liberal response to the problem of domination—the democratic response—in discussing the problem of freedom and order, but remarks he makes at other points in the book about democracy are germane. Most fundamentally, Unger sees little reason why liberals committed to value subjectivity should experience majorities as anything more than accidental coalitions of particular wills. The basic utilitarian posture that each of us must be committed to maximizing aggregate utility is, for Unger, too strong an objective value assertion to be consistent with what he understands as liberalism. In part, I think, Unger simply misreads the Anglo-American, non-Continental liberal tradition by so thoroughly ignoring its utilitarian-democratic strain; in part, I think, modern liberals underestimate the difficulty of squaring their very strongly stated and held beliefs in value subjectivity with less well defended democratic beliefs.

Obviously our legal culture forever battles the problem of the fear of ruler subjectivity, particularly in its obsession with the problem of the illegitimate personal domination we purportedly experience in the face of activist judges.[13] (In routine court-centered American constitutional law dialogue, the problem of subjugation of a minority to majority wills is simply brushed aside, on most occasions, except when First Amendment and Equal Protection issues are raised. Though the commitment to value subjectivity implies that the will of the majority is nothing more than an accidental confluence of whim, only the right-wing libertarians experience all legislation as fundamentally suspect[14] in the way mainstream lawyers think of judicial decision as suspect, rather than some smaller subcategory of majority action that interferes with "fundamental rights.") Efforts to contain judicial oppression are manifold, but each advocate so effectively critiques competitors that we suspect that the problem must linger forever. If reason and desire are completely separate, how can judges decide cases on the basis of reason rather than their own subjective desire? The litany (and the critiques) of purely rational techniques is familiar: textualism,[15] historical intent reconstructions,[16] political process correction,[17] ends-means rationality review,[18] even recognition of the shared values of others[19] all represent efforts to silence the persistently disquieting fear that we are subject to the wholly arbitrary whims of the judges. The obsession should remain as long as our core fantasy image of oppression is individual, the subjugation by one arbitrary will of another equally arbitrary, equally entitled will (rather than, to take an equally unreal image from the utopian left, an image of oppression as nonparticipation in the moral dialogue that frames and forms all wills).

Thomas Heller's account of the contradictory demands posed for a workable liberal theory of the state, given the underlying liberal commitment to subjective value and objective fact, appears to follow from Unger's observations, but it seems to me to sharpen and clarify the nature of the dilemma considerably.[20] Since there is no objective good, only preference satisfaction has any moral claim; thus, good social systems simply accurately aggregate private preferences (for example through markets and voting systems). The aggregation technique must be objective and scientific because of both our epistemological stance and our political theoretic stance. Epistemologically, the point is that the preferences of individuals are facts, and as facts they should, like all other facts, be knowable if our fantasy of the universality of knowledge is to be realized. Politically, if aggregating state administrators rely on anything but objective knowledge in their summing-up process, they may well covertly dominate others, impose their own values.

The problem that Heller notes is that liberalism's positivist method fails to meet its normative needs, that it has never been fully comfortable to apply traditional positivist technique to the material that is to be studied here: human desire. Even in dealing with simple cases of market choice, we are thrown back on an obviously poor presumption, which

I shall discuss at great length in Chapter 4, that revealed preference is a reasonable surrogate for true desire. The claim is hard to square, of course, with the existence of regret, mistakes, or ambivalence. Worse, in many cases there are reasons to believe that people will systematically *lie* about their preferences or intentions, and that behavior does not invariably reveal state of mind. We believe that people systematically understate preferences for collective goods, have no reason to reveal the sort of malicious criminal intention required to deem them culpable when they harm others, have no reason to reveal that they are motivated by consumption desires when their objective spending behavior looks consistent with a motive to earn more income. This poses intractable legal and technical issues. Sections 162 and 262 of our tax code (in which we try to distinguish between deductible business and nondeductible consumption expenditures) are hopelessly vague and circular; in criminal law we despair of interpreting personal motivation when we don't implicitly assume that an action is taken for typical reasons. (Thus, in attempt law, we look for acts that bespeak a particular intention "on their face," and we worry, almost obsessively, in "impossible attempt" cases that when an action is temporally complete, we won't be able to infer that the actor was trying to accomplish a criminal end, trying to do something a bit different from what he actually did.) But more significantly, it poses the political theoretic problem that the state may be unable to act as purely rationally as it needs to act to avoid the possibility of nonneutrality and domination.

Operational Problems

The commitment to value subjectivity and fact objectivity appears to make both a substantive and a procedural demand on those exercising state power: substantively, the demand is to refrain from judging the worthiness of the desires of citizens; procedurally, a commitment to rules coupled with a sense that values are not held intersubjectively leads to a demand to draw up norms of conduct so that they refer only to externally verifiable objective facts, not to inevitably interpersonally variable value judgments.

Problems with Theories of Entitlements
The supposition that we have an unwavering commitment to the idea of end neutrality is simply impossible to square with the granting of entitlements to parties in situations where their desires clash (clean water

versus cheaper goods; religious uniformity or the nonexpression of her-
esy versus free exercise). Unless one believes that, barring the inevitable
rational errors of judgment that might be made by those in power, each
entitlement we put in place would in fact have been generated by a
transaction-cost-free bargain among persons with given subjective preferences and economic power, one cannot believe that assigned rights
match up solely with desire.

First, though, the theory that rights might mirror the outcome of
transactionally costless bargains is inexorably indeterminate in that there
is no way to determine which rights people possess when they enter this
universal bargain to determine rights, and no way of determining how
much market power each person has *unless* one has already determined
those rights.[21] (Take the rape example I mentioned earlier: women as
a group, particularly before many entered the labor force, almost surely
would have been unable to outbid would-be rapists for the right to
determine whether sexual relations would occur if they did not have a
preexisting right to be free from unwanted sex that could be waived
only at their asking price, which did not have to be purchased at their
bid or offering price. Whether the bids of men who desired that women
have that choice would have outweighed those of men who didn't is
surely problematic. To determine *whether* women should have the right
to determine whether sexual relations can occur simply by mimicking a
market requires knowing whether women have the right, whether they
have at least the illiquid wealth to block certain changes they desire to
block.)

Second, the notion that rights might in fact be set only to mimic
hypothetical markets ignores two critical features we associate with them:
both that they are frequently set by majorities (without regard to the
wealth or market power of voters) and that they are often designed to
protect minorities against the transient subjective desires of majorities,
whose desires might well be manifest in hypothetical market transactions
as well as through voting if we were interested in these transient preferences. The unpopular religious figure may be granted a right to worship as he chooses precisely because he could not persuade, cajole, or
bribe others into tolerating him even through costless voluntary transactions, *not* because free exercise would be the outcome of costless
bargaining.

More traditional utilitarians avoid some of the economists' problem.
First, their theories are formally egalitarian: they try to measure the
intensity of desires without regard to capacity or power to meet one's

desires. Second, they are formally compatible with democracy, which
serves to (imperfectly) register or sum utilities. But the utilitarian scheme
is itself indeterminate in its own way. Even ignoring the typically noted
technical problems of no particular concern to me here (whether rights
should be assigned so as to maximize total or average utility, whose
utility should count, and so on), the chief difficulty is that the rights
assignment issue is simply never adequately distinguished from ordinary
goods assignment issues. The ordinary utilitarian preference for markets
could conceivably coexist with an opposite assumption that neither markets nor market-mimicking devices are presumptively utility maximizing
in assigning entitlements, but I've neither seen nor can I imagine a cogent
utilitarian defense of that proposition. Why we should allocate some
consumer goods (food and housing) through a market but not others
(clean water), why we should allow some tastes to be acted on in the
market (social distance from the poor) but not others (social distance
from the religious heretic or religious fanatic) should not be for the
utility maximizer by any means an obvious proposition.

Theories of Value in Contract Law
The ostensible commitment to the idea of end neutrality in contract law,
the most privileged domain of subjective end seeking, is also often far
from complete. At the abstract and principled level, we seem to scorn
the commitment to "just prices" or voiding all but substantively fair
exchanges as premodern, and tend to resolve the issue of identifying
unfairness in wholly procedural terms.[22] Still, practice seems to require
the covert reintroduction of substance in both obvious and somewhat
more hidden ways.

Most apparently, the purely procedural interpretations of unconscionability appear increasingly defective as they are scrutinized to a
greater extent. No interpretation that posits that illegitimacy arises from
disparities in bargaining power can survive the obvious fact that in cases
in which bargaining power is most obviously unequal, cases of pure
seller monopoly, contracts are by no means routinely voided.[23] In fact,
monopoly prices are not per se substantively unreasonable, nor is non-
competitive market structure procedurally suspect per se.[24] Similarly, no
interpretation that posits that illegitimacy is grounded in informational
disparities can adequately explain why superior information is, at least
on some occasions, just another aspect of the marketable power one
trading partner might have,[25] a factor to be thought of as *determining*
income distribution, not one that *hampers* the operation of a market,

given existing income shares. Finally, any interpretation that posits that the basis of the unconscionability inquiry is an inquiry into the possibility of the exploitation of those lacking purely *rational* capacity to judge whether their ostensibly respected ends will be met will inexorably fail as a procedural explanation in at least one of two ways. First, we may well tend to infer what we would call general capacity from our judgment of the irrationality of the particular choice rather than void the contract after we have looked at "general" capacity, may in fact believe that "capacity" is always situationally specific (the capacity to make the particular choice on the particular occasion).[26] Second, in judging whether an agent's acts advance supposedly respected ends, we will inevitably have to impute general "objective" ends rather than inquire into the details of particularized subjectivity, since we ordinarily simply infer ends from acts but claim we cannot here because the acts are so inapt.

The same problem crops up when we look at efforts in modern contract law to purge consideration doctrine of a substantive dimension, to avoid inquiry into the approximate equivalence of the exchanged goods by purportedly focusing only on the sufficiency or presence, rather than the adequacy, of each promisor's consideration.[27] Measuring when consideration is absent (in Second Restatement of Contract terms) or insufficient (in First Restatement ones) still requires knowing when a promise is worthless or empty, and it is not immediately obvious that we could objectively measure worthlessness without having a clue about how to measure worth. A court may void a contract where a party does no more than agree to do something he is legally required to; but then again it may not, if the *form* the parties' bargaining took enables the court to conclude that something must have been gained, given all the fuss. If one is *purely* formal (only in cases where the promisee has gained nothing he was not already formally entitled to will we void his promise), one will surely make substantive errors (people surely often get far *less* in their deals than assurances that some formal obligation will actually be met or met in more than a formally satisfactory way). But when we move away from pure legalistic form (as we often do), we acknowledge our capacity to know substance. If one is transactionally formal in divining that value is received (by presuming that consideration exists wherever parties bargain fussily and declare that they believe it exists), one has incorporated the subjective conception of value most fully. No one can tell anyone else who really thinks he has gotten something that he hasn't, so our only concern should be to ascertain whether the party subjectively thought he had gotten *something* at the time he contracted.

But this effort must flounder. In part, it must fail because it denies the objective court the capacity it must be granted given the very existence of the requirement of *some* consideration, of a requirement that contracts be more than bilateral agreements. In part, too, it conflicts with our more general desire to avoid inquiries into unknowable subjective intention, to focus only on objective manifestations of subjective intention rather than intention itself, in order to keep the judicial process rational, universal, fact focused. Perhaps the standard is simply one in which we void only *extremely* unequal contracts. But then, it is not really one that denies our capacity to ascertain objective value; it is simply one that either is not much concerned about anything but terrible cheating, or holds that objective values lie in a range, not at a single point.[28]

Void-for-Vagueness Doctrine

Once we assume that values are both arbitrary and nonuniversal, we cannot precisely command groups of people to act in accordance with values and expect them to know how to act. The law "Don't do *bad*" is the paradigm of vagueness precisely because people's accounts of what is bad are unshared, subjective.

Of course, the claim of vagueness is not strictly *necessary:* one could well *know* other people's values without *adopting* them, and references to values might explicitly be to common values or values of particular others (I might believe that there are no "dirty" words but would still easily be able to obey an injunction not to say "dirty" words in class). Unger[29] (and Simon, precisely following Unger in this regard)[30] claims that one cannot know other's values in a thought system committed to a fact-value distinction and the arbitrariness of value. (Simon makes this point in trying to explain why lawyers simply impute materialistic selfish ends to clients rather than try to discuss actual subjective ends.) Unger's claim seems to be that if one is to know desires, one must know them in accord with usual scientific ideas of knowledge, as determined events with causes, but that such a conception of desires is incompatible with the liberal theory of personality in which desires are seen as the basic self-generated building blocks of individuality. The point seems mistaken though. One could know others' values by confession, an epistemological stance consistent with a belief in their arbitrariness and subjectivity rather than their having intelligible general essences, without these being either determined responses or aspects of a more universal humanness. It would be *possible* to argue persuasively that confession is untrustworthy or unreliable, that people can't listen empathetically enough (particularly in a world of class, race, and gender division) to discover others' wishes. But this simply is *not* Unger's point. He says, instead, that to know others is to undermine their subjective personhood; this statement is true only if one "knows" them by imputing (determined) ends "appropriate" to their situations rather than assuming that ends are subjectively, intentionally chosen to *create* their unique identity.

Still, even if values of others are discernible, it is hard for believers in subjective value to imagine believing that official discretion will be adequately constrained or that demands on citizens will be clearly comprehended if laws explicitly refer to values in defining terms essential to their interpretation. The void-for-vagueness doctrine, the constitutionalization of the principle that official discretion must be limited and clear warning be given to citizens by demanding that legislatures clarify their commands, is ultimately a paradoxical effort to eliminate value terms (because they are inapplicable, since their content is unshared, hence indeterminate) when (and only when) bad substantive results occur (which, of course, demands that the courts know what a bad substantive result is). At times a statute proscribing certain forms of "unreasonable" behavior is acceptable; at times it is not. Reasonableness is, in standard senses, a value term, without explicit factual or objective reference. Statutes using such words may well be struck down, though only when the conduct that may be chilled when citizens are uncertain of the statute's reach is affirmatively desirable (for example political speech) rather than undesired by the court (for example arguably atypical sexual practices) or when the court fears that the statute could reasonably be thought to comprehend behavior that substantively ought to be allowed (for example, vague descriptions of vagrancy seem at their clearest in proscribing aimless strolling).[31] Given the supposed commitment to the subjectivity of values, laws proscribing the bad or the unreasonable must be utterly uninterpretable, subject to each individual's interpretive whim; the back-door reintroduction of a conception of the good universal enough to permit constitutional decision making enables us to determine which of a slew of such value-referring statutes are in fact intolerable.

The Problem of Acting in Role

The simultaneous contradictory commitment to both rules and standards is presented by both Kennedy (explicitly) and Simon (more implicitly) as implicating a deep ambivalence toward others. Playing (only) by the rules, denying the inevitable poor fit between the general and the particular, abstract theory and practice, is a characteristic response to the nightmare of intrusiveness: I will do only so much, I won't break the rules. Simon's bureaucrat who tells the welfare applicant that she, a case worker, cannot continue to provide benefits (without even mentioning that an intake worker might provide the applicant the same benefits) adopts the characteristic posture of distance, isolation, going about one's (delimited) business. But their view of this contradictory commitment fits easily within a paradigm of thought committed to arbitrary value: the private, whimsical demand for fusion makes one seek love, community, situation-sensitive altruistic obligation; but since others are prone to *use* us, egotistically, for their own ends, one might well want to ward them off, to describe quite precisely where one's obligations to them end.

In his early work, though, Unger describes the ambivalent relationship between the self and others in ways that centralize the question of whether values are indeed private and whimsical, rather than treating the ambivalent relationship as the result, arguably, of conflicting whimsical tastes for unity and distance. Epistemology is once again most critical; the book is not called "*Knowledge* and Politics" for nothing.

The self, says Unger, experiences itself as weightless, trivial, as having only some accidental, insignificant desires without meaning or pattern. The moral world is opaque, either simply unknown or unknowable in theory, depending on how self-consciously the actor is committed to the arbitrariness of moral codes: what is good, what one should seek, is a mystery.

To acquire coherence as a self, one seeks *recognition* from others. Without the validation of others, one has no faith that one's life plan is at all serious; there is simply no other way to check its validity. Moreover, one seeks to persuade others of the validity of one's perceptions of what is true because there is no test for the validity of moral propositions; the assent of others to one's perceptions must do.

The dilemma is that one inevitably seeks recognition by acting in role, living up to defined expectations, and in role one doesn't really get one's subjectivity affirmed but rather denies it by limiting one's expressions and interests. Similarly, one seeks affirmation of the truth of one's beliefs by altering the beliefs until they are nothing but conformist babble, until they have the commonsensical, everyday platitudinous sound that gains one intellectual respectability. One seeks validation of one's subjectivity by papering it over; the commitment to subjectivity leaves one utterly weightless unless one denies one's real experiences of subjectivity.

One solves the problems of opacity and weightlessness within a culture that denies that one can transcend the arbitrariness of desire only by *resignation* (a despairing submission to a social order whose claims are inwardly despised) or *disintegration* (revulsion against the external world). Only in the supposedly private realms (love, religion, art) does the unalienated self flourish; but these domains are viewed as being untouched by reason so that the self is once more torn asunder, divided into reasoning and purely emotive sides.[32]

Kennedy structures his analysis around the theme of how contradictions in legal ideas correspond to certain personal stances. Thus, it is both reasonably apparent why he believes that the rules pole in legal discourse is at least culturally connected to a distancing attitude toward others and how his claim might at least partly fail, at least if it is (wrongly) perceived as a predictive claim of necessary connection. Unger does not explicitly analyze his material as I have presented it. Thus, there is no reason to believe that he even means to suggest that instances of the breakdown of the commitment to value subjectivity in legal discourse (for example in entitlements assignment) represent attempts to overcome the characteristic personal attitudes he associates with the commitment. In part, this is true because Unger presents those attitudes in their debased, unworkable form (role-oriented conformism and babbling, resignation, disintegration, retreat into the private and emotional) rather than in the arguably utopian form in which Kennedy presents the individualist's commitment (as the rights-respecting seeker of a personal life plan). Still, one might reasonably posit that the legal (collective) commitment to a Nonplatonic value objectivity, a nontranscendent, historically conditional quasiobjectivity grounded in the discourse of free subjects, is a weak and fleeting shadow of a fuller collective and political life, a life where one would bring one's actual uniqueness of belief and behavior to ongoing collective inquiries into the good.

I am puzzled by this formulation, in part because I am at base puzzled by Unger's epistemological focus, the way in which he privileges the question of moral opacity. It is to the question of Unger's utopianism, his focus on the conditions of moral lucidity, that I shall turn in the last section of this chapter.

But for now I want to make a different point. While Unger's observation about the connection between weightlessness and self-denying conformism seems to me both profoundly true and profoundly *concrete,* its connection with the deep epistemology of liberalism seems much more problematic. I cannot see from Unger's account why one could not utterly eliminate the domain of reason, do away with the fact-value distinction by eliminating facts, without even touching this profound sense of weightlessness, which seems to me grounded not in *dualism* but in *value subjectivity*. There seems to me absolutely no reason to believe that strongly antipositivistic social scientists need find the ethical world any less arbitrary for finding the facts of the social world more so. One could also, as best I can tell, think of values as attributes of groups rather than persons, but experience the world as composed of highly diverse groups none of which has any obvious moral claims, and still seek the approval of larger, more prestigious, more powerful groups. As best I can tell too, one could even experience values as objective but outside one's ken because one is simply lazy or stupid and still feel rather weightless, still look to others as the arbiters of the good, and believe one can gain approval only through mindless aping of routine practices. Even if one believed that *political* liberalism must maintain the dualistic stance, because social order would be impossible unless we shared *something* (at least facts, if not the values moralistic conservatives or socialists believe we share), I simply cannot see that any of Unger's observations on role playing are meaningfully connected to a belief in the objectivity of facts.

Unger's Epistemological Utopianism

For Unger, the most pressing issue we face is moral opacity, the need to transcend the two prevalent defective conceptions of knowledge of the good: the liberal conception that there is no good to be known, just arational tastes, and the classical Platonic conception that the good is implicitly an objective feature of objects, the realization of their true nature. The transcendent solution Unger offers is a relatively familiar one for those conversant with nonlegal critical theory. The good is historically contingent, nonuniversal; it is not an attribute of objects but an attribute collectivities assign to objects. Thus, it is good for people to express their nature, as Unger says, but their nature is neither constant across culture or time nor is it independent of the collective work that goes into trying to ascertain it. Collective solutions to inquiries into the good become increasingly trustworthy as the spiral of domination within society is broken; as all speakers express their beliefs in an open discourse, free from the self-seeking we associate with preservation of hierarchical privilege and free from both the constraints of deference to status superiors and the constraints of scorn for status inferiors.

Unger's view seems to me most peculiar for its focus on the centrality of moral knowledge, ungroundedness, despairing nihilism. In part, to the degree that the claim is about *individual* needs for lucidity, it seems to me a much less psychologically plausible organizing experience than the experience of integration and separation from others that Kennedy centralizes. Issues of separation and individuation are not just chronologically prior in each person's life to issues of moral development;[33] they seem far more potent and universal in form. Each of us must learn early on to trust, must find relief in dependence, on (it is to be hoped) loving and beneficent parents, but this is soon coupled with the need to assert independent control, given both the parents' inevitably partial beneficence and their factual incapacity to mediate all external traumas. We clearly recapitulate this theme again and again; we surrender and yet feel suspicious in the face of all potentially intimate relations; constant "approach and avoidance" of others demonstrates the centrality of this experience.

The development of any particular sense of morality or life plan in any particular individual, though, seems more a banal process of identification with the coincidental practices and prejudices of the family. (In psychodynamic terms, it probably occurs when one mimics the same-sex parent to resolve the Oedipal crisis.) The collective conditioning of the family in which the moral message is learned is surely more complex, but for each person there is far less reason to believe that the experience of moral learning is nearly as charged or constantly conflict laden as the fundamental attitude of ambivalence about others.

Unger's focus seems ill conceived even if it is thought to be operative only at the collective level (that is, *political* action is problematic, given social division over ends, unless one can resolve disputes without recourse to force or louder insistence on one's whims). A battle between those demanding greater levels of collective care and those demanding greater freedom of private action has most consistently defined the political spectrum as we know it. I simply cannot interpret *any* historical political movement (including antifeudal liberalism) as fundamentally metaethical. The opposition by liberals to, say, the legitimacy of efforts by particular hierarchies to define the good may well be carried out in the name of an apparently metaethical supposition that the good cannot or ought not to be defined, but, as I've tried to demonstrate by showing the inexorable departures from genuine value skepticism within liberal legal culture, the depth of the epistemological commitment seems far weaker than the substantive opposition to the particular assertions prior hierarchies had imposed.

Unger's view seems peculiar too because of its false promise of resolution. It is perfectly commonplace, but perfectly telling, to note that Unger's scheme for identifying legitimate values is circular. If we could identify the proper conditions for *discourse* on values, recognize non-dominative discourse grounded only in *legitimate* hierarchy, we would know the answer to the most significant question we would want decent moral discourse to answer: when are hierarchy and distinction legitimate?

To note, as Unger does so persuasively, that we are stuck, that we have set up a string of problems that are insoluble given the terms of solution to which we are committed, is a valuable service, but it is not one that demands a remedy. The remedy (shared legitimate values) is utterly unreal anyway; it strikes me as almost purely formal and rhetorical (that is, as what's left over to complete the set, the mathematically whole universe, once one has decried liberal subjectivity and classical objectivity), without real punch. Advancing a "remedy" in such a situation, then, becomes little more than making a statement of global hope, a form of denying the possibility of acting in the absence of global hope.

Kennedy's position is, of course, far more skeptical of at least the offers of hope the classical individualists and altruists have given. At the level of high theory, Kennedy is denying the individualist, Adam Smithian claim that we can hope to avoid the clash between self and others by channeling pure selfishness through formal legal institutions (like competitive markets) so that others are inexorably helped by one's selfish conduct. Simultaneously, he is denying Marx's early utopian claim that true individualism is in no danger in a world of more total formal collective power because each of us will find it in his selfish interest to encourage diversity, for each can realize his own species-being, his collective potential as a person, only through the efforts of many. We might each be hunter in the morning and critic at night, to recall the classic Marxist phrase, but if we sense that we won't see what it is to be human unless we are a lecher, a celibate, a fanatic athlete, and so on, and that we can experience that sort of range only, at least in part, derivatively, we will never impose collective conformism. At the more concrete level, Kennedy's view is that we must always worry on the one hand that our reading groups will turn into Moonie cliques and on the other hand that in seeking what we first see as our own advancement, we will soon realize that we have nowhere to go, that the fate of each of us is inseparable from the fate of the whole society.

Day-to-day practice is to be informed constantly by a clear understanding of the centrality of this dilemma, but there is no formal or implied claim that an intermediate synthetic term, neither altruistic nor individualistic, should or could be sought. I sense that Kennedy's stance is antisynthetic but not the least bit resigned: that Unger is optimistic about a synthetic resolution, but the terms of the resolution are so abstract and empty that it provides no real spur to political action. Unger seems most useful when we rethink a concrete problem, more aware of the ways we are prone to construct it, given the dualistic structure of liberal thought we are inexorably drawn to; he is not so useful when we attempt to test a variety of possible political stances by reference to their capacity to contribute to the development of a nondominative community whose moral decisions we could view as transcending the traditional and unsatisfactory polar positions.

CHAPTER THREE

Intentionalism and Determinism

In Critical Legal Studies, liberal discourse both self-consciously and unself-consciously makes use of intentionalistic as well as deterministic description. Intentionalist discourse pictures human action in phenomenological, forward-looking, free-will–oriented terms, emphasizing the indeterminacy of action and, correlatively, the ethical responsibilities of actors. Determinist discourse pictures conduct in structuralist, backward-regarding, amoral terms, holding that conduct is simply a last event we focus on in a chain of connected events so predetermined as to merit neither respect nor condemnation.[1] Once more, though, liberal discourse privileges one of these opposed terms, here intentionalist discourse, just as it privileges a commitment to the Rule of Law, individualism, and value subjectivity. Forms of privileging, though, are certainly not invariable. The rule form is generally thought to dominate any system committed to legality, most unwaveringly in the criminal area. The dominance is viewed as so thorough, is so taken for granted, that we are prone both to describe our social system as having those virtues it might have if it were strongly rule governed whether it has them or not, and to attribute the actual presence of virtues to rules whether they accompany rules or not. Likewise, moral individualism is thought to dominate altruism so thoroughly that in everyday parlance it is difficult to explain altruism as anything more than the introjection of another's desires by a particular selfish subject. The subjective value conception is privileged in a slightly different way: the clearest domain of value objectivism (rights assignment) is somehow precipitated out from ordinary practice, so that we are able to make a wide array of value-skeptical, antipaternalistic, "pluralistic" arguments without any reference to our unacknowledged use of value-objectivist arguments.

In the intentionalism-determinism conflict the form of privileging is not one that *denies* determinism *a* place; it is simply one that claims (falsely, I shall argue) both that we can *descriptively* identify domains of freedom and distinguish them from domains of choicelessness *and* that, to the extent that social life is increasingly occupied by presumed domains of freedom, it has improved. It may well be that all social systems have wrestled with problems of distinguishing domains of free will from domains of determinism; what is interesting to explore in looking at our own culture is, first, the degree to which recognition of the ubiquity of the problem is repressed, and second, and more important, the particular choice of intentionalist domains. Liberal thought may not, for all I know, repress determinist limits on blame particularly differently from other thought systems; it can be practically *defined*, though, by its peculiar insistence that there is some definable collective life that is coercive and determining and a definable domain of private empowerment in which free intentional action occurs.

The CLS analysis of the liberal posture should be a familiar one by now. The first claim is that it is simply inaccurate to believe that we know when it is appropriate to apply determinist analysis and when intentionalist analysis is more appropriate, that it is more accurate to say that we are actually *simultaneously* drawn to each form of description, so that our relationship with the discourses is, once more, *contradictory,* not one in which two *complementary* discourses are used, each correct or appropriate in its place. I shall elucidate this claim in three ways: first, by noting the degree to which the general practice of punishment is *morally* unstable insofar as it rests on the acceptability of intentionalistic assumptions, even if we can predict with confidence that these assumptions will sometimes operate; second, by showing that in many instances a more covert battle between intentionalistic and deterministic discourses goes on in the criminal area precisely because each discourse is so available to us; and third, by showing that even in areas where one rarely focuses on the issue of the clash between intentionalism and determinism (like the interpretation of testator's wills in situations in which circumstances have altered), the unconscious oscillating attachment to each of these discourse forms renders justificatory schemes, if not daily practice, indeterminate.

I shall then criticize the most significant, system-defining liberal effort to distinguish the domain of freedom from the domain of necessity, the public-private and voluntary-involuntary distinctions. Having attempted to recapitulate the standard CLS depiction of the liberal posture on the question of descriptive discourse choice, I shall then argue that some CLS scholars have tried to use this depiction to bolster methodologically antipositivist positions, positions that hold that we cannot objectively discern the reality of human conduct and social life. The motivation of the antipositivists, though, is not at all lucid to me.

Finally, I shall argue that those who have focused on the issue of the contradictory commitment to intentionalist and determinist discourses have yet another view of the problem of the relationship between self and others. It is distinct both from the Kennedy-Simon position, which focuses on the self's ambivalence about intrusion, and Unger's, which focuses on the problematic status of the self's seeking validation by conforming to others' expectations of one's proper role.

The Descriptive Contradiction in Practice

Blame in the Criminal Area

The social practice of punishment can be formally justified without reference to the capacity of actors to control either their *desire* to violate criminal norms or their criminal *conduct*. Certainly to the extent that the aim of incarceration is simply incapacitation or isolation, an effort to ensure that a person's only available victims are other prisoners, one need not believe that criminals have any capacity at all to alter their behavior. While deterrence-oriented theorists must believe that actors have some capacity to control their conduct, that they will be less likely to engage in criminal activity when it is more costly to do so, they need not believe that actors can control their level of temptation to do what we call wrong. To use economics jargon, actors may not have much control over the location of their "demand curves" for crime. Even if they are able to make moves *along* a given curve, the location of the curve may well be an unchosen given, in the terms of the deterrence theorist.[2] X may proceed to commit a battery if he is to be fined $10 but not if he is to be jailed; Y may commit one if he is to be imprisoned for only one year but not if he would face ten years in jail. The differences between them may result from determined factors, but deterrence theory is premised on their capacity to make choices, to commit the battery or not depending on the cost of so doing.

It is rare, though, to find commentators utterly willing to disclaim any interest in assigning *blame*. The most characteristic stance that Anglo-American criminal law theorists take is deterrence oriented in its general justifying aim (for example, the general purpose of outlawing murder is to diminish the number of murders) but retributivist as to the distribution of punishment (for example, it is wrong to punish someone who is not blameworthy even if it would diminish the number of murders).[3] Likewise, the near-uniform opposition to pure preventive-detention systems (ones grounded solely in the prediction of dangerousness of citizens not even accused of violating a criminal norm) is only in part *evidentiary*, only in part grounded in skepticism about our factual capacity to predict future dangerousness. Opponents almost invariably strongly denigrate such a system because it punishes those who have not yet behaved in a blameworthy fashion.[4] Because blame has been treated as a theoretical predicate to punishment, and because we so rarely infer blamelessness once certain acts are performed unmistakenly, we privilege, at least implicitly, the intentionalistic descriptive account that renders the blaming practice morally unobjectionable.

What is problematic is that it is simply impossible to construct an adequate theory of individual blameworthiness that is left untouched or secure in the face of the obvious fact that circumstances clearly beyond the control of the actor have, at a minimum, a strong bearing on the possibility that he will commit wrongful acts.[5] Moreover, the fact that we can specify *some* factors that alter the probability of certain actions suggests that it is at least conceivable that if we could model an individual's life more fully, we could predict *all* conduct with certainty. Alternatively, we might well believe that there is some residual flux left after we have finished explaining all influences on behavior but question whether the flux is adequate to ground blame.

The connection between deterministic description and blamelessness has probably never been adequately specified, in part because there is likewise no definitive account by intentionalists of the minimal conditions for blame.[6] At times the determinists use purely causal or attributive metaphors that seem rather primitive: the act is attributed not to the defendant but to anthropomorphized background conditions (the act is a product of insanity; the act is a result of child abuse).[7] These metaphors seem grounded in a psychological desire to find blame at the level of some agent, to create an agent if need be to substitute for the most obvious candidate because the most direct causal agent is treated like a puppet who *must* have some puppeteer.[8] At times the determinist claim seems to focus on the assurance of those of us privileged to judge others that we can label them deviant or deeply different. Unless we are certain that those we would blame have different (worse) reactions to a set of circumstances than we would have, rather than that they simply face worse circumstances, our capacity to condemn diminishes.

The capacity to blame in personal life may thus be an artifact of a partial illusion that those we know, in our own social setting, *could* behave just as we do, something we find quite hard to assert with confidence in dealing with those more distant from us either socially or psychologically.[9] At times the argument seems to be one that treats the capacity to be deemed blameworthy as a simple correlative cost of privilege. Once again, the argument is at a wholly metaphorical level. It is as if some inexplicit contract has been made: in exchange for receiving any number of positive things one has no particular moral claim to (money, talent, a stable upbringing), one receives a negative thing one has no strong moral right to resist, given one's privileges—demands for good behavior that, if unmet, call for condemnation.[10] Finally, even those who, like Michael Moore, think that they can deny the moral relevance of determinist accounts still attribute blame only to individuals with what they consider a strong rational capacity for self-governance.[11] But it is surely ambiguous whether rational capacity or "agency" is not itself something we think people have more or less of depending on their (determined) degree of self-control and clear perception of the consequences of action to themselves and others.

Moreover, it is not obviously just for those who face enormously distinct (unchosen) internal demands to behave more or less acceptably to be treated the same as those facing different demands, even if they do have one thing in common—their presumptively equal rational capacity. Moore's system depends on believing both that the world is divided noncontinuously into the clearly insane and the rational and responsible *and* that *factual* inequality of opportunity to avoid crime is acceptable as long as everyone has equal *formal* capacity to avoid it. Yet the idea that a defect of the sort Moore must treat as rational—for example the degree to which one fails to understand that others have feelings like one's own—is either present or absent, rather than more or less present, in part as a result of all sorts of background conditions, is hard to fathom. And Moore gives no reasons at all to believe that factual distinctions in exposure to the risk of condemnation should be of no concern.[12]

It is surely *possible* to deny blame-evading determinism (as libertarians like Thomas Szasz do)[13] or to believe that blame is *never* appropriate because one imagines that all of our failures to condone are based on our *own* failures to understand behavior adequately, a feature not morally relevant to the defendant.[14] It is also surely the case, though, that the vast bulk of people simply oscillate uncomfortably between intentionalist and determinist accounts, with no discernible metaprinciple to discover which is appropriate to particular situations. It was indeed true that utopian Marxists denied the pull toward political individualism, and utopian market theorists believed that one could adequately attend to altruist demands by properly channeling purely selfish behavior; but our dominant *actual* practice in that arena has been to waver uncertainly between the individualist and altruist poles while nominally privileging the individualist position.

In this case we privilege intentionalism either by wishing away the profundity of the issue of discourse choice or by purportedly *confining* determinist discourse. We may be openly "pragmatic," making statements that amount to: we must pretend we can blame to convince ourselves that it is all right to do something we want, but we realists know it is just a myth needed to put people away.[15] The cynicism of the effort is bothersome, though, in part because those who give voice to it generally try almost immediately to justify what they have just claimed has no need for justification, and in part because we lack a socially acceptable theory of which people should purvey and which accept false myths.

We may also privilege certain limited forms of explanation, implicitly denying the validity of others. Given our allegiance to hard science, it is not surprising that a finding of insanity, a quasimedical determinism, is privileged over sociological determinisms,[16] particularly since it is also the case that the sociological determinisms seem to undercut *most* of our blaming practices while the insanity defense is exceptional. Still, the extent to which the insanity model can maintain a truly medical pedigree is in strong doubt, and the possibility that legal insanity could ever match up with clinical categories (assuming, heroically, that such categories are biochemical, "hard" scientific ones) is highly doubtful. The instability of all efforts at denial and self-reassurance are quite transparent. We simply have two discourses available to us when we consider human conduct, and they are not integrable or compatible. Newspaper readers may find it preposterous that John Hinckley and Dan White were, respectively, wholly and partly excused; to become *serious* about these or any other cases, to immerse oneself in the defendants' conditions, is to abandon a smugly cheery faith in intentionalist assumptions, to recall the mysteriousness of each person's motivations, to recall that we may both exaggerate our own sense of self-control and distort our capacity to control what we see as the meaning of the options we may think we choose between.

Hidden Discourse Shifts in the Criminal Law

If CLS scholars are correct that the choice between an intentionalist account and a determinist account of an event is fundamentally a choice between two readily available discourses, then we ought to find that we can plausibly refocus apparently settled views of existing cases, make other actors in our legal culture see that accepted instances where intentionalist accounts have dominated could be supplanted by determinist accounts and vice versa. It is moreover important to emphasize that we often use determinist discourse, despite our nominal commitment to intentionalism, even in a situation where the determinism is obviously "impure"—that is, where no one could claim that a certain result inexorably follows from certain causes.

Voluntaristic or Intentionalistic Interpretation of Events

Voluntary Acts   It is commonplace hornbook law that a defendant cannot be held liable unless he has voluntarily performed the prohibited *actus reus*. It is equally common to interpret the following situation as one in which the defendant has taken no voluntary action: the defendant is apprehended at home while drunk and brought to a public place, where he is arrested for public drunkenness. In a typical case, like Martin v. State,[17] the court says that the statute presupposes a *voluntary* public appearance, and that such an appearance is involuntary.

It is likewise clear that one can convict a defendant who was unconscious (clearly not acting voluntarily) at the time he performed a prohibited act if he had earlier taken voluntary actions that created a risk that he would later perform the proscribed conduct in an unconscious state. Thus, in People v. Decina,[18] the court sustained a defendant's conviction for negligent homicide, although at the time his car struck the victims he was not conscious as a result of an epileptic seizure, on the theory that his decision to drive was not only a relevant act but a culpable one, given his awareness of the possibility that he might have such an attack while driving.

Of course, the suppressed voluntaristic interpretation of the material in *Martin* should be elucidated by *Decina*. The defendant in a case like *Martin* may well have done *something* voluntary to get himself arrested, either at the time of arrest (if, say, the officers had come to intervene in a domestic dispute) or on some past occasion (if, say, he was simply picked up on an old warrant). Only in the rather unlikely case that

Martin was arrested for no reason at all related to him (such as mistaken identity) is the contention that his public appearance is utterly outside his control at all an obvious one.

I can explain our interpretive practice here, in the sense that I would have predicted the outcomes correctly for reasons I can share with others, but the explanations hardly negate the alternative intentionalistic discourse. Suppressing the voluntary or intentionalistic account of the behavior obviates the need to deal with the case as raising antilegalist (and therefore unprivileged) defenses. The case could be said to raise either issues of justification (although being drunk in public is formally proscribed, it is on balance desirable in this case, given that the alternative is to resist the police) or the excuse of entrapment (the police are too entwined in the violation). But while we may understand *why* we use an ordinarily unprivileged *descriptive* discourse here (to preserve a distinct, *normatively* privileged discourse), we must recall that it is our simultaneous access to each discourse that makes the practice available.

Status Crimes   Politically liberal judges, like Judge Wright and Justice Douglas, argued that it is illegitimate to punish drug addicts either for the status of being addicted or for incidents of the status, like drug possession, because they are not voluntarily addicts or voluntarily drug possessors.[19] Once more, though, it is only through an arational, narrow time-framing decision that the determinist vision seems adequate or preclusive of the intentionalistic alternative. Assume, with Justice Douglas, that addiction is a sickness. The Justice claims that we are ordinarily reluctant to blame people for *being* sick. But it is not at all obvious that we don't frequently blame people for *becoming* sick, for having taken actions we tend to characterize as intentional that leave them subsequently in a choiceless state. (The fact that venereal disease is clearly an illness hardly precludes people from blaming their lovers for getting it.) Assume, too, that we take Wright's deterrence-oriented focus and agree that at the moment at which an already addicted person decides whether to violate laws against drug possession, his desires are so determined by his status that no punishment will affect his behavior. It is still not obvious why we should not focus on earlier, more chosen decisions to use drugs that *resulted* in his becoming addicted,[20] and note that the person might have been deterred from those earlier uses (which would, of course, have made him less likely to make the particular subsequent use for which he was arrested) if he could be arrested *whenever* he used drugs, not just before he became addicted.

Again, while Wright and Douglas used determinist accounts, a perfectly plausible intentionalist discourse is available as well; it is simply
suppressed in their scheme, but perfectly understandable to all of us.

Uniform Hostility to Strict Liability   As I discussed in Chapter 1, the
debate over the propriety of strict liability can most profitably be seen
as an instance of the general battle between the rules form and the
standards form. Nonetheless, at least in part to avoid open advocacy of
the normatively nonprivileged standard, the majority of commentators
attack strict liability without attacking its formal flaws, the flaws inherent
in its being too rulelike (just as treating *Martin* as a rare case in which
determinist discourse is appropriate ducks the open invocation of standards). The argument is that the defendant convicted of a strict liability
crime is choiceless, determined; his wrongful conduct is out of his control. H. L. A. Hart, for instance, speaks of actors who "could not have
done otherwise,"[21] Joel Feinberg of penalizing persons for offenses "they
could not help."[22]

Whatever one's vision of the ultimate propriety of strict liability, it
ought to be apparent in the ordinary cases that the strictly liable defendant can easily be seen as having voluntarily placed himself in an
unusual position where he is aware that his failure to avert harm will
be punished. Someone who takes a controlling position in a company
that ships drugs in interstate commerce, who is then strictly liable for
illicit shipments, can hardly be said to have had *no* choice at all about
violating the statute even if it turns out that no one who took such a
position could stop the illicit shipments, at least as long as we have
reason to believe that he was or could have been aware of the risk that
such illicit shipments could occur. He was certainly not simply taking
steps inevitably incident to survival on earth that posed a risk of causing
harms we punish for. Indeed it would be odd as a general policy matter
not to outlaw assumption of a particular position if we believed one
would inexorably cause unacceptable harm by filling it; a legislature
would be unwise to outlaw the harm rather than assumption of the
position if it believed that it were impossible for someone in that position
to avoid excessive harm. Still, viewing the case solely from the vantage
point of the *defendant,* of justice to the individual rather than prudent
social policy, his conviction should hardly be seen as the result of determined conduct that he was powerless to control unless one believes
that he was forced to assume the position.[23] Once more, an intentionalist
account of the misconduct is readily available, as we should expect, even

given the common practice of viewing the conduct through a determinist lens.

Deterministic Interpretation of "Intentionalistic" Events

Opposition to Negligent Crimes   While most modern Anglo-American commentators sympathize with predicating liability on negligent behavior,[24] the more common traditional position was that negligence was an inappropriate basis for criminal liability.[25] The modern authors interpret carelessness in an intentionalistic fashion: though one does not *choose* to harm carelessly (if one were subjectively aware that one was harming, one would be deemed reckless or intentional), one has some meaningful control over how careful one is. The traditional authors, though, saw intentional maliciousness as chosen, but interpreted negligence as determined. In Glanville Williams's words, "Some people are born feckless, clumsy, thoughtless, inattentive, irresponsible, with a bad memory and a slow 'reaction time.' "[26] Of course; but some are, arguably, born malicious, hateful, thrilled by the sight of others' blood, and so on. The ready availability of determinist discourse permits the traditionalists' argument to make perfect sense within our legal culture, just as the availability of an intentionalist account makes the acceptance of at least some level of liability predicated on carelessness seem perfectly reasonable as well.

Provocation, Duress, and Subjective Entrapment   Intentional killings were traditionally characterized as manslaughter rather than murder when the killer was provoked, or when his conduct was a partly determined response to external circumstances, a reasonably predictable outcome of prior events. The traditional view was that one could readily confine the list of incidents we would label provocative, maintain the unbending methodological commitment to intentionalist accounts of defendant decision making, except in cases where the defendant had been physically assaulted. But it is clear that we could also either expand a discrete list of causally determining provocations (to include, for example, witnessing adultery in progress or learning of adultery, illegal arrest, and so on)[27] or allow an open-ended determinist inquiry (for example, the Model Penal Code allows a fact-finder to determine that a defendant was provoked when a reasonable person would have been abnormally likely to be tempted to kill).[28] Again, the question is simply when do we *try* to explain a killer's motivation and negate blame by having explained it. Arguably we can, once more, explain our practice; we may believe, for instance, that the more generally determined killer is likely to kill again, the provoked killer less likely to face circumstances in which he would (and the incapacitationist is mostly interested in identifying would-be recidivists). But to the degree that we *justify* it as an effort to identify the blameworthy, the expansion of determinist categories in this area suggests the wider-spread availability of the discourse form.

The identical issue of the expandability of determinist discourse could, of course, arise if we decided to accept defenses of nonincidental duress: for example, if Patty Hearst had been allowed, as a formal matter, to base her defense to bank robbery *not* on being forced at gunpoint at the crime scene to commit the act but on being emotionally remade into a bank robber by months of isolation and torture.[29] Likewise, assume (mistakenly) that courts accurately describe our practices using the "subjective" defense of entrapment they claim to apply.[30] According to this account of the entrapment defense, we acquit those entrapped by government agents not simply to deter government agents from taking undesirable steps to induce crime,[31] but because we believe that the conduct of entrapped defendants was significantly determined by the agents' conduct (that is, that the defendant was not otherwise predisposed to commit the crime). It is apparent that we could readily describe the conduct of solicited, pestered, and aided defendants in determinist terms as well, create and then expand a now nonexistent category of private entrapment,[32] if we truly believed that we could do a determinist analysis in cases where official agents solicit. The decision may both flow from and reinforce the usual liberal public-private distinction; even when different defendants are influenced by an agent's efforts, we assume that only the agent with government authority is coercive, determining.

Impure Determinisms

Perhaps the most familiar explicit methodological defense of the privileging of intentionalist discourse is that those who proffer determinist explanations are incapable of predicting behavior with any real precision. They might, for instance, tell us that beaten children as a group go on to commit more crimes than others, but can neither claim that *all* beaten children will commit crimes nor tell us *which* beaten children will and which will not; further, they might predict that a generally violent disposition will result from certain conditions but cannot tell us

whether a person with a generally violent disposition will strike his wife
once or go on a mass murder spree. Those in CLS committed to the
idea that we are simultaneously drawn to both deterministic and intentionalistic discourse need not reject this description of determinist practice but must show that it is frequently simply ignored as a critique. It
functions less to squelch the discourse form at a general level than to
provide a handy, ever-available argument when it is to be rejected for
some other reason. Covert or overt inexact determinist predictions are
often treated as acceptable.

A Second Look at the Drunk-in-Public Statutes   Assume we are willing
to characterize the defendant's public appearance in *Martin* as involuntary, even though we may actually recognize that he voluntarily performed acts prior to arrest that make us believe that his ultimately
appearing in public drunk should be deemed voluntary. The statute he
was charged with violating requires that perpetrators be both publicly
drunk *and* boisterous.[33]

It seems apparent that if the court believed that boisterousness was
fully voluntary, even for drunks, best described in ordinary intentionalistic terms, there would be little hesitation in convicting someone even
though he had not performed each element of the offense voluntarily.
(Public exhibitionism statutes require *both* being in public and disrobing,
yet a defendant who disrobes after being dragged into public could surely
be convicted. Similarly, one need not dial the phone to be convicted of
placing an obscene phone call, although the statutes ordinarily speak of
both phoning and addressing obscene language to another.) Likewise,
it seems equally apparent that the court cannot believe that boisterousness is a fully determined universal response to the excessive consumption of liquor, that it is absolutely inevitable once one is drunk,
because to accept such an account would render the second part of the
statute redundant. If the court believed that boisterousness is fully determined but nonuniversal, absolutely inevitable for *some* but not all
drunks, conviction of a Martin dragged into public where he is doomed
to be unruly would indeed be unfair, but conviction in ordinary cases
where the public appearance is voluntary would also be highly suspect,
being based on a fact outside the defendant's control. (It would be like
arresting only those public drunks with blue eyes.) Only under a very
far-fetched interpretation (that is, that boisterousness is fully determined
for some, but that those few *know* that they will become boisterous and
can ordinarily stay at home when drunk to avoid the offense) can we

reconcile the practice of acquitting Martin and convicting the routine boisterous public drunk under the notion that we assume conduct to be intentional except when it is absolutely uncontrollable. The far more plausible interpretation of our practice is that we view boisterousness as partly or impurely determined behavior, difficult to control, predictable if not *exactly* so. Thus, unless drunks have the chance to stay out of public, they have not had a fair chance to avoid criminality, since it is at least relatively difficult to shut up once in public, though by no means utterly out of anyone's control.

Explicitly acknowledging that we reach decisions based on partial or impure determinist views threatens the privileging of intentionalism to the extent that we ground the rejection of determinism in its inevitable impurity; so the *Martin* court simply never discusses the boisterousness issue at all. Nonetheless, we can readily see that if we were not drawn to an impure determinist account of a drunk's boisterous behavior, we could not explain our actual practice in this area.

Abandonment of Attempts   Many jurisdictions allow a defendant whose conduct would already constitute an attempt to commit a crime to exonerate himself by renouncing or abandoning the course of conduct. Of course, the abandonment must be understood in intentionalistic terms if it is to do the defendant any good. Just as we do not ordinarily blame a person for engaging in criminal conduct unless it is intentional, we surely would not credit a person for abandoning a criminal plan unless the abandonment was understood as intentional.

The point for our purposes here is that instances of supposedly involuntary abandonment—instances of deterministic discourse—arise in cases where a defendant's conduct could hardly be said to follow inexorably from past events. Thus, in the standard case of LeBarron v. State[34] the defendant ceased his sexual assault on his victim when she informed him that she was pregnant. The court found the abandonment of the attempted rape involuntary, out of the defendant's control, analogizing it to the failure of a defendant to kill because the pistol he was using was not loaded.[35] It is obvious, though, that such mechanical determinism is acutely overstated: the abandonment was obviously neither totally out of the defendant's control, unmeditated, nor by any means utterly predictable or inevitable. (It is clear that not all would-be rapists would desist from raping a victim because she was pregnant; effect does not follow cause with certainty.) But because the conduct seems impurely determined, at least partly predictable, we are not at all confident that the defendant won't rape in other situations, not confident that his decision on this occasion will generalize adequately to other confrontations; nor do we give moral or legal credit to his ceasing an immoral course of conduct. We clearly use the determinist account here, while suppressing the degree to which we use it despite its methodological impurity, by employing analogies to more pure cases of nonintentional conduct.

Intentionalism, Determinism, and the Testator's "Will"

The dispute between intentionalist and determinist discourse is known to frame the most general debates about the propriety of criminal blame; even in the more particular controversies in the criminal area which I have just detailed, where the significance of discourse choice is more hidden, I doubt that many would be surprised to find that this fundamental difficulty crops up. If the contradictory commitment to intentionalism and determinism is to prove a fertile source of insight into liberal legalist thought, it must be embedded in other controversies as well. I shall claim later on that it is central to what is perhaps the most ideologically significant duality we note—that contrasting the private domain of free choice with the public domain of coercion. For now, though, I want to discuss it in the context where it is most invisible, largely to demonstrate that, like the unavoidable rules-standards problem and the unavoidable subjective-objective value dilemma, it too is pervasive.

Take a typical case in which a testator has left his money to support scholarships at an all-male school, and has specifically said in his will that he wishes to educate "young men."[36] The trustees of the school, who have recently decided to admit women, go to court to get permission to use the testator's scholarship fund for female students. The trustees argue, in part, that circumstances have so changed that, if the testator were able to consider the situation today, he would approve his money being spent on women students. (The problem is obviously hardly unique to interpreting bequests. Assume that one feels committed to following legislative intention or the framers' constitutional intention. Assume too, for instance, that we know with certainty that each of the framers approved a particular practice, for example the death penalty, that we now wish to condemn as violating *their* injunction against cruel and unusual punishment. Is it consistent with their intention to bar the practice?)

It is possible, of course, that we simply don't care what the testator wanted at all, that with the passage of time, our desire to do what we want with the money swamps any desire to discern and respect his wishes, particularly if they strongly contradict our own. But as a matter of both rhetoric and practice, we follow to an extent the appropriate intentionalist discourse, treating the testator as a self-created person with individual and individuating tastes who *chose* objects of his bounty in accordance with a meaningfully free will. We see this *rhetorically* when we look at the court's subjunctive language: courts claim to redraft the document to express the intentionalistic subjective will of the person brought back to life under new circumstances. We see this *practically* because grants are not simply thrown out wholesale, nor rejected simply for being generally viewed as substantively quirky or frivolous.

But despite the nominal commitment to intentionalism, the subjunctive reconstruction of the testator is fundamentally impossible to square with a full-blown commitment to intentionalism. If we construct a testator's desire to educate only boys as nothing more than the typical belief of people of his class and time, simply relativize his intentions and assume that were he alive today, he'd undoubtedly have today's typical beliefs, which include at least a formal commitment to sex blindness in education, we treat his literal written will not as the outgrowth of a personal, subjectively chosen "will" but as the determined result of his historical status and role. Our capacity to comfortably project a testator into the present is, of course, a tribute to the ready availability of determinist discourse, to a picture of our beliefs and attitudes as objects of collective forces, not the subject-based source of the collectivity.

It is conceivable that a committed intentionalist might respond to my argument by claiming that we believe that personalities have structures that transcend their particularities without believing the structures themselves to be determined. One might thus treat a particular testator as intentionally "politically progressive" or "bigoted" and simply look to do whatever progressive or bigoted people do. The structures, though, that give that sort of coherence to character are almost certainly social; the idea that the range of understandings we label as constituting "progressiveness" or "bigotry" could be individually imagined and created is implausible. To treat particular beliefs as instances of a belief structure rather than the building blocks of a belief structure is to flip the intentionalists' methodological commitment: the particular is derived from the general, detailed subjectively from structure, rather than building structure by summarizing discrete chosen desires.

One may well believe that the shift from nominal intentionalism (following a subject's chosen desire) to obscured determinism (deconstructing subjective desire through a focus on the cultural relativity of ostensible desire) is simply the outcome of an irrepressible urge to be freed whenever possible from the commands of the past (at least as long as current would-be donors won't see too clearly that their "wills" will be overturned as soon as possible). But the *possibility* of the ready shift clearly rests on the availability of these contradictory pictures of human conduct.

The Medical Care Deduction

The fertility of the recognition that the often undefended recourse to either intentionalist or determinist discourse can effectively appear to resolve a complex legal dispute can also be seen by its appearance in yet another sphere of law, outside the criminal area, in which we hardly expect the issue to crop up routinely: tax law. Yet the dispute between proponents of the deductibility of medical expenses and opponents of the deduction can in large part be seen as a controversy over whether the expenditures are intentional or chosen (hence, like most consumption expenditures, presumptively both pleasurable and taxable) or fundamentally determined, a necessary response to disease, an external fact.

The appeal of William Andrews's justification of the deduction is almost surely that spending for medical care should be seen not as freely chosen, in utility-enhancing terms, but rather as restorative of a baseline utility position of good health from which the taxpayer involuntarily departs. The claim that a taxpayer who spends $10,000 on health care and earns $40,000 is no better off than one with a $30,000 income and without medical bills is premised on the idea that the $10,000 gives him nothing beyond what the healthy nonspender has, that he has just responded to the external circumstances of disease.[37] The attacks on Andrews's position emphasize the considerable income elasticity of health care expenditures—how much they vary with wealth—precisely to counter the claim that disease mechanically triggers certain expenditures (both because people *define* disease differently and because they embed different levels of both amenities and quality of care in their health care bill). They also emphasize the extent to which bad health may result

from voluntary decisions to take health risks, that even if at the moment
of deciding to go to the doctor one is relatively choiceless or determined,
one may have been intentional (and utility seeking) in risking ill health.[38]

Obviously neither position is descriptively complete. There are undoubtedly some medical procedures that people invariably seek unless
resources are limited, and diseases that some tolerate and others don't
(that is, there are domains where one or the other description would
seem especially inapt), but the controversy inevitably goes beyond the
purely descriptive. The observer's interpretive decision to emphasize
the intentional aspects of behavior (such as risk taking) or the determined aspects (the unwanted, hence involuntary nature of diseases, once
acquired) is difficult to defend or attack, given the availability of each
discourse.

Spheres of Freedom and Spheres of Coercion

One might conceivably believe that people consent to or choose nearly
every aspect of public and private life, that they, in essence, intentionally
construct the world they inhabit. Emigration is always the final potential
act of willful choice, which, if untaken, can be deemed to demonstrate
consent to all that one hasn't left. In fact, while it seems a bit forced to
speak of staying in one's home country as a strong form of approval of
particular collective practices, it is common for legal economists dedi-
cated to federalism to argue that local governments compete with one
another for citizens, that exit is the standard effective weapon to control
bad local government practice.[39]

The mainstream right-centrist legal position, though, is not that people
choose everything but that there is a fairly distinct line between the
domain of intentional choice and freedom (private life, contract) and
the domain of coerced choicelessness (public life, mandatory law, subjection to political sovereignty). It is generally easy, in fact, to locate
people on our traditional political spectrum by ascertaining to what
extent they are committed to describing life in those spheres "unregulated" by the state as free, chosen. For instance, politically left-of-center
economists are prone to see unemployment as fundamentally determined by macroeconomic forces that inhere in the private sector and
are certainly beyond the capacity of any single person (or plausible
privately formed group) to control, forces that the state might conceivably alleviate but did not create.[40] Politically right-of-center economists
are prone to picture unemployment either in voluntary terms (for ex-

ample as a function of rational long-term contracts or of extensive but rational job search)[41] or as imposed by wrong-headed coercive state power (through minimum wage laws).[42] In discussing income inequality, right-of-center economists, while obviously recognizing the considerable degree to which marketable talents are unevenly distributed in ways beyond the control of individuals, are far more prone than those to the left of center not only to emphasize obvious factors perhaps better described in intentionalistic terms (like work effort) but also to point out nonobvious intentionalist sources of nominal income disparities (for example differences between actors in their attitudes towards risk, which make some choose lower but more certain earnings paths).[43]

CLS commentators have made two basic criticisms of mainstream efforts to draw distinctions between private and public spheres. First, they have reiterated and sharpened a little-noticed Legal Realist position that the state is inextricably involved in the supposedly private realm. Second, they have noted the extent to which coercion and choicelessness can readily exist in the realms traditionally denominated private.

The Inevitability of Coercive State Action

The notion that there is a meaningful private domain, dominated by consensual contract, obviously depends on ignoring the extent to which the state inevitably regulates the steps one can take to induce others to contract. Little-known Realist writers like Robert Hale have noted that every contract into which people enter can be seen, to use the CLS terms, as an intentional or privately rational adjustment to background conditions that, from the vantage point of the actor, are taken as determined or given.[44] A choice to give a mugger the money he asks for is perfectly intentional once the background conditions are settled. The price I am willing to pay you for shoes likewise depends on your state-protected right to withhold the shoes from me. The Realists' greatest contribution in this area was to point out the degree to which the basic background conditions we tend to take for granted (like the state's regulation of physical force) represent coercive decisions with vital distributive consequences (altering the power those more capable of mustering force can wield).

They also did a great service in demonstrating the degree to which certain bargaining techniques have been permitted or forbidden historically within a fundamentally continuous legal culture. Hale, for instance, talks of contingent distinctions in the degree to which one can

take generally legal steps for bad reasons. He notes that while one can
ordinarily collect all checks drawn on a bank from that bank, one cannot
collect checks to force the bank to keep unreasonably large cash reserves; likewise, he notes that one is often allowed to block an actor
from using one's property unless he pays in advance, even if he must
pay a monopoly price, and other times one must allow an actor to use
one's property if he pays damages, where the damages are figured not
on the basis of the price that would have been reached through contract,
given the actual parties' bargaining position, but on the basis of some
hypothetical competitive market price.[45] John Dawson demonstrated the
degree to which definitions of duress expanded widely within a fundamentally preregulatory environment. In the thirteenth century promises
to pay were undone only when they were induced by imprisonment or
threats of serious bodily harm. Later, courts refused to enforce promises
to pay for return of property that had been wrongly seized or detained,
even when the promisor had the theoretical alternative of seeking replevin. Duress continued to expand: promises could be voided when
the promise misused state-conferred monopoly power; used far broader
forms of "undue influence" or exploitation of the improvident, particularly improvident heirs; threatened even warranted criminal prosecution.[46]

The existence of a developed law of quasicontract (and less clearly
stated quasi contractual interpretations of express contracts) also belies
the claim that the state passively responds to private volition in the
"private" sphere of contract. Quasicontractual obligations are generally
thought to derive from unstated volition, but inevitably in practice, the
state imposes obligations on the basis of unchosen status and social
positions. As Clare Dalton explains,[47] reinterpreting much of the Realist
material from a CLS perspective, liberal legalists have tried to maintain
strict boundaries between the *unusual* contracts implied in law, seen as
a pure creature of collective force, and both contracts implied in fact
and express contracts (enforced by the state but grounded in expressed
or assumed private volition). But she notes that the line between im-
plied-in-fact and implied-in-law contracts invariably blurs. Courts inexorably *assume* that they know what the parties would have desired not
by examining particular relationships but by presuming that they inevitably would have wanted to replicate customary relationships; in effect,
courts thus *demand* that parties replicate typical arrangements even
though they are supposed to do this only in finding implied-in-law con-

tracts. Thus, for instance, a son is or is not deemed to have worked for his father without promise of financial benefit on the basis of *general status suppositions*—status-grounded suppositions about the extent to which family members help one another out of love, though strangers rarely do—without regard to the particularities of their relationship. The importance of this, Dalton's first observation, may be somewhat blunted, though. When contracts are or are not deemed to be implied in fact, the court has done no more than *interpret* conduct; it has not *barred* explicit contracts to correct mistaken perceptions of their subjectivity by a court that inexorably imports objective ideals into a nominally subjective inquiry.

But Dalton's point cannot be so readily confined. Even supposedly express contracts *become* express contracts only when the court has made a wholly public, wholly political decision to treat the parties' expressions of intention as binding or contractual. A decision, for instance, to treat the promises of unmarried cohabiters as contractual words rather than as alegal words of commitment puts public force behind what is otherwise legally vacuous. It is hard to see the decision as resting in any significant sense on any particular party's volition, rather than a collective decision about the proper nature of the relationship. In part, courts contractualize or decontractualize the explicit promises by interpreting what the general *subject matter* of such would-be contracts actually is. If the contract is deemed an exchange of sex for money, no court will enforce the contract. Unless, though, the courts accept a formal way out and heed the parties' purely formal declaration that the contract is a legitimate one, not sex grounded, the decision as to whether it is *all* a case of sex for money seems invariably to rest not on voluntaristic and particularistic but rather general normative assumptions that men *want* and women *use* sex. In part, too, a nonvolitional focus must occur because it is questionable whether in this case there is anything permissible, in subject-matter terms, to contract about—whether one can contract privately or whether the failure to order according to the institutions of marriage preempts the supposition that private ordering was really intended. Even courts that are not *overtly* public in failing to enforce a cohabitation agreement (for example, by saying that the contracts should be voided by an active judiciary seeking to enforce pro-marriage public morality or voided by a passive judiciary that would expect the legislature to regulate the field) are left with the inevitable dilemmas of interpretation: contracts might arguably have comprehensible express *terms*, but people cannot simply declare that they have created a contractual relationship unless the court goes along with that characterization.

The Realist attack on the notion that there is a distinct private realm unordered by political decision has focused largely on the impossibility of specifying a coherent regime of contract, independent of substantive public norms, that both specifies what one is entitled to "threaten" or "withhold" and implicitly grounds contracts in supposedly defunct status relationships. It has also focused, to a lesser extent, on the impossibility of a nonpublic tort regime. In order to imagine that a purely private sphere exists although the state demands that some pay others for harming them, one must believe both that (1) uncontroversial private initial entitlements can be defined at an abstract level, and (2) at the level of application, we can accurately ascertain when one party has diminished the value of a protected entitlement and by how much. I have already discussed the extent to which the first supposition is philosophically problematic if one tries to maintain a commitment to subjective value: an entitlement is a sort of elevation of one kind of desire over another (for freedom from battery over battery, for clean water over cheaper, more plentiful manufactured goods).

But the practical problem is just as significant. Unless one believes that causation judgments are objective and scientific, it is unavoidable that tort law will continue to redistribute income collectively rather than simply maintain some (presumed) desirable *status quo ante*. As Morton Horwitz notes, the notion of objective causation was essential for the late nineteenth-century apologists precisely because they were so committed to a vision of tort law as apolitical, as simply *maintaining* a purely private equilibrium.[48] Assume that air pollution increases the incidence of cancer; assume too that breathers are legally entitled to noncarcinogenic air. A particular breather sues a polluter, but we cannot know with anything approaching certainty whether the plaintiff's cancer was caused by the pollution or even know the shifts in probability of the incidence of cancer among a plaintiff population. If we attribute too few cancers to polluters, victims will be expropriated; if we attribute too many, polluters will in essence bear a nonuniformly applied tax to fund medical insurance programs. The problem is surely most dramatic when one talks about epidemiological causal uncertainty, but it is present in all mundane torts as well: the level of emotional distress that victims feel when they have been injured is simply beyond our ken to evaluate. The problem is only worsened, of course, when one realizes not only that we cannot make technical judgments of but-for causation but that vague and circular liability limiting devices (such as proximate cause and foreseeability) are built in that seem to imply that a certain degree of victim expropriation is systematically acceptable.

I by no means want to imply that problems of causal uncertainty are unique to liberal capitalism. Any openly collective administrative decision on permissible risk taking must face the same issue. What is more particular to liberal thought is the *dream* of an order that fundamentally simply *protects* or replicates some natural precollective set of relations. It is that dream that is shattered when one realizes that more and less expansive definitions of cause reorder relative social power.

"Coercion" in the "Private Sphere"

It is perhaps most illuminating to illustrate the problem of private coercion with a nonlegal example. Assume (quite unheroically) that a group of students dislikes the way I teach my first-year class and demands that I change it. There is, according to CLS thought, a response I might make that closely follows a routine mainstream depiction of the private sphere, but that one can readily see is silly in this context: the students chose to come to Stanford Law School (there was no problem of monopoly since other choices were available and the choice is a private contractual one with no sovereign interference with the privilege to choose), where there was some *ex ante* risk that they would be taught by me; therefore they have chosen or consented to the teaching they (mistakenly?) now claim to want altered.

Economists like Albert Hirschman have done much to capture the point that the CLS writers have emphasized by noting that while consumer exit (shopping around, taking one's business elsewhere) is *a* technique for controlling those with whom one interacts in the private sphere, voice (direct collective control) may often be preferable or necessary.[49] Hirschman emphasizes a market-structural reason for this. If the dissatisfied customers of one supplier simply shift to another supplier, while those equally dissatisfied customers of the second shift to the first, exit won't harm the market share of either supplier; direct control would be needed to overcome the dissatisfaction.[50] The CLS commentators have adopted this view in part, but they also stress the problem of "bundling" to a greater extent—the problem that contractual terms may be grouped together that could feasibly be separated (a Stanford degree without exposure to my teaching is a technically feasible option that students might prefer among all available options, though they might prefer Stanford and the risk of me to the next best possibility). The inability to control the availability of all technically feasible unbundled packages is undoubtedly an enormous source of impotence and determined choicelessness in private life; economists who simply find it peculiar for workers to say, "I took a dangerous job because it was better than no job," cannot simply assume, but must demonstrate, that all technically feasible safety-pay combinations that might have been desired were available.

The bundling analysis is helpful even in dealing with mundane legal issues like the problem of covenants running with the land. A landowner promises his neighbors that he and all his successors will do something or forbear from doing something; are those who succeed him necessarily bound? Courts have historically refused to enforce some such promises against subsequent owners,[51] using vague and circular language (for example, the covenant will run to purchasers only if it "touches and concerns the land"). Writers in the Law and Economics school have claimed that the courts strike down covenants that the subsequent purchaser would not have renegotiated with the promisee had renegotiation been costless, even when the original promisors declared that they intended that the covenants run.[52] I agree that a covenant that would not be renegotiated is, in a significant way, unchosen. Still, the Law and Economics commentators have not adequately explained why, in this particular case, they suddenly assume that the initial landowner, a formally uncoerced private party, would make a promise that would bind subsequent purchasers, knowing that if the fully intentionalist model of private life is true, he would be paid less for his land upon sale, unless he were paid more to make the promise than he would lose on resale (and hence it is worth more to the promisees than it costs the promisors).[53]

There is simply no room for anyone to be coerced in the optimistic private model. The promisee pays only what he wants for a promise, and only as much more to have it bind successors as it is worth it to him to have it do so. The promisor accepts this offer only if it gives him more than selling the land unbound. The promisor's successor pays only as much for the land as it is worth burdened by the promise.

Presumably, the courts have rightly rejected an analysis that assumes away the problem of purely private coercion that such an analysis implies: the courts may justifiably believe that subsequent purchasers may not adequately reevaluate the large bundle (say, a home in a particular location) based on a small feature (a mildly annoying covenant). It may well be the role of the state to free the purchaser from the private restriction if there is no reason to believe that the agreement is adequately intentional from the purchaser's viewpoint (that is, adequately compensated for by the purported discount on the house) or to free the initial promisor from his foolish promise if, to take the weaker case, continued enforcement of the contract is not as optimal an arrangement for all parties concerned as getting out of the covenant would be, given the degree to which the benefited party would pay for the covenant itself today and what the burdened party would ask to be paid to perform it, if all parties were focused solely on the single promise.

The historical decline of "assumption of risk" doctrine in tort law reveals a precisely parallel focus on bundling.[54] It is simply not clear whether the plaintiff would have explicitly contracted to bear a particular risk for the wage premium he supposedly received when he signed a work contract in which a risk actually inheres (and a premium might or might not).

At times, the newer CLS attacks on the public-private distinction seem purely historical, but the historical attacks are probably largely rhetorical. Gerald Frug, for instance, sharply attacks Robert Ellickson's belief that cities ought to be treated as involuntary, fundamentally coerced associations and homeowners' associations as voluntary because of their historical origins, pointing out that while some cities originated in unanimous consensual arrangements, many homeowner association "agreements" were written entirely by developers before residents had ever interacted.[55] But I take it that Frug's historical point is largely a debater's one: Plymouth is surely no more or less coercive than Palo Alto because it was initially formed by a unanimous process. The *theoretical* point is that one can readily see people's relationship to local government authority as at least as voluntary as one's relationship to private corporate authority; it is not at all obvious that a resident of a municipality that bars political speech is not both more able to move to another municipality (exit) or to alter the public decision (voice) than that an employee of a corporation that bars on-premises speech can better pick a more hospitable employer (given, at a minimum, plant-specific skills that pose inevitable transition costs) or have impact on the policy. Whether the municipal or corporate limitation will squelch the content of speech more thoroughly is likewise an open question. In neither case are all outlets closed off; in both cases certain sorts of audiences and opportunities are restricted.

Intentionalism, Determinism, and Antipositivism

The Incomplete Commitment to Positivism

Thomas Heller's primary point about the split between liberal methodology and liberal norms follows from Unger's observation that liberal culture is committed *both* to the subjectivity of values (their indeterminacy and arbitrariness) *and* the objectivity of facts (their determined universality).[56] A properly functioning social system grounded in these basic liberal postulates must be a preference aggregator: markets and self-interested voting mechanisms are the standard liberal institutions because only preference satisfaction has any moral claim once one believes that there is no objective good.

The key point is that the preferences to be aggregated must be known through *positivist* method. The aggregation techniques must be purely technical, purely scientific, for two distinct reasons. First, if aggregating administrators rely on anything but objective knowledge in toting up preferences, they may covertly dominate others, impose their own values in the guise of reflecting others' desires. Second, since liberals are committed at the methodological level to the universality and accessibility of facts, the preferences of individuals, as facts, must be knowable.

In theory, then, intentional discourse governs the normative world; determinist discourse (positivism) governs the descriptive world. The problem, Heller notes, is that the positivist method poorly comprehends the material that must be known: subjective desire or intentions. Even in the simple case of market choice, a theory of revealed preference is a poor surrogate for a theory of desire; what people *choose* need not be what they *want,* given the possibility of mistake and ambivalence.[57] Worse, state officials must frequently act in situations where there is reason to believe that people will systematically *lie* about their subjective intentions and desires. The desire for public goods is thought to be systematically understated; criminals cannot be trusted to tell us what they wanted to do when they performed harmful acts; taxpayers will claim nonpersonal business motives for all expenditures if only business expenditures are deductible. At a technical legal level we despair that our positivist techniques will work, so we state operative legal tests in circular terms that clearly preclude rulelike fact-finding (for example, tax if the motive is personal, punish a criminal act if it is intended); we rely on political action, like congressional logrolling, to serve as a poor surrogate for the revelation of preference for collective goods. At the theoretical level the failure to know intentions, the failure to believe

that our sense of others' intentions is determined by what those intentions really are, poses the standard nightmare of ungoverned, unconstrained governors.

CLS Antipositivism

Heller also reversed the traditional way that people on the left deal with
liberalism's fact-value distinction, emphasizing the relativity of facts rather
than the potential quasiobjectivity of moral discourse (as Unger did).[58]

His basic antipositivist position can be understood in two distinct ways.
First and foremost, if there is both an available determinist account and
an intentionalist account of every human action, there is no *truth* about
conduct, just paired rhetorical stories. There is no factually correct
account of why someone killed or what a donor really wanted, just two
perfectly acceptable ways of looking at the issues. Second, positivism
seems (at least metaphorically) to be a form of incomplete determinism:
"facts" can be seen as "determined" by some external reality. But if
"facts" are just answers to a select grid of questions that we (choose
intentionally to) ask, just whatever we need to understand to achieve
particular purposes, then the positivist vision is, at the least, incomplete.

While this attack on positivism has been common in CLS, I have
never really discerned its relationship to the movement generally. It is
clearly associated with the antitechnocratic strand prevalent in Frankfurt
school thinking, though its failure to stress the overcoming of liberal
reticence on moral discourse separates it from, say, Max Horkheimer's
antitechnocratic antipositivist work.[59] I take it that some believe that
there is a relatively strong cultural association between a belief in positivist social science and various kinds of destructive technocracies (an
antienvironmental desire to dominate nature, an acceptance of our destructive nuclear capabilities) or right-wing technological determinism,
but I can't fully fathom the claim. The verbal metaphor or analogy is
certainly weak: while one can readily say that the desire to understand
action is a desire to master or dominate the world (which sounds a bit
like saying you don't care about the fate of the little snail darter), it is
as easy to say that the desire to understand is a desire to see one's place
in the scheme of things, that determinists and positivists think of themselves less as powerful subjects than as imputed objects. Likewise, while
there are right-wing functionalist determinists, who justify the status
quo by saying that we must study and understand how all existing institutions fit together, positivist Marxists obviously believed that an ob-

jective understanding of social forces would enable us to see how rapidly the existing order was crumbling, not to apologize for it. Leftists certainly continue to share many Enlightenment ideals: a belief in false consciousness is surely a belief that there are truths that can be seen if one is opened up to them. Nonetheless, it is useful to note that the recognition of this discourse split has been used in this antipositivist program regardless of what might *determine* such a program's existence.

The Deconstruction of the Self

In the discussions of rules and standards and the subjectivity of values, I focused on ways in which the existence of the conflicts might be seen to have a strong relationship with characteristic dilemmas the self faces in social life.

Rule-bound individualism was seen to express the fear the self has of engulfment, of conformist pressure, of role-oriented inauthenticity; more generally, it can be seen as manifesting a subjective desire for distance. Kennedy and Simon surely posit a self—one with conflicting desires for both fusion and separateness.

Unger's self is less secure in its identity; the utopian self is surely one that experiences itself as being at one with the community it helped to constitute and that would in turn constantly reconstitute it in a morally acceptable fashion. But he surely saw *a* self at sea in the liberal world of value subjectivity, a self seeking recognition by acting in role, knowing that the recognition it received would be not of some true self but of the masked role player.

Heller's focus on the split between intentionalism and determinism paves the way for a fuller deconstruction of the self.[60] The self is simply a creature of intentionalist discourse; a world of selves is just one way of imagining the world. One can just as readily see oneself as a "crossroads," a locus where things occur, a place in which action is just one result of past actions, known and unknown. The image of a self-other split, in this view, simply *assumes* a consistent hold on the experience of selfhood, which is just a restatement of the ungrounded privileging of intentionalist discourse.

Once more, the point of this exercise escapes me. It seems useful to integrate the realization that the self is not *just* subject but object, especially in recognizing the limitations of normative systems (like economics) that both posit the existence of meaningful selves and posit these partly imagined ghosts' satisfaction as the only social end. But

someone who has fully integrated the one-sidedly *self-less* vision seems
to me to have integrated nothing. He would not ever be *led* to passivity,
as some fear, since the question of whether he would in fact be passive
would be experienced as an externally controlled phenomenon: there
would be no way to *become* more passive, no way to become. To note
that our bad experiences of acting in role *depend* on the experience of
a self, either in sensing some split between action and authentic subjectivity or in believing in one's subjective negative feelings of distance
and isolation from other selves, seems a worthless truism. Obviously
nothing one does matters to the extent that one doesn't feel one exists,
chooses, feels contingently. Still, once again, the full-blown deconstruction of the self is a reasonably significant aspect of CLS and Critical,
antiindividualist theory more generally, and it is important to see that
it can be grounded in the recognition of the availability of determinist
discourse. Beyond noting that, I haven't got a clue as to why some Critics
give such importance to this issue.

CHAPTER FOUR

Legal Economists and Normative Social Theory

Critical Legal Studies is not infrequently paired in observers' minds with Law and Economics, in part because both became prominent as academic movements at the elite law schools in the middle and late 1970s, in part because each represented an attack on the dominant law school stance: centrist, ostensibly pragmatic and antitheoretical, process centered, case-law oriented. Moreover, Law and Economics was frequently thought to represent not just a new *method* of thinking about legal issues but a *substantive* attack from the right on the consensus views of the propriety of mildly liberal political policy, while CLS was often seen as the attack from the left on these same policies. Finally, since a fair number of CLS writers attacked Law and Economics writing, either in detail[1] or in passing,[2] CLS was often viewed by outsiders unfamiliar with the range of CLS work as predominantly an anti–Law and Economics group, some kind of negatively charged satellite. In my view, the relationship between CLS and Law and Economics is in fact quite intimate: I believe that to the extent that one can discern general themes within the Law and Economics movement, it is the best worked-out, most consummated liberal legal ideology of the sort that CLS has tried both to understand and to critique.

The next two chapters are attempts to elucidate two distinct broad themes. In this chapter I try to locate Law and Economics within liberal thought, claiming that it can be understood in part in terms of its stance vis à vis the central contradictions I discussed in Chapters 1 through 3 and in part as a general theory of the state that one would predict would emerge if one recalled those forms of discourse that are privileged in liberal thought. I shall then recapitulate the CLS critiques of Law and Economics, concentrating on problems in normative welfare economics, to complete the chapter on the relationship between Law and Economics and liberal thought. In Chapter 5 I shall focus on certain technical problems in translating these (defective) norms into practice, problems that CLS theorists believe have been understated in the Law and Economics literature, in large part either to support its pretense to systematicity or "wholeness" and in part to bolster its typical liberal commitment to rule-bound individualism.

Law and Economics as Social Theory

To the extent that one can generalize about a movement that is reasonably diverse, Law and Economics has been both an academic school that has advocated, normatively, a certain general vision of state function as well as particular implementing practices *and* a movement that purports to present a general descriptive theory of existing legal practice.

The descriptive agenda, significant largely to the Chicago school of legal economists, has had two main messages. First, the claim is that judge-made common law has tended to be efficient or wealth maximizing, promoting legal results that "increase the size of the pie";[3] second, legislatures and administrative agencies are dominated by the more or (frequently) less legitimate distributive demands of groups that tend to capture these bodies.[4] The first point has obviously been the special province of *Law* and Economics scholars; the themes of illegitimate regulation and legislation have been adopted largely wholesale from conservative economists with little general interest in law.[5]

The specific descriptive claim of legal economists that judges have unself-consciously adopted efficient rules preoccupied Chicago school Law and Economics scholars for a period; in fact, a significant sub-industry developed that tried to explain the *mechanisms* by which this counterintuitive result could occur.[6] But, unlike the normative claims, this claim has had little impact on law teaching or legal scholarship in general, probably because it is almost wholly unpersuasive. In part, the failure of impact is a bit of a historical accident. The general claim that the common law promotes efficiency was often conflated with a well-known but dubious example, Richard Posner's assertion that the common law courts adopted an economically efficient negligence standard in torts in the nineteenth century.[7] But as both Gary Schwartz[8] and Robert Rabin[9] have demonstrated, there is little evidence that the courts in fact ever adopted the negligence test across the board, even if Posner is right in holding that negligence is the efficient standard of care. Schwartz emphasized variations between jurisdictions. Rabin emphasized that even where negligence was supposedly adopted, there were both significant pockets of immunity from *any* tort liability and enormous problems in framing a viable negligence test in terms that in any serious way mimic an *efficient* negligence test, particularly given the difficulty of imagining all *marginal* precautions the defendant might have taken to reduce harm rather than judging the activity more generally as reasonable or not.

At a more general level, the positive theory is inevitably untestable unless we are sure which decisions are actually efficient, and there is little reason to believe that we can ever identify such decisions. This point will be demonstrated further in the next chapter, where I review the CLS argument that it is unlikely that *any* general legal rule will induce selfish actors to behave efficiently. But the implausibility of Posner's positive claims clearly struck even those people unfamiliar with the CLS critiques. It is surely *plausible* to say, as Posner does, that the English rule protecting access to light but not view is efficient since it saves the transaction costs of negotiating only those agreements that would generally be negotiated;[10] but the statement that the American rule (ensuring no access to either light or view) represents the hypothetical end point of hypothetical negotiations is surely just as plausible.[11] There is an ad hoc, grab bag character to the bulk of the arguments for the efficiency of actual rules that is hard to miss. Posner actually argues that the English rule protecting light may well have been economically rational in England, while the American rule was rational here, given the fact that we had more room (and were thus less likely to block light than the crowded English).[12] His argument seems wholly unpersuasive: a rule that provided that neighbors not block one another's light would be no less sensible in the United States because land is more plentiful; we would simply expect it to be applied to fewer cases, since neighbors would presumably block light less frequently, given the less crowded conditions. Indeed, the fact that land is plentiful should make a rule against blocking light *more* efficient, given that the cost of *not* blocking light would presumably be *lower* for the blocker where land is more plentiful.

The normative claims have been far more influential, in part, I would claim, because they so assertively deny the omnipresence of those central, painful contradictions that CLS writers have tried to show are inevitably characteristic of liberal discourse.

It is, in my view, in its normative *social theoretical* mode—the mode in which it most clearly adopts certain stances toward the basic problematics of the formation of the self, the relationship of self to discrete others and social life more generally—that Law and Economics has been a unified and significant movement. One needn't be a Law and Economics adherent at this social theoretical level to *do* microeconomic analyses of particular legal programs, with more or less market-oriented biases or presumptions, with more or less concern over the distributional impacts of a decision. But I do not think that Law and Economics would, or should, have been discerned as a particularly significant *movement* had it been no more than a collection of policy analyses of the probable impact of particular decisions. Much of the work would have been, when empirical, indistinguishable from traditional Law and Society impact studies,[13] and when theoretical, simply a better-informed, more sophisticated version of the hypothetical analyses of rules that policy-oriented Legal Realist law teachers had long been doing.[14] It has not, however, simply been a discrete series of microstudies.

Posner has been the more influential figure in establishing Law and Economics as a school of thought than Guido Calabresi, not because Posner's rather quirky *Economic Analysis of Law*[15] is more informative or better reasoned than Calabresi's breathtaking book *The Costs of Accidents,*[16] but because it is infinitely more imperialistic, complete, catechismic. It may offer mind-numbingly off-target answers to many, many questions, but it does have an answer for *every* legal issue, and, perhaps more important, the answers can be derived from a very short list of normative and descriptive propositions about individuals, markets, and the political process. Posner's massive outpouring of work has occasionally been economically unsophisticated (as where he confuses many-seller markets with fully competitive markets without any regard for variations in buyer behavior);[17] occasionally unfathomable (as in his efforts to define a meaningful concept of wealth maximization,[18] or worse, to claim that this wealth-maximization criterion avoids many of the horrors of classic utilitarianism, though it is quite clearly subject to all the standard deontological rights theorists' critiques of a system that can sacrifice the individual to the whim of others);[19] occasionally downright comic in its effort to explain all court-centered legal practice as derivative of the search for efficiency (as in his claim that premeditated murder is punished more severely than unpremeditated murder because we must equalize the expected punishment of all killings, and premeditated killers are more likely to get away with their crimes).[20] This really doesn't matter, though; Posner gets the underlying *world view* completely right, probably even *more* right by being so obstinate in his drive for completeness, in his powerful urge to flatten human experience and deny complexity in the service of a desperate Panglossian optimism about the "straight" world of middle-class barter and an utter cynicism about the worlds of the outsiders and those who at least claim to care for them. It is, I think, *because* Posner would *never* have written a book called *Tragic Choices*[21] (as Calabresi did, along with Philip Bobbitt) that he is the culturally, social theoretically central figure in the Law and Economics movement.

But it is not solely my claim that the Chicago school is the truly significant one because it brought its simple message to an academic and social world in search of simplicity while both the old economically influenced Realists (like Calabresi, Bruce Ackerman, and Richard Markovits) or the prominent neoinstitutionalists (like Oliver Williamson, Charles Goetz, and Robert Scott), who focused on transaction-cost reduction in organizational and legal form, gave too few simplistic answers. It is my claim that even the more sophisticated thinkers (like Calabresi) in fact *must* adopt, more or less consciously, the social theory of the Chicago school adherents, even if they genuinely bristle at any summary statement of the theory, because it really *is* the social theory of economics, of a coherent liberal individualism that sees society as fundamentally successful when it *responds* to the will of individuals, and mediates the conflicts between individuals simply by making everyone pay his way.

As social theory, Law and Economics starts with the supposition that values and desires are the arbitrary assertions of individuals. In fact, legal economics much more wholeheartedly embraces value skepticism than either of the main antecedent liberal movements, libertarianism and utilitarianism. Unlike the libertarians, legal economists try to assign initial entitlements without any regard to the preferred status of particular activities. Battery, for instance, is tortious *not,* as for the libertarians, because the taste to be free from battery is morally preferable to the taste to batter, but because we seek either to eliminate needless transactions (it is an *empirical* proposition that those who wish to be free from battery would end up having to pay off those who would batter them) or to assign entitlements as they would have been assigned in an auction among people with arbitrary desires to gain the entitlement.[22] There is also no sense that anyone is bound by any nonwhimsical moral or political imperatives. The utilitarian, of course, believes that we are bound to seek to maximize utility. Though wealth maximization is the preferred collective goal for the legal economists, it is preferred not because it is a morally right end but because, as a factual matter, following a collective wealth-maximizing strategy ought to redound to each person's whimsically selfish benefit in the rather short run.[23]

Legal economics claims further that one can construct a state that is consistent with the premise that values are arbitrary yet does not suffer from what Unger calls the problem of "order" (and which Kennedy might call the problem of "selfishness" or "excessive individualism"). First, rules are established without regard to morality: end states either are the product of actual negotiation or are established in accord with hypothetical negotiations. Similarly, people's initial lots are altered, in this social theory, only when there is actual consent (explicit contract), implied consent, or hypothetical consent, at least at some level of generality.[24] Thus, victorious plaintiffs in tort suits arc deemed to consent to compensated losses (that is, compensation is supposed to be set at a level that would have induced prior consent to injury had bargaining been plausible). Even those would-be plaintiffs who must bear the losses others inflict (arguably) nonnegligently are deemed to consent to these particular losses by having consented to a *system* in which that is the casc, on the supposition that a series of similar decisions in like cases will ultimately redound to their personal benefit. Thus, the smoothly functioning system permits no harm, allows no room for worry that the selfish will "grab" benefits.

The sense of contradiction that dominates CLS writing is utterly absent in legal economic literature. At the technical level of the choice of *form* of legal pronouncement, the rules-standards "dilemma" is reduced to an argument over the relative costs of substantively misgoverned conduct and administratively costly case-by-case fact-finding.[25] At the philosophical level, the conflict between individualism and altruism simply disappears, because the very notion of altruism is unfathomable. It is simply reduced to (even perhaps defined as) an individual's arbitrary taste to incorporate the interests of others in making his own selfish calculations, and like other tastes it is neither to be condemned nor encouraged.[26] To the extent that (apparent) altruism is ever to be applauded, it is simply in situations in which one party (for example a helpless child) is transactionally disabled from negotiating with others to purchase help; thus, a parent's emotional concern for a child is needed solely because we cannot readily substitute enforceable contracts in which a child agrees to trade some of the future wages she will earn if cared for in exchange for better care in early life.[27] Finally, as I have indicated, the fear of disorder or excessive individualism simply disappears: proper background rules can restrain harm, ensure that everyone's interests are properly accounted for in the incentive structures each of us faces.[28]

The legal economists maintain a strong commitment both to the general adequacy of intentionalist discourse *and* to drawing the traditional line between the private domain of intentionality and the public domain of coercion. Actors are treated as sufficiently self-determined to respond to price signals, to alter and control their behavior. Law is generally treated entirely as an objective price constraint that tells actors what it will cost them to obtain a certain good (for example, a battery "costs" X dollars in fine or Y days of imprisonment, an in-kind fine substitute).[29] Thus, punishment is a guide or restraint on presumptively *self-determined* action, not a person-creating, determinist force affecting, say, whether people will *want* to batter or not.[30]

Moreover, implicit contracts are assumed to dominate private life, expanding the assumed domain of self-determination: people hypothetically consent to nearly all conditions in private life because the exit option (working elsewhere, buying a different product, leaving a battering husband) is invariably *formally* available, legally *privileged*, not precluded by sovereign command.[31]

Law and Economics, as a social theoretical movement, has a fundamentally complete or gapless vision of what law should aspire to as well as a remarkably inclusive short list of rules of thumb for realizing the ideal in practice.

Law *should* promote all alterations in social arrangements that are Pareto efficient (that is, those in which at least one party's position is improved while no one's is worsened) and those that are *potentially* (or Kaldor-Hicks) efficient (that is, those in which the party whose lot is improved doesn't actually compensate the harmed party but *could* do so to the point where the initially harmed party would be indifferent between the new and the old regime, while remaining better off himself).

The commitment to Pareto efficiency is thought, generally, to be utterly uncontroversial politically. In a sense this claim is right but banal: *if* there were consensus on what it meant for a party's lot to be improved or unchanged, it is hard to imagine why anyone would *oppose* steps that helped some and hurt none. What *is* politically charged is simply unstated in applying the usual Pareto test: the notion that people are obviously better off in state X than state Y if they "voluntarily" trade

Y for X. If (but only if) we do not have to inquire into either the formation of our desires or the background conditions under which trades are made (that is, if we assume that "voluntariness" is a simple, self-defining concept), then we have the reasonably technical, politically uncharged welfare criterion that technocratic legal economists seek, albeit one that would rarely be applicable to concrete controversies, since most choices in legal decisions clearly harm *someone.*

A commitment to the Kaldor-Hicks or potential Pareto efficiency test is not nearly as uncontroversial, but the controversy can be framed, at least in theory, as technical and empirical rather than openly politicized. The empirical claim is simply that the uniform use of the Kaldor-Hicks test to resolve *all* legal issues will yield *actual* Pareto efficiency *over time,* even though in any particular case some people will certainly be hurt by particular decisions.[32] If, though, there is no reason to believe that the losers in any case are atypically likely to be losers in other cases (a claim that grows increasingly plausible if one believes that losers are a random, unidentifiable hodgepodge rather than a definable class),[33] then it may seem that *everyone* will ultimately benefit over time from a procedure that self-consciously seeks to give benefits *on average.* If one is strictly Paretian, of course—committed to the philosophically individualist stance that makes it impermissible to balance the gains to one party against gains to another because each person is profoundly *separate*—this empirical claim is obviously either wrong or unfathomable. It is surely wrong if the point is that for a society that views itself as making a relatively small number of legal decisions in a given period, no individual will be harmed by one more than he is helped by all the others (for example, it is almost surely the case that a rise in marginal tax rates or an uncompensated condemnation of property takes more away from someone than all other explicit legal decisions "give"). If the point is that, on balance, nobody is worse off in a regime pursuing efficiency (even when one efficient solution seems to sting badly on a particular occasion) than he would be in a regime (1) without law, (2) that relentlessly pursued deliberately inefficient results, or (3) that pursued results without regard to efficiency, the point is either trivial (since no one who attacks the efficiency standard does so in the name of either lawlessness or constant deliberate inefficiency) or seemingly impossible not only to *prove* but even to have a particularly strong empirical hunch about.

If this *technical* claim for potential Pareto efficiency is wrong, if a particular legal economist doesn't believe that actual Pareto efficiency will result from following the potential efficiency mandate on each discrete occasion, then he simply *qualifies* his support of the standard. He may favor only those Kaldor-Hicks improvements where the winners are distributively more *worthy* than the losers, either because, at some general, aggregate income distribution level they are needier *or* because, in terms of moral desert in the particular case, they are more entitled to benefit.[34] (Some people whose predominant concern is economics, such as Richard Markovits, would demand that "moral worthiness" and a respect for rights be a part of any decision-making rule, even if they believed that the across-the-board use of the Kaldor-Hicks test would ultimately help all, since they quite clearly view economistic social theory as incomplete; but once more, I am trying to deal with what strikes me as the meaningful core of a world picture, not the practices of each person more or less inclined to adopt the whole world view.)[35]

Law will, in this version, generally promote the ends it *should* promote, provided legal decision makers follow some rules of thumb. First, "free" contract must be permitted since parties won't reach agreements unless at least one party is helped and the other unharmed by their compact. No substantive contractual terms should be explicitly imposed or refused. While some terms might be inferred in the face of the parties' silence, thus implicitly raising the transaction costs of striking atypical bargains, no terms ought to be nonwaivable.[36] The privileging of "free" contract is most specifically manifest in opposition to judicially enforced compulsory terms (such as nonwaivable habitability or merchantability warranties),[37] statutorily enforced compulsory terms (such as OSHA regulations of workplace safety features),[38] judicial strictures against substantively unfair contracts (unconscionability),[39] and legislative prohibitions against certain forms of contracts (such as prostitution contracts, usurious interest rates, price controls).[40] Certainly, both more and less politically liberal Law and Economics practitioners will vary in their beliefs about the degree of information parties must have (or can be presumed to have) before their decision is sufficiently well grounded to be thought of as self-promoting.[41] Likewise, they will differ about duress, the degree to which the enforcement of bargains made in the face of unusual pressures on one of the contracting parties, whether the pressures derive from the other bargainer or external forces, can be presumed to be as beneficial as a regime that voided such contracts.[42] But the presumptive permission of contract remains the basic starting point, the *exceptional* nature of inalienable property rights the rhetorical correlate.[43]

Second, when transaction costs seem to preclude bargaining, legal economists tell us either to choose rules that lower bargaining costs, *facilitating* parties in transferring "entitlements" to a given end state to that party who values the end state most highly,[44] or to mimic a hypothetical bargaining transaction, designating that end state as a position to which the beneficiary is entitled which would ultimately have resulted had bargaining been feasible.[45]

It is not entirely clear, within the legal economic tradition, what one is to do if these decision rules clash, as one might assume they frequently would. For instance, assume we are trying to decide whether the public has access to beach-front land or whether private parties ought to own it initially and simply sell access to the beach if they so choose. It is certainly the case that assigning the land to private parties facilitates transfer, helps *develop* a market. Should the general public initially have rights to exclude and a private party desires to purchase a right to exclusive use, it is inconceivable that the private party could effectively negotiate with all entitled public users a promise on their part to stay away. (Even if dispersed public "owners" could be costlessly assembled, these parties would have no reason to state their true asking price to give up beach access since each might try to hold out and capture the would-be private users' surplus.) Users from the general public, however, *could* buy out an initially vested private owner. But it is conceivable that the transaction costs of buying off a private owner are significantly higher than zero; at a minimum, the private owner must hire guards and ticket sellers in order to transact with would-be users. We might well believe that while the public values the beach *more* than the private user, they don't value it by *enough* more to cover these transaction costs. Thus, in a transaction-costless market, the beach would wind up in public hands, and arguably it should be so assigned; assigning it to the public effectively, however, prevents bargaining.

More generally, and far more significantly, it is almost surely the case that the use of clear rules will generally *simplify* and thus facilitate bargaining between parties, but that, given the residual transaction costs that keep bargaining costly, one might want to apply an unclear standard that *mimics* a hypothetical market but by no means helps to develop a real one. For instance, imagine choosing between a clear rule that any party can block his neighbor's light and a situation-sensitive standard that one can block light only if it is economically reasonable (that is, if the damage to the neighbor is less costly than the cost of averting it). It will probably be simpler to bargain in the shadow of a clear rule; it is perfectly certain who has to pay whom, and there is no risk or uncertainty introduced to complicate bargaining in which parties might diverge in their probability estimates of the outcome of a dispute should they not presettle. But it could well be that there are significant residual transaction costs, such as strategic behavior, in which a party fails to accept a deal that would in fact better her position in order to try to capture more of the gains from trade, thus bearing the risk of getting *no* gains from trade on a particular occasion with an eye toward capturing more on future occasions. Given these residual transaction costs, it could well be the case that the *rule* (light can be blocked) will result in an outcome (light blocked) that would not be the outcome of a transaction-costless bargain even though the *rule,* relatively speaking, makes bargaining *less costly* than would a standard (light can't be blocked if it is unreasonable to do so).

Nonetheless, despite the fact that the supposed rule of thumb for situations in which transaction costs preclude contract (either facilitate or mimic the market) is surely not mechanically applicable, as generally understood, there is good reason to believe that this second rule is not *experienced* as causing a gap or a sense of disorder. My sense is that the mimic-the-market approach is *normatively* or ideally prior for most legal economists.[46] Given the distrust most legal economists have of claims of administrative or state expertise, though, many will undoubtedly feel that it is generally the safer practice to try to *facilitate* the development of a market.

Again, some of the clashes that would have arisen over this issue had it become more visible would be overtly political. Those economists with more committed libertarian philosophical sentiments would be prone to be far more bothered by establishing a legal rule that cannot be effectively "corrected" by autonomous private action than they would be by substantive inefficiency. We can guess this because we know, explicitly, that libertarians are far more worried that certain legal rules (for example a negligence standard in torts, no mandatory Good Samaritanism) would be expropriative than they are that the opposite rule (strict liability, enforced duty to strangers) would lead to Kaldor-Hicks inefficient outcomes.[47]

Obviously the translation from either the short list of standard operating procedures or the more grandiose welfare criteria to actual legal practice is not likely to be especially simple. For the Law and Economics movement to fulfill its grandest promise both to provide a *normatively neutral arbiter* of disputes and a technical *answer* to every case, it is important not only that the list seem theoretically complete but that it be generally applicable. It is certainly *theoretically* possible to separate claims of normative completeness from claims of technical applicability. One could readily believe quite rationally that the Kaldor-Hicks standard would be an unexceptionable guide to each legal decision yet believe that it is simply impossible to ascertain what the standard demands. And certainly no one makes the extremely strong claim that efficiency dictates particular outcomes in each and every case. (In fact, everyone who does this work says, quite reasonably self-protectively, that some cases look utterly indeterminate and that in others only rough approximations of efficient solutions can be attained in particular cases.)[48]

But it would be folly to ignore the factual historical connection between the claims of theoretical completeness and practical applicability. It seems to me there are at least two reasons for the connection. First, Law and Economics (like Critical Legal Studies) can be described not just as the *legal* instance of a more general aspect of political culture (CLS was to Critical Theory as Law and Economics was to the non-moralist-nontraditionalist aspects of the New Right consensus emerging in the United States in the late 1970s and early 1980s), but as an attempt to respond to an ongoing internal legal academic crisis, the difficulty of justifying the separation of law and politics that has beset post-Realist legal academics who have been taught that legal rules are nothing but policy-oriented decisions. In this regard, the domain of law was recaptured or resuscitated as the domain of one sort of consequentialist reasoning, reasoning to achieve efficiency; the domain of politics and legislation was basically separated (and basically denigrated) as the domain of distribution, of tampering with efficiency to grab a few of the crumbs that would have been a lovely pie if people had not grabbed so quickly. Now, at first blush, law could still be separated from politics solely in terms of the *intentions* of those practicing law, without regard to the technical possibility of translating the legal economists' program; but it is clear that, if nothing else, lawyers didn't intend to pursue efficiency (but instead to pursue "justice" or follow precedent or whatever).[49] That meant that if law were indeed different, it was because hidden forces made it *turn out* differently; only we external observers know this hidden side of law because we know an efficient result when we see it and can observe that these results have in fact taken hold. If we *can't* know efficient results, and therefore can't know that they have been adopted by lawyers, we once again can't assume that the legal process is truly distinct.

Second, Law and Economics really *is* conservative ideology, and it really is central to any status quo–preserving ideology that the distribution of benefits be seen as impersonally justified. Those who can call on state force (to enforce a contract the other party now regrets, to refuse to share, to fire a worker they just don't like) should be able to see that the rules that give them these entitlements were adopted with general and uncontroversial aims in mind and are applied to more specific situations in a fashion that does not subvert the neutrality of the process. The rule that lets me move my plant and shatter your community cannot be seen as any more helpful to me or people like me than to you and the people in your position; the decision-making criteria must be impersonal, general, unbiased, uncharged, and they must be sufficiently applicable to concrete controversies that we can assume that they were applied in such a general manner when we adopted the particular rule that leaves you without redress in the face of a staggeringly dislocating calamity.

Thus, CLS commentators on Law and Economics have been compelled to focus *both* on the ways in which the supposedly weak normative claims needed to sustain the commitment to the legal economists' program are deeply problematic *and* the attempts to derive practice from the critiqued theory. Many of the critiques of the normative premises simply revive in slightly different jargon the unprivileged poles of general liberal discourse (determinism, paternalism, altruism); the critiques of the applicability of the norms to cases are meant to denigrate both the claim that any actual legal regime could ever be as neutral as its (actually politically charged) underlying normative premises and the claim that the clash of individualism and altruism can be wholly mediated through law.

Welfare Economics: The Normative Critique

Choice and Desire, Ambiguity and Paternalism

The basic Pareto efficiency criterion can operate only where we are sure that we can discern meaningful content to individual will, can discern when a party's position has improved. Even if we assume that each person is the ideal arbiter of his own good—that is, even if we set aside the paternalist critique I'll return to later—we need to know how to discern what a person truly *wants*. Liberal social theory sees society as want satisfying; it is surely an empty theory if the concept of wants is contentless. And, as Heller points out, liberal *political* theory depends on the capacity of technocratic governors to aggregate preferences until wants are satisfied to the maximum degree possible, given technical constraints on production. But if we can't *know* what preferences are in a technocratic way, can't directly observe them or count them since we observe only behavior, which may or may not reflect desire, then governors may be unable to realize their purely technical program.[50]

The Complexity of Desire

Economists try to duck this difficulty either by falsely conflating choice and utility, by asserting that chosen positions are actually desired, or simply by so thoroughly backing off the claim that the "desires" of others can be understood at all that we have no alternative but to focus solely on choice. In my 1979 article "Choice and Utility" I attacked both these strategies in ways that are fairly typical of Critical Legal theory.[51]

First, I dealt with the neoclassical strategy of denying the possibility that one can talk meaningfully about desires at all, much less the connection between particular chosen positions and desire. It is surely the case that at the *definitional* level, neoclassicists have stripped the concept of utility of all psychological meaning: good X is of more utility than good Y only in the sense that Y is given in exchange for X. Choices are thought to be the only observable, scientific data.

It certainly would have been possible to argue that this position renders the neoclassical argument vacuous. After all, it would not be unreasonable to ask why anyone should care if institutions permit people to get what they choose unless there are virtues either in getting what is chosen, because it is somehow better for the person who chooses, or in the process of both choosing and being stuck with even the adverse consequences of choice because it somehow educates people about managing their lives. Robin West's comparison of Kafka's and Posner's world views in fact sharply questions both these possible substantive defenses.[52] To summarize far too briefly, West notes that many chosen positions are chosen not because they help fulfill a person but because we are sometimes masochistic and sometimes prone to give ourselves over to the demands of authority, to surrender self-control (because freedom seems too burdensome). Such choices may on some occasions both stunt our self-governing development and substantively wreck our lives; we must analyze particular choices before concluding that all consensually chosen arrangements help the chooser.

By contrast, I tried to argue that the neoclassical position is disingenuous and thus, in a sense, false: that we indeed treat it as possible to say more about a choice than that it was made, to relate choice to underlying desire in a way that makes it wrong, a priori, to dismiss the possibility that it is coherent to speak of bad choices, ones that *poorly* fulfill desire.

The basic attack on the position that we observe only choices, not choosers as people putting objects to uses we can understand, is that we are all routinely able to categorize choices, something we'd surely *not* be able to do if choices were the only scientifically observable events. When the chooser picks one Snickers bar off the candy shelf, we believe with fair certainty that if he were to drop and lose that one before he got to the cash register, he'd more likely pick *another* Snickers bar than some random candy bar, or that he'd just as soon have picked up any Snickers bar as the one he actually chose in the first place. The first chosen bar is seen as an instance of a *category*, Snickers bars, though as a simple instance of *choice* (without regard to subsequent use, without regard to our sense that the choice is connected to a substantive desire), there is absolutely nothing conclusive in the actor's motions of choosing to tell us what he would do on any other occasion.

One might be analytically sloppy and assume that the second Snickers bar is simply *indistinguishable* from the first and that we're just presuming that the first choice process would be repeated (though, on reflection, one should realize that the goods are indistinguishable only in terms of their relationship to desire, revealed as indistinguishable only in use). Still, we clearly know a great deal about demand for obviously nonidentical products because we believe that we know why people want things, what substantive desires the goods generally meet. Even if we've seen only whole apples sold, we know that more people would buy coreless apples than apple cores. We even know something about which people are more likely to order Stolichnaya vodka from knowing which people are more likely to buy certain styles of clothes or imported cars or beers, because we have a sense that one form of gratification from the choice of a brand of vodka is in making social-class-locating statements about oneself.

Some neoclassicists attempt to rescue their claim that we can't "know" about anything but choice by asserting that we discern choice categories or patterns not by deducing them from implicit theories of the choosers' desires but by *inducing* the categories from behavior. The inductionists' claim is that we know that people go back and buy a second Snickers bar simply because we've *seen* people do just that. The claim is almost surely disingenuous as a description of our practice (we might well believe that Snickers bars are a choice category without ever having seen anyone go back and purchase a substitute one). More profoundly, the position suffers from the typical problems of inductionist arguments: induction would simply not be possible without an implicit theory that enabled us to pick categories to observe and count. A person might *claim* to know that people in the tropics buy air conditioners rather than heaters without regard to knowing the *use* that is made of air conditioners, simply by observing that a particular kind of box (air conditioners) was purchased repeatedly and another (heaters) was not; but one would never think to make this claim about *all* people in the tropics, to generalize from the infinite variety of observable facts (rather than, say, make the claim about all people you happen to see, or all people in the five stores in a particular city you've been to), unless one had a desire-grounded reason to believe that *climate* was the appropriate category. One knows that the typical chooser goes back to the Snickers bars—not to candy bars at a certain height above the ground, to bars with brown wrappers, to bars in bins with twenty pieces of candy—because one knows what candy bars are desired for.

Having engaged in what many would consider extreme overkill of a position that would almost certainly be viewed as politically trivial if it prevailed, I went on to discuss the far more serious political claim that we can generally presume that people in fact desire what they choose, that choice-satisfying institutions (generally thought to be markets and market mimickers) meet individuals' actual *ends*. My claim was that a theory of individual will that identifies chosen positions with desired positions is primitive at the individual psychological level, unable to cope with regret and ambivalence, and primitive at the sociological level, unable to deal meaningfully with the omnipresence of constraint and duress or to define when constraint is legitimate.

At the personal psychological level that point is really quite simple, though its implications are not easily dealt with. Given the existence of ambivalence and regret, it is unclear what a preference-satisfying decision maker should do. A friend tells you that he's going on a diet, that he will beg you to let him eat some chocolate cake, but that you should refuse him steadfastly. Ulysses begs to be bound to his ship's mast to resist the temptation of the Sirens. Later, the friend begs for the cake and tells you that he was vain, shortsighted, or just not hungry enough to think lucidly when he told you to turn down his perfectly reasonable request. Ulysses wants out of the shackles. What does the preference satisfier do?

Choices are manifest at particular points in time, but individuals have ongoing identities. There is some "person" who transcends the chooser. In fact, we generally experience ourselves as having metatastes as well as momentary preferences—that is, tastes about the tastes we'd like to have at each moment.[53] It might be easy if there were some "governor," some dependable arbiter whose decisions always counted,[54] but that's clearly mythic. There is no sense in which we can reliably claim that stated *aspirations* should always be deemed to reveal "real" preferences more accurately than particular choices, just as choices don't swamp aspirations. Rather, the notion is, as I said in the piece, that "all choices are part of a never-equilibrating, dynamic process of self-discovery. We continually try to establish conditions in which more desirable selves, with particular preferences, will flourish. Then, we reevaluate our vision of whether the chooser we create by working to establish those conditions seems more or less realized, then work some more to redo background conditions."[55]

While the piece did not really emphasize the point, it surely adopted the familiar notion that neither particular momentary desires nor *stated* aspirations can define all of a person's possibilities. Any set of desires is learned, not so much through the sorts of explicit demand creators that left-liberal critics often focus on (like advertising)[56] but by adapting one's needs to the whole fabric of social life (learning to value what is available in one's culture).[57] Thus, any particular revealed preference might clash not only with an *explicitly* stated metapreference but with ones we could readily imagine having developed if a given individual had been formed in a somewhat different setting. Once we accept and integrate a view of the self as both defined by its determined boundaries and as transcending these limits, at least in one's potentiality, both determined and intentional or existential, the desires of the concrete self can never exhaust our underlying possible desires.

This more determinist perspective, which sees individuals as significantly created by circumstance, of course implicates the issue of the sociological primitiveness of the standard economic theory. All agree that choices that are perfectly coherent and rational at the moment when they are made pack little normative punch if the chooser was under something that can be described as "duress." It may make perfect sense to *choose* to hand over your money to a mugger or to *choose* to have sexual relations with an armed rapist; if the option set really is "your money or your life," giving over your money hardly seems exceptionable.

If coercion-determined choices are not presumed to be satisfying to the chooser, the neoclassical economist's commitment to equating choice and desired positions is thoroughly undermined unless he believes either that the chooser doesn't truly make coerced choices in a way that makes any intentionalistic discourse plausible (a hard claim to swallow, given that the choices seem *less* ambivalent or regretted or irrational than choices typically deemed legitimate) or that we can both *define* coercion and assume it is present on only a few discrete occasions. But to do this we'd clearly need a theory of rights and/or illegitimate duress, as well as a picture of the ideal setting in which choices are made. As I said earlier in discussing duress in contract law, one simply cannot define duress independently of rights: if the beneficiary of the chooser's decision is *entitled* to determine the choice conditions, the choice is not a product of duress (if I am *entitled* to slash your throat, your choice to hand me money rather than have me exercise the right is definitionally uncoerced). Moreover, if the unhappy chooser has a right to be free from unwanted background conditions (whether facing a monopolistic seller or being unable to feed himself without accepting employment), his choices are "unfree."

The fact that there are some conventionally and uncontroversially *illegitimate* "bargaining tactics" (like mugging, like traditionally defined rape) hardly demonstrates that there exists anything approaching a clear sense of *legitimate* choice conditions. The problem would be hard enough even if we believed that illegitimate pressure came *only* from the beneficiaries of the restricted chooser's decisions. The essential problem is a restatement of more general rules-standards dilemmas: is a person entitled to exercise a *generally* available privilege for no particular purpose on a particular occasion except to induce conduct beneficial to him? We all know that it is rape for a man to tell a woman that she will be physically hurt unless she agrees to have sexual relations with him; but if he tells her that he will disclose to a would-be employer negative information about her that he is legally privileged to disclose unless she has sexual relations with him, is this something *like* rape? Or should the woman feel that her choices are needlessly unsatisfactory? Are these the same question? The general problem, of course, is even more serious. People make choices in circumstances that are not explicitly attributable to any particular person's conduct but that seem to influence or pressure them to make choices that are unsatisfying. The question of whether these choices can best be thought of as utility maximizing, given "objective constraints," or unsatisfying adjustment, because other background conditions are technically feasible though not socially available, turns to a great extent on a question that seems unlikely to elicit uniform responses. Beaten women may "choose" to stay with a particular assaultive man on a particular occasion in a world of great gender inequality, in a world in which women's options may be limited in ways that may or may not be socially remediable. To the extent that the conditions *are* socially remediable, the "choices" reveal little about women's desires but a great deal about our collective (male-determined) will to satisfy women's desires.

"Choice and Utility" specifically disclaimed the most common neoclassical interpretation of the psychological problem of intertemporal preference instability, the interpretation that focuses on the inadequacy of information available to a chooser *ex ante* about the attributes of a chosen position that would be revealed with use. The example I focused on was the child abuser, whose regret at the decision to beat a child need certainly not diminish as he beats more regularly and learns more about how badly he feels afterwards. Some legal economists have reacted to this example by taking refuge in the usual rigid, vacuum-bounded intentionalist-determinist dichotomy, interpreting child beating as uncontrollable, determined behavior (which one could either aspire to avoid or regret), while "ordinary" economic behavior is pictured as intentionally self-controlled, and thus readily altered on future occasions if one feels regret once.[58] I believe that, like any effort to treat intentionalist or determinist accounts of experience as utterly determined by the "subject" of the inquiry, this argument fails dismally. Child beaters can be pictured as having some capacities for self-control, while each of us making ordinary economic decisions (picking a good for its status associations, picking a high-paying, meaningless job because we have become habituated to having access to certain goods we had earlier lived without comfortably) can be pictured as will-less objects of social forces far beyond us. Certainly there is no "empirical" case that goods addiction—that is, powerful habituation to a particular lifestyle[59]—is "cured" more often than a predilection to engage in child beating or drug dependency, "choices" traditionally filtered through determinist lenses.

I also specifically disclaimed the less significant neoclassical interpretation that people only *seem* to regret the choices they make, but that the choices are in fact maximally satisfactory, given the side constraints the choosers face. It is certainly common to note that people maximize utility, *given* an income constraint: one may choose hamburger rather than steak not because one would prefer it in a world without scarcity but because each of us faces scarcity. At times, neoclassicists reinterpret regretted choices as choices that respond to a scarcitylike constraint (for example, one can interpret a drug addict's regret at choosing drugs rather than food for her children as resulting from a desire to have both food and a freedom from the desire for drugs, which makes it sound rather as if she just wants more goods). But the income constraint reinterpretation is clearly unsatisfactory (so clearly, I suppose in retrospect, that I once more feel that I may have brutalized a rather lifeless object) since the desire to be free from a desire is really not significantly *similar* to a desire for more income, at least in the sensible sense that it would hardly help it be met if the society's productive resources were to increase.

The most significant question, looking back at the effort I was making in "Choice and Utility" to discredit neoclassicism, was whether this rather *theoretical* attempt to undermine the purported nexus between choice satisfaction and utility translates into a serious political-legal attack on neoclassical social theory. It would certainly be perfectly coherent to believe either that one simply doesn't have a clue as to what to do to satisfy preferences when people express ambivalence about their choices over time or that one *must* fall back on one's own judgment about their best interests, while believing either that people are frequently unambivalent or that there is no systematic way of responding to ambivalence that is superior to responding to each instance of momentary desire. Moreover, one could certainly believe that the tastes we actually see demonstrated are themselves a product of complex social forces, and thus just one set of many potential choice sets, while still believing either that tastes are *not* particularly manipulable by consciously altered political decisions to change these complex forces *or* that it is best to respect desires, even knowing them to be perfectly contingent, since they are, once implanted, effectively unalterable or mutable only by inflicting great pain on those one would like to change.

Once more, the preliminary strategy was to try to make the critical cases seem less exceptional, just as CLS scholars have invariably tried to do when dealing with all the basic contradictions in liberal thought. Expressed ambivalence might or might not be common, but it is certain that we frequently *presume* that people are both temporally divided choosers and subject even to short-term external influence. The frequent demand for waiting periods before certain choices are made operative (whether by antiabortion advocates[60] or by those worried about high pressure door-to-door salesmen[61]) is clearly responsive to the notion that we may make momentary choices that would not survive reflection. The parallel fact that even those most committed to a "right" to take one's life or to refuse extraordinary medical care demand that these decisions be made deliberately and reaffirmed over time[62] expresses our understanding that even in the absence of explicit ambivalence, we *assume* that certain momentary choices are not the choices we would ordinarily be most likely to make. Similarly, the fact that we frequently believe that we can shape people's decisions, while not formally limiting their legal privilege to make any choice they desire, by altering the context in which they choose is evidence of the fact that we are aware that the same biological person can readily make a range of distinct choices, without our believing that we are dealing with a truly different person with different underlying desires or motives. Once again, the abortion debates are instructive: both opponents and proponents of abortion recognize that requiring a teen-ager to discuss a decision to abort with a parent might alter the substantive decision (even disregarding what might arguably be deemed parental force compelling a particular decision),[63] even though that teen-ager can meaningfully be thought of as basically the same decision maker whether she consults with her parents or not. It is also true that we believe that the discrete decisions that help form the actor's milieu don't simply respond to tastes but recreate a new world of tastes: men "forced" to do dishes or change diapers almost surely have systematically different tastes relating to these tasks than do men who have never performed them (and these tastes may well be reflected in decisions with a more traditional economic ring; for example, the labor supply curve may be affected if such men cannot separate from their children as readily as "traditional" men).

Still, there is a sense in which arguments by the Critics and the economistic social theorists continue to seem skew to one another. Even those economists most sympathetic to the Critics seem to think that the issue of whether stated preferences are to be respected boils down fundamentally to a (quasi)empirical question about both the plasticity and "political-ness" of desire. It is really not enough to know, they say, that economics is psychologically primitive in dealing with complex and self-contradictory desire unless one believes that the significant choices at stake when we debate the choice of public institutions resemble the ambivalent dieter's contradictory demands. And it is not enough to know that we could all have been very different choosers—that the day-to-day desires of someone raised in New Guinea bear only a distant resemblance to those expressed in Palo Alto—if we don't believe that the self-conscious political efforts to alter our preferences, traditionally associated with the resocializing efforts of revolutionary regimes or smaller communes, have much real punch.

I think that the first skeptical counterclaim, that complex ambivalence is restricted to politically empty cases (like Ulysses and the Sirens, the dieter), is simply wrong. I certainly don't believe that every consumer choice is in any sense weighty or conflicted; even choices made under uncertainty need not involve the sorts of intertemporal divisions I've been speaking of. (Though you're not *sure* that the Honda you're choosing is better than the Toyota you forgo, there may be no intrapsychic clash at all about the *attributes* you seek, just a longing for technical information you can't obtain.) But I do believe that most society-defining economic choices are laced with exactly the sorts of intrapsychic conflict I have described. I simply think that each of us is more or less ambivalent about the relative rewards of obtaining material goods and working to serve needs one discerns are unmet by a market; about the status meaning of different goods and the significance of status acquired through goods; about taking health and safety risks; about the value of self-control and skill development at work; about the pain of being deferential or subordinate (particularly when there are rewards for being subordinate); about both the pains and joys of the mobility that fluid economies reward.

The second skeptical counterclaim, that expressed preference sets are contingent only on factors far beyond our conscious collective control, is certainly significant, but it also invariably threatens to turn into a vacuous, overblown argument about the elasticity of human nature.

In theory, it is possible to narrow this potentially open-ended inquiry by "testing" the impact on taste of some potentially taste-creating collective decisions (Did the 1964 Civil Rights Act or desegregationist court decisions alter people's feelings about racially integrated public facilities or schools?[64] Has OSHA shifted workers' sentiments about job risks?). But it is hard to imagine any test of such propositions that a reasonably skeptical reader would find more than merely suggestive.

It is certainly possible, too, to make at least some a priori guesses about the goals of explicit collective taste-creating choices. Collectively imposed uniformity may seem to deny the possibility of distinctions between people, but it may well be needed to *rationalize* a choice that few can make unless it seems utterly out of their hands, even though they would in some sense like to make it. A system that seemingly leaves people no alternative but to use a safety device (for example legislatively mandated seat belt interlocks) might be thought to manifest an aspiration to use the device on which few would act unless they felt choiceless. Similarly, people may collectively mandate costly work-safety programs knowing that, if given the appearance of choice between more wage income and safety, they'll always be drawn to the immediate payoff of wages. A less intuitive example, where collective efforts naturalize a "good habit" that is difficult to choose, comes from the field of public finance and taxation: it may well be that both our incentive to work and our taste for sharing voluntarily when others claim a portion of the products of our labor are anything but collectively immutable or trans-historical. It might well be true that the sudden and surprise seizure of 5 percent of one's product by the self-proclaimed needy would cause people to flee from producing, as might the *first* imposition of a low-rate income tax, while an ongoing 50 percent income tax could be integrated in such a way, treated as equivalent to a physical constraint on one's productive powers, as to have next to no incentive effect. Similarly, few might volunteer to give away 50 percent of the income they treat as theirs, even if free-rider effects were eliminated by some sort of contract in which donations were required only after a certain percentage of would-be donors pledged, though they might in a sense *want* the collectivity to make them share both by making them feel choiceless on particular occasions and by ensuring (as in a withholding system) that they never have control over the money in the first instance.[65] Whether these collective efforts have in fact solidified or rendered less ambivalent many people's commitment to the aspects of character they may well have sought to strengthen is certainly as problematic and hopelessly contestable a contention as the claim that prohibitions on the *manifestation* of unwanted character traits (like racism or excessive risk taking) ultimately affect the character trait itself.

In the final analysis, I suppose I believe that one's attitudes about the *ultimate* plasticity of human nature may well be less important than conservative ideologues believe. One can certainly, at the "private" political level, alter the traditional division of household labor or at the "state" political level work to employ state force to discourage sexual harassment in the workplace without having anything resembling a developed theory about which gender differences are biologically ineradicable or mutable only through extreme and unacceptable resocialization efforts. One need not have developed opinions about the global possibility of inducing work effort without *any* traditional extrinsic incentives (like money or glory) to believe that collective efforts to promote greater levels of equality have proven compatible with tolerable work effort or that pass-fail grading has had little impact on the genuine educational attainments of many students in certain sorts of settings.

Clearly, those of us committed to radical politics must be particularly sensitive to the possibility that our suppositions about how we will respond to our efforts to transform the world that frames us are *wrong,* that our dreams simply won't *take.* It seems to me that it is vital to be sensitive to the resistance we may see to our efforts to change tastes. This is true whether the resistance is focused and relatively nongeneralizable—as opposition to mandatory seat belts was, given that there was no across-the-board opposition to mandatory auto safety devices like crash-proof windshields or partly collapsing steering wheels[66]—or fairly generalized, as opposition to agricultural collectivization in the Soviet Union was.[67] But awareness of the need for this sort of sensitivity seems far more vital to me than the capacity to make correct *ex ante* decisions about human malleability, given that these decisions will almost surely be fundamentally groundless restatements of general political bias.

Paternalism

If one reads the CLS critiques that focus on ambivalence and regret broadly enough, one can seemingly overturn or deride any particular choice without recourse to traditional paternalistic justifications. Given the availability of a determinist picture of the self, it is not surprising that there is no clear line between paternalistic interventions that avowedly disrespect a chooser's will and appeals to the individual's own preference structure. If some hypothetical self significantly distinct from the concrete person we encounter, "created" by a different social framework, is always *imaginable,* we can always claim to appeal not to "true" judgments of the good but to this hypothetical self's judgments of the good. In practice, too, traditional paternalism and sensitivity to ambiguous choice are inevitably entwined. Without the attitudes traditionally associated with paternalism—some sort of conviction that we think that some choices are simply intrinsically better or more satisfying than others—it is unlikely that we would recognize any of the *implicit* cases of ambivalence, doubt, or potential regret. The acceptability of the idea that X would probably regret doing Y is hard to disentangle from the idea that Y is just a bad idea. Yet the divided-chooser analysis may temper traditional paternalism as well by reminding the decision maker that the subject's long-term reactions to his interventions serve as one significant check on the decision maker's judgment.

Still, despite the fuzziness of these concepts, there seems to be an ineradicable core of purer paternalism, of judgment that a particular person may make particular decisions that harm him, and that no one we can readily think of as that same person would choose any better, no matter how much we rearranged the background conditions under which he chose or how often he got to reconsider the decision. My sense, though, is that most of the CLS writers have tended to emphasize the political importance of ambivalence and denigrate the significance of purer paternalism. For instance, in Simon's discussions of the need for attorneys to interact less passively with clients rather than serve the clients' stated ends, he emphasizes not so much the superiority of the lawyers' judgment about clients' "real interests" as the inevitable ambiguity of the ends the clients can readily be made to perceive themselves to have.[68]

Perhaps this focus on ambivalence is a cowardly concession to the power of the liberal choice-satisfying paradigm. In a sense, the divided-chooser analysis respects liberalism's value skepticism, assumes that some sort of want satisfaction is normatively desirable, yet deeply questions the received understanding of wants. While the paternalist program can also readily be stated in terms that are consistent with liberal social theory—particularly if a "responsible" person's tastes become the substitute for or arbiter of the good for a person lacking "rational capacity" to govern himself—it is just as frequently associated with nonliberal beliefs in false and true consciousness, objective good, vanguard classes.

Perhaps, too, CLS has run away from traditional paternalist analysis not simply because of its left-totalitarian Stalinist pedigree but also because of its right-elitist-racist-sexist pedigree (in which white male Anglo-Saxons forever describe women and people of color as incapable of knowing their own true interests, in need of the protection of the literal or figurative father).[69]

But it is ultimately neither possible nor desirable for the Critics to disclaim the legitimacy of paternalist motives entirely, particularly once one recognizes how unexceptional the activity we often try to exceptionalize and isolate really is. Once again, the CLS strategy, typified in Kennedy's article "Distributive and Paternalist Motives in Contract and Tort Law, with Special Reference to Compulsory Terms and Unequal

Bargaining Power," was to remind us that paternalism could not be confined, just as other instances of unprivileged normative commitments could not be limited to "exceptional" circumstances.[70] It is easy enough for liberals to acknowledge that delusional schizophrenics are constantly restrained, and easy to divide the world into the wholly incapable (children, the insane, the senile) and the self-governing. The ubiquity of paternalism is more readily seen when we think, as Kennedy invites us to, about whether to recommend that a writing-blocked colleague simply be *asked* to deliver an important address, without interfering in the least with his formal legal privilege to accept or decline the offer. The paternalistic impulse is then seen as omnipresent in two distinct ways: it is not confined to situations in which we explicitly overturn a stated choice but includes situations in which we deliberately alter the circumstances in which the actor chooses, nor is it confined to "crazy," unordinary people. If we truly respected the writer's block, treated it as a substantively desirable or unexceptionable decision, it is unlikely that we would want to tempt someone to break his habit. (Perhaps, too, of course, "tempting" doesn't capture what we think will happen when we begin our manipulations; we may, for instance, simply know that our colleague is reluctant to refuse direct invitations.) Whether we justify our actual decision by reference to the ambiguity of his prior decision not to write or by reference to our belief that his "real" interest is in shedding this dreadful affliction, we surely shouldn't have recourse to the self-deluding position that we simply gave him an option, left the ball in his court.

Kennedy's justification of what he dubs "ad hoc paternalism"—paternalism grounded not in a general judgment by the paternalist of another's incapacity to choose well but in the paternalist's capacity for empathy for individuals in particular situations—is based in richly textured stories in which one sees ways in which a decision maker can gain a great deal of insight into the difficulty of the situations the would-be chooser faces. He talks at length, for instance, of someone watching an old woman struggle to make decisions about receiving care for her terminal illness, and I believe that he conveys quite effectively the need to help make judgments for others, the moral opacity of simply claiming to defer to some other's will, and the capacity we may have to make decisions for others even in the face of our profound doubts about our own judgment. Paternalism in such a situation is intimately tied to love and altruism, to making less rigid distinctions between one's self and others than the individualist claims we inexorably do. The ad hoc empathetic paternalist feels that the decision is terribly difficult and weighty, but not because the other's sentiments are truly inaccessible to him; indeed, the most significant point is not that the right choice is lucid but that the decision would be just as difficult and weighty if made about oneself. The paternalist's capacity is grounded in his seeing the choice as an intensely problematic *human* choice with consequences for the disabled-to-choose actor that the paternalist can know *precisely* because our nondiscernible differences in this situation are far outweighed by some combination of our similarities and the differences we can understand from empathetic listening and an authentic desire to hear another's voice.

But Kennedy's plea for ad hoc paternalism seems strained in one sense and incomplete in another. Kennedy, quite reasonably, wants to distinguish his love-empathy account of paternalism from the paternalist position more compatible with liberalism, which claims to respect all decisions made by persons with "capacity" to choose. In doing this, though, Kennedy denies that "capacity" is a meaningful concept at all, claiming that there is no coherent account of capacity that is distinct from "capacity to make a particular judgment," which one would presumably discern simply by directly deciding that the particular judgment was right or wrong. If he means this only in a forward-regarding sense— that is, that one cannot decide once and for all that a person cannot make any good decisions—the point seems unexceptionable. I have trouble believing, though, that a backward-regarding judgment about capacity—based on knowledge of other decisions the chooser has made on other occasions—would not bear on one's judgment of whether the particular choice helps advance a discernible and respectable life plan. Perhaps Kennedy so fears that traditional capacity judgments have so clearly reflected traditional social hierarchies that he thinks it politically safer to root out all talk of capacity. But if the effect is that we focus only on the narrow, time-framed choice situations the would-be chooser is now in, and exclude all other knowledge about her, the argument certainly seems unpersuasive and peculiar.

More significant, Kennedy's attempts to justify paternalist motives in *legal* life by using stories of intimates seem somewhat disingenuous. In a sense, Kennedy uses overly transparent rhetorical tricks. First, he makes us see that we believe in our paternalistic *capacity* by making us think of situations in which we know a great deal about what the disabled chooser has generally been like and can test our initial instincts about the propriety of her preliminary decision by observing how this person whose moods we have long had to understand reacts to our intervention. Then, he implies that the only thing that makes paternalism toward nonintimates a more difficult issue is that there are some serious but fairly abstract hierarchical barriers that make one systematically underestimate the intelligence of social-status inferiors. If, though, one can overcome elitist presuppositions, public, impersonal, legal paternalism poses few special problems. But, of course, if the account of the possibility of paternalism is grounded both in deeply caring (which makes one really hurt if one makes a wrong decision for another) and a profound ability to discern the other's life plan (grounded, I would imagine, in long-term observation), then it is not clear that we can know anything at all about the propriety of a paternalism based on nonparticular general suppositions about people (to cite one of Kennedy's examples, that people are childish about risks, systematically underestimating them) by thinking about a paternalism grounded in intimacy.

Perhaps the problem is really just one of literary style. The decision about whether to let the old woman die in peace (and possibly pain) is easily pictured and captured on paper, easily made rich and emotional. It is not one, though, in which the would-be paternalist necessarily *knows* more about her relevant agenda or concrete needs, or even one in which he really cares more about consequences than he would in the less well focused, less emotionally freighted decision to stop unnamed others from subjecting themselves to certain health hazards. Still, it is certainly troubling that we are led to understand paternalism as a process grounded in intense and focused love and then simply asked to assume that it must be a less obvious version of that love that guides us in making decisions for faceless others. It is not obvious why we ought not deny our public paternalist capacity rather than assume that it exists and must be similar to our private paternalist one.

Is the Kaldor-Hicks Position Coherent?

Even if we believed that we could *recognize* Pareto efficient moves, that we knew for all important moral and political purposes that parties who agreed to move from state X to Y either preferred or were not harmed by the move, we would obviously know very little that would help us in making legal judgments. While a belief in Pareto efficiency might seem to require that exchange be permitted, there are few other significant legal issues in which one can even imagine invoking the pure Pareto efficiency criterion. Particular legal rules invariably create losers as well as beneficiaries. (I should note, though I've no particular stake in the point, that the adoption of a regime in which exchange is permitted is almost certainly not Pareto efficient either. Doubtless some people will be hurt when others are allowed to exchange for the first time, if only those who had been favored by the customary modes of assigning goods to particular parties, or those once given allocational authority for the group who will be disempowered when universal free exchange supplants their allocative role.)

Law and Economics theorists have claimed, of course, that there exists an alternative welfare criterion that would help us decide actual cases. This welfare criterion can be described as demanding either rules that maximize wealth, rules whose benefits outweigh their costs, or rules that help beneficiaries enough so that they can compensate losers to the point of indifference between the status quo ante and the new regime while still themselves favoring the new regime (Kaldor-Hicks or potential Pareto efficiency).[71] Obviously this variant of a decision-making rule has been significant not only at the abstract legal academic level—where analyses of various traditional tort and property controversies regularly proceed on the assumption that entitlements can be assigned in accord with a cost-benefit analysis—but, more important, in public regulatory policy, where the Reagan administration asserts that all administrative regulations should (and can) be subject to cost-benefit analysis.[72]

The CLS claim, quite simply, is that there is absolutely no politically neutral, coherent way to talk about whether a decision is potentially Pareto efficient, wealth maximizing, or whether its benefits outweigh its costs. Essentially, Critics cite two distinct reasons for indeterminacy, each of which makes it impossible to ascertain which rule one ought to adopt to be efficient without already knowing what rules are in place, including the rule that is at issue when one undertakes an efficiency analysis. The first concerns the problem of wealth effects; the second involves the disparity between offer and asking prices.

Law and Economics commentators invariably acknowledge that wealth effects exist, but they trivialize the phenomenon.[73] Surely, they say, there will be *some* impact on the downstream user's demand for clean water if she is made richer by assigning her a right to clean water, but since the increase in aggregate wealth represented by granting her this entitlement is minor, it will undoubtedly have trivial effects on her demand for each particular good, including clean water. While one can imagine cases where the initial rights assignment would always prove efficient owing to wealth effects (for example, where the only bottle of water is assigned to one of two parties desperate to survive in the desert and neither could purchase the water from the other once the other received the entitlement to it) such cases have little to do with our usual concerns.

There are three sorts of problems with this dismissive, minimizing response, only the last of which has particularly preoccupied CLS commentators. The first is that there are significant legal disputes that are far more like the water-in-the-desert dispute than the marginal-shift-in-pollution-rules dispute. For instance, assume that one is trying to decide whether Native American hunters and grazers are making the sort of "efficient" or "best and highest" use of the land that economically justifies their ownership claims. Ordinarily, we assume that land is put to the highest use as long as it is freely alienable, so that the party who desires (values) it most will purchase it. It would surely be far easier to decide that Native Americans are *not* efficient users if one were to imagine their effective demand for land, *given* that we have already made a decision that they don't own any land because they use it inefficiently. Clearly, Native Americans stripped of their land rights could not purchase back the land assigned to European settlers, but it is at least a great deal more ambiguous whether the settlers could have purchased it from the Native Americans had the Native Americans been considered its owners.

The second problem is that it is simply unclear why we treat any rule as marginal, rather than recognizing that we must simultaneously assign all entitlements if the regime as a whole is to be efficient.[74] If it is not the case that there are only trivial wealth effects from the assignment of *all* entitlements, it is unclear why we can ignore the general wealth effects of entitlements by assuming that we have correctly set all other entitlements except the one we are discussing.

Finally, and most interesting, the Critics have emphasized that serious wealth-effects problems must occur if we picture people being granted entitlements to manifest their moralistic attachment to particular end states—that is, given the power either to be bought off or to refuse to waive a right to maintain a state they approve of.[75] Here is an example: In one entitlement scheme, mine workers have no right to safety that I, a concerned moralist, can enforce. If I want to make the mines safer for workers, I must pay the owners to do so. If, however, I must be paid by the owners to waive my right to insist on a particular safety level, I might not be bought out at any imaginable price. Even if I have no such enforceable right, the cost-benefit analysis we may reasonably use might demand that we measure the *value* of my attachment to the end state (the benefit of the rule) by reference to the dollar value I would place on waiving the benefit. Thus, just as the bottle of water in the desert seems to be efficiently assigned no matter who starts out with it, because the party without the right cannot induce voluntary transfer of the right, so either a legal regime with a right to safe mines or one with no right to safe mines would appear efficient or wealth maximizing, since the sum of the hypothetical bids of workers and moralists to improve the mines cannot induce the change from the unsafe situation, while the hypothetical bids from those who find it cheaper to operate unsafe mines cannot shake the moralists' desire to exercise their right to maintain safe mines.

This last CLS critique can be silenced only by recourse to a rather controversial moral assertion that the preferences of people who don't produce enough to back up their claims with expendable dollars ought not to count, that it is impermissible to create rights to emotionally desired end states. This was Posner's precise strategy. As he said, "[A]ny theory of consent that is based on choice in the original position is unsatisfactory . . . because the original-position approach opens the door to the claims of the unproductive . . . In effect, the choices of the unproductive are weighted equally with those of the productive. This result obscures the important moral distinction between capacity to enjoy and capacity to produce for others."[76] But Posner's position certainly doesn't describe our actual legal practice: parents, for instance, have the right to be *paid* to bear the emotional distress of seeing their children injured, without regard to their market productivity; the right to be free from sexual assault was granted to women with no market power at all. Worse, from Posner's vantage point, his is anything but a value-free technical proposition; in fact, it expresses rather peculiar antiegalitarian, preliberal values, ontologically discounting some people's desires on the basis of a fact (productivity) over which they might have little control.

Alternatively, one can simply claim to decide, as Markovits does, that we in fact *have* a procedure to deal with the problem that opposite moves will appear efficient depending on the initial entitlement scheme.[77] Markovits claims that the "proper" procedure is that losers from a change must be able to outbid winners, each loser constrained by the wealth he would have after the proposed change and each winner assumed to be as wealthy as he would be if he had gained the entitlement. But Markovits's position is clearly of no help at all either normatively or descriptively. Normatively it is of no use because one can hardly recognize who has won and who has lost from the adoption of a rule unless we decide (for some unknown reason) that *some* status quo ante is normatively privileged. If we begin with the supposition that goods are ordinarily allocated by markets, I suppose Markovits would claim that the rich who use dialysis machines would have to outbid the enriched third-party moralists if we decided to change the rule to one that allocated the machines according to need, because the moralists would "win" and the rich would "lose" by the change. But there is no apparent reason to begin with that supposition. Descriptively it is surely the case that Markovits did not mean to imply that the *practice* of cost-benefit analysis of entitlements has been to follow a single procedure (even if one could imagine what that procedure might be) in terms of picking the appropriate budget constraint for all affected parties. The only point Markovits makes that seems at all helpful is that the CLS position would certainly be wrong if it were read to imply that there would not be any cases in which a certain rule appears to dominate another *regardless* of the budget constraints of all affected parties. But, I believe, the CLS position simply implies that there would be few politically *significant* legal disputes (for example over the validity of safety regulations, the desirability of a private property regime that generates high levels of income inequality, and the like) in which efficiency cannot be invoked by either side, given the problem of valuing the interests of third-party moralists, any one of whom could single-handedly block the imposition of a morally undesired regime if he were understood to be entitled to preserve a morally favored one.

The issue of valuing the desires of the third-party moralist ties into the second of the major CLS critiques of the potential Pareto efficiency criterion: the critique that there is a disparity between offer and asking price *separate* from that caused by wealth effects.[78] The descriptive claim is that the amount a person might *pay* to attain an end state might frequently be lower than the amount he would have to *be paid* to forgo the end state. The implication is that, once more, if both a legal rule and its opposite can be efficient because neither affected party can induce the other to waive the initially assigned rights, then either legal rule seems to be wealth maximizing.

This issue first arose in the context of the critique of the invariance proposition of the Coase Theorem, the central postulate in Law and Economics, which asserts that in the absence of transaction costs, the efficient value-maximizing accommodation of the conflict between competing uses will be adopted, regardless of which party is granted the legal right to exclude interference by the other.[79] The Coase Theorem can be explained easily with an example. Assume that profits are at a minimum for a manufacturer if he uses a production process that keeps the water pristine, $190 higher if the water is made moderately dirty, $200 higher if the water is filthy; in other words, some filtering costs $10, extensive filtering another $190. The user "values" pristine water at $100, moderately dirty water at $50, and dirty water at zero (see Table 1). If the user is entitled to pristine water, the water will still end up moderately dirty, because the manufacturer gains $190 by not having to make the water pristine, and can use a bit more than $50 of that gain to more than compensate the user for the loss of pristine water. But the manufacturer won't pay the user to allow him to make the water filthy, since that would gain him only $10 and the user won't allow it unless he is paid at least $50. If, though, the manufacturer is entitled to do what he wants with the water (the opposite liability rule), the water will *still* end up moderately dirty, since the user will pay the manufacturer up to $50 to make the water not filthy but only moderately dirty, and the manufacturer would gain only $10 by insisting on using no filtering at all. But the user won't be able to induce the extensive filtering that would render the water pristine since it costs $190 and is worth but $50 to him.

The problem with Coasean analysis can be seen equally easily. If the "value" of pristine water is different depending on whether it must be purchased or whether the party must simply refuse bribes to give it up, there will be situations in which the choice of legal rule will certainly affect allocation. If, in our example, the user would not give up pristine water for less than $200 but would pay only an additional $50 to get it, the granting of an entitlement to pristine water would make *that* the substantive end state, while the granting of the entitlement to the man-

Table 1. Hypothetical illustration of Coase Theorem (all values expressed in dollars).

Condition of water	Manufacturer's total profits	Manufacturer's marginal cost	Total value to water user (offering price)	Marginal value to water user	Join prof
Pristine	0	190	100	50	100
Moderately dirty[a]	190	10	50	50	240
Filthy	200	0	0	0	200

a. The water will be moderately dirty regardless of the liability rule (assuming transactions are costless); the parties will always arrive at the outcome that maximizes joint profits, though the mutual gains from picking the efficient outcome may be split differently in different negotiations.

ufacturer to use the water as he wished would lead to only moderate water quality. The manufacturer's offer of up to $190 to dirty the water somewhat would be refused (see Table 2); the $50 offer by the user to clean up the water would not be sufficient (see Table 1).

The difference in valuation, though, may well *not* be the result of a general wealth effect. If the user had been granted some *separate* entitlement equal in aggregate value to the right to clean water, his demand price for clean water might not have changed. Instead, people may simply cling to existing states rather than seek parallel substantive ones; they may value more highly the things that they are declared to be entitled to because these things are sanctified by the entitlement; they may be averse to valuing things except when comparing items they are choosing to purchase, so that they typically are able to do no more than imagine a selling price valuation for items they already own that bears no relation to any offer they might conceivably receive ("Sure, I'd sell my house for a million dollars").

We see many instances of this in daily life and observable markets: for instance, people may not sell goods they own when they wouldn't buy the same goods for the selling price net of the costs they must bear in selling the goods. (In my first piece on the Coase Theorem, I cited as an example someone who turns down a $50 offer from her roommate to purchase an extra black and white TV set she owns, although she would not have gone out and spent $50 for such a set); people often refuse fairly high offers to give up airline seats on overbooked flights although they would almost surely pay far less to retain their seats; baseball owners may have refused to pay as much to sign players after the advent of free agency as they implicitly used to spend on them when they refused to sell them to other owners in the regime in which players were bound to sign only with the team that "owned" them.[80]

The problem of evaluating third-party moralisms is difficult because

Table 2. Illustration of asymmetry problems in Coasean analysis (all values expressed in dollars).

Condition of water	Manufacturer's total profits	Manufacturer's marginal cost	Total value to water user (asking price)	Marginal value to water user
Pristine	0	190	300	200
Moderately dirty	190	10	100	100
Filthy	200	0	0	0

both wealth effects and nonwealth-based disparities between offer and asking price undoubtedly exist. A third-party moralist might pay less to save the miners than he would ask to be paid to waive his right to insist on safety *both* because he is being granted enormous illiquid change-blocking wealth if he is given the right to enforce his moralistic concerns *and* because we may systematically pay out less to manifest our moral concerns than we would have to be paid not to, in part because we might feel that we had *caused* the victim harm, rather than simply failed to prevent it, if we waived a protective right. It also implicates, once more, the profound problem raised in discussing the ambiguity of desire or defining "wants." In the absence of asymmetry between offer and asking price, it would be easier to convince ourselves that people's moral tastes can be understood as privately held individual preferences for particular end states that they define. Collective decision on social or-ganization could be seen as potentially responsive to these tastes. But what seems to be demonstrated by the existence of the price disparity is the impossibility of defining desires for end states without recognizing that the end states can scarcely be understood without reference to the collective and legal background. There is no single-valued "desire" as such for miners to be safe; there may be a discrete desire to purchase mine safety and a desire not to waive a right to insist on a safe mine, but neither is an abstract, presocial, authentic representation of the "real" desire; each is simply the contextually influenced understanding of both a want and an end state that cannot be abstracted from the legal setting in which one understands precisely what it is that one is seeking.

At any rate, the existence of an offer-asking problem not only calls the empirical validity of the Coase Theorem into question but also poses the same definitional problems for the potential Pareto efficiency test that a widespread wealth-effects problem would. When judging a pro-posed legal rule, it is simply unclear if it meets the test if the "loser" could neither buy out the "winner" nor the "winner" buy out the "loser." When both a rule and its opposite seem efficient, depending on who has the hypothetical burden of paying compensation or the benefit of resisting bribes to change, a judgment that one of the rules is efficient will almost surely be made by covertly privileging one party's interests, for unstated political reasons. Again, Markovits's claims—that there exists a prepolitical normative criterion that identifies which party is the loser and tells us that losers must outbid winners for the wealth they would gain if they possessed the relevant entitlement while the winners are presumed to have the entitlement, or that there will be at least some cases in which the price disparity problem does not exist—seem uncon-vincing in the first case and irrelevant to most significant politically charged issues in the second.

Posner thought that one could simply evade issues of how to design the appropriate hypothetical compensation procedure by declaring that the aim of legal rules both is and should be to maximize wealth.[81] A change in legal rules is good, he said, not if as a result winners can compensate losers but if the dollar value of the goods produced in the world rises as a result of the change. CLS theorists have played a very small part in the attack on the coherence of this position; it was left to others (like Jules Coleman,[82] Mario Rizzo,[83] and Lewis Kornhauser[84]) to note, and for CLS writers simply to reiterate,[85] that changes in the dollar value of goods is a terrible measure of how well off a society is, since prices will generally ultimately reflect production costs, not the subjec-tive valuations of consumers. Posner thought that he could evade this problem by recourse to the idea that he was maximizing not the aggre-gate of the *prices* of goods but their value to consumers, that he meant to take account of consumer surplus. But consumer surplus is a mean-ingful, theoretically measurable (though still concretely unobservable) concept only on a good-by-good, partial equilibrium basis. The invention of machines that lead to across-the-board superabundance without any work must still be thought to impoverish a society in Posner's terms, since consumer surplus cannot be accounted for in the general equilib-rium setting, and the value of leisure cannot be monetized except in relation to particular valued goods. Likewise, monopolization of all industry, raising prices and lowering output, might similarly seem to increase wealth. Moreover, a wealth-maximization criterion simply ig-nores the value of all goods in which markets cannot be organized, for example as a result of the impossibility of excluding nonbuyers. Further, even if we were to define a society as wealthier only when there are more of *all* goods available, it would simply not be the case that there had necessarily been an increase in wealth, for this would depend on how those who received the goods valued them.[86] Finally, and more conceptually, a Critic would note that Posner has given us no reason to believe that we ought to care only about the valuation of what he calls "goods"; if people subjectively *care* about an abstract end state (for example the level of equality in the society they live in), they are wealth-ier when "more" of the desired end state is "produced." The distinction between desired "goods" and desired "moral states" should be wholly arbitrary and unsupportable to a consistent economist.[87]

The political point of all these technical attacks on the Kaldor-Hicks criterion is really quite simple, although it is undoubtedly obscure to many CLS sympathizers with a deep aversion to the jargon of economics. The point is to revive the political person's instinct that there really is no *technical,* prepolitical way to determine that one society is materially better off than another, or better off under one regime than another. When we get more widgets at the cost of more widget workers' lives, we can use different, technically coherent procedures to value this change that will make us think, alternatively, that it is either perfectly dreadful or completely unexceptionable. Choosing between the procedures will so often reflect underlying substantive debates about whether materialist or life-preserving value structures are preferable that the notion that there even exists a separate procedural technique for evaluating the polity, grounded in simple responsive preference aggregation, is, while not invariably wrong or self-deluding, so frequently wrong that it is almost certainly a pernicious myth.

CHAPTER FIVE

Legal Economists and
Conservative Preferences

Even if the legal economists used politically unexceptionable welfare criteria, their role at the law schools would still be politically regressive. The welfare criteria are undoubtedly *inevitably* politically biased: it is hard to imagine how one could separate economistic social theory from certain distorted assumptions about individual desire and the relation of the self to the collective. Yet much of the concrete institutional study done in the Law and Economics movement, particularly by those whose work has been readily integrable into mainstream law classroom teaching, is biased, not because of an inevitable social theoretical tilt but rather either because the people doing this work explicitly and substantively favor certain traditional right-wing positions that they have argued for rather disingenuously or because, in their frenzied desire to demonstrate the possibility of an economistically governed utopia, they distort or deny the insuperable difficulties legal institutions would have in overcoming the problem of "otherness," the problem that selfish people will inevitably harm others, no matter how we try to *channel* their selfishness. Much of this biased institutional work can be exposed for its distortions without questioning the social theoretical economics paradigm at all; in fact, most of the critiques of institutional bias offered by CLS commentators make use of conventional microeconomic analysis to question the validity of the work of others purportedly using the same tools. In a sense, then, the material in this chapter is in no way uniquely *Critical*. It is more typical of the work of those in the politically liberal mainstream who attack politically conservative uses of microeconomics. Only in its focus on the Panglossian insistence on wishing away the problem of selfishness does the work deeply resonate in the Critical tradition.

Basically, the institutionalist message of these politically complacent legal economists can be summarized readily. First, private property regimes generally or presumptively serve to maximize social welfare, as do more particular decisions that assign exclusive rights to certain people to retain what they produce and dispose of scarce and valued goods as they wish. Second, in many-seller markets all goods (and attributes of goods) will be available at their marginal cost—therefore, from a social perspective, neither under- nor overutilized. Interference with any of the terms of trade (price or quality) in competitive markets will harm at least some of the actors in the market, who will either be forced to purchase something they don't want or be unable to purchase an item whose resource cost is within their means. Selfishness (exploitativeness) by sellers is never a problem; sellers will be constrained by competition to offer the best physically attainable deal to buyers. Third, relations among strangers (noncontracting parties) must be governed by explicit legal rule rather than the minimalist strategy of nonintervention appropriate to dealings among contracting parties so as to avoid the possibility of some parties harming others. Once efficient tort rules are put in place, though, parties may act fully selfishly without fear of harming others. Efficient tort rules, which demand payment either for all non–cost-justified accidents or for all harm the plaintiffs cause, will induce parties to behave just as they would have if the party they harmed had been in no way "other" (that is, if the "active" and "victim" parties were a single individual with the same substantive judgments about the utility of the desired conduct and the disutility of the undesired damage that the conduct entails that the actual active and victim parties have). And fourth, while economic power can conceivably be marginally affected by the choice of tort rules, the fundamental distribution of income is a function of prelegal productive power, the capacity to withhold one's more or less socially valued productive capabilities. Frequently, "reformers" believe that they can redistribute power by altering legal arrangements—for example, by declaring that the more politically sympathetic character in a typical transaction (the tenant, the durable-goods buyer, the worker) is formally entitled to some desirable end state (a habitable dwelling, safe products, a less risky workplace)—but the legal economists believe that such efforts to redistribute income will inevitably fail, that the underlying price of the goods or dwelling bundle (the good with a certain risk rate, the dwelling with its level of amenities) or "total" wage rate (money wages adjusted for variations in risk) is set by supply and demand factors fundamentally unaffected by the legal regime.

CLS writers have argued that these conclusions are invariably grounded in unwarranted a priori theorizing, and that proving them valid in particular cases would require empirical evidence that is either utterly unavailable or far less convincing than the proponents of the positions would wish.

The Economic Case for Private Property

Defining *private property* rigorously would obviously be a difficult task.[1] The problem is not *simply* technical, although there are of course problems of completeness and analytical accuracy in assembling a summary characterization of a complex body of rules. The more intractable *theoretical* problem, though, is that proponents of "private property" frequently conflate whatever legal rules are in force in Western societies with private property rules, so that they are unmoved by attacks on the presumed normative dominance of private property that are grounded in analyses of Western legal institutions that might, at a more technical or analytical level, be extremely difficult to characterize as private property institutions.[2] Moreover, most reasonably sophisticated legal economists state, at the grand theoretical level, that they do not in fact presume that either lawlessness or collective ownership is intrinsically inferior to private property. The question is whether one can understand the *practice* of mainstream legal economic thinking without assuming that the practitioners are actually using fairly strong presumptions about the preferability of private property. In a sense, the economists are very much like the typical legal educator playing Realist or positivist, declaring at the grand level both that entitlements can exist only to serve collective purposes (since they are clearly established collectively) and that the very definitions of the entitlements can be understood only by explicit reference to the collective purpose, since politically charged words have no interesting fixed meanings, while suggesting, in their more revealing day-to-day classroom speech, that it is helpful both to derive proper practice from strong presumptions about individual rights and to derive practice in concrete cases from abstract reflection on the meaning of the words that have been used to define these rights. Having listened to law teachers for many years, as a student and colleague, I have no real faith in either the proposition that legal academics make few presumptions about the economic wisdom of private property or the proposition that consequentialist, nonconceptualist thinking has truly supplanted Formalistic rights orientation.

In their piece entitled "Are Property and Contract Efficient?" Duncan

Kennedy (of CLS) and Frank Michelman (who, if law school were international politics, might well be considered the most eloquent leader of the nonaligned nations) attacked five standard arguments for the presumed efficiency of private property.[3] They did not attack the efficiency criterion itself, questioning neither its meaningfulness nor its normative appeal. Instead, they contrasted three prototypical regimes—private property, the state of nature, and a forced sharing regime—and concluded that there is little reason to believe *any* of the a priori arguments that more "value" would be produced in one regime than another. Their basic definitions of the regimes correspond to the politically significant classroom uses. In a private property regime, all valuable and potentially scarce resources are owned in the sense that state force exists to back up an owner's desire to exclude others from appropriating the value of the resource. Moreover, all that is initially owned is fully alienable. In the state of nature, there is no organized, legitimate enforcement of any claims, though obviously some claims to use or exclusion will "stick," given the factual balance of physical force, guile, the capacity to form alliances with others. While contracting is of course permitted (since nothing is collectively prohibited) in the state of nature, there is no organized collective sanction against breach. In a forced sharing regime, the state exists to sanction interference with individual rights. But the traditional private property regime right to exclude others from use of one's property may frequently be trumped by others' needs, which may be defined relatively generally or situation specifically as well as more or less mechanically.

It is important to note that the "state of nature" or "forced sharing" can be thought of as both generalized legal organizations or pockets of legal rules within a system that contains many pockets of private property as well. For instance, we are clearly, in this legal regime, in a state of nature regarding others as to many relationships that *could* be governed by entitlement or property rules: harming strangers emotionally without intent commonly gives rise to no legal claims; holders of a *profit à prendre* in the same body of water generally have no legal rights *inter se*. Similarly, there are surely both large and obvious pockets of forced sharing in private property regimes (income taxation used for redistributive welfare programs) and smaller, more obscure ones (for example, airspace above our land is subject to expropriation by "needy" overflying craft).

Kennedy and Michelman address five distinct arguments for the presumptive economic superiority of private property, arguments based on

incentive effects, the need to transfer goods to their highest use, uncertainty, wasteful precautions, and coordination and knowledge of costs.
I shall try to summarize, criticize, and supplement their arguments; in
fact, my first act of supplementation has been to rearrange their list of
five arguments into a somewhat different list.

Incentive

This standard economic argument for private property is fairly straightforward. If people are basically selfish—that is, if they strongly prefer
either to consume valued goods themselves or to consume by designating
explicit loved ones who will more directly use the goods, *and* if they
value leisure—it is inconceivable that they will produce as much in a
state of nature or a forced sharing regime as in a private property regime.
Aggregate social product will therefore rise if a private property regime
is adopted, presumably therefore maximizing wealth (skirting the thorny
problem of how we value goods in one regime versus leisure in another,
given the distinct set of initial property rights in the different regimes).
If people will always be able to appropriate the value of their leisure,
the incentive argument is simply derivative of observations about routine
substitution effects (observations that people choose X more than Y as
the relative price of X declines). Assume that in a private property
regime, one can either enjoy an hour of leisure or produce two baubles,
so that the implicit price of an hour of leisure is two baubles. One might
then choose to produce the baubles. But in a forced sharing regime with
a 50 percent tax rate on income or a state of nature where marauders
grab half the baubles one produces, one might not choose to give up
an hour of leisure to obtain a single bauble. As the relative price (in
forgone baubles) of an hour of leisure rises, less leisure will be consumed,
hence more goods produced.[4]

Kennedy and Michelman counter this a priori argument by noting
that, in comparing a private property regime to either a state of nature
or a forced sharing regime, income effects run counter to substitution
effects and may or may not outweigh them. Further, in comparing private property to the state of nature, the argument simply underestimates
the possibility that force can induce output.

The income effects argument is quite simple in the traditional form
Kennedy and Michelman present, and it can be readily explained in two
distinct ways. First, one can imagine that producers have an *ultimate*
goods consumption target that requires *more* work effort to meet if the

producer is unable to appropriate his whole initial output, either because of the state-enforced claims of the needy or forceful seizure by the strong and unrestrained. If the person we mentioned in discussing substitution effects *really* wants to consume two baubles, and there is a 50 percent tax rate, he will have to work two hours, not just one. Alternatively, one can point out that if leisure is a normal good, it will be valued more highly as a person's income rises; as one retains less of one's initially appropriated product, one will value leisure less, forgo fewer goods to get it.

For Kennedy and Michelman's purposes, it is sufficient simply to note that the choice of regime is indeterminate on a priori grounds, that it is therefore an empirical question whether one regime will yield more goods than the other, not a question whose answer can be deduced from uncontroversial assumptions about human motivation. It would undoubtedly make their claim even stronger to note that the empirical issue has hardly been conclusively resolved. Obviously, the existing forced sharing institution that generates the most general information for us on incentive effects is the income tax system, which obviously calls on state power to make people share with others some portion of the product they initially produce. While the main theme of supply-side economics is that high marginal tax rates indeed reduce work effort— that substitution effects dwarf income effects—the conclusion is hardly uniformly accepted. In fact, there seems to be something of a professional consensus that work effort for male heads of household is unchanged by shifts in the rate of appropriation of product (tax rates), although the work effort of secondary female workers is affected.[5] While I do not see the findings of limited incentive effects as conclusive (at a minimum, it is hard to imagine that studies that focus largely on the number of hours people work under different tax regimes indicate much incentive effect, given the fact that the bulk of workers are contractually committed to working fixed hours) neither can I foresee that there will soon be convincing studies that demonstrate that significant substitution effects dominate.

Actually, the empirical literature analyzing the impact of taxes on work effort is quite ambiguous as to whether strong substitution effects are counterbalanced by strong income effects or whether *each* effect is actually weak.[6] It is obviously sufficient for Kennedy and Michelman's purposes to note that it is ambiguous, on a priori grounds, whether goods production will increase in a private property regime. But if they had been interested in helping to construct a more radical economic theory, more generally consistent with the insights of the Critical Legal Studies literature, they might have explored the implications of those studies that suggest that there are neither powerful income nor substitution effects. In a nonconventional, sociologized economic analysis, work effort is no longer seen as ahistorically responsive to exogenous tastes, whether about the disutility of work, the value of privately appropriated goods, or the value of others' consumption. Instead, work effort may reflect, to a far greater extent, customary responses to institutions that are perceived as more or less just, that is, people may work hard as long as they consider their rewards fair, either in relation to particular others whom they use as a reference group[7] or in terms of historically available rewards.

One can draw the contrasts between the theories in several instructive ways. Assume, first, that one is analyzing the imposition of a 10 percent income tax. In standard theory, one simply looks to the move along the demand curve for leisure created by the fact that the producer appropriates less (presumably, he places nearly no private value on his contribution to the collective in standard theory, since it will do little to alter collective spending even on projects he approves of) and that he is a bit poorer. In sociologized theory, one might assume that an ongoing 10 percent tax would have much less impact on incentives than the first imposition of such a tax would have, given that work effort is responsive to expectations about both the ordinary return to effort and the politically fair return. This sociologized vision might explain why those who were most skeptical about income taxes, both in the late nineteenth century and in the wake of the Sixteenth Amendment, predicted dramatic disincentive effects,[8] despite the fact that top rates were lower than the lowest rates in today's tax,[9] while today's supply siders assume that *lowering* rates to 10 to 20 percent would ensure that all possible work effort would be unleashed.[10] The sociologized theory might be more consistent with a second observed pattern: that although people frequently earn different amounts for identical jobs in different sectors, they seem more sensitive to relative pay differences among their co-workers (which indicate to them whether they are fairly or unfairly treated) than they seem to care about the *aggregate* amount of goods they appropriate by sacrificing a certain amount of leisure.[11]

While Kennedy and Michelman's primary attack on the a priori assumptions of inefficiency in a forced sharing regime is that income effects may well offset substitution effects, this is just one of three points they raise in countering claims about the inexorable inefficiency of the state of nature. The second point is that it is not at all unambiguous that the terms of trade between leisure and work will be altered if a state of nature supplants private property; simply because people are (legally) *allowed* to take some of the product others produce doesn't mean they will do so. It is wrong to confuse the *permission* of forceful appropriation with its *practice,* which may well be constrained by private force, morality or custom, or indifference to material goods. Third, and most important, there is surely neither a priori nor empirical reason to believe that a stable regime of force can't develop in which some *make* others produce a large quantity of goods. One "incentive" to work may indeed be the hope of private acquisition; another may well be the fear of violence if one shirks. It has certainly been a topic of much inconclusive debate whether slavery in the American South was ever an effective system for maximizing cotton production.[12] There is likewise little reason to believe that women's production of household services would always be (or would always have been) higher if women were wage workers with private property rights in their household output rather than workers more or less outside the law, subject to the barely restricted force of their husbands, and making their own claims for material goods without the backing of significant state power. Obviously, there are independent moral reasons for detesting slavery or the subjugation of women; but if the point is that such systems are obviously incompatible with inducing the production of more goods, it is simply unconvincing.

Finally, though Kennedy and Michelman choose to frame their attack on the defense of private property by focusing on the possibility that the competing regimes might perform quite adequately, it would certainly also be possible to note the extent to which plausible accounts of the *unproductiveness* of private property can be constructed. The claim would be that self-interested private actors would tend to construct legal arrangements that lack the standard features of private property in order to maximize income, given these standard problems of private property. Let me mention just two: agency problems and sharing problems.

Agency problems are created whenever actors must trust another party to manage or employ their assets but find it difficult to monitor the performance of this worker. The theoretically pure agency relationship is one in which the agent has a property interest in his labor, and the principal all residual property rights in the profits from the assets the agent utilizes. Given the difficulty, though, both of describing the work the agent has contracted to perform (the implicit *res* "owned" by the employee) and of monitoring work contract compliance,[13] parties frequently substitute a property arrangement more consistent with collective property ideals (for example some form of profit-sharing arrangement in which the success of the agent is explicitly tied to the success of the principal).[14] Neither the agent nor the principal retains all the fruits of the property he initially owns, whether labor or assets.

Sharing problems are undoubtedly more interesting politically. They occur whenever there are social gains from sharing but an individual may privately gain from not sharing. For example, a seller may have information about a product's defects that, if shared, would increase the joint wealth of the buyer and seller, because the actual product, rather than the product the buyer imagines he is getting, might be more highly valued by the seller than the buyer. Since the seller can't ordinarily appropriate any of the benefits the buyer would gain from *not* buying the good by offering to sell information about defects (since the offer to sell such information would itself signal the defects), it may be the case that the good is inefficiently transferred. We may overcome this standard problem through legally imposed sharing rules, whether compulsory disclosure laws, laws establishing collectively funded information-gathering agencies, or laws granting the right to rescind contracts for goods that prove defective.[15] An example that may well be less intuitive or familiar to lawyers is that information sharing among workers may well increase plantwide productivity, but workers with information about in-plant machinery and work processes may be reluctant to share this information with newer workers for fear that they will thereby make themselves more replaceable. Purer private property systems (for example piecework, in which workers are paid in accord with their personal marginal product) might then, even if otherwise feasible (given probems of measurement of output, morale problems caused by resentment of speed-up, and so on) be supplanted by systems much closer to forced sharing systems. If workers then have claims on (maximized) aggregate plant product based on matters like seniority, perverse incentives to withhold information from new workers might be eliminated.[16]

Avoiding Undervalued Uses of Property

The standard argument here, as in the incentives case, is again clearly accessible. In the absence of alienable private property and the correlative prohibition of theft, protecting the right *not* to alienate, goods will not inevitably end up in their highest valued use. There are, of course, always at least potential Pareto gains when a good winds up in its highest valued use. If a ring is worth \$100 to the person who would be the owner in a private property system and only \$40 to the "thief," transfer of the good to the owner leaves both parties better off: there is \$60 of surplus to split between the parties. Only if the thief has to *buy* the good to possess it can we be sure that it is worth more to him to have it than it is worth to the owner.

Kennedy and Michelman note, though, that if one assumes, counterfactually of course, that there are *no* transaction costs—that is, that bargaining is free—it is clear, given standard Coase Theorem assumptions, that the ring will wind up in the owner's hands whether there are rules against theft or not. Either the thief will be unable to buy the ring from the owner (the expected result in the private property regime), or the owner will pay the thief not to take it (the expected result in the state of nature or an enforced sharing regime in which the party who values the ring less highly has some sort of "needs"-based claim to that particular object). The instinctive notion that Kennedy and Michelman's claim might be valid for two-party bargaining games but not for larger social groups in which there would theoretically be nearly endless numbers of potential takers to buy off is simply a function of the difficulty of imagining a *truly* transaction-costless situation. In such a situation, though, all people can costlessly engage in a mass bargain to split the gains from assigning all goods to the users who value each one most highly, and breaches of agreements could be costlessly policed.

Once we recognize that transaction costs can preclude the assignment of goods to their most valued use, we should recognize that it is private property rules that will sometimes block efficient goods assignment, not rules consistent with the alternative legal regimes. Take both an obvious and a less obvious situation in which we may believe that forced sharing regimes must supplant private property. The more obvious instance is that while we believe that airlines and airplane users value distant airspace more highly than surface owners, we also believe that forcing the airlines to purchase use rights from initial private property owners would carry such high transaction costs that use rights might not be transferred at all; so we instead establish a forced sharing rule that strips the private property owner of his ordinary right to exclude, given the claim of need by these sorts of users. Less obviously, some legal economists (like Posner) have argued that a negligence standard in tort law must supplant the strict liability standard more consistent with private property assumptions.[17] Although the initial entitlement holder would ordinarily be presumed to be protected against uncompensated, unbargained-for diminution of the value of his rights, we may so fear that efficient users of the "victim's" entitlements will be transactionally disabled from buying waivers of these entitlements that we force the entitlement holders to share their holdings with those others who, in essence, need them (that is, because they have no socially cheaper mode of producing goods). In a negligence regime, the downstream water user has no pure private property right to clean water; instead, she must "share" her water with the manufacturer if the manufacturer cannot avert the damage to her at lower cost than the cost of the damage, for fear that transaction costs will preclude her from selling her entitlement to clean water to a would-be willing buyer.

Kennedy and Michelman also note cases in which pockets of state-of-nature alegalism would dominate private property because the transaction costs of a private property regime are thought to preclude effective assignment of goods. Abandoned property, for instance, is in a state of nature because it is thought to be too costly to locate an owner who can either dispose of the property through ordinary means of alienation or retain it if she values it most highly.

Uncertainty

This argument for the presumptive efficiency of private property is perhaps the hardest to fathom or make lucid, but the gist of it seems to be as follows: Even if we ignore the impact that uncertainty over one's capacity to keep the goods one initially produces would have on production incentives, there is an efficiency cost attached to unwanted uncertainty itself. Since uncertainty is something people would pay to limit (the existence of insurance proves that), a regime that limited it would, all else being equal, be wealthier.

The argument, though, is hard to take seriously. It is hardly obvious that a private property regime most effectively eliminates even the significant form of uncertainty that proponents of this argument seem to focus on: uncertainty over how much of the product of one's labor one would appropriate. It is simply not clear, for instance, that in a forced sharing state with stable tax rates, people would be the least bit *uncertain* about how much of their initial output they were entitled to keep. But worse, even if one were convinced that private property eliminated the uncertainty *some* people faced about how much income they would have at any time, it would surely increase the level of uncertainty for others. A move from the state of nature to private property might lead to greater uncertainty for those inclined to grab goods; a move from a forced sharing regime to a private property regime might well make those people with socially recognized needs and limited productive capacities far more subject to shifts and vagaries. It is hard to imagine how anyone could make a serious claim that some aggregate level of uncertainty is inevitably higher in one regime than another, that one regime produces either fewer fluctuations in income or more predictable ones.

Kennedy and Michelman try to solidify what might seem an already obvious point by noting that there seems to be a kind of law of conservation of aggregate uncertainty in altering legal rules, a law derivable from fundamental Hohfeldian insights into the correlative nature of legal relations. If, as appears to us logically necessary, each creation of a right for one party implies a duty for another, so that each creation of a right wipes out a prior privilege elsewhere, uncertainty can only be *redistributed* through legal shifts, not eliminated. One can, to take the authors' example, protect the contractual promisor from the uncertainty of large judgments by restricting consequential damages to foreseeable damages (the famous Hadley v. Baxendale rule) only by exposing prom- isees to the risk of large losses. The creation of a privilege (state of nature pocket) in promisors as to harming promisees in remote and nonforeseeable ways wipes out a possible right in the promisee. To take a more politically charged historical example, one can create a private property right in the animals on an owner's land by seriously crimi- nalizing poaching only by eliminating formal or "in effect" historic priv- ileges to hunt on property treated as commonses.[18]

Precautions and Waste

Advocates of private property argue that (inevitably) selfish people will inexorably want to appropriate products for their own use, and will waste resources ensuring that they will keep what they produce, rather than investing in producing more. The avoidance of wasteful expendi- tures to preclude others' appropriation is thus supposedly an advantage of private property systems. The ordinary abstract argument usually contrasts private property with a state of nature, and notes that in the absence of private property, people will waste money hiring guards and building fences, or will concentrate their efforts on producing imme- diately consumable goods rather than either producing durables or in- vesting (since either of these moves poses the risk of theft, of failing to appropriate preclusively).[19] In the more politically relevant form of the argument, associated predominantly with debates over more highly redistributive income tax systems, opponents of the forced sharing or redistributive regime note that people will waste resources producing in ways that minimize taxable income (by investing in tax shelters or overspending on less desired but deductible items) or waste resources hiding income (by partly withdrawing from the money economy) even at the expense of producing less.[20]

Kennedy and Michelman's primary counterargument to the antiwaste claim for private property is again fairly simple. Even accepting the claim that protective efforts against "theft" are "wasteful," it is not obvious, a priori, why the collective expenses to define and protect property rights that must be incurred in a private property regime (for police, courts, lawyers, and so on) would necessarily be cheaper than private efforts in a state of nature. Once more, of course, it would depend in large part on the factual *extent* of grabbing goods in a formally lawless regime, as well as the factual extent of grabbing goods that must be restrained by explicit state force in a particular private property regime. (It would, of course, also depend on things like how expensive it is to operate a police force compared to how expensive private guards are.) Surely, it is plausible that the inegalitarianism associated with private property so increases the persistence and dedication of would-be grabbers that *more* is spent on precautions in a private property regime (whether an obvious wasteful precaution like police, or less obvious ones like taking taxis instead of subways, or building in the suburbs to get away from the urban poor) than in a more egalitarian regime, even one where there are no state-based sanctions against grabbing. Likewise, to think that one can compare, on either purely theoretical grounds or the basis of any available empirical work, the "waste" associated with efforts at tax evasion with the "waste" that would be associated with resisting the material demands of people unaided by a functioning welfare state is surely folly.

One can also, once more, make even more radical CLS-style claims than it was necessary for Kennedy and Michelman to make by exploring the idea that only certain expenditures are "wasteful." As best I can tell, the traditional picture of "waste" invokes some supposed dichotomy between goods consumed for their own sake and goods purchased either to ensure that desired goods can be consumed or needed to provide incentives for desired goods to be produced. Thus, a policeman's salary is both a necessary expense (given the presence of potential thieves) and yet wasteful in the sense that one desires his services not because one enjoys them but because they are needed to ensure that one can enjoy the goods one desires and because, in his absence, goods might not be produced as plentifully. Lawyers are needed in the actual world and considered wasteful in an ideal world in the sense that without their work, incentives to produce might be blunted; but no one directly desires their services. Now, here is what is *technically* troublesome in this account: distinguishing "wasteful" expenditures from needed intermediate expenditures—necessary costs of production—depends on making hidden assumptions about which costs are "physically" necessary to produce items and which are only "socially" or contingently needed. The distinction is often quite arbitrary. Do we "waste" money when we move to the suburbs to avoid the very poor (and incur all the increased costs of a dispersed infrastructure), even if, given their presence, we concretely desire social distance? Can we know this unless we also know what the world would be like under alternative arrangements and how our taste would respond to that distinct world?

Of course, one could try to differentiate wasteful and nonwasteful expenditures in terms of a substantive theory of human needs: only expenditures that meet "legitimate" aspirations to develop one's human potential would be nonwasteful. Obviously, such a move is wholly inconsistent with the ordinary liberal commitment to value subjectivity. Moreover, it certainly threatens the claim that private property regimes are presumptively less wasteful, since these would seem to be the regimes in which there is most clearly a strong private seller's interest in inducing others to desire what they might not otherwise desire, the regimes in which we would expect to see people make their living inducing substantively wasteful spending. (Obviously, there would be no formal bar to such behavior in the legal state of nature, and there might or might not be in a particular forced sharing regime; but, certainly, salesmanship is a cultural artifact we associate with the development of private property rights and the culture of acquisitiveness.)

Coordination and Knowledge of Costs

This last argument for private property is probably the only one that the more sophisticated Law and Economics adherents would advance overtly and with confidence (the others tend to sneak into casual classroom discussion, though they are known, at some level, to be suspect). The idea behind this last argument is that only in private property regimes will actors have adequate information about the "true" costs and benefits of their activities, as well as adequate motivation to act on this information. Because they will know the true cost of all activities— and every activity will affect an owner's interest since everything of value is owned—they will make correct, "natural" trade-offs between activities, unlike in a system of incomplete private property, where people make wrong trade-offs between the consumption of one (owned) good and another (unowned) one or between (owned) leisure and (partly owned) goods.[21] If air is unowned, hence free to harm, there will be too much air pollution; if no one owns the grazing land and thus cares about maximizing its long-term value, it will be overgrazed. If work effort is expended in part to produce goods for others, people may not work as much as they would "naturally."

Only a full-blown private property regime can hope to avoid the tragedy of the commons, which results when people need not account selfishly for the harms they generate. When no one has a property interest that is directly interfered with when the actor causes harm, harms are externalized from the vantage point of the actor. Even if each person would prefer that *everyone* avoid these external harms, coordinating efforts to ensure that *all* avoid the harmful externality is difficult; since these free-rider coordinational problems can't ordinarily be overcome, property rights must be established that force each person to account for the impact of his conduct.

Kennedy and Michelman directly critique the idea that certain trade-offs are more or less natural than others by pointing out that *different,* equally natural substitution decisions between goods will occur depending on the choice of initial endowments. To say that one gets the "right" mix between baubles and air pollution under private property is folly. The amount of air pollution would certainly depend on who owned the air in the first instance, and what the bauble lovers of the world initially owned. Kennedy and Michelman formalize this point, noting quite uncontroversially that the final distribution of goods 1, 2, and 3 among parties A, B, and C with preference orders of 1, 2, 3; 1, 2, 3; and 1, 3, 2, respectively, will vary with the initial entitlement scheme. If the initial distribution of ownership interests is that A gets 1, B2, and C3 or A1, B3, and C2, the final result is A1, B2, C3, but if the initial distribution is A2, B1, C3 or A3, B1, C2, the final result, equally "natural," is B1, A2, C3.

Perhaps, though, their point was both clearer and punchier in its less formalized form. Assume that there are actors on a string of desert islands who are making work-leisure trade-offs in their farming activities.

In one legal regime there is something like private property in farm products with extremely limited duress rules and sharing obligations, so that if one islander's crop fails, he will have no claim on others' crops and will be held to any contract he signs after crop failure. Obviously, we can imagine many variations on that regime, some consistent with certain visions of private property though partaking of the altruistic flavor of a forced sharing system: the victim of crop failure may be able to make claims on others' crops (perhaps only if he was faultless or not lazy in the crop failure, perhaps as a more unconditional claim); he may be able to void long-term (labor or borrowing) contracts he signs after his crops have failed, or perhaps they may be made only on certain terms. Depending on the regime, the trade-offs all parties make will surely be *different*. People may, for instance, work more or less: they have to save for the claims of others, but not as much for themselves; they face distinct income and substitution effects, given that they don't keep all their product, and so on. There may be more or fewer personal services purchased (if, for example, becoming a servant is one of the ways those whose crops have failed can most readily support themselves); there may be more or less spent on security from marauders. But the notion that one set of trade-offs is "natural" in some sense, that one set represents the reactions one has facing the "real" cost of things, seems little more than an inexplicable fantasy. The "real" cost of destroying sacred Native American sites certainly depends on whether the Native Americans *own* the sites, or *own* anything at all; it can't be the case that conduct that is clearly natural and efficient if one side wins the land wars is clearly unnatural and inefficient if the other does. Each is simply responsive to the price signal generated by a particular initial endowment set.

While Kennedy and Michelman don't quite as directly address the claim that the tragedy of the commons results from the coordinational failures of non–private property regimes, it is important to note that the tragedy of the commons might be presumed to affect *common* or unowned areas but certainly not *collectively owned* areas. In fact, it is frequently the case that collective property solutions have been used to *overcome* the ordinary coordinational problems of private property systems. For instance, given the transaction costs of vindicating a large number of individually small private claims for violation of rights to clean water, or resolving a series of private disputes in which proof of causation problems would leave formally entitled health victims of air pollution without effective remedy, we frequently see collective, regulatory solutions in which, in effect, the air or water is collectively "owned" in the limited sense that certain breaches of duty thought to harm particular people are remedied at the behest of the state, not the harmed individuals.[22] It is also vital to note that even as to the traditional commons, which might be considered to exist in something like a state of nature, the authors' general point that one ought not confuse the legal *permission* of conduct (here, overuse or waste) with its *practice* is once again salient. There is little reason to believe that the commons were in fact overgrazed in medieval England, which is not surprising, given the presence of nonlegal obstacles (like the social disapproval of neighbors) to misbehavior.[23]

Competitive Market Efficiency

Just as the law classroom's legal economist makes certain false presumptions about the efficiency advantages of private property regimes, so does he tend to paint a picture of the beneficial working of many-seller markets that is, once more, little more than a complacently right-wing assertion of faith. In this mainstream picture, the presence of many sellers legally permitted to compete freely results in the provision of all bundles of attributes (the actual physical product, contractual terms in respect to the product, the product's risk of malfunctioning or harming) at their long-term lowest cost of production, given technical constraints. Consumers invariably receive all attributes for which the marginal consumer's offering price covers the long-term lowest cost of production, and price signals are also cost signals, so that people will avoid waste, never substituting higher- for lower-cost goods that they want equally.

Interference in a many-seller market may be at best needless and at worst pernicious. The regulation of a quality term (for example, mandating certain levels of product safety, or making habitability warranties in leases nondisclaimable) is either unnecessary (desired terms are already provided) or unwise (it may force the consumer to substitute the "extra" feature of a good he wants for some other attribute he wants more, or force supplier exit if consumers are unwilling to pay the added cost of the mandatory term).[24] Parallel arguments are made where the "good" is sold implicitly rather than explicitly; for example, since in many-employer markets, workers are thought to "purchase" safer jobs by forgoing wages, legal economists generally believe that explicit safety regulation is ordinarily preempted by the market.[25] Price controls and quantity restrictions are even more uniformly condemned than quality-term regulation,[26] which is sometimes defended by more politically liberal legal economists in situations where buyers are thought to be misinformed about product attributes or to systematically misprocess available information.[27] (It is common for the more politically liberal economist to cite psychological literature to demonstrate that people subjectively discount the expected harm when looking at events with very low probabilities, of exactly the sort that are frequently at stake in product or job-safety decisions.)[28] Price controls (an example most commonly discussed in the law schools is rent control) and competition-restricting government cartelization (such as prederegulated air and ground transport or professional licensure) are thought both to prevent some willing buyers from purchasing items that would be available if sellers could legally charge full cost, and to distort substitution decisions by breaking the ordinary nexus between price and production cost.

In my piece "Trashing,"[29] I noted that it is possible to define a competitive market as one in which price drops to the level of long-term production costs. It would be wrong, however, to identify any particular market as competitive on the basis of readily recognized factual features (many sellers) and legal institutional features (absence of price, quality, or quantity regulations). My point was that even if one utterly ignored the commonly recognized barriers to beneficial competitive performance (most significantly, misinformation), the *theoretical* justification for the standard model would be as inconclusive, a priori, as the case for private property, and the empirical arguments quite suspect.

Income and substitution effects are generally recognized to run counter to each other when we consider whether a particular economic actor will be induced to work less or more when he keeps less of the product he produces. There are parallel, but far less recognized, factors that motivate entrepreneurs in opposite, perhaps offsetting, directions when they make pricing decisions. There is surely some tendency to lose volume if one raises prices—that is, sells at prices above cost—since there is *some* tendency for consumers to try to buy at the lowest available price, and *some* possibility that a competing seller will offer goods at cost. But the standard model assumes that all buyers will instantly flock to the seller of the lower-priced identical good; the best image is of a large magnet or giant vacuum cleaner sucking up all the eager little bargain-seeking buyers. Of course, to the extent that large numbers of buyers are price insensitive, utterly unwilling to comparison shop at all, it is surely a plausible profit-maximizing strategy a priori to raise prices above cost and increase revenue by selling at higher cost to slightly fewer buyers, to lose the few price-sensitive buyers (*if* any other seller chooses to go after them) while making more money per sale.[30] It is even more advantageous if the seller is able to "price discriminate" among potential buyers, selling above cost to the price insensitive while still competing for the patronage of those who shop around.[31]

I simply pointed out in "Trashing" that the second set of ideal strategies (uniformly high prices or price discrimination) can certainly exist in an unregulated many-seller market, at least as long as a reasonably large number of buyers are price insensitive, a point that is hardly unfamiliar in economics generally, though its inroad in legal economics has been quite minimal. Once one moves from theory to data, the question is hardly resolved: some empirical evidence suggests that the second strategy is common, just as the first strategy appears prevalent.

I did three things in trying to deal with the empirical claims that legally unconstrained many-seller markets ultimately would reach equilibrium by offering all features at cost: I cited some existing empirical data that indicated that that was not the case; I presented simple new empirical examples from a local consumer market; and I criticized a few of the politically significant studies purporting to demonstrate the validity of the competitive-markets hypothesis.

Existing empirical work suggests, though it obviously cannot fully *prove* as a generalization, that prices are quite dispersed for seemingly homogeneous goods in single geographical markets,[32] and that wages and prices in labor markets neither clear the market (even ignoring places where minimum wages formally preclude market-clearing prices)[33] nor equalize for equal work.[34]

I then focused at some length on an example of the failure of mainstream theory to account for actual economic behavior—specifically, the fact that the price of the full-service term that is offered at Palo Alto gas stations had clearly not fallen to cost (for five months when the article was written, and for well over two years as of this writing). Price remains significantly different for the different grades of gasoline, although the cost of the term can't conceivably differ for regular, unleaded, and premium; it remains far higher in the Palo Alto market than in some others, and it remains significantly different from station to station. It would seem clear that each gas station operator is price discriminating, segmenting the market into price-sensitive self-service and price-insensitive full-service customers. (The conclusion that the stations price discriminate is bolstered, incidentally, by data unavailable at the time "Trashing" was written: aggregate full-service prices have tended to remain stable, while the price of the full-service *term*—that is, the difference between self-service and full-service price—has varied widely with shifts in wholesale gas prices.[35] This suggests that the station owners have picked a quasimonopolistic revenue-maximizing price for non–price-sensitive customers and have stuck to it.) Price discrimination and non–cost-related terms exist in this market despite the fact that it clearly meets the legal economist's well-known conditions for competitive market performance: the product is relatively homogeneous; there are many sellers; there are no government constraints on price competition; information about price is visibly posted, hence maximally available; and "shopping" consists of the simplest of acts—driving a short distance to the cheapest station.

Finally, I criticized several studies that argued that there is strong empirical support for the competitive-markets theory in areas in which important policy issues are at stake; one claimed that there are compensatory wage premiums for risky work (implying that workers purchase the level of risk they most desire), while another claimed that antiusury laws diminish investment. My point was *not* that the particular studies were poorly executed or badly conceived but that the conclusions they drew from inevitably paltry and somewhat irrelevant data were unduly confident restatements of a priori faith in the competitive-markets model.

Thus, W. Kip Viscusi's empirical work on wage premiums asserts that workers are indeed compensated for risk on the basis of a study that shows nothing of the sort.[36] At best, Viscusi shows that workers on jobs grossly classified as "dangerous" rather than "not dangerous" receive more pay, all else being equal. But he doesn't even purport to show any marginal increases in wages for shifts in danger within a dangerous occupation; the idea that, say, miners may get some premiums for hazard as compared to shoe salesmen tells us very close to nothing about whether particular employees receive compensatory wage hikes because their workplace is abnormally dangerous. Since, at the political level, controversy would center on regulations of already hazardous activity (for example, bringing all mines up to a safer, though still "dangerous" level), the study hardly implies that in the absence of regulation workers are already compensated for, or choose, desired safety levels, given the objective cost of greater safety. Moreover, there is next to no correspondence between workers' descriptions of their job as "dangerous" or "not dangerous" and our (admittedly imperfect) capacity to measure objective danger. Only 60 percent of workers in groups with the second-highest industry injury rate report their job to be dangerous, while 43 percent of the workers in the second-lowest group, a group with less than one-third the injury rate, report that their jobs are dangerous; roughly a quarter of workers receiving risk premiums are on jobs that, as best Viscusi can (imperfectly) discern (given that he is looking not at particular jobs but at industrial categories), are the safest around.

Steven Crafton's study of antiusury law, which reiterates the usual attacks on price control, purports to demonstrate that some consumers don't get to take out loans that they would otherwise willingly pay for when usury laws are in effect.[37] But the empirical *demonstration* is in fact of a very different point: states with antiusury laws have lower mortgage-lending and construction rates than states that do not regulate interest. The fact that there is capital outflow to higher-interest areas from lower-interest ones, though, says nothing at all about whether the supply of loanable funds would have been significantly lower had a *universal* interest or price control been in effect. The fact that investors prefer a certain 10 percent rate of return to a certain 5 percent of return is obvious; whether people save more in the aggregate (have more funds to lend) when interest rates are 10 percent than 5 percent is one of the hardest to resolve questions in public finance.[38] There is nothing in Crafton's data that advances the argument about the sensitivity of saving to the rate of return—nothing, then, necessarily connected with the claim that price controls will cause shortages. Again, the point is not that either Viscusi or Crafton has failed to come up with a convincing picture of how labor or capital markets work (to call such a task impossible might be to understate its difficulty) but that they clearly *believed* that they had. Their work, then, becomes just another building block in the relentless ideological effort to convince us that the complacent world vision of beneficial markets has in fact been *proven,* the belief that there have somehow been so many pieces in the *Journal of Law and Economics* that reaffirm the creed that, even if none of them really proves much, the creed must be bolstered.

Efficient Tort Rules

The legal economics insight that has almost surely had the greatest impact on law school classroom teaching is that it is possible to order accident law so as to minimize social costs—the costs of accidents minus the costs of accident prevention. In a transaction-costless world, parties would bargain to reach the joint cost-minimizing strategy; in a world of strangers, entitlements should be established to induce the defendant to pay for all those precautions, but only those precautions, for which the marginal benefit (damage averted) exceeds the marginal cost of taking the precautions. Both the Hand negligence formula and strict liability, in their ideal forms, can be analyzed as meeting the goals of cost minimization. If we assume that the plaintiff can't in any way control harm, designing efficient liability rules looks easy; if courts have perfect information, they can induce proper precautions by charging defendants for all non–cost-justified damage. If suits are costless, all proper precautions will be taken when defendants are strictly liable.[39]

The claim that there are potentially efficient liability rules has not just reorganized academic tort analysis; it is one of the central ideological tenets of economic social theory. Will selfish people harm others? Not if competitive markets harness self-seeking by making it possible to sell to others only by providing goods at the lowest possible cost *and* if we must pay a toll, equal to the damage we cause, on at least those occasions when we harm strangers when it is not socially beneficial to do so. The problem of "other-ness" is supposedly obviated by efficient tort rules: the tortfeasor acts as she would were she herself the tort victim, with the victim's "tastes" about damages, taking only those steps that harm her that simultaneously help her more. But just as the competitive-markets claim fails, just as there is no reason to believe that the selfish will act in harmony if we get the background *market* institutions right, so does the claim of efficient tort rules fail. There is simply no reason to believe that we can put tort rules in place that would induce people to act just as they would if bargaining were costless, to act just as they would if they were both perpetrator and victim.

First, as I noted in "Trashing," if we fail to account for pecuniary externalities (changes imposed on parties through price shifts), we simply cannot say with certainty that it is correct to impose liability on a party, even if the party is clearly negligent (that is, the party failed to take a cost-justified precaution). Placing the whole joint cost of the active and victim party's conduct on the negligent activity, as we do when we find a negligent defendant liable, will clearly decrease the demand for that activity. The "value" of those lost units of production must be ascertained by looking not at their equilibrium price but at the subjective value put on them by all those who demanded those units. In other words, the lost value is the lost consumer surplus. Only if the consumer surplus that is lost by raising the price of the negligent activity (as we do when we impose the joint cost on that activity) is greater than the sum of the consumer surplus gained when we raise demand for the victim activity by implicitly lowering its price (by making the victim bear none of the joint cost) *plus* the saved joint cost (the excess of the original joint cost over the cost of precautions) will it be efficient to force a negligent party to *pay* for the precautions, even though it is clearly efficient that these cost-justified precautions be installed. If there were no transaction costs, each consumer who would have purchased the items that are no longer produced would pay what the goods were worth to continue the production; that will not happen in a market in which tort judgments against the negligent are simply added to cost. Whether this sort of inefficiency occurs is a function of the relative elasticities of demand for the tortfeasor and tort victim activities. Since we don't ever seem to have information on the shape of demand curves, it is certain that liability decisions will be made without regard to this sort of inefficiency, and likely that this sort of inefficiency will occur frequently. (Even if demand curves were not so differentially elastic that findngs of no liability are frequently justified in the face of negligent conduct, cost splitting or allocation of *some* of the joint cost to each party to minimize consumer surplus losses would almost surely be the most common efficient solution.)

Second, if courts, given the limitations on their capacity to gather and process information, focus solely on the *marginal* benefits of *marginal* precautions in applying the supposedly efficient Hand negligence formula, then supposedly constrained selfish actors will end up harming others. The point, first raised in a rather confusing fashion by Kennedy,[40] is by now a perfectly acceptable mainstream point in Law and Economics: not only does it show up in Steven Shavell's "Strict Liability versus Negligence,"[41] but it is also explained in A. Mitchell Polinsky's wholly mainstream work *An Introduction to Law and Economics.*[42] Assume that a factory can operate with no scrubber at a profit of $15 and cause $20 in damage; operate with a moderate scrubber (profit of $11, causing $15 in damage); with an excellent scrubber (profit of $5, causing $10 in damage); or not operate at all, of course neither profiting nor causing damage (see Table 3). If the factory is operating with a moderate scrubber and the courts ask whether *marginal* increases in precaution taking are optimal, the answer will be no: an excellent scrubber would cost $6 while conferring only $5 of benefit on the victim. Joint profit (operator's profit minus damage) is maximized, however, when the factory is not operating at all: it is zero then, and negative in all other cases. The point is easily generalized to other torts contexts. When we try to ascertain

Table 3. Interaction between manufacturer and pollution victim (profits and damages expressed in dollars).

Mode of operation	Profit to manufacturer	Damage to victim	Joint profit
None	0	0	0
Excellent scrubber	5	10	−5
Moderate scrubber	11	15	−4
No scrubber	15	20	−5

if a driver who hit a pedestrian was negligent, we ask whether he was driving too fast, not whether he ought to have been driving at all. It is far easier to believe that we can determine whether an activity one has undertaken should have been done differently than to imagine whether it is economical to substitute entirely distinct activities. If that is all we can ascertain, though, the dream of efficient tort rules may be unattainable in practice, at least in a negligence regime.

Third, if both parties can take steps to reduce joint cost by altering their activities, as is almost invariably the case in real torts contexts, the hope that the parties will arrive at the joint profit-maximizing solution constrained only by simple rules fades even further.[43] Unless we can both *bar* recovery whenever the plaintiff has not taken efficient precautionary steps and *demand* recovery when the defendant has failed to act optimally, the parties will be misdirected, not adequately selfishly motivated to reach the selfless solution. Unless the *same* level of precaution taking is always most cost effective for a party, regardless of the precautions the other party is taking, it is hard to see how one could establish general rules that guide conduct rather than simply trying, in essence, to order the parties to the most efficient accommodation. But, in fact, the level of joint cost-minimizing steps either party *should* take is not uniform but depends on what the other party has done: the factory should install *different* antipollution devices dependng on whether the people whose health or property values might be adversely affected by the pollution live far, close, or at points between, whether they also smoke cigarettes, vacation at home or away, or paint their houses white or gray, just as pedestrians ought to wear brighter clothing, or walk different routes, or just stay home, depending on what drivers are doing. There is simply no reason to believe that a general judgment—use X level of scrubber or pay damages, walk only Y distance from the road or you'll get no recovery—inevitably induces efficient behavior. Once more, commentators outside CLS (like Jerry Green)[44] have certainly suggested this point, but its impact on the social theoretical claims of legal economics has been emphasized only in the CLS literature.

Fourth and finally, the notion that selfish actors will be forced to account selfishly for all the unwarranted harm they are tempted to cause, and thus ultimately cause none, is grounded in the supposition that factual causation judgments are accurate.[45] Defendant unleashes toxic wastes; plaintiffs contract cancer. If we use a negligence standard, defendant pays only if the cost of better waste disposal is lower than the cost of damage caused. But if we don't have a good idea of how much cancer has been caused, we may either underdeter inefficient waste disposal (by underestimating the amount caused, or requiring proof of causation in particular cases by a preponderance of the evidence) or we may overdeter by asking the toxic waste disposers to pay for environmental cancers not of their causing. A move to strict liability is obviously of no help: the defendant then simply pays for all the cancer it causes; if too many cancers are attributed to the defendant, perfectly efficient activity will cease, and if too few are, inefficient activity might persist.

The problem is just as serious if we focus on expropriation, on justice between the parties, as if we focus on mimicking transaction-costless markets. Attributing too many cancers to the disposer in essence places a groundless health insurance funding tax on a normatively random party; attributing too few expropriates the victim, strips him of an entitlement (whether the entitlement is to be free from caused injury or to be free from nonnegligent injury).

The problem does not go away if we know that the fact-finder must be able to make *some* estimate at the end of trial about the shifts in probability of cancer brought on by defendant's activity. Let us assume that the courts discarded the preponderance-of-evidence test that requires that the cancer be more likely than not attributable to the waste and instead used a causal attribution system requiring the defendant to pay, say, for that portion, and only that portion, of the victim's damages that could be attributed to defendant. In other words, if the defendant raised the odds of getting the disease from 100 chances in 1,000 to 150 in 1,000, the defendant would pay one-third of the damages in a causal attribution system, while he would pay nothing under a preponderance-of-evidence standard, since the plaintiff could not prove defendant caused his illness.[46] Courts would still be faced with an extremely politically sticky question: how *sure* of its probability judgment must the fact-finder be before it disturbs the pretrial status quo? Obviously, fact-finders could

be more or less confident of their probability judgments; given information costs, becoming close to *completely* confident might cost far more
than the amount at controversy. But to reach a conclusion once we see
that causal uncertainty poses problems, we must make both tricky efficiency judgment (for example, should we, as Shavell hints, discourage
inevitably costly litigation when the causal links are uncertain and we
are as likely as not to over- rather than underdeter, or do we by so
doing systematically underdeter damagers?)[47] and equity judgment (for
example, is it fair to lump payors together as a defendant class, believing
that the class will be treated fairly but particular individuals within it
confiscated? Is it as fair as can be expected if the alternative is to expropriate some plaintiff-class members? Does it matter how people are
assigned to each class? Whether people value gains and losses in suits
symmetrically?).

    One simple conclusion to a discussion of causation is that in a tort
system like ours, which has no workable answer to the problem of causal
uncertainty but simply systematically underdeters harm causers by demanding in the bulk of cases (with the apparent exception of medical
malpractice)[48] that plaintiffs prove causation of the particular injury by
a preponderance of the evidence, selfish actors will surely harm others
more than they would if they were in the plaintiff's shoes. The problem
of "other-ness" remains wholly unsolved.

Can Economic Power Be Redistributed
through Legal Rules?

Mainstream legal economists generally divide controversies into tort and
contract disputes in discussing whether shifts in legal entitlements can
alter the underlying economic power of actors in the dispute.[49] The
analysis is fairly straightforward. One can, say the legal economists,
redistribute income to a plaintiff class in torts cases by shifting the rules
of the liability system in fashions that favor plaintiffs' interests, whether
by establishing a new cause of action (for example an entitlement to be
protected from negligent infliction of emotional distress), by using a
standard of care that expands defendant responsibility (strict liability
rather than negligence), or by expanding damage awards (for example,
by allowing injunctive relief rather than market-measured damages where
plaintiffs subjectively value an entitlement more than its market price).
One cannot, however, ordinarily redistribute power or income to one
of the two sides of a contractual relationship through shifting legal rules.

If plaintiffs are entitled to an expanded remedy (such as expectation rather than reliance damages) or are entitled to receive some substantive term (such as a nonwaivable warranty of merchantability or habitability), they will simply have to pay more for the expanded contract right. The underlying value of the good or relationship that is bargained over is set by forces extrinsic to the legal system—production costs and consumer tastes—and efforts to transfer goods at less than value will simply fail unless people can be compelled through state force to provide goods at less than cost.

Legal economists also have a characteristic set of opinions on the normative *propriety* of using legal rules to redistribute income in cases where it is feasible, a set of opinions basically consonant with the Process theory most consistent with the Law and Economics movement. Redistribution through shifting entitlements is almost invariably thought to be a poorer choice than redistribution through tax and transfer systems, largely because it is thought that both the losers and the beneficiaries of entitlement-based redistributions will inevitably match up poorly with the groups intended, according to income class, to have their positions changed. Even where, at a general level, the entitlement-rule beneficiary would be expected to be of the "right" class (for example, tenants will generally be poorer than landlords), winners will be just a subset of the poor and will inevitably include some nonpoor; neither will the loser group be entirely as intended.[50] This position is hardly the only one consistent with legal economics, though it does give an appealing economic logic to the deeply problematic question of the division between law and legislation. Depending, though, on how one compares the efficiency losses from inefficient legal entitlement with the efficiency losses inherent in either excise or income taxes (which obviously must shift the relative pretax prices of goods, leisure, future versus present consumption)[51] and whether one thinks that people have some distributive entitlements utterly separate from their income-class status, dependent instead on their part in a particular conflict (for example, "victim" of a "wrong"),[52] one *could,* as a legal economist, undoubtedly embrace the propriety of distributive goals in rule choice.

CLS commentators have focused very little on the explicit normative question of the acceptability of rule-based distribution, in part because, given their descriptive analysis, the question seems badly posed. *Any* legal regime produces its own distinct characteristic distribution: no set of legal rules *re*distributes income from some normatively privileged base; each simply creates its own distribution.[53] To the extent that one can see the CLS work as engaged by this controversy rather than simply skew to it, it is in noting two important points. First, implicit in CLS work is a point that I shall try to make explicit: the division between tort and contract that is posited by the legal economists has long been discredited in legal academic thought in general, so that one would expect that a hypothesis that it is possible to redistribute in "tort" situations but not "contract" ones would be extremely ambiguous in practice. Second, the CLS work I have already discussed has stated explicitly that the notion that the model of competitive markets that posits that all goods are inevitably traded at production cost is wrong; further, depending on the shape of demand and supply curves for goods with desired traits or terms to which the law entitles a buyer, the buyer *class* may well be enriched at the expense of the seller class by even the most minimal entitlement shifts, ones establishing compulsory terms, even though particular buyers may be hurt by the imposition of undesired compulsory terms.

It is surely the case at the purely *doctrinal* level that there is little reason to draw a bright line between torts and contracts. For instance, issues of whether one must compensate another when one has yet to form a contractual relationship with that party can surely be answered using either tort or contract language (the failure to bargain in good faith can be seen as a tort toward the party whose resources are redirected by the hope of contract or seen as a breach of an implied form of agreement); remedy questions that have been answered differently in the two areas are not clear in practice (the availability of consequential damages often turns on characterizing, say, a failure to deliver chattels as a contract breach or a wrongful conversion of the undelivered chattels, but either mode fits many sets of facts); many areas are doctrinally associated with tort, although the parties have contractual ties (medical malpractice, product liability). The question, though, is whether the economists have implicitly found a more viable distinction than the crumbling traditional tort-contract one, a distinction between intervening in cases where the parties bargain with each other (which would include both traditional contracts issues, like the extent of damage remedies, and traditional torts issues, like malpractice) and those where they don't (like auto accidents involving pedestrians, like polluter-pollutee relations).

The problem with the economist's model is that decisions about the definitions of the most basic constitutive limits on the validity of the contracting process—how to define when contracts can be invalidated as a result of duress and/or unconscionability (which, for my purposes here, can be seen as a surrogate for fraud and duress judgments)—can clearly be cast in tort language (fraud- or duress-based transfers are like conversion or theft), but their reform can also clearly affect distribution between the parties.

Assume that we are trying to decide whether the distribution of income between buyers and sellers will change if there is a defense of fraud to an action against a defrauded buyer, or a recission remedy for defrauded buyers. Though this question would ultimately prove to be a fairly complicated one if looked at in realistic detail, we can start out with a deliberately oversimplified example. Assume first that buyers have absolutely no information, *ex ante,* about inferior product quality, knowing neither that particular products are defective nor that defective products exist and thus that there is a certain probability of receiving one. They do, though, discover all defects *ex post.* A fraudulent seller, by contrast, is both aware of product defects and produces defective products at lower cost than good ones. In such a case, contract recission for the fraudulent sale, effective prohibition of sale, a fraud defense against breach claims in executory contract situations, or a nondisclaimable warranty of merchantability would all effectively redistribute income. Let's look at an example. There are many used cars available, some of which are safe, some of which aren't, and the unsafe ones cost dealers less to obtain. The demand curve for the actual used cars in the world is the same as the demand curve for safe used cars, since that is all that buyers know of *ex ante.* A particular seller passes off a cheap but unsafe used car as a good used car; a recission remedy upon the discovery of the defect will simply transfer excess profit from unscrupulous seller to buyer.

The case becomes increasingly complex as we get closer to realistic assumptions about the impact of misinformation. Buyers may perceive that there is some possibility of defect, so the "good" they demand is a probability of receiving a nondefective commodity. Some sellers are more likely than others to sell defective cars (and not all consumers can recognize interseller variations). It is likely, though, that fraud would not exist if it did not redistribute either from scrupulous to unscrupulous sellers or from buyers to sellers; its existence implies some systematic misperception of particular product quality.

Now, the problem for the legal economist is that fraud—this quasitort, quasi–"contract constituting" doctrine—can clearly be defined in more or less buyer-protective fashions, and every shift in the fraud rules will partly constitute a distinct legal regime with distinct distributions of income. Crafty liars and perceptive buyers will be relatively disempowered as information-sharing obligations grow; the terms on which actual goods trade will simply shift, not reequilibrate at some level we think we could define independent of the degree of information buyers possess.

The duress case must be analyzed differently, but the result is pretty much the same: shifts in rules explicitly or implicitly affecting the situations in which parties can void or alter a contract because they were inadequately "free," given the pressures others put on them, will lead to distinct distributions.

First, take a simple proposition: economists would obviously concede that rules that shifted a market from monopolistic to competitive or prohibited a monopolist from charging more than competitive prices would shift monopolists' surplus to consumers' surplus. Obviously, given a beneficial entitlement to a competitive price, consumers wouldn't simply continue to pay the monopoly price they paid before they were given the favorable entitlement. Many duress rules (as well as explicit contract-altering law like antitrust), though, can certainly be thought of as rules that deny a seller the benefit of a monopoly or quasimonopoly position.

More generally, shifts in what one contracting party is initially entitled to do *to* or withhold *from* another party will often clearly affect what the buyer will pay to be provided a benefit. It is easiest to recognize this issue when we imagine creating additional affirmative duties to potential buyers. If we declare that one can't sell lifesaving services to a readily rescued drowning victim either because one must provide the services to free oneself from criminal liability or because any contract to sell such services is void as grounded in duress, it will clearly *not* be the case that the distribution of income between drowning victim and saver will be unchanged. But surely the problem is far more widespread. It obviously exists in cases where the parties have only *one* significant interaction; for instance, can one receive payment not to build a spite fence, or is the would-be builder entitled to put up any fence on his own property that he wishes, for any reason, as long as it is not a nuisance? Can a would-be donee of a gift or bequest take steps that may or may not be deemed voidable "undue influence" to influence a donor shifting both the distribution between himself and other potential beneficiaries and himself and the donor?

It is obviously more complicated to determine if redistribution will

occur when we alter rules in ongoing relationships, since it is conceivable, but hardly inevitable, given the difficulty of predicting when or
whether extra compensation might be earned, that the ultimate gains
the "threatener" will earn might be deducted from the initial contract
price. Can workers receive a bonus for not engaging in a secondary
boycott, or do they have no entitlement to do so? Can they receive
money for not staging a collective "sick-out" to which they are, as
individuals, apparently formally entitled? Can they pass on information
learned on the job to other would-be users (even industrial spics) in the
absence of explicit contractual prohibitions or sell to their initial employer their entitlement to use the information? While it is *possible* that
such rules don't matter (since the agreed-on price when the initial contract terms were set could be lowered so as to incorporate the value of
later gains received through taking advantage of the rules), it is by no
means inevitable that the parties will set, *ex ante,* discounts that eat up
the *ex post* gains the rule beneficiaries end up earning.

CLS writers have also reiterated or expanded at least five routine
neoclassical economic arguments that suggest that buyers may be benefited at the expense of sellers even in the cases that seem most subject
to the traditional analysis. Even in cases where the *only* legal alteration
in the contractual relationship between parties is to make a term or
terms compulsory, although the law neither limits price shifts nor alters
market structure or permissible bargaining techniques, redistribution
may occur.

Let's look first at the relevance of the earlier argument on the failure
of seemingly competitive markets to meet their presumed goals. Not
only could a legal regime redistribute from sellers to buyers by an explicit
price control (for instance, in the gas station example I discussed, by
fixing a price for full service), but it could also conceivably effectively
transfer from sellers to buyers by making full service a compulsory term.
Many self-service buyers would certainly be unwilling to pay the price
currently charged the price insensitive for the term (or else they would
already be buying it at that price); thus, price would have to drop,
perhaps until it reached cost, at which point further drops would induce
seller exit. Some buyers would be hurt (they would be forced to pay,
at cost, for a term they didn't want), but others would be helped, namely
those who are currently paying their demand price, not a cost-based
price. Whether on balance consumers as a group are helped or hurt is
an open question, depending on the degree to which current self-service

customers value full service and the size of the price-discriminatory margin, but there is no doubt that sellers could be systematically hurt.

Second, Kennedy notes in "Distributive and Paternalist Motives"[54] that even in a competitive market, depending on the shape of supply and demand curves, the buyer group may be helped by a compulsory term. Building on Bruce Ackerman's defense of housing codes,[55] Kennedy notes that if the supply curve for a good is fairly inelastic, and the demand curve has the form that marginal buyers would pay very little more for the good with the compulsory term than without, while infra-marginal buyers value it highly, then price will rise just a little and quantity fall just a bit. The few buyers who exit the market lose, and the sellers may lose quite a lot, both through providing the compulsory term and through lost producer's surplus, while the inframarginal buyers who value the term a great deal more than its new equilibrium cost are helped a great deal. The new equilibrium is competitively stable; all producers cover the marginal cost of producing the new product (the good with the new compulsory feature) that their industry now produces, but it has a *different* distribution of surpluses than the old equilibrium.

Third, the effect of the imposition of a compulsory term may be to lower the *long-term* cost of producing the term. The claim that compulsory terms (such as safety regulations) "force technology" is grounded in a behavioral assumption that innovation tends to be produced by shocks in the environment; that while in theory it might, for instance, be the case that to the degree to which labor market wages are sensitive to safety variations, entrepreneurs *always* work to minimize safety costs, real innovation occurs predominantly when there is an organizational jolt.[56] The "redistribution" from such innovation-inducing shocks, if they indeed exist, is complex. Presumably, in this case, workers may receive the benefits of new technology—lower real resource-cost provision of things they want—at the expense of others (for example customers with an interest in new product) whose demands are ignored for a bit while technical skill goes into satisfying this particular set of demands.

It is worth noting that a parallel postregulatory transformation may occur on the demand side; tastes for the term may be changed, just as the costs of providing the term change as a result of regulation. If this occurs, the beneficiaries of a term may be helped, although their pre-regulatory demand for the term would not cover the postregulatory cost of provision. Thus, for instance, consumers may learn to value a safety feature more once it is mandatory, both because they become more aware of the danger they faced and because they become accustomed to using the precautionary device. At times the "demand" and "costs" sides may both be altered because a regulation is explicitly designed to be preference transforming: regulations against sexual harassment in the work place may well, if their political and educational effect takes hold, both cause women workers to devalue harassment more and male supervisors to value their "freedom" to harass less, thus altering preregulatory estimates of both the extent to which women value a harassment-free workplace and the "cost" of such a workplace.

Fourth, if entitlement-granting programs are administered in such a way that the entitlement granter is able to identify, and seize only the surplus of, inframarginal providers, those with costs below industrywide marginal costs, income will be redistributed. If, for instance, a housing administrator grants only those tenants of landlords with lower than typical costs a right to greater amenities, which they were unwilling or unable to pay for, they'd be enriched, and there would be no shift in the supply of housing.

Fifth, and finally, there are cases in which it is simply unclear, a priori, who is the buyer and who the seller in a relationship, so the legal rule is needed to clarify who is the financial beneficiary, given competing wants. The troublesome real case I have in mind in this regard is the creation of tort or civil rights causes of actions for women workers against sexual harassment, but to clarify the analysis of that case, I will also make reference to a frivolous imaginary case. The problem in the serious case is that it is ambiguous in the unregulated world whether harassers "bought" the right to harass from women workers—that is, paid them *above* marginal product—or whether women workers had to implicitly buy back a harassment-free environment from bosses, so that total wages for nonharassed workers were less than marginal product. (I am assuming, quite unreasonably, just for this analysis that the labor market generally meets the legal economics ideal model: that women workers are informed about the risks of being harassed at particular jobs and that wages *differ* from one job to another depending on the risk of harassment.) If the second scenario is the correct one, granting an entitlement to a harassment-free environment would certainly raise a woman's economic power, would, at a minimum, turn potential harassers into the buyers. The underlying question of which description is more likely to be right seems to turn on whether women could, in the unregulated environment, effectively withhold their "harassability," for if they could not, they would not have to be paid to stop withholding it. (One might also look at the issue by asking whether being harassed is a *marginal* cost of work, hence having an impact on labor supply, or a sunk cost borne upon entry into the market.) Now, here is the frivolous parallel: imagine a competitive seller of a soap that, when a small number of people washed with it, produced a valuable mineral residue on their hands. Would the soap sellers have to pay the lucky buyers for the mineral, or would the buyers have to pay the sellers to keep it? If sellers must pay buyers, the net amount they receive is less than the marginal costs of manufacture if they are to "retain" the mineral. Yet we'd guess that, in the absence of a legal entitlement to the "product of the soap"— the minerals—sellers *would* have to pay buyers, since they couldn't dissociate the mineral production from ordinary sale of the soap and hence capture what amounts to the consumer surplus gained by the lucky mineral-producing buyers. (In addition, the "loss" of the minerals is not a marginal cost to the producers.) If women workers (similarly) can't dissociate harassability from working, then they too probably must "buy back" freedom from harassment and receive less than their marginal product, unless they are given an entitlement to freedom from harassment, for example by making a harassment-free workplace a compulsory contract term.

Under any of these five conditions, then, which may certainly exist in the real world, the mainstream supposition that economic power cannot be redistributed by altering norms of contract law is untrue, even where the alteration is most minimal—that is, where one compulsory term is enforced while all other terms are allowed to vary and permitted bargaining techniques remain unchanged.

Once again, the *descriptive* practice of actual mainstream legal economics, even accepting the more deeply suspect social theory that lies behind *any* conceivable economistic thought, is to justify complacence, to make the existing social world seem either inevitable (as in this last case, the argument for the immutability of the power of contracting parties) or beneficial and conflict free (the defenses of markets and private property, the myth of efficient tort rules). Resuscitating the near-instinctive sense of outrage at gross inequality, selfishness, and the glorification of anticommunitarian exclusiveness requires faith that efforts to rectify these injustices are not, a priori, fanciful and unreasonable. Some of us in CLS, perhaps wrongly, have been preoccupied with the fear that many of the students who pass through law school *feel* sympathetic to progressive goals, but can most comfortably *argue* right-wing economistic politics, as if the case for a private property scheme with considerable faith in undisturbed markets had been convincingly made. We aim to overcome this separation between mind and spirit, to show that the rationalistic claims for resignation are, quite simply, overblown, manipulative, and frequently false.

CHAPTER SIX

The Deification of Process

Despite its difficulties, legal economics, in my view, provides the most coherent and intelligible realization of the liberal social theoretical agenda. The *application* to concrete legal disputes of the ideal of satisfying subjective desire is surely far more troublesome than the legal economists concede; philosophical ambiguities in discerning desire, the intractability of the problem of establishing a legitimate rights framework that determines the extent to which a person is empowered to have her desires accounted for, and the difficulty of ascertaining which concrete institutions would meet even a well-defined welfare maximizer's agenda all contribute to the indeterminacy of the program. Still, it is fairly apparent what the legal economists' basic *vision* is; the same cannot be said for the other dominant academic "school" prevalent in mainstream legal education, that of the Legal Process institutionalists.

In fact, the main problem I face in describing the "confrontation" between Critical Legal Studies and process-oriented scholars is that neither I, nor the Critics I have read, have yet done much to capture (and then confront) the deep utopian yearnings of the Process scholars. While it is relatively easy to identify and then attack the legal economist's utopia—a fully demand-responsive society that distributes power as equally as is compatible with maintaining high levels of production—there is no equally obvious *vision* underlying the Legal Process school. (Perhaps my incapacity to see clearly the deep yearnings behind Process rhetoric while I find the economistic writing so lucid is in some part a function of an obvious historical accident: CLS is *contemporaneous* with the development of legal economics, while the real groundwork in Legal Process thinking was laid while the bulk of the Critics were children. We simply haven't seen, close up, the development and working out of the dream.) I sense, in a very undefined way I could not begin to define, that the most basic image that underlay and animated Legal Process work was the image of the liberal democracies defeating Nazism and Fascism in the Second World War, and that the Legal Process school was, at its core, an effort to give a legal-system–oriented *definition* of the distinction between profoundly good and profoundly evil social systems. But this deep background utopian image (if it is the correct image) translates oddly into the concrete series of propositions the Process school has enumerated: tales of the potential tyranny or limited competence of judges or stories about the need to protect the vitality of popular local institutions against centralized authority by delaying federal *habeas* proceedings until certain state remedies are exhausted seem so far off the point that it is easy to ignore or forget that there *is* a point. The failure of the Critics to confront the Process theorists directly is perhaps even more exaggerated in the case of federalism issues than with issues of judicial and legislative competency and legitimacy. To the degree that there *is* a meaningful core to Process-oriented concerns in the area, rather than a mound of abstract babble about the relationship of federal and state courts, the Critics seem to share, not dispute, the Process theorists' concern. I believe that both groups find *powerful* decentralized and central institutions incompatible in almost precisely the same way.

Perhaps, then, it would be most fruitful to understand the fundamental Process posture not by focusing initially on its stated interests—the allocation of decision-making authority between "private orderers" and the state, between central and local government, between court and legislature—but by placing them in more traditional, nonlegal, political spectrum terms. But the translation from their political centrism to their actual program has so eluded both the Critics and, I believe, the Process writers themselves that issues may never seem joined.

Having expressed a deeply felt skepticism that I will be able to capture the heart of the debate over Process in the way I believe either I or a more lucid expositor *could* capture the debate between legal economists and Critics, I shall nonetheless try to outline both the basic tenets of Process-fixated thought and the occasional attacks on this thought by the Critics.

Broadly speaking, the Process school seems to have the same basically utilitarian vision of the state as the economists. Obviously, well-defined social welfare functions are hard to specify. One can easily founder trying to weigh the degree to which violation of individual "rights" is so "costly" as to amount to a side constraint on the pursuit of welfare; it is hard to say how one could uncontroversially sum utilities across individuals even once one has accepted a formal egalitarian vision that everyone's interest counts equally; determining whether "immoral" (for example sadistic) pleasures deserve satisfaction is likewise difficult.[1] But these problems could readily be skirted, given the fact that, unlike the economists, the Process theorists never focused on which particular *substantive* decisions would meet their vague general goal of "maximizing the satisfaction of valid human wants." Their "utilitarianism" served less as a guide to concrete action than an uncontroversial (they hoped) consensus backdrop for avoiding debate over state function: isn't the idea to make people happy?

Much more important than the extremely vague backdrop of utilitarianism was the concrete vision of state function assumed to correspond to want satisfaction. According to this vision, the state does more than simply specify the rights of private citizens *inter se* and establish some self-limiting rules to protect citizens against tyrannical state overreaching; the Process school's synthesis was *not* the late nineteenth-century classical synthesis. At a minimum, far greater attention is paid to the expanding provision of collective goods and the role of the state in rectifying income maldistribution.[2] Of course, the expansion of legitimate state function requires an increased focus on restraining state power. To the extent that power is not significantly restrained, as it was for the classicists, by a sense that functions beyond rights declaration are inherently out of bounds, *ultra vires,* a more elaborate structure of state-restraining devices had to be adopted: the law of legitimate law had to be, self-consciously, more complex.

Still more important than either the utilitarian backdrop or the post-classical vision of state function, though, was the focus on institutional design, the working out of a system of power allocation that would, in theory, be sure to meet both the general stated substantive end (valid want satisfaction) and the more particular, unstated ones (the political program of centrist postwar technocrats, the mildly activist state). In institutional terms, there were two main obsessions: federalism and a strong court-legislative split.

The argument for federalism—the coexistence of local and central power, each autonomous in its sphere—has been fairly consistent. First, the strength of localities must be preserved in order both to maximize the number of decisions that are made proximate to affected parties and to reduce the number of occasions on which nonparticipants are affected by decisions.[3] Second, competitive models of products markets are extended, by vague analogy, to localities: satisfaction is more likely when the provider faces exit than when service provision is centralized, implicitly monopolistic.[5] Ordinary economistic theories of fiscal federalism in a sense have combined these first two Process school observations: assuming that people have divergent tastes for public goods, waste of two forms (overprovision of public goods to some parties who would demand less and technically inefficient provision of a desired level of goods) can be minimized by offering a variety of public goods packages. Focusing on overprovision, people's location decisions will match people with certain tastes with jurisdictions offering packages that suit these tastes. Each locality will come to consist of a relatively homogeneous population, in terms of public goods preference.[5] Third, in the more legalistic-political models, localities are "laboratories for political experimentation," permitting tests of governance strategy that can either spread by example or die a deserved death.[6]

At the same time, the central government must maintain strong powers against localistic splintering to create a common market, enabling both the realization of scale economies and consumer access to cheapest-cost goods;[7] to avoid the peril of regulatory flight, of jurisdictions being unable to regulate more harshly than the least stringent locality;[8] to tax and transfer, to some extent on the supposition that the national community may frequently be the appropriate one when making aggregate income distribution judgments;[9] to protect minorities, given the strength of the cosmopolitan commitment to diversity, which may be threatened by less diverse provincials;[10] to protect against the imposition of extraterritorial externalities by particular states, especially when affected parties are unrepresented in the decision-making process.[11]

The arguments for strong separation between legislature and judiciary have taken two distinct forms, each associated with a "process" fixation. In one traditional mode, most fully and lucidly expounded by John Ely in *Democracy and Distrust*,[12] the argument is one largely from democracy: suppositions are made about the democratic character of legislatures, the nondemocratic character of courts, and the advantages of democracy as a register of wants that are believed to define appropriate institutional roles. In the other, associated with Henry Hart and Albert Sacks, the argument rests far more on considerations of specialization and technical competence than democratic theory or legitimacy.[13] For Hart and Sacks, welfare maximization requires two fundamentally distinct sorts of decisions to be made: first, rule applications, settling past disputes within a preexisting framework, based on "reasoned elaboration" of the implications of the rule structure, and second, "free adaptation" of the legal system to new circumstances. In their view, courts will do the first job well not just because they become good at it by doing it again and again but because "reasoned elaboration" is a skill one hones in a work environment just like that in which judges work: one in which workers are isolated, in which there is no real chain of command to permit abdication of responsibility; one that affords the worker high status, with an emphasis on craft as the basis of status; one where written explanations of one's decisions are needed. Not only does the basic work environment favor the development of the skill, but the reward system supports it: strong cultural and professional norms serve as a control here, along with peer review whose primary effect is to reinforce these norms rather than strip a bad decision maker of power.

Legislatures will do the second task, that of "free adaptation," well because it is, say Hart and Sacks, a task intrinsically suited to a collegial group, representing such broad constituencies that decision makers will be attuned to social trends and shifting needs, able to see the necessity of compromise in dealing with the new and unsettled, aware of what decisions will be accepted by a heterogeneous population when change is needed. Moreover, the dominant control mechanisms—election, veto, occasional judicial overruling (all explicit institutional checks on the exercise of power)—are well suited to correcting the errors of zealotry that legislators may make, just as professional snubbing restrains the errors of reasoning that judges might be prone to.

Though people still cite the canonical Hart and Sacks materials as if it were quite influential in defining Legal Process concerns, the fact is that most mainstream legal academics' vision of the Process school is much closer to the vision expounded by Ely (or Jesse Choper, or Alexander Bickel). Not surprisingly, then, most of the CLS *critiques* of process orientation confront the arguments for federalism and the "democracy"-based arguments for a presumption of judicial reticence and legislative legitimacy, though there are limited confrontations of the Hart-Sacks "competence" model.

CLS commentators have addressed the Process school's positions on courts and legislatures in a number of ways: first, in a sense, by using the traditional CLS technique of "flipping," or showing that arguments made about one institution can be made reasonably well for the other and second, by noting the troublesome status of democratic theory in liberalism. The published attacks on the Process school's federalist obsession have been sporadic and rather unsystematic, though I shall suggest positions that I believe the CLS commentators might be comfortable with.

The mainstream picture calls for a remarkably cheery view of the legislative process, consistent with decidedly optimistic pluralist political science models (for example the early Robert Dahl).[14] There is a strong presumption of legislative validity in cases in which excluded (generally racial) minorities are unaffected, given both the assumption that indirect or representative democracy is the proper solution to the problem of summing and registering the welfare-seeking desires of individuals *and* the assumption that existing legislatures come reasonably close to meeting the ideals of representative democracy. The presumption that actual legislatures are, in fact, "democratic" depends, of course, on assumptions that they are not unduly influenced or captured; that nonparticipation by some constituencies in the electoral process doesn't preclude some groups from being heard; and that no majority is so permanent as to be able to ignore the interests of any potential allies—that is, that pluralistic power is dispersed by the need to form shifting coalitions, that there is no class of perennial winners and none of perennial losers. The assumption that legislative action should ordinarily dominate referenda is based in large part on its unique capacity to reflect distinctions in "intensity of preferences" on issues and in part on a fear of misinformation and sporadic, class-biased participation in frequent referenda.

The process-oriented picture of the judicial role, particularly in its grandiose, constitutional mode, is largely complementary to the optimistic picture of the legislature in Ely's picture. The judiciary must provide structural protection of two distinct types: it must allocate decision-making authority to the proper body, policing the boundaries between state and central authority, between adjudicating courts and policy-making legislatures; and it must ensure that the legislature in fact functions as democratically as it should, cleaning up self-interested antidemocratic process decisions by legislators desiring to preserve their own power (for example through reapportionment decisions, or by barring discrimination in voting rights). The judiciary must also recognize that the cheeriest assumptions about democracy will occasionally break down, that some groups will be relegated to the status of perpetual losers, even when the courts have ensured that they are entitled to *participate* in the legislative process. Courts must substantively *correct* legislation that prejudices the interests of groups who tend to remain powerless, unaccounted for.

Most mainstream Process adherents disclaim any belief that judges are uniquely capable of protecting individual rights, believing instead that rights are validly declared when their pedigree is proper (that is, determined as an outcome of a functioning democratic process in which no group's interests are discounted). There is surely, though, also a centrist Process tradition (associated with constitutionalists like Tribe,[15] Perry,[16] Karst,[17] Fiss,[18] and Epstein[19]) that postulates that the courts are uniquely qualified to protect one version or another of individual rights against zealous majorities who are too willing to sacrifice particular persons expediently to benefit the mass. People who believe in the court's *obligation* to "protect" individual rights generally do fear that the definition or declaration of rights might become a pretext for courts to make political decisions they believe ought to be committed to the legislature. Generally, their recourse is to one of two distinct postreligious visions of natural law. First, they may believe that courts are able to observe profound, widely shared values in declaring what is to be protected against legislative overreaching (see, for example, Wellington or early Perry)[20] and that "natural" rights are defined by widespread convention. Second, they may believe that concrete rights can be derived by calling on a generally acceptable theory of justice (see, for example, Michelman on Rawls,[21] or Epstein in large measure on libertarians like Nozick)[22] that people may not (know that they) agree on the definition of particular rights but *do* agree on the sorts of arguments one can make to justify one's views, and that once a certain justificatory procedure is adopted, only particular rights will in fact be justifiable.

Courts and Legislatures

CLS critics have ultimately denied that there is much to be gained by paying attention to these traditional process concerns. Kennedy's introductory aside in "Distributive and Paternalist Motives" may be unusually dismissive of process obsession, but I doubt that it is atypical of the CLS position in anything but its candor: "I will have nothing to say about the impact of 'institutional competence' considerations on the motives for lawmaking I discuss. I assume that the only grounds for distinguishing between courts, legislatures and administrative agencies as lawmakers are (i) that the false consciousness of the public requires it or (ii) that the decisionmaker has a quite specific theory about how his or her particular situation should modify his or her pursuit of institutional objectives."[23] How did CLS scholars get to this point? I take it that the erosion process has resulted from their battering simultaneously at the integrity of both traditional poles, wearing away the vacuum boundary between court and legislature by denying both the traditional privileged status of the legislature and the traditionally asserted infirmities and virtues of the courts.

The Problem of Legislation

There seem to be two distinct traditions within CLS criticizing the presumed legitimacy of legislative choice. One, most closely associated with Unger, calls into question whether even truly democratic collective choice can be legitimated within liberal social theory.[24] A second, perhaps most lucidly presented by Richard Parker[25] but associated with Mark Tushnet[26] as well, questions the degree to which actual functioning institutions come close enough to meeting the Process theorists' vision of a democratic utopia to deserve the deference owed to a more pristine legislature.

Unger's critique has two messages, broadly speaking, neither of which strikes me as representing quite as sharp an assault on the traditional picture as he seems to imagine. The first one is, in a sense, a restatement of the liberal individualist attack on the collective. If the group is fundamentally artificial and only the individual truly natural, within liberal thought, then group decisions should be seen to express nothing more than an arbitrary consensus of particular others. The decisions cannot be right *for the group,* cannot express its nature or purpose, not just because liberals are value skeptics, invariably unsure of what is right for anyone, but because there simply is no sensible entity with interests to be advanced. The decisions may be right for *many* (maybe even nearly all) particular others, but that does not, in and of itself, sway any particular person who is disadvantaged by a collective choice; this is so, first, because an arbitrary desire is no less arbitrary because widespread and, second and more important, because one's own losses are readily emotionally separable from the gains of others, are related at all, in fact, only if one chooses (privately, subjectively, arbitrarily) to make them so.

In a sense, even if democracy functions perfectly to advance utilitarian ends, the altruism of the perfect utilitarian stance, which demands that each person adopt a posture of complete neutrality between his own and others' ends, is incompatible with the fundamental *cultural* attitude of individualism, even if it expresses itself as impeccably individualistic, doing nothing more than adding up the satisfactions of isolated nomads.[27] As is often the case, I think that Unger is inadequately attuned to the nuances of Anglo-American utilitarian thought to criticize it completely fairly. As I discussed in Chapter 4, postutilitarian legal economists have felt the need to purge utilitarian thought of its selfless objective moral content, preferring to argue that wealth maximization is a selfishly beneficial strategy rather than a mandatory moral stance. But utilitarians believed, not entirely unreasonably, that they had mediated the tension between moral objectivists and subjectivists by emphasizing the plurality of conceptions of well-lived lives (as the subjectivists did), while demanding, like the objectivists, an extremely weak, limited, nonegotistical duty not to discount others. (The objective moral conception might even be thought to be *bolstered* by value subjectivism generally, insofar as a traditional argument for discounting the fulfillment of others' dreams was that their dreams were "objectively unworthy," a position the value skeptic finds unfathomable.) If the utilitarian effort fails as a mediation of the contradiction between subjectivism and objectivism, as I believe it does, it is because the "objective values" that give rise to the duty to maximize utility are based on far *stronger* ethical presuppositions than utilitarians like to suggest in emphasizing their strongly subjectivist side. Neither its equality of regard for each actor's satisfaction, nor its focus on pleasure and pain rather than self-realization or salvation as goals, nor its failure to recognize distinct attachments to community members is a weak ethical postulate. I am simply uncertain whether Unger's account of the ultimately contradictory liberal accommodations to democracy and utilitarianism is based, like mine, on the supposition that the utilitarians falsely portrayed their "objective" commitment as far weaker than it really was, though, because Unger's account of utilitarianism are so cryptic.

While this first criticism seems reasonably applicable to a Process theorist like Ely, who neither puts explicit limits on the democratic agenda nor justifies how the morally compulsory altruism of traditional utilitarianism can be squared with his general value skepticism,[28] it is surely possible to conceive of a limited-agenda utilitarian democrat who would be unmoved by Unger's critique. If, say, the legislative agenda is limited to setting demand for technically nondivisible goods (such as defense or air pollution control efforts), and preferences for these goods must be registered *somehow,* given the incapacity of markets to provide them at optimal levels, since it is impossible to preclude nonpurchasers from benefiting, then legislation is simply the best of the second-best options. At the same time, if it is conceivable that no legislation is legitimate that involves the *transfer* of consumption power from one person to another, then democracy need not threaten thoroughly non-altruistic individualism. In order to give his critique the bite he wanted, Unger would have had to address the conceptual and practical impossibility of limiting legislation in such a way that only desired collective goods would be purchased, and in such a way that the world of actors in a hypothetically stateless setting would otherwise be unaltered. While many of the CLS critiques of the legal economists that I sketched in the last chapter do indeed address and try to refute the claim that one can imagine an entitlements framework that would have no impact at all on the relative power of individuals, Unger's first criticism seems, in its wholly theoretical form, rather empty.

It is only when one looks at the second critique as well that one can see the problem Unger may have been addressing in making what for him appears to be the wholly separate first point. Unger's second argument is that the *task* of democratic institutions is ambiguous, even if recalcitrant individuals believe that they should experience the express desires of the group as anything but a tyrannical confluence of particular tastes. The argument is one between what might be thought of as republican and pluralist conceptions, between legal theorists (like Cass Sunstein)[29] who view the legislature as seeking to enunciate consensus values and those (like Ely or Choper)[30] who think that the legislature should simply try to aggregate private desires as well as possible, attempting to minimize the possibility that some will get their way too often through being part of a permanent majority.

Under the first view, *many* political positions taken in daily legislative life are suspect (even if, for republican theorists like Bickel, no institution ought to correct them);[31] only positions taken from a disinterested perspective, with an eye toward public goals, are privileged. But nothing would tell us whether legislators' solemn invocations of ideals of commonweal are a hypocritical cover for self-seeking constituents or if a habit of public-spirited *talk* actually restrains private self-aggrandizement; nor would we know if there really *are* consensus values to be enunciated rather than winners and losers in value clashes. But Ely and Choper may jump too quickly from the idea that values actually clash to the idea that the clashes are legitimately presented as battles of desires rather than battles of perception of the correct *public* policy. To take an easy analogy, you and I might disagree over the speed of a passing vehicle (just as we might dispute the proper distribution of income) without believing that our disagreement is simply a clash of tastes. The basic point, though, is that, given this ambiguity over the fundamental democratic task, any assertion that "democracy" meets some unambiguously desired end seems a bit hasty. The pluralist horse-trading legislature lacks the republican virtue that legitimates for some, but the republican legislature may not even resemble a limited-role collective-goods purchaser, which simply registers a limited class of selfish preferences. The republican assembly may be unlimited in its reach because its failure to announce openly and confront the fact that there is nothing but selfish desire leaves issues on the agenda that would be unthinkable if spoken of as private bounty seeking. Talk of self-seeking clearly reveals the problem of individuals experiencing themselves as victims of individual arbitrariness at the theoretical level, since the pluralist makes no attempt to separate collective from want-satisfying discourse. But talk of consensus values may leave us more vulnerable to what the egotist should see as a redistributive grab at the *practical* level. It is in a regime of open, collective value affirmation that one can find oneself losing out to others on *any* topic; it is only in such a regime that there are no obvious limits on legitimate state agenda.

It is almost surely the case, though, that the political strength of the mainstream romanticization of the legislature is undermined to a greater extent by CLS reiteration of the standard left-liberal political science critiques of pluralist description, their picture of power dispersion in both the legislature and the society. Parker's list of six critiques of Ely and Choper is fairly typical.[32] His first line of criticism is that there is no convincing reason to believe that the large number of people who do not participate in the political process either acquiesce in current decisions, simply feeling that the decisions being made without them are much like the ones they would make, or are just random individuals with random views who have integrated the calculation that it is too costly to participate, given the objective probability of affecting outcome. They may instead be discouraged, disengaged because of their powerlessness, withdrawn because they are aware that they would be unable to bring their distinct agendas to fruition.

Second, he claims that the capacity to act in the political sphere is not just randomly distributed but class correlated. Pluralists like Ely acknowledge that some discernible groups are perennially disempowered, but they assume that disempowerment is predominantly a function of racism. While Parker would hardly deny the significance of racial prejudice, he notes both that vast numbers of people participate ineffectively, either because their interests as a class are discounted or their class-specific cultural style of self-presentation is devalued, *and* that race and class prejudice are inextricably intertwined. Ely's model of racially disempowered citizens, dependent as it is on the notion that the racial majority treats racial minorities as "other," as distant, not quite human creatures, has as its corollary that racism can be overcome by increasing social contact between the races, thus overcoming "other-ness." Parker points out that the weakness of the corollary casts doubt on the main premise: if racist attitudes are systematically reinforced rather than eliminated when middle-class whites increase their contact with lower-class blacks, then it is not simply race that divides us, not simply race that leads to systematic disadvantage.

Third, pluralist theorists who applaud the extent to which no discernible group perennially wins out in a series of discrete public policy disputes underestimate the importance of agenda setting: what counts as a plausible topic for legislative debate may be far more class biased than decisions within the constricted agenda would appear to be. Fourth, the legislative process is hardly as open as the romanticized model would imply. Neither Ely nor Choper deals particularly effectively with the existence of lobbying, of back-room dealing, of unscrutinized last-minute changes in technically complex legislation about which some constituencies are far better informed than others. Fifth, groups that tend to be outsiders in the political process (like prisoners) may be better heard when their views are directly solicited (as they might be in class-action court hearings, depending on the capacity of socially distant but well-practiced judges to hear distinct voices) than when they are represented by people who may have only a general, weak concern for their welfare. They may not be "disregarded" as a group, in the very weak sense that Ely speaks of in chastising majoritarian handling of racial minorities; but since legislators are *not* themselves prisoners, they have little sense of what it is like to be one, and since prisoners do not *as* prisoners form a significant pluralist voting bloc, there is little reason to believe that much effort will be made to solicit their concerns in a legislative context.

Sixth, and finally, the pluralist model assumes that dispersion of power in the legislative process is tantamount to dispersion of significant power; to the extent that a subset of nominally private parties exercises some of the same sorts of power that we often fear the state will exercise over others, equal access to control of the state would mean less than the pluralists desire, even if it were in fact available.

It is only in exploring the last of these points that I think one can gain some sense of the exasperation Critics sometimes feel at solemn discussions of traditional Process issues. (I have no doubt that the Critics' exasperation in turn exasperates the Process theorists, who wonder what contribution the CLS faction intends to make to the question of the proper degree of deference to be paid to legislatures.) Few Critics denigrate the real significance of traditional electoral participation in the Western democracies; I, for one, certainly have no doubt that, because we can vote, we are significantly empowered to control aspects of the direction of community life that would be far harder to control by other means (such as passive resistance to especially onerous government policy). The Polish people could far more readily control their collective destinies if permitted to vote than they can through more or less repressed general strikes. Process scholars sometimes go partly astray in overstating the responsiveness of state officials to the entire citizenry; but if that were their main flaw, I think the Critics could engage some variant of the Process debate to a greater degree, joining up with either judicial, constitutional, or legislative reformers out to rid the legislative system of various forms of corruption (for example, by engaging in campaign finance reform, or trying to shift rules on access to public forums). And indeed it does seem to me that one of the frustrations Critics sometimes feel with the incessant focus on the antimajoritarian powers of the courts is that those fixated on those powers may not pay nearly enough attention to the parallel antimajoritarian powers of, say, congressional lobbyists.

But the Critics, perhaps more traditionally Marxist in this regard than in any other I can discern, are probably more concerned by the "public" focus of those ostensibly concerned with disempowerment. Most of our daily experiences of thorough disempowerment, of subjection to the kinds of power we associate with truly totalitarian imagery, are in relation to people who are in the liberal imagination's *private* sphere, whether teachers, husbands, or, most significant in the Marxist tradition, bosses. The disempowerment one faces at work, though, goes so far beyond the scope of what is usually comprehended by Process-analyzed pleas for formal democratization of the workplace that all election-centered talk seems utterly beside the point. In the Critical picture, disempowerment is not peripheral, a result of the exclusion of workers' representatives from some nominally powerful board or other, but is enacted in innumerable daily battles. To use Marxist language, workers sell their labor power (capacity to work), while bosses require labor (work), and daily work life is a struggle to extract labor from labor power on terms as close as possible to those the boss desires.[33] Workers are by no means simply victims in this struggle; they are empowered partly as individuals operating in markets (through the capacity to leave, to work elsewhere) partly by the explicit efforts of the state (through protective legislation), partly by their collective capacity to resist. Most Critics probably believe that it is in honing the capacity to resist that the greatest gains will lie, not in altering state protective functions; as I shall discuss in Chapters Eight and Nine, one of the key state functions may be to dull the capacity to imagine appropriate forms of resistance. Whatever the route, the struggle for fuller empowerment in that critical sphere seems so skew to the issue of, say, overreaching courts that one wonders whether the Critics and those in the mainstream are observing the same world of powerlessness.

The picture appears similar if we focus on gender hierarchy rather than hierarchy in the production process. Routine subjection to sexual violence is central in and constitutive of women's lives, in their daily disempowerment.[34] Once again, like workers vis-à-vis bosses, women are not utterly disempowered vis-à-vis men: they have some, imperfect, exit options (parallel to the exit options workers have) to shun long-term abusive relations, and they similarly receive some protection from the state through antibattery and antirape laws. I don't mean to be purely rhetorically manipulative, though, when I suggest that few women felt nearly as disempowered by the extramajoritarianism of Roe v. Wade as by the pervasiveness of sexual violence. And while the *attack* on sexual violence can itself be partly directed by a responsive state (I suppose rape law reform is the classic example), there are real limitations to focusing political energy on the state in this area.[35]

The Problem of Adjudication

In trying to denigrate the Process school's emphasis on maintaining a strong separation of powers, the Critics have not only questioned the presumption of deference to the legislature but have decried the presumption that courts have any special abilities that entitle them to some separate, legitimate sphere of power. It is, of course, not predetermined what message one should take away if one believes simultaneously that there is neither any uniquely legitimate judicial process *nor* any theoretically or factually legitimate set of democratic institutions. It is, I believe, in their attacks on the Process school that CLS adherents can justly be viewed *within the Process tradition* as wholly negative. The point is not that CLS has a different theory of power allocation than this judicial activist or that proponent of judicial restraint; it is rather that the attempts to generalize about *types* of institutions and the outcomes they are likely to produce, given their archetypal traits, is largely beside the point. To focus on the problem of judicial tyranny—as if the alternative were the fabulous empowerment we all get by voting for our Congressmen, as if any degree of empowerment wholly within the traditional public sphere were adequate—is simply, as I have noted, a blinding deflection. At the same time, to look to apolitical courts to protect our "rights" is chimerical: judges are just actors with some command over state force and socially acceptable chatter; they are not acting in some privileged domain of reason that can or ought to be protected from openly political conversation.

The Hart and Sacks model of "reasoned elaboration" of established rules, the process of deciding cases *under* the rules, seems hopeless as a description of an apolitical method. At the preliminary epistemological level that Unger focuses on, the problem is that courts are caught in what he sees (not entirely convincingly) as a hopeless bind: neither Formalist nor purposivist adjudication seems a plausible option. Purposivism alone is consistent with modern, liberal accounts of knowledge, of the way we categorize. Categories (the names of the "things" to which the legal rules judges elaborate refer) are established to further the interests of the categorizers, and they are accurate not when they correspond to some fixed, Formalist understanding of a term but when they advance interests. But a purposive reading of rules is at base inconsistent with both the separation of powers and the more general liberal commitment to fixed entitlements on which individuals can rely. Unger focuses on the fact that a multiplicity of ends will be served by any conceivable rule, and that decisions about how to balance these competing ends in deciding how to apply the rule will thus always be politicized. Were I to defend his claim that purposive adjudication is inconsistent with "reasoned elaboration," I would emphasize an even more ineradicable problem in thinking of the purposive applications of rules to facts as technical: since there are no metarules to tell us when to ignore and when to tolerate a general rule when its application to a particular case may violate its ostensible purpose, it is hard to imagine either that any individual could readily describe his "rights" or that anyone could be certain that the court was simply trying to meet legislative ends, given judicial freedom to determine at what level of specificity the ends must be met in particular cases. Unger is surely more convincing in noting that while Formalism restores the separation of powers and diminishes the fear of judicial domination, it is inconsistent with modern liberal accounts of knowledge, relying on either socially discredited correspondence views of language, in which words simply match up to objects in the world that naturally differentiate themselves from one another, or ideals of intelligible essences.[36]

This set of observations can be illustrated readily with a familiar type of case. Assume that the question confronting a court is whether a shopping center owner can have unwanted pickets arrested as trespassers. Unger's point is that the purposive judge is in a bind when she looks to the list of reasons that justify invocation of state authority to stop trespass and sees that some purposes will probably be met (for example, the desire of an owner not to feel contaminated by seeing his property made useful to advocates of positions he loathes) while others might be frustrated (for example, if the purpose of trespass law generally is to ensure that property is used in the way in which it is most highly valued, by ensuring that there is an owner who controls its alienation, then it is unclear whether the law should be used when transaction-cost problems preclude groups from manifesting their factually intense desire to use the property). I would emphasize instead the degree to which the judges are free from constraint because we cannot tell whether it is appropriate to apply the rule whose purpose is met in "like" cases to *this* case: the desire to protect the privacy of private property owners might or might not be invoked when there is a weak fit between purpose (privacy protection) and the instance of the category (expelling people from private property generally may protect privacy; the shopping center is an instance of private property, but privacy interests are hardly at their strongest in this context). Finally, the Formalist effort to show that decisions follow mechanically from language may also be doomed: we may say that the state intervenes whenever owners of private property want someone removed, but there will be innumerable interpretive difficulties. (Is this truly private property, or private property held in some sort of public trust? What do we make of the fact that people are invited generally onto the premises? Are corporate managers of shopping centers with a general policy against pickets the sort of "owners" of parcels we had in mind when we first described trespass law?)

The problem is almost surely even *worse* in some ways than Unger initially implied. If the CLS commentators are correct that we are simultaneously drawn to contradictory world pictures, whether at a descriptive level (for example, the choice between picturing activity in intentionalistic or deterministic modes, the choice between models of production incentives grounded predominantly in protecting the producer's security and those grounded in beliefs that the insecurity generated by competition maximizes product) or the normative level (for example, the choice between paternalism and nonpaternalism, between self-reliant individualism and altruism), then the judges will always have to make profoundly political choices in elaborating any rule structure, since each one has within it philosophically clashing elements. Reasonably noncontroversial ends, then, will always clash, even if we could assume—quite heroically, of course—that judges could regularly discern the factual impact of decisions on any particular end. Of course, perceptions about the sorts of instrumental judgments judges regularly must make will almost invariably turn on philosophical or political predispositions, given the unavailability of convincing data. For example, to take a case from Kennedy's earliest (unpublished) attack on Hart and Sacks,[37] neither the actual deterrent impact on murder of refusing to allow a testator's killer to become a beneficiary nor the impact of overturning precise will language on a testator's confidence that the state will respect her wishes can conceivably be known with any certainty at all, and "intuitions" on the issue are largely reflective of the sorts of assumptions about human nature that ground all political choice.

The notion that courts have a unique reasoning capacity to discover and protect moral or political rights is just as suspect as the claim that they are uniquely able to enforce and elaborate a preset legal rights framework. Whether the source of court-declared substantive rights is supposed to be shared values, elaborated social theory, or whether the court's role is ostensibly more restricted, limited to ensuring that the rights declared by the legislature are legitimate, properly pedigreed in a sense, the actual content of court-certified rights will be as much the product of political debate as any legislative outcome could be.

For some (like Harry Wellington or Ronald Dworkin[38]), of course, a special judicial sensitivity to deeply shared values gives judges a legitimate *technical* rights-declaring power. The critique that judges are expressing private political preferences in announcing rights is silenced because judges are simply *discovering* the principles that are both common, not divisive, and outside, not within, them. Moreover, the court is not just legitimately nontyrannical but *needed*. The legislature does not, in process terms, adequately register deep collective values, since legislatures often are mired in reflecting day-to-day whims, not long-term collective principles.

Some of the CLS critiques of this vision of judicial role closely resemble the critiques that advocates of relative judicial passivity, such as Ely, have made. Tushnet points out that the existence of contrary legislation that the court seeks to overrule makes it doubtful that deeply shared values are violated by the enactment, except on the dubious assumption that the legislature profoundly misunderstood the impact of its choice.[39] Further, both Paul Brest and Tushnet note that the idea that shared values exist at all depends on the assumption that the society is far more politically and culturally unified than would seem to be the case. As Brest emphasized in his attack on Owen Fiss's invocation of shared values language, a group of largely upper-middle-class male Anglo-Saxon judges may often falsely discern that certain subcultural commitments are far more universal than they really are; conceptions of privacy, distinctions between rights and powers, ideas about both the nature and centrality of expression are hardly insensitive to our distinct life experiences.[40] Once again, though, the attack is not readily differentiable from ones that mainstream advocates of restraint, such as Ely, make.[41]

Unger's critiques of the privileged rational status of shared values adjudication do seem somewhat more peculiar to the CLS perspective. The first criticism simply echoes Unger's critique of legislative legitimacy within liberal thought: given the liberal premise of value subjectivity, even the most deeply shared values are like shallowly shared political goals, the accidental congruence of particular wills.[42] Second, to the extent that natural rights are supposed to derive from a common sense of what is truly socially constitutive, what bedrock notions define the society, then they blur the fact-value distinction so critical to liberal epistemology. Even if judges could *factually* discern what principles were required to maintain an existing, recognizable social structure, the judges could not permissibly derive an "ought" from an "is," could not legitimately privilege that existing social structure.[43]

For others who see a special judicial role, rights enunciation is derivative of the reasoned interpretation of acceptable moral theory. Unger largely addresses the constitutional theorists' tradition (most trenchantly elucidated by Michelman) that sees the Rawlsian theory of justice as embodying a moral framework that judges can utilize in reaching concrete results.[44] Tushnet likewise engages the Rawlsians (like Michelman) and, to a lesser extent, the libertarians (like Epstein).[45] Both believe it is impossible to imagine that judicial reasoning grounded in social theory can be usefully separated from ordinary political discourse. Unger's focal point is, as usual, epistemological: he notes that to the extent that Rawls's theory is grounded in hypothesizing the social contracts that would be reached by people functioning behind a veil of ignorance of one's circumstances, with only the universal capacity of reason, not the individuating particularity of taste, it cannot generate concrete, particular results, since abstract people can have no actual programs. If, though, one posits that people know their actual ends, it is impossible to imagine how one could reach universal agreement on any principle that interferes with particular ends. Unger's point, though, simply fails to address Rawls's effort to avoid the problem he poses, his attempt to posit an intermediate category between universal reason and particular desire, the category of "primary goods," which are things (like security, material well-being) that we all, as abstract universal thinkers, know that we would seek once rendered concrete. Whether we could in fact construct concrete political disputes over "primary goods" is deeply troublesome, but Unger does not do much to advance the debate by simply ignoring Rawls's efforts.[46]

Tushnet's critique seems harder to dismiss. In the absence of social consensus, acceptance of the Rawlsian theory by some standards of truth would hardly validate the theory. The point is obviously strengthened when one recognizes the existence of *competing* moral theoretical traditions within liberalism: the mildly altruistic Rawlsian one, Nozick's libertarianism, pure utilitarianism. Even if judges could divine the implications of any one of these moral theories, the choice of theoretical starting point would hardly seem an outcome of neutral reason. Tushnet also notes that the legal system may simply never raise issues of rights as understood by a general theory of justice. To put the point concretely, given the fact that courts are rarely asked to decide cases systematically involving the distribution of income, it is unlikely that they could explore and explicate all the facets of a justice theory with distributive implications (like Rawls's difference principle or Nozick's principle that past injustices must be rectified by current redistribution). Once one recognizes that the courts cannot institutionally enact the preferred theory, one would need some sort of rational "second-best" account that gives judges guidance as to when it is worthwhile to realize parts of a program that might make sense only if fully implemented.

The Critics have been equally skeptical of claims that judges can avoid supposedly illegitimate politics simply by seeking, as Ely would have them do, to determine that the existing entitlement framework was legitimately established. All declared rights are valid in this view if the legislative process is nonexclusive and if the losers from a particular declaration of entitlements were not victims of dismissive prejudice. The attacks on the notion that the courts' special role is to certify pedigree is fourfold.

First, to the extent that there is controversy over the extent to which legislatures are democratic, judicial decisions about the degree of deference they will pay to actual decisions is a result both of quite overtly political judgments about what adequately participatory democracy is and covertly political descriptive visions of what actually goes on in legislatures.[47]

Second, Brest and Parker[48] (as well as commentators outside CLS like Tribe)[49] have argued that it is meaningless to insist that courts should step in to correct process breakdowns manifested in prejudice against excluded groups unless one has a substantive political theory of when "prejudice" against a group is legitimate. (Gays' interests may obviously be minimized, but if gayness is legitimately impermissible, the exclusion is hardly unwarranted. Neither the validity of prejudice against homosexuality nor the validity of homosexuality itself can be assured by noting that *decisions* about its legitimacy are made with less than full input from gays.)

Third, Brest points out that almost any substantive political decisions could readily be justified in process-oriented terms, so that the supposed restriction of courts to process correction would pose little actual restraining power. Ely's favorite bête noir, the decisions striking down blanket prohibitions of abortion, could certainly be framed as simply correcting the long-standing, exclusively male legislative perspective on the abortion issue.[50]

Fourth and finally, Tushnet,[51] and Parker[52] in particular (as well as Tribe),[53] straightforwardly castigate Ely for his emphasis on process. If, says Tushnet, even perfectly democratic decisions fail to meet important substantive goals, why should we support them? Tushnet especially emphasizes civil rights and antiwar activity as involving significant ends, comprehensible without reference to whether racist or prowar activity is being supported by legislatures. [54] Moreover, process-related goals, he notes, must be explained by reference to substantive ends (for example, democratic decision making is desirable insofar as it contributes to the development of people's capacities to make decisions), while substantive goals are hardly justified by reference to process-related ends. Parker makes a parallel point in a fashion I find even more persuasive: since it is impossible to imagine framing any direct distributive claim in process terms, and since there is always a perfectly acceptable procedural reason for failing to alleviate maldistribution, apart from the ontological dismissal of some citizens' concerns (that is, that it is costly to alter income shares), the "rights" that can be enunciated by a process-fixated court are inevitably limited in ways that hardly seem compelling.[55]

Federalism

There is little critical legal writing that addresses either the institutionalists' general fondness for federalism or the more particular ways in which the theoretical virtues of federalism are purportedly realized in our legal universe. Al Katz[56] and Tushnet[57] have certainly *discussed* traditional federal courts issues, but it would be difficult indeed to translate their discussions into the sort of confrontation or dialogue with the obsessed federalists that Tushnet, Brest, or Parker have had with those fixed on the allocation of power between court and legislature. Gerald Frug's article "The City as a Legal Concept"[58] could be read as an attack on both the theoretical possibility and the actual existence of a commitment to federalism within a liberal polity, but, once more, it does not obviously dispute the Process school's version of its federalist commitment. Only Thomas Heller's recent essay on the possibility of European economic integration[59] directly addresses the federalist program, and it is largely a historical account of shifts in the allocation of power between central and local authority that accompanied the shifts within liberal models from an infant-industry–developing activist state to a laissez-faire state to a market-failure-correcting activist state. It is not at all clear that the Critics have made unique contributions to the discussion of federalism.

   Katz has used the historical unfolding of federal courts issues to illustrate one of his central themes—the penchant of liberal thinkers to avoid duality, confrontation, and political choice by establishing mediating terms between potentially conflicting vacuum-bounded categories. Thus, for instance, the Erie Railroad v. Tompkins question (whether federal or state law applies in a diversity suit in federal court to questions that may or may not be substantive rather than "purely procedural") is transformed over time from an overt battle to determine which competing sovereign has absolute authority to regulate a partic-

ular form of activity into a far less well defined question of federal judicial
deference to (federal) Congress, which can always choose to expand
federal authority (through either greater substantive preemption or expansion of court power under the diversity clause). What was once a
battle between substantive ideals—in that some people might believe
that diversity jurisdiction promises better central resolution of disputes
while others might favor the experimentation of localism, of many state-
by-state solutions—is covertly transformed into another glorification of
the *mood* of judicial deference or passivity. But I cannot really gather,
reading Katz, whether he thinks that the underlying federalist claims
themselves would be sensible if not submerged by *other* process concerns, or whether he believes that a more authentic attachment to federalism would be worthwhile or realizable.

Frug argues that the ostensible liberal commitment to strong local
authority is simply bogus. Municipalities have never been allowed much
authority in liberal society. Most important, they are formally precluded
from engaging in any number of traditionally private enterprises, although such entry by cities might radically expand the domain of life
controlled democratically. Moreover, there are limits on their public
authority: to tax, to borrow, to regulate. His argument has an odd
structure, though. While one could discern some fairly simple descriptive
claims and policy recommendations (that cities are restricted in the
activities they have been allowed to perform, that the world would be
better if cities could start banks, insurance companies, and so on to
serve those uncovered in a private market), the bulk of the piece seems
to be focused less on the virtues of a genuine commitment to both
localism and government-run enterprise than on explicating the connection between a supposed aspect of liberal consciousness and the legal
infirmities of municipal corporations. Frug's claim, which he derives in
part from his reading of Unger and Kennedy, is that liberal thought
must be characterized by vacuum-bounded dualisms, that the liberal
world picture is most reassuring when it classifies an event as falling
within the sphere of reason or desire, freedom or necessity, threatening
state or contractual freedom expansion in the private sphere. It is interesting to note (and, to my jaundiced eye, revealing of the difficulty
of claims made about "thought systems" at this general a level, without
adequate attention to demonstration through example) that Frug never
addresses Katz's almost diametrically *opposite* claim, that liberals invariably try to establish mediating, permeably bounded categories,
abhorring the moral absolutism of vacuum-bounded dualities. Kennedy,

incidentally, tried to resolve to some degree the discordance between the Katz and Frug positions by arguing that liberalism requires a complete set of arguments for dualism and a complete set for permeable boundaries;[60] Heller's claim is that permeable boundaries are associated with interstitial, "technical" professional questions, while vacuum-bounded categories are associated with popular legal ideology.[61] I remain skeptical that there is any bite at all to general theories of categorization modes, whether anything interesting can be said about a cultural or political system in terms of its purported preference for one or another form of boundary theory. At any rate, a significant duality Frug wants to explore is that between individual and state; to the extent that the city is an intermediate organization, neither as central as the state nor as free from group aspects as the isolated subject, it is suspect.

Frug's account of the disempowerment of cities is not wholly unpersuasive, but it seems significantly overstated. First, there seems little reason to believe his claim that, in the absence of restrictive enabling legislation, localities would engage in far more collective economic activity than a highly antistatist United States is willing to support politically (that is, he overfocuses on formal legal inhibitions to certain activity). And second, there is no reason to believe that there is much immediate promise of changed political practice in locally run enterprises; municipal electric systems, cable television, and the like have hardly proved to be politically transformative institutions.

His claim that liberal *thought* is inexorably dualistic and that liberal *institutional practice* reflects whatever tendency there might be toward dualistic thought by weakening intermediate institutions is even less persuasive though. The epistemological claim not only seems to fail to confront the sorts of examples Katz provides of permeably bounded categories; it characterizes a system of thought at a highly general level without proposing any good theory as to why the claimed general trait might advance any systemic interests. The associated individualism-altruism, rules-standards dilemmas that Kennedy claimed were constitutive of liberal thought were obviously an *incomplete* account of a thought system; since it is inevitable that no single observation can encompass a whole complex body of practice and justification, it is unsurprising that if Kennedy is interpreted as advancing a highly general predictive theory (that rules advocacy is associated with individualism), that theory will often be wrong. But there are good reasons to believe both that issues of the relationship between self and others are central ones facing actors in any imaginable culture *and* that a rule or standard orientation will advance distinct visions of dealing with the dilemma; moreover, the *overt* political postures of liberal thinking implicate both concerns about legality (rules) and the formal individual rights that legality may vindicate. Frug's purported organizing principle seems more suspect: he has failed to describe any basic human issue that the unvarying use of dualistic rather than mediated categories would tend to serve, nor can he demonstrate any *explicit* liberal political commitment to dualism itself or any of its (supposed) implications. Whereas the use of some dualistic categories (like the public-private one) undoubtedly has important implications, it is difficult to imagine how one might sustain the claim either that the origin of the important distinction is in dualism or that vacuum boundedness itself helps to sustain the particular vacuum boundary.

The empirical claim is dubious too. Even if one accepts what strikes me as Frug's plausible claim that municipal corporations are impotent, he has hardly dealt with the more general claim (perhaps most often associated with Tocqueville)[62] that America, a liberal society, is quintessentially group pluralistic, *dominated* by the very sorts of intermediate institutions that Frug denies can maintain vitality. Even if the sorts of intermediate groups Tocqueville observed (churches, fraternal organizations) have lost some vigor, it is surely not clear that they were never significant during periods Frug would surely admit were dominated by "liberal consciousness."

At any rate, if one reads Frug strictly as CLS commentary on the Process school's commitment to federalism, his work can be seen largely as a denial of the strength of that commitment. Since, however, he never expressly disputes the claim by mainstream Process theorists that the local institutions they supposedly seek to maintain and strengthen (like independent state courts) are either less significant than those he wants to revive or, in fact, just as powerless as municipalities, it is hard to see that his criticism represents, or was intended to be, a potent part of the skeptical anti–Process school literature.

Tushnet seems most openly skeptical both about the connection between the usual federal courts issues and a coherent federalist philosophy *and* about the substantive vitality of localist claims in our cosmopolitanized nation of mobile workers. The arguments intersect in the following way. The constitution made small government units the building blocks for larger ones as part of a general plan to restrain power, on the supposition that at the local level, where face-to-face bargaining among those who respect one another would predominate, overreaching in the service of economic growth would be restrained. The development of an open, dynamic capitalist economy so weakens people's roots in the community, and so homogenizes national culture, though, that it is hard even to think about the localist structural protection of freedom in a way that parallels the Madisonian vision. Courts, then, are stuck protecting the forms of federalism with absolutely no conviction that they are protecting any of its initial political substance. Invocations of abstract rhetoric that one preserves the vitality of significant local institutions by deferring to state court fact findings in federal *habeas* cases amount to nothing more than ritual incantation.[63]

Tushnet also implies, I believe, although somewhat less clearly, that the basic federalist commitment, even if its tribute to a liberty-protecting localism were less fanciful, is far more contradictory than its proponents acknowledge. Once more, the battle between CLS and mainstream commentators may be understood in part as a reinterpretation of "balanced" or "competing interests" as simple irreconcilable contradiction. The federalist balance between centralism and localism, between two sovereigns, each dominant in its proper sphere, is seen instead as yielding hopeless conflict. For instance, it is not really possible to balance a typical virtue of localism—its purported capacity to serve as a laboratory for the diversity of regulatory schemes, for political experimentation—with its standard flaw, the problem of regulatory flight. The regulated relocate or threaten to do so until either all localities enact uniform but inadequate regulation or central coordination produces adequate but uniform results. The two phenomena cannot be played off against each other; they are simply contradictory interpretations of the same decisions. Likewise, Tushnet notes that the National League of Cities v. Usery controversy (over federal authority to regulate state and local government wages) can best be seen as a simple conflict between central authority to set income distribution policy and local authority to control taxation and spending levels. While federalism purports to have a theory of the side-by-side coexistence of different authorities, Tushnet implicitly turns it into a theory whereby people randomly invoke complete arguments for localism on some occasions and complete, incompatible arguments for centralism on other occasions. Heller's essay "Legal Theory and the Political Economy of American Federalism"[64] makes this point more vividly and concretely. If centralism's least controversial normative commitment, the desire to open borders, is fulfilled and markets are integrated to avoid the obvious negative impacts of protectionism, centralist economic controls will also ultimately be needed to counteract exit from local positive regulation, at least if one is committed to an expansive view of market-correcting government activity. Free movement of capital, labor, and products is necessary to guarantee that economies are maximally productive; ensuring that mobile capital does not flee public control (such as environmental regulations, highly redistributive tax obligations) requires centralization of regulation. In descriptive terms, the impetus for centralist preemption will come from the demands of the most activist regulating localities. In the United States the more politically liberal northern states would have required the protection of centralist legislation in the Progressive and New Deal eras. With the decline in the power of the more progressive states, decentralization, inevitably in part a code word for deactivization of *all* governmental power, becomes more acceptable.

Historically, descriptively, the thesis is ultimately parallel in one sense to Frug's and Tushnet's: the commitment to federalism must invariably become wholly empty and banal. The nineteenth-century commitment to economic integration had to be followed by the twentieth century's evisceration of local regulatory authority; a generally strong localist commitment simply cannot survive capital mobility, unless each and every locality is either committed at the local level or restricted by (central) constitutional authority to the negative state ideals. The "new federalism," then, *must* be the old laissez-faire: if the central government is *formally* precluded from regulation, perhaps for the seemingly coherent process-related reason that variations in tastes for different mixes of public goods can be met more effectively by ensuring that public goods purchases will be made by smaller and ultimately more homogeneous units, the *activist* states will be effectively precluded from regulation by capital mobility. (Heller notes that the activist states won't instantly be rendered utterly impotent, in large part because the open-borders policies are still incomplete; while overt, tarifflike discrimination against interstate commerce is generally blocked, many forms of functionally equivalent local subsidies are still legally permitted, perhaps because their functional equivalence is still invisible.) But for the non–laissez-faire Hart-Sacks political centrists, the dream of meaningful local authority must remain largely chimerical.

I suspect, ultimately, that CLS writing on the peculiarities of the mainstream federalist fixation is sparse in considerable part because CLS adherents, by and large good New Left decentralizers by disposition, retain a fondness for revitalizing local authority, while acknowledging (as socialist-influenced thinkers must) the need for centralism. It is un-

clear that there is *any* significant distinction between the basic contradiction between central and local authority faced by the federalists
influenced by Hart and Sacks and that faced by the communitarian
decentralizers. Thus, a focus on contradiction here is in no way a focus
on peculiarly liberal contradiction, nor does it seem to explicate any
blind spots in mainstream thought. Moreover, there is no privileged
term (as, say, individualism or intentionalism was privileged) that helps
define a complacent liberalism repressing dissident chords.

CLS commentators may be distinguished here, if at all, only in their
feeling that mainstream thinkers both overestimate the diverse vitality
of standard local public institutions (particularly state courts) and underestimate the need for nontraditional local collectives (for example,
at the workplace level, both Karl Klare[65] and Katharine Stone[66] have
emphasized the vital significance of worker control efforts, and Frug
explicitly states that the "cities" he would like to see empowered are
not those currently constituted but more utopian collective experiments). I suppose that the general tone of disengagement from the
typical debates is a predictable response to the alarming unreality of the
mainstream fixation on the supposedly vital relationship of federal and
state courts, despite an absence of historical or sociological support for
the proposition that significant political gains have been made by carefully preserving these particular local institutions. One might guess that
the mainstream theorists have unconsciously fixed on a clash of insignificant sovereignties to avoid facing the pain of the irreconcilability of
real clashes: the exaggerated tribute to localism and diversity can be
sustained only when no significant local power exists to be exercised,
for real local power tends either to be normatively perilous or factually
short-lived.

CHAPTER SEVEN

Visions of History

Much of the Critical writing has been historical; to the extent, in fact, that one can discern how CLS scholars generally understand law and its connection with sociopolitical issues, it is often through reading both accounts of shifting legal practices written by Critical legal scholars and the works of historians not directly associated with CLS that writers in the movement most frequently cite. There is also a significant strand of CLS writing that does not portray the history of legal consciousness and practice but that instead categorizes and critiques the historiographic processes that have dominated mainstream legal education. Critical writers have, in this regard, identified three significant attitudes toward history from which they claim to want to distance themselves. In the first, the past is seen as a *privileged* source of values, a time to be studied as a normative oracle, a Golden Age.[1] The typical Critical response, most lucidly expounded by Paul Brest in the context of constitutional law, denies both the *possibility* of governing oneself in accordance with the principles of some privileged past oracle and the desirability of doing so even if one could.[2] In the second tradition, history is seen as *progressive,* as directed, teleologically, toward the greater fulfillment of humankind.[3] The role of the historian is to discern the benign historical path so as to help hasten our collective jump onto the bandwagon of progress. The Critical response, perhaps best enunciated by Robert Gordon, is skeptical of descriptive claims that general patterns of shifting practices can be discerned as well as normative claims that whatever shifts might exist would inevitably be desirable or "progressive" in all but a temporal sense.[4] Third and finally, those in the mainstream frequently take a timeless view of normative discourse, claiming that the role of legal theorists is to elucidate norms that lack historical or cultural specificity.[5] But just as Critical thinkers deny the presumptive normative *superiority* of either the past or the (imagined) future, so do they deny that norms can be intelligently discussed without regard to changing social conditions;[6] in fact, Critical scholars often use a certain style of historicist inquiry to remind us how unlikely it is that things we may take for granted will always be so, because we can so readily see that things once taken for granted have hardly proven indispensable.[7]

I should note that it would surely be possible to confront more fully the relationship between mainstream functionalist *history* and its CLS critics at this point; but since it seems to me that the functionalist view is more significant and potent as an ongoing account of the *role* of law, which simply uses historical material as illustrative, I shall defer both the fullblown critique of functionalism and the alternative conception of the interpenetrating connection between law and society that has emerged in CLS until Chapters 8 and 9.[8] In this chapter I shall simply explicate the Critics' account of mainstream work, and then briefly, at the chapter's close, to analyze the Critics' own historical inquiries, making use of the typology they have found helpful in looking at the work of others.

History as Nostalgia

Within mainstream thought, it is largely in the tradition of American constitutional law that the past is especially privileged. Obviously, *originalism,* the glorification of either the constitutional text or the precepts of the founders that the text may only partly elucidate, may be defended without recourse to any form of historicist nostalgia, whether in the form of a substantive preference for the values expressed by those in power here in the late eighteenth century or of a yearning for continuity of *any* reasonably acceptable principles. One could, of course, either defend the deification of the Constitution as necessary to constrain otherwise intemperate judicial decision makers, who might otherwise believe that any "significant" values had supermajoritarian force, or defend the recourse to originalism on the ground that the governed have consented only to participate in a community framed by the original political understanding, regardless of whether or not it was a wise polity to form.[9]

Brest's attacks on constitutional originalism are quite thorough: any form of originalism (whether textualist or interpretivist) is not only untenable but not worth striving for, whether one strives for it because one believes that originalist values are prone to be superior or because one believes that other values (such as legality, stability, democracy) are best served by originalism.

The attack on textualism (the belief that constitutional adjudicators can rule on the validity of practices predominantly by reference to the words in the Constitution) is, like much of the CLS constitutional scholarship I discussed in referring to legal process concerns, hardly unfamiliar. It is not markedly dissimilar from the attacks of nontextualists, who make up the bulk of mainstream scholars, on the few remaining textualists.[10] Even if one believes that some precepts in the Constitution are essentially rulelike, fairly mechanically applicable, it is quite clear that almost everything of significance in the Constitution has no such clear meaning. A few provisions may, within our culture, be readily linguistically determinate, susceptible to few interpretations (for example, that the President must be at least thirty-five years old); a few others may be less obviously *referentially* determinate, but the purposive readings are still reasonably rulelike as a result of common social practice and context (for example, knowing that the requirement that the President be "natural born" excludes immigrants rather than those delivered by Caesarean section does not seem to require going "outside" the text in any interesting way). Brest is surely right, however, that there is in no way a core linguistic meaning to the requirement to provide "due process" or to the duty to refrain from the "impairment of contract" or to the power to regulate commerce. It is not simply the case that many actual practices would be neither clearly permitted nor barred if one tried to square the practice with the textual rule (do existing textual prohibitions on state power to interfere with interstate commerce permit infrastructural subsidies that may have parallel economic effects to direct tariffs?). But ruminating on the text does not in any way *help* determine the legitimacy of the practice.

Having dismissed, as most do, the possibility of a significant textualist commitment, Brest then looks at "intentionalism," the belief that one ought to govern one's constitutional conduct by mimicking the constitutional practice one believes the constitutional adopters would themselves have used had they anticipated the myriad detailed cases that have actually arisen.

Brest's first strategy, is, I think, to quibble with intentionalism. The arguments are not "quibbles" in the sense that they are either easily answered by intentionalists or insignificant if one is committed to intentionalist method; but they seem quibbles from *Brest's* critical perspective in the sense that even if each of these arguments were inapplicable, his fundamental technical objections to the vision of translation from past to present would still be unmet. The quibbles, though, are still worth mentioning. First, because the Constitution was the work product of so many people (both many writers and, equally significantly, even more adopters, in a variety of state legislatures, theoretically representing a still wider variety of constituents), it is ambiguous how "intention," seemingly a feature of an individual, could be ascribed to the relevant subject, a group. Different writers may well have meant different things, yet we have no conceivable summing scheme to register competing understandings. Moreover, many delegates (and still more state legislators, and even more voters) clearly intended nothing at all about particular provisions but rather simply preferred the whole constitutional package to what they must have viewed as the likely alternative. Second, it is unclear whether an intentionalist is bound to follow the privileged subject's canons of interpretation of his utterances rather than what the interpreter himself sees as the subject's true intentions. This would clearly be quite bothersome if the privileged subject's canon of interpretation was that his commands should be interpreted loosely, giving great discretion to those in new circumstances, but it even poses something of a problem given that our Constitution was probably drafted by textualists. Does it truly follow the constitutional scheme to interpret the Framers' underlying intent when an aspect of their intent was to be interpreted only through their words? To distinguish substantive intentions from procedural or interpretive intention may be nearly as difficult as drawing any line between substance and procedure. It may well have been a significant substantive belief about proper future government function that it would be better to follow the written document and permit or prohibit a practice when the Framers would actually have done the opposite, faced with the particular case, than to try to inquire into intention.[11]

Even if there were but one adopter, though, one source of privilege, and even if she wanted to be interpreted by those looking to follow her intentions, it is quite clear that Brest would be extremely skeptical of our capacity to follow the intentionalist path. The problem, according to Brest, can be seen when we consider judging practices that simply did not exist when the privileged subjects were around to form intentions; one then recognizes the ubiquitous insolubility of the problem when one realizes that no practices exist across time with precisely the same meaning.

The fact that some practices we must now judge simply postdate the Framers and therefore raise issues that they never considered (such as copyright of the products of nonprint media) could be overcome if we had a ready rule of thumb to deal with unanticipated cases (for example, permit whatever state conduct the privileged Framers did not think to prohibit, or prohibit whatever they didn't think to permit). Neither such rule of thumb commends itself, though, on interpretivist grounds: current attitudes about judicial activism or deference would almost surely determine one's position, if one chose to take any position at all in such a purely procedural controversy.

More significant, of course, the bulk of practices have different *meanings* in today's setting than they might have had when initially envisioned. As Brest notes, it is hard to say that the death penalty we see now is the *same* death penalty that the Framers surely tolerated. At the deepest level, it is hard to know whether death itself has the same meaning in a largely secular society in which few die young of natural causes that it had in late eighteenth-century America. (Brest does not belabor the point, but the death penalties of two different periods would have to be put in any number of historically shifting contexts: What other punishments are prevalent or available, and how is each of these perceived? What crimes is the penalty reserved for and how common are these crimes, or how are these crimes perceived? Murder, for instance, may be strongly disapproved of now as it was then, but it may well be far more common now. Does the "mere" death penalty represent a "liberalization" of even more extreme punishments, or is it the most severe? What is the relationship between this society's practice and that of other generally comparable societies?)[12]

The problem is widespread. In judging the constitutionality of police surveillance of the home, it is surely insufficient for an intentionalist to note that a particular parallel act of surveillance was tolerated. The toleration may have been an outgrowth of unstated assumptions about how prevalent such surveillance was, given its technical feasibility (and the associated limits on police resources), that may no longer be applicable (in addition to the possibility of more profound shifts in our concepts of physical privacy, or the growth of visions and fears of technological intrusiveness). In judging the constitutionality of state conduct that might arguably prejudice interstate commerce, shifts in assumptions about how common certain nonprejudicial ends are might well influence assumptions about the permissibility of arguably unchanged practice. State subsidies that might have seemed valid to Framers used to thinking of short-term infant industry protection might look invalid, while the expansion of the domain of collective goods purchases (for example, to include different levels of environmental preservation or safety) may legitimate restrictive practices that could not once have been envisioned as anything but illegitimate localist monopolizing efforts.

Interpretivists try to get around this difficulty in two ways, one conscious, the other far less so, and it is in responding to these techniques that the Critics probably speak in their most characteristic voice, speak less like one branch of mainstream constitutionalists attacking another.

The first technique is to look for something like the "principles" of those in the Golden Age, rather than their views of particular practices.[13] In a sense, this can be seen as a rules-to-standards shift (in which the standards tend to be of an extremely high order of generality) in the adjudicatory posture. Instead of commanding that the judge treat any mechanically identifiable practice as his normatively privileged forebear would have, he is asked to step back, discern, and state the *reasons* he imagines the Framer had for evaluating a situation as he did and simply apply the reasoning. The statement of such broad-level principles, though, can have little impact. If, for instance, one interprets the Framers' support of the death penalty within the "cruel and unusual punishment" clause as nothing more than support for punishments that offend few morally sensitive people or don't morally degrade the society that practices them, this "principle" can give rise to the experience of delimiting a practice that stays reasonably settled only as long as consensus over the practice remains steady.

The second technique, which I first discussed in the chapter on intentionalism and determinism, is to abandon, covertly, talk of *subjective* intention, to transform the Framers' principles into beliefs "typical" of people (perhaps of a certain class or general political sentiment) of their time, and assume that they desired only that such "typical" beliefs govern. Not only does this shift the discourse from an intentionalist one (in which subjects, like the Framers, define themselves by their beliefs, rather than having beliefs that are defined by the circumstances they happen to be framed by) but, as a practical matter, it effectively strips away all past-regarding constraints. If today's decision maker says that a past subject's substantive belief about X should be understood only as a typical belief of the time about X, and assumes that the subject's intention was simply to ratify typical beliefs, then the *particularities* of past cultures no longer sway us. If we interpret the previleged decision makers as having decided, in essence, to ratify commonplace values *because* they were commonplace, if we decide that their underlying core intention was to deify the commonplace, it is surely *today's* common values that have constitutional power.

Brest is not just dubious that originalism is a feasible interpretive technique; he is dubious that it is desirable. He perceives defects in all three traditional affirmative arguments for originalism—that it alone is consistent with the dictates of popular consent, with stability, and with legality—and offers two additional arguments against its acceptability.

Brest denies both that the concept of ongoing social contractual consent is meaningful at all and that, if one imagined that each generation consented to broad governing principles, one could convince oneself that it is the original Constitution to which people today swear particular allegiance. The first point is a perfectly familiar reiteration of standard objections to social compact theory: even if one could imagine that the initial adopters assented affirmatively to a particular form of governance, their progeny have not consented in any strong sense. Only by interpreting their failure to emigrate as a confirmation of governance principles can one treat current citizens as constitutional adopters. If, though, one did choose to emphasize this intentionalist, contractualist interpretation of staying put, one should probably interpret those who have "chosen" to stay as choosing to ratify the *existing* governance structure—which clearly includes nonoriginalist decisions by the Supreme Court—rather than a hypothetical one. Only by deciding that people actually consent by staying *and* that they consent not to existing *practice* but to the existing originalist Law Day *rhetoric* that judges tend to use in confirmation hearings, perhaps because they have little way of knowing that practice is frequently nonoriginalist, can one make even a weak argument that some "we" has consented only to the original understanding.[14]

Brest sees the argument from stability as equally defective. Used retroactively, as a guide to deciding which past decisions are legitimate and should be sustained, it would certainly cause great turmoil and instability to overturn all nonoriginalist decisions (at least if instability is seen simply as a product of any rapid, massive change). Overturning, for instance, school desegregation, reapportionment, or anticonfession decisions because all the condemned practices were certainly (in some sense) known to and tolerated by the Framers would hardly advance the cause of stability. Even using originalism only prospectively, to navigate currently uncharted waters, would hardly engender as much continuity as proponents pretend. Brest notes that the histories that are generated to illuminate original intention change as frequently as attitudes and values do. Changing case law to keep up with the latest revisions in historiography might lead not only to rapid and destabilizing substantive oscillation but also to a meaningless, unacceptable sort of oscillation. It is hard to imagine enormous popular sympathy for the idea that the work patterns and quirky interpretive styles of current (normatively nonprivileged) historians should govern practice.[15]

The argument from legality—that any form of nonoriginalist review is unconstrained or ungrounded in valid external authority and hence despotic—is more subtly flawed. First, says Brest, it is not clear how the Constitution gains ultimate legal authority simply because it proclaims it has it. Obviously, a particular congressional enactment that declared itself supreme to the Constitution would have no particular force if we remained committed to some sort of constitutional review. Similarly, statements internal to the constitutional text that purport to set up its precepts as legal reference points likewise have no obvious weight.[16] The second argument is more complex: it might be the case that particular constitutional precepts have no special claim to legal authority but that judges who decide to be originalists will have an appropriately restrained attitude. It might be that legalist principles call for judicial restraint, and that originalism is a theoretically irrelevant source of restraint that in fact ends up restaining. Brest questions why one would ever feel compelled to use *indirect* means of attaining self-restraint—whether originalism or the traditional procedural modes of self-restraint (declaring cases moot, unripe, or otherwise nonadjudicable)—rather than simply reflect while making decisions on the powers and problems of one's institution.[17]

I think that Brest actually *underestimates* the problems of this legalist argument: the connection between judicial restraint and legality is really far from clear, both theoretically and practically. One can certainly believe that legislative decisions are *legitimate* even when they derive from no past principles—that is, when they are not deduced in any sense from an existing set of norms—but this is not really an argument from "legality." *Process* arguments, of the sort I discussed in the last chapter, about the supposedly democratic nature of the legislature, might validate nondeductive decisions, but the fact that decisions are democratic hardly makes them any more deductive, any less a product of will, than judicial decisions. If the thrust of the traditional legalist argument is that decisions are to be made not by willful particular people but simply by reference to ongoing principle, judicial activism in the face of expansive legislative will could well be appropriate. Of course, if this "legalist" argument is just a stand-in for the "process" argument that legislatures are ordinarily normatively perferable to courts and that originalism is just another good technique that leads to judicial deference, then we are left with two difficulties: Brest's problem (why not simply be deferential?) and two variants thereof (will originalism either maximize the degree of deference or exercise it at the "right" times?).

In practical terms, the connection between originalism and deference is perhaps even less lucid. While many of the leading activist decisions of the postwar era have surely involved nonoriginalist interpretation (most prominently the school desegregation, abortion, and reapportionment cases), it is equally clear that colorable originalist justifications can undoubtedly be made for an extremely activist reactionary court (one that might, for instance, dramatically curtail federal regulatory efforts as an undue expansion of the Commerce Clause powers or local land use planning as an illicit uncompensated taking).

Brest is not just interested in elucidating the practical difficulties one would encounter in attempting to privilege the initial constitutional moment and in debunking standard arguments for the desirability of trying to do so; he argues as well that there are two affirmative reasons for not even *trying* to be an originalist. First, the Framers were just particular people, neither gods nor prophets with direct divine access. In fact, they are not an especially attractive group of people to use as models, but rather an overtly racist, slaveholding or slavery-tolerating group of privileged white males. Moreover the society they lived in was different enough from our own that one would be surprised if they didn't draw some political lessons from their experience that we would find irrelevant: their society was predominantly agrarian; most production occurred at the family level; and the existence of the frontier provided a viable option for many of these agrarian workers when conditions became intolerable.[18] Second, Brest argues that one can see, without any reference to the past, the distinction between nonconstitutional and constitutional values (both in the broad sense that one could argue that the values are "constitutive" or society defining and in the American institutionalist sense that we fear that short-term fluctuations in popular mood may tempt majorities to trample longer-term culture-defining efforts in the absence of either judicial intervention or constitutional self-consciousness by legislators or the executive). In essence, there seems to be a short list of recurring issues of this grandiose sort, and we simply change our precise understanding of how to translate broad principle to constitutional practice. Nonetheless, we do sense, rather unproblematically, that the major general constitutional *domains* are the protection of minorities from exploitation and fear of suppression of cultural diversity by the majority, as well as the policing of some aspects of the existing distribution of political authority. But there seems to be little reason to think that the possibility of a shift in understanding in which minorities or politically disempowered groups can be exploited (for example women or Latinos as well as descendants of the black former slaves with whom the Framers of the post–Civil War amendments were concerned) should be dismissed because those in the past did not share our understanding, whether or not ours ultimately proves to be a wise one.[19]

The Historical Bandwagon

In the adaptationist traditions that Gordon has outlined, history is progressive. Things get better. There are obviously politically distinct teleological pictures of the march of history, different visions of the progress we have made and the expected progress to come. What the theories have most in common, beyond their generally bubbly optimism, is that they picture a similar role for the legal historian: once she recognizes the pattern, the direction in which things are going, her role is to counsel the acceleration of historical change, critique remaining atavistic anomalies. (Obviously, it is wholly unclear why the existing *pace* of historical change and the existing mix of future-regarding and backward-looking practice is any less functionally ideal than the hurried introduction of everything we now see in the wind would be; but since most theorists want to have some minimally critical bite, simply describing and endorsing all past progress hardly makes for an adequately detached scholarly program.)

In the traditional mainstream *conservative* view, the basic historical shifts are threefold: first, the "involuntary" status relationships associated with medievalism are replaced by "free" contractual relationships;[20] second, formal legal inequality is displaced by formal legal equality (that is, ascriptive status privileges die out);[21] and third, voluntary associations, separate from either state or individual, flourish.[22]

The mainstream political "liberal" has her own stories of historical progress. It was once appropriate for the law to promote economic growth and to reflect individualistic values, because in a preindustrial economy of rough equality, people could readily protect themselves from the overreaching of others and the vagaries of social life. Moreover, economic growth was more essential, so decisions that were experienced, at least in terms of initial incidence, as raising nonrecoupable production costs for infant industries had to be avoided. Now that these rugged frontier days are but a dim memory, and societies are "complex" and "interdependent" and the demand for justice can be readily met, the laissez-faire policies that were appropriate to the nineteenth century no longer are, as a descriptive matter, prevalent or, as a normative matter, appropriate, given the progressive trend toward human fulfillment.[23]

In the standard left-radical picture, the past is not only not privileged—as it is in the constitutionalists' nostalgic mode—but actively decried: past practices simply expose the temporary constellation of class interests that happened to dominate the polity at the time (whether the particular radical theory views dominant classes as substructurally determined or as at least semiautonomously politically formed). The move from past to present, though, exposes the nascent promise of ultimate liberation. Particularly in the more traditional teleological Marxist views, each major historicolegal shift involves the growing realization of universal freedom. The standard moves the radicals picture are from a legal regime sustaining the formal inequality of feudalism to one enacting the formal equality of capitalism to one protecting the desire for equality of outcome (left-liberal welfare capitalism or Marx's precommunist socialism). Finally, communist society is both postlegal and posthistorical: it is postlegal in the formal sense that the state has withered away with the withering away of class conflict, and it is posthistorical in the sense that fundamental social relations are no longer determined by either technical productive forces or the existing mode of production, that human activity is for the first time the product of intentional choice.[24] It is obviously easier, in day-to-day legal terms, to see what mildly critical stances the mainstream teleological historicist should take than to divine those open to the Marxist. The conservative should recommend expanding the domain of free contract when the opportunity arises; the liberal should recommend an appropriate protectiveness and socialization of risk when she sees the chance. The Marxist, presumably, simply allies herself with the real interests of that class whose concrete self-interest is in fact humankind's universal interest, the proletariat, in all its struggles, with the thought that it is the political triumph of the class, not the legal institutionalization of any single aspect of that historically progressive class's ultimate program, that hastens the desired end of history.

CLS commentators, most clearly Gordon, have by and large been extremely skeptical of all varieties of adaptationism, both its *descriptive* claim that past history can readily be understood as the unfolding of a short list of general themes and its *normative* claim that the present is inexorably an improvement on the past, so that, correlatively, we should assume that all discernible trends are to be welcome.

The mainstream conservative notion that status relations tend to be supplanted over time in more and more domains by contractual ones has enough significant exceptions that one would be hard pressed to recall the rule. While judges did indeed tend to blather on in the 1960s and 1970s about the fact that modern landlord-tenant law disclaimed the status-based feudal conveyancing tradition in favor of the notion that the lease is a contract like any other,[25] innumerable observers have recognized that nearly all the modern landlord-tenant reforms have adopted that portion of modern contract law that transforms contract relations back into something much like status relations. Surely, while the adoption by courts of nondisclaimable terms (such as nonwaivable habitability warranties) hardly meant that landlord and tenant would henceforth have a *traditional* status relationship (grounded in birth or fairly immutable social position), it certainly did not mean that they had a readily alterable or individualizable *contractual* relation.[26] Likewise, many workplace relations have been decontractualized; whether collective bargaining agreements are in force or particular courts or legislatures have adopted strictures against at-will discharge, few workers and bosses define their relationship through anything like direct, *individualizable* (let alone *individualized*) bargaining.[27] The only major area in which one could make a plausible case that the present movement of the law is toward loosening status strictures is, perhaps ironically, the only one in which mainstream conservatives seem to be nostalgic for traditional status roles.[28] To a limited extent, family law has been contractualized,[29] at least as to property relations between spouses and nonmarried cohabitants. But, of course, conservatives frequently worry that the family, which they often view as a critical institution, will be weakened if the legal system validates any nontraditional arrangements, backing either shifts in the duties of people who demand to be called married or allowing people who aren't married the right to enforce contracts that make demands on others parallel to those status duties that are traditionally implied when one marries.

Similarly, both the notion that formal equality inevitably displaces formal inequality and that voluntary associations grow in prominence are highly suspect. Formally egalitarian law has been under frequent successful attack both from the left (for example in affirmative action programs[30] or demands for comparable-worth pay for women workers[31]) and the right (for example, backlashes against measures protecting gays).[32]

One would certainly be hard pressed to claim that churches, fraternal organizations, or charities have consistently and steadily gained either in importance or in purely legal status in the United States.[33]

It is, of course, plausible that the conservative adaptationist picture is meant to be so general that it cannot be defeated by counterexamples: that is, if *more* arenas of social life are contractualized over very long periods of time, we have met the loose test for trend. But I take it that the normative force and significance of all adaptationist strategies depend on spotted trends being encompassing and universal; if all the adaptationist has said is that castelike controls on labor mobility broke down as the closed medieval economies collapsed, he hasn't said much to guide our practice.

The standard liberal descriptive claims seem equally implausible. As both Gordon[34] and Betty Mensch[35] have emphasized, the notion that nineteenth-century buyers were, as a rule, better able to take care of themselves than their twentieth-century counterparts is not at all obvious; the idea that people "in the good old days" were less subject to economic vagaries outside their control is not just unobvious but almost surely wrong, given the severity and duration of business cycles up through and including the Great Depression. Not only is the claim unconvincing that people now "need" the typical welfare state reforms more; the idea that the liberal welfare state has steadily and consistently supplanted laissez-faire traditionalism is equally wrong. Just because the UCC has formally adopted a code section on unconscionability does not mean that substantive contractual relations have altered a great deal, that substantive fairness of exchange is guaranteed. It is also just as true that the active regulation of auto safety has faded in the 1980s as that it came to life in the 1960s and 1970s;[36] similarly, real dollar welfare levels have hardly risen continuously.[37]

The legal Marxists' claims that formal liberalism inevitably supplants something like feudalism and that outcome-oriented legal visions of equality inevitably dominate formally egalitarian liberalism seem just as suspect as the mainstream claims. The first claim, of the inevitable rise of formal liberalism, is hard to square with the rise of the mass fascist regimes in our century; the notion that liberal societies inexorably progress toward a more developed welfare state is readily belied by Thatcherism and Reaganism.

In part, the CLS skepticism about the simple adaptationist claims is just part and parcel of a twofold general antifunctionalism that I'll discuss in more detail in the next chapter. Suffice it to say for now that particular legal development paths are unlikely to be seen as predestined if one believes both that relatively similar social organizations can coexist with widely diverse legal rules *and* that there is likely to be no independent social development, comprehensible without regard to past legal decisions, that could be thought to generate concrete needs that the legal system would then meet.

Moreover, many of the typical adaptationist statements are simply nonsensical in the CLS lexicon, so it is hard to imagine them as descriptively *accurate*. If one says, for instance, as some liberal adaptationists do, that the state was once uninvolved in income distribution but has become increasingly so,[38] the claim seems, on its face, impossible if one believes that *any* legal regime creates a particular distributive pattern. An argument that there are trends toward or away from the "regulation"[39] of contractual relations is difficult to interpret for those who have strongly integrated the Realist insight that even the "freest" contract regime is a regime that regulates what is and is not permitted in bargaining.[40] While these typical adaptationist arguments could be *translated* in a way that Critics would find sensible (for example, the liberal adaptationist might simply be referring to the historical growth of explicitly income-transferring tax and benefit programs or to particular consumer-protective rules), the arguments that are routinely made often seem to adopt, covertly, ideologically charged, mistaken pictures of conceivable practices.

Finally, the CLS writers have tended to believe that social formations are, in a sense, simply too complex to develop in the orderly fashion the adaptationists see. Even Unger, the major CLS writer most given to historicist taxonomies, pictures particular legal development paths as a product of the *confluence* of enough distinct social forces that to assume that any particular development path would represent either a descriptive norm or a duplicable inspirational model would be folly. The ordinary legal ideals associated with liberalism depend, he says, at a minimum, on the existence of a particular confluence of group pluralism (the absence of a stable social hierarchy) and a transcendent religious consciousness. As a result, "it may be impossible to find a single telling example of [a legal order] outside the modern Western liberal state."[41]

The Critics have devoted considerably more attention to denigrating the descriptive claim that legal history follows a simple, steady path than to addressing the claim that one should endorse and endeavor to hasten whatever developments one sees. My sense, though, is that at both the social and personal levels, CLS writers have been skeptical of models that equate development with growth, temporal with moral progress.

At the historical level, this is most obvious in the more or less explicit sentimentalization of aspects of preindustrial life that one sees in both Morton Horwitz's *Transformation of American Law*[42] and Unger's *Law in Modern Society*,[43] as well as in sympathetic citations by CLS writers[44] of E. P. Thompson's work, which more explicitly condemns the factory system for destroying communities and routinizing the work lives of laborers who had earlier been able to use their artisans' skills.[45] The break from Marx's snide attacks on the banality of rural life, or his comparatively nonironic praise of the impact of capitalist inroads on precapitalist cultures, is quite dramatic.[46] Similarly, it is obvious that once one notes that genocidal fascism and Stalinism may be perfectly plausible steps in the social development path, one does not necessarily open one's arms to the future.

At the personal level, it strikes me that one of the most obvious distinctions between the European "Critical Theory" associated with the Frankfurt school and our similarly named Critical Legal Studies is that the Europeans, most obviously Jürgen Habermas, have tended to try to overcome the traditional liberal fact-value dualism by positing that there are "mature" values that are morally privileged. Echoing the work of moral development theorists like Lawrence Kohlberg, who believe that there are ever higher states of moral development toward which people tend to develop or ascend, the Critical Theory adherents tend to see certain sorts of universalistic moral discourse (much like the "veil of ignorance" discourse in Rawls) as the morally developed discourse that would be the proper base for the resolution of value issues.[47] CLS did not explicitly join in the attacks on moral development theory (until some Critical feminists endorsed Carol Gilligan's critique that it supports a typically male form of rhetoric as advanced moral thought),[48] but it is surely the case that CLS writers draw at least as many pictures of the tendency toward personal moral *devolution* as evolution. For instance, in "Choice and Utility" I made reference to the notion of goods addiction, a tendency for people to come to need, but not truly enjoy, all the goods they have become accustomed to consuming, so that they feel decreasingly free to make choices that threaten their access to their accustomed bundle.[49] The life cycle, given a goods addiction model, is one in which one becomes more addicted, less open as one ages, especially if one simply adds new addictions as time goes on. In criticizing Ely's hypothesis that racism could be overcome by social contact, Parker makes a devolutionary claim as well: people may have fewer prejudices *before* cross-class contact than after.[50]

While neither of these models purports at all to be a universal account of personal development (Parker explicitly refers to the regress of group relations in a grossly inegalitarian society), they surely are *not* accounts that sentimentalize experience as such. Though I would have trouble finding explicit textual support for the point, my overall sense is that if one had to describe CLS work as either romantically sentimental toward innocence or admiring of wise experience, it is somewhat more sentimental toward the presocialized. While Kennedy does not adopt the model in "Legal Education and the Reproduction of Hierarchy" that recalcitrant law students are converted en masse into corporate tools by the law schools, he certainly paints a far brighter picture of entrants than of typical graduates.[51] Similarly, Catharine MacKinnon's pictures of sexual relations between men and women are unremittingly gloomy (all heterosexual intercourse invariably bears a great deal in common with what the legal system has defined as rape);[52] but since she adamantly refused to *biologize* or *naturalize* this situation as a presocial conflict in sexual desires, I take it that the devolution of heterosexuality is socially based.

Timeless Discourse

It is easier to understand the thrust of both nostalgic and adaptationist uses of history than to comprehend the third mainstream posture, that legal truths and discourse should *transcend* historical particularities, thus eliminating the need for historical inquiry. In part, this third, antihistoricist posture is hard to specify because it demands not that one utterly ignore shifting circumstances in talking about law but rather that one draw some sharp line between historically contingent *practice* and historically invariant *principle*. If, for instance, one's "principle" is that actors ought to be liable if and only if they have not taken precautions whose cost is lower than the damage the precautions would avert, one's "practice" (whether to find a particular defendant liable or not) will change as the world in which the defendant operates alters. As precautions get more or less expensive with technological change, as the damage caused is disvalued to a greater or lesser extent, and so on, defendants taking superficially identical acts will face different consequences. Obviously, it is easy to think of cases where the line between principle and practice is blurred. For instance, to refer to an example I mentioned in discussing nostalgic uses of history, it is obviously difficult to tell whether we have a principle against certain forms of police surveillance (such as looking inside a house) or a principle protecting some less definable quantum of privacy or security that may or may not be violated by a particular form of surveillance ostensibly comprehended by some vision of principle. (For instance, television monitor surveillance may not violate a principle that holds that it is all right to look from the outside into the inside, but it *may* violate a principle based on the level of instrusion.) But the point, for now, is not to criticize often unworkable efforts to distinguish (broad) principles from (narrower) applications.

What the "timeless" posture seems to require, and what CLS commentators refuse to concede, is that some meaningful ends are in fact reasonably universal, that law governs behavior so that discussions of universal "right rules" can be tacitly understood as discussions of right governance, and that we can have some faith that we are not utterly deluding ourselves when we perceive a particular principle as universal and significant, even if such principles in fact exist.

To counter the notion that operative principles of a nontautological sort (principles less banal than, say, "Do less harm to others if you can") persist over time and across cultures, the CLS commentators simply try to locate all the supposed universals in historical space and time. So, for instance, Gordon treats the "eternal verities" embodied in the Constitution as the peculiar beliefs of late eighteenth-century Whigs[53] and treats today's purportedly timeless efficiency analysis not as a universally valid view but as the world picture of people seeing an atomized, secularized social world.[54] The Critics see the universals not only as *time* specific but as specific to particular people at any time, perhaps intellectually dominant within a class or particular social milieu but not pervading the whole culture.[55] The constitutional vision was hardly *everyone's* vision in late eighteenth-century America but was obviously a victory for certain positions in political struggles (between, to name just a few groups, inland debtors and seaboard creditors; "nationally" oriented mercantalists and local precapitalist agrarians; slaves and slave owners). Likewise, those fixated on efficiency may well constitute a social group far less concerned with socioeconomic inequality or the breakdown of community than other groups.

CLS adherents also use historical and sociological analysis to deride the ordinary mainstream supposition that reaching some normative or intellectual consensus on legal principle will invariably transform actual social life. One of the claims of those who are interested in perfecting positive law, putting it in harmony with universal principle, is that positive laws govern behavior, that they are complied with and universalized within their sphere of influence.

Historical observation, though, may show us that law is just one of many forms of governance (alongside, say, more or less local custom or force).[56] In fact, given enforcement and procedural problems, law is often not a form of governance at all but an expression of pious hope or of hypocritical self-presentation.[57] This vision turns the "normal" case in the mainstream search for right rules—a law enacted to be universally applied in order best to meet an uncontroversial instrumental end—into an oddity, a quirk, a specific situation whose existence must be proven in each case. It is not, of course, *logically* impossible for the universalizing antihistorical scholar to toss nonpositivist ends into the list of needs his perfect law is designed to further: mainstream thinkers do indeed say that laws may make symbolic assertions or form a counterenclave to undesirable but pervasive custom. But the actual antihistoricist practice seems to be to divide the world of law into two distinct spheres. In one sphere (almost invariably exemplified by Prohibition and laws against consensual sex) are rules designed mainly to express a symbolic value; in the other are the core private and constitutional law rules that law students are forced to debate and master, and the assumption in these cases is that rules will be translated into practice. Few contracts teachers remind their students what historian-sociologists have taught us: that the choice of a "rule," say of offer and acceptance, may have little impact on the richly textured, multifaceted social world. Since parties rarely enforce contracts strictly legally, a decision that purports to tell them whether they have made a legally enforceable contract may be of less moment than the rule perfecters pretend.[58]

CLS adherents also use history to remind us how prone to self-delusion we are likely to be when we announce that we have discovered universally valid principles. Just as some of the critical biologists have implicitly questioned modern theories of biological determinism by reminding us of some bizarre past efforts to prove that certain social problems have biological bases (for example, craniologists' explanations of crime or nonproductivity),[59] so do the CLS historians often try to remind us how essential to the preservation of civilization and liberty certain now peripheral or rejected legal practices seemed to past commentators. In "The Structure of Blackstone's Commentaries," for instance, Kennedy frequently points out the ways in which Blackstone celebrated certain features of English law virtually on the eve of their utter collapse. To Blackstone, the soon-to-disappear writ system was a central bulwark of liberty, yet he makes nearly no mention at all of judicial review of legislative action, so dominant a preserver of liberty in modern American mainstream thought.[60] (Blackstone also not only defends but sees as socially constitutive a variety of legal relations that soon proved dispensable feudal remnants, for example the bulk of the incorporeal hereditaments.)[61] Morton Horwitz even treats the historiographic discourse of mainstream lawyers as historically relative, noting that at different points in American legal history, judges and commentators have embraced progressive adaptationism, sentimentalism, and timeless discourse as necessary features of intelligent legal discourse.[62]

In part, attacks on our ability to perceive timeless truths about law often follow more general CLS attacks on functionalist legal explanation, which I shall focus on in the next chapter, in large part because functionalist homilies are the most common sort of timeless truths that mainstream theorists perceive. Thus, for instance, a commonplace "timeless" truth is that capitalist merchants, particularly those managing large enterprises, require rule-bound law to reduce risk by increasing legal certainty.[63] Mensch successfully criticized this mainstream Weberian assumption, noting, first, that the loose standardlike UCC, with its emphasis on enforcing reasonable commercial practice, is often now pictured as particularly appropriate for merchants, and second, that there is little reason to believe either that large enterprises would not be *better* able than smaller ones to protect against risk through diversification or self-insurance or that the risk of unforeseen legal decisions represents a particularly important source of enterprise risk, compared, for instance, to that of business cycles.[64]

Suffice it to say, for now, that an analysis, like the CLS analysis, committed above all to the notion that liberal discourse is *defined* by its basic contradictions is one in which one would expect to find, looking at history, not *single* truthful answers to sociolegal questions but oscillating, contradictory ones. Using historical research to find, as Kennedy did, that at times criminal sentencing has been considered a uniquely appropriate field for imposition of discretion-limiting determinate sentencing rules and at other times uniquely appropriate for ad hoc standard-based decision making only confirms and strengthens the a priori CLS theoretical position that legal practice cannot properly fulfill social needs because liberal discourse in fact sees *conflicting* needs.[65]

Gordon believes that the mainstream antihistorical posture is sustained, even in the face of historically relativistic descriptions of value schemes, "Law and Society" pictures of the frequent nonpenetration of abstract norms in social practice, and reminders of the foolishness of those who have thought that they had correctly perceived legal universals by means of three modes of denial.[66]

In the least interesting but most commonplace mode, mainstream theorists defend their belief that principles are universal by focusing on principles of such a high order of generality that they simply lack bite. To the extent that, for all politically relevant purposes, we do not find any historical instances of cultures that tolerate murder or the causing of harm, we may, at first blush, seem to have found a universal; but it is obvious that critical distinctions arise when the cultures *define* murder or the causing of harm. (Is it a universal truth that cancer-causing polluters are or are not murderers? That certain forms of provocation do or do not reduce the moral gravity of an intentional killing?) Gordon does not explicitly deal with the most assertive of the moral universalists, commentators who, like Michael Moore, explicitly defend the idea that there is a "moral reality";[67] but Moore's efforts have scarcely advanced the less well focused, less theoretical antihistoricist cause. Moore fails to demonstrate even that the critical moral terms he uses (such as *malice, death*) have a conventional meaning (there are, for instance, widely divergent beliefs about the relevance of various forms of determinisms, like provocation, in debates about whether a killer acted with malice, and widely divergent beliefs about when someone is "dead" enough to justify our making certain decisions in certain contexts as if he were more certainly dead), let alone providing even a hint of a theory of how moral truths could have any nonconventional, nondivine genesis.

In a more interesting but less common mode, antihistoricists simply assert that there is but *one* ahistorical organizing legal principle, and that it permits the social order to change over time. That principle is that the universal role of law is to facilitate private ordering; the actual content of social life will, of course, vary over time as private desire changes over the course of history, but the principle of accommodation to private desire will endure. Gordon does not emphasize the fact that this particular timeless model might well be morally unappealing,[68] that others might believe that it would be *bad* if this were the sole aim of law, but instead notes that, on any reflection, it is an utterly illusory goal as well. Once one recognizes that even the nominally facilitative rules of private ordering, like rules that tell people when they have formed contracts, have a substantive bite, it is unclear whether we can describe any legal rule as *simply* facilitative.[69] As I discussed in detailing the contradictory commitment to both rules and standards, norms of contract formation could never *simply* facilitate private ordering, but rather would invariably imply different degrees of protectiveness toward people in different positions, and would similarly imply distinct levels of altruistic commitment by parties. A rule that demands high levels of formality cannot simply be said to *facilitate* private ordering, but may instead facilitate ordering only for certain legally sophisticated parties with particular expectations about their dealings with others. Any rule expanding or contracting the domain of contracts voidable for duress or fraud can readily be framed either as facilitating or hampering parties' efforts to organize their own lives.

Finally, Gordon argues that mainstream antihistoricists often purport to develop universals by what he dubs "Cartesianism,"[70] by deducing all principles through systematic logic. I find Gordon's description of Cartesian ahistoricism by far the hardest of his accounts to follow: both examples of Cartesianist thought systems he offers (late nineteenth-century Legal Formalism and modern legal economics) indeed use deduction of detailed rules from a short list of principles, but it seems to me that they would require some *separate* form of antihistoricism from their day-to-day focus on deduction to explain how their organizing principles gain universal legitimacy. Perhaps Gordon's implicit phenomenology of the Cartesian impulse has a few hidden steps, for example, that the Cartesians have a hidden commitment to the universal validity of systematic thought and believe that *only* the principles they expound permit one to deal with social life in the systematic way they demand. The correctness of the world view is a function, then, of the unique way in which it can be expounded. *If* this is indeed the implicit account of Cartesianism, it is obviously suspect, both because there is no particular reason to believe either that systematicity is a moral or legal system's prime virtue *or* that the laissez-faire core beliefs of late nineteenth-century liberalism or the efficiency-oriented beliefs of twentieth-century Chicago school adherents are nearly as contradiction free or easily interpretable as the proponents believe. I am, though, quite unsure how the deductive temperament serves, in even a minimal way, to block the feeling that values are historically relative.

Brief Notes on Critical Histories

If mainstream thinkers suffer from a failure to recognize the historical specificity of attitudes and values, an inexplicable yearning to live as in the past, and a tendency to discern nonexistent developmental trends, so, on at least some occasions, do the CLS historians. Little of the published Critical historiography has been particularly self-critical, but as the CLS antifunctionalist position on the role and history of law crystalizes, I suspect that many of the insights of the earlier CLS histories will have to be tempered or reformulated.

Let's take the problematic image of timeless discourse. While Critics justly attack the idea that operatively significant universal norms can be comprehended cross-culturally, they quite frequently imply, with equally little justification, that meaningfully unchanged "contradictions" or "clashes" continually dominate the legal agenda. Kennedy, for instance, in "The Structure of Blackstone's Commentaries," surely implies that something very much like the Fundamental Contradiction that I detailed in Chapter 1 has always existed in Western society.[71] There may be some way of constructing ongoing, philosophical or social dilemmas that implies that there is always some need for mediation between the self and others, but it is surely also the case that our particular understanding of the contradiction is anything but historically invariant. The conception of a coherent self with a life plan and secret, private dreams that are threatened by the demands of others, particularly the demands for role-appropriate behavior from others occupying positions of bureaucratic authority, is hardly age old. Mensch is likewise surprisingly blind to the extent to which the conflicts she perceives as having perpetually dominated legal life are in fact the "same" conflicts: for example, clashes between abstract ideas like "security" and "freedom," clashes between the notions that people want to avoid "risk" and yet believe that without "risk" no production will occur, may have no more cross-culturally constant meaning than do the universal norms that antihistorical scholars frequently advance.[72]

Undue CLS sentimentality is not quite as easy to spot as the mainstream constitutionalist's nostalgia, since CLS adherents worship neither a sacred test (or set of intentions) nor a discrete historical moment when all universal political problems were solved. Nonetheless, there are certainly times when the Critic's sentimentality seems as flimsily grounded as the mainstream theorist's. For example, Kennedy's implicit reference to the pre-Socratic days before the Fall, before the Fundamental Contradiction left us in the mess we're in, seems nothing but a bad twentieth-century existentialist literary device;[73] the idea that we have an interesting clue as to how pre-Socratic Greeks experienced themselves or others or the striving for perfection is enormously suspect. Likewise, while Unger does not thoroughly sentimentalize precapitalist "organic communities," he fails to explain adequately the ways in which their social structures might be not just *undesirable* (because grounded in domination) but nonreproducible (because the one relevant feature he is focusing on, the stability of their values, cannot be lifted out of historical context, just as the favored constitutional values, such as federalism, cannot be lifted meaningfully from theirs).[74] Again, too, while it would be unfair to say that Horwitz completely sentimentalizes the medieval notion of just price, to the extent that he implies that it reflects a greater commitment to nonexploitation, he is surely partly misportraying the ongoing normative relevance of an institution that, to the limited extent to which it ever held sway, may have reflected either the desire to restrict economic mobility or simply the then-prevailing factual absence of certain sorts of shifting circumstances.[75]

Most to the point, I think that the CLS historians initially adopted traditional pictures of a discontinuous development from feudal to capitalist social relations that would likely strike many of them now as implausibly neat, unduly dualistic. In the traditional CLS typology, preliberal (feudal) consciousness seems to have had at least five discernible traits, while liberal (capitalist) consciousness has at least four. Whether this typology, even if interpreted as having no more than heuristic ideal typical force, can truly survive both Critical theoretical skepticism about the noncontradictory nature of any thought system and empirical skepticism about the neatness or definedness of regimes is doubtful. Like adaptationists' notions of legal development, the early CLS view of feudal-to-liberal development often profoundly misses the boat.

The traditional CLS view was that preliberal society and social thought were principally constituted by five features. First, preliberal thought was committed to the idea of just price, to objective visions of the worth of objects. Not only did external objects have nonsubjectively grounded values, but *people's* worth was, in a sense, objective as well: ascriptive status dominated meritocratically earned status, the sort of status forever contingent on the whimsical and changing tastes of others about the value of one's work and the desirability of one's traits.[76] Second, there was a weak distinction between status and contract in preliberal ideology. There was no sharp line between duties that are socially set, generally by custom, and those that derive from individual commitment. Our tort-contract distinction was either absent or, if not utterly absent, weak. Likewise, the expectancy damage measure and executory contract rights were undeveloped, because the idea that one could individually create a property right, in the benefit of one's good bargains, is hard to fathom when property rights generally derive solely from customary social relations.[77] Third, the Fundamental Contradiction was mediated not by rights, as in liberal culture, but by defined role.[78] As long as everyone acted in role, according to customary obligations, one both had realized one's own ends (which inevitably coincided with the realization of one's role) and was assured that one had not been illegitimately dominated. Thus, the two operative perils highlighted by the Fundamental Contradiction analysis were eliminated: the problem of sacrificing one's true self for the sake of others that Kennedy and Unger both discuss was eliminated because there simply *was* no true self outside of role, and the problem of the fear of illicit domination was removed because no one expected deference or perquisites beyond one's station. Fourth, the "state" was no more than one of many limited actors on the social scene, with its own interests and concerns, rather than the institution that mediates all the conflicts within civil society. One can see this in formal legal terms by noting that writs were not available to vindicate all customary claims; that is, each right did *not* have a remedy. Many claims were vindicated, if at all, by local, indigenous institutions, while writs were available only when this socially separate body of state officials was thought to be involved.[79] And fifth, the concept of universal rights inhering in individuals, radically distinct from powers or privileges that could inhere in any particular entity, individual and natural or corporate and artificial, was very weak. Blackstone scarcely distinguished between the rights of individuals that constituted the basis of social organization and the powers and prerogatives of legislative and executive entities. Moreover, for Blackstone, the law did more than establish universal rights with correlative remedies to vindicate them; it certified customary status relationships that could be quite nonuniversal.[80]

By contrast, the traditional CLS vision of the ideology and practice of liberal society stresses four factors. First, the state is separate from society; it has exclusive jurisdiction over the regulation of civil society. Its regulatory function, though, is limited to ensuring the enforcement of contract and establishing rules (of tort and crime) to prevent harm to strangers.[81] (As liberal economic theory developed, the importance of the public provision of collective goods was stressed as well.)[82] In social theoretical terms, all social relations can be understood through the prism of the tort or free contract model: the world is divided into strangers who must respect one's entitlements and those one fuses with on limited, self-defined, voluntarily selected terms. Thus is the Fundamental Contradiction mediated: one can fuse with others, as long as they respect one's rights. In jurisprudential terms, Blackstone's defense of legal hypertechnicality—that is, that as a matter of descriptive fact, all legal rights in England happen to have remedies—was an early defense of the liberal ideal that the organized collective world could be fully constituted and understood as a rights-vindicating mechanism. The *absence* of a right in X—for instance, a situation in which X is injured but in the large domain of *damnum absque injuria* (injury without remedy)—*defines* what it is to be hurt without being exploited or unjustly dominated. There is no free-floating or prior notion of injustice to alter judgment about what rights are in particular situations; thus, the "late" or postliberal deconstruction of the notion that "every right has a remedy"—the deconstructed notion that the statement is utterly circular because we can list people's rights only by seeing what remedies we have given them—is not yet sensible. Second, "free" exchange generates normatively satisfactory results; since value is arbitrary and subjective, the *fact* of exchange proves its worthiness, and exchange alone proves relative values.[83] There are thought to be no significant problems of definition of "unfree" exchange as a result of ambiguities in defining fraud or duress.[84] Third, while the decision to contract or not is to be as free from legal impediment as possible, contracts, once made, are binding. A property right is established in the wise contractor's expectancy (unlike in preliberal contract), permitting, in essence, people to treat executory contracts as if they were fulfilled. Questions of when a contract is formed and when discharge is permitted are, once more, thought to be answered with adequate determinacy to permit people to treat their expectation interests as determinate property rights.[85] And fourth, while the state is not just another actor but the sole legitimate definer and defender of rights, it is constrained by the Rule of Law, so that no conflict exists between establishing a mediator over "civil" disputes and the strong desire to avoid the domination of this newly empowered superparty. Blackstone, for instance, partly defends legal hypertechnicality as a technique of avoiding tyrannical judicial discretion in rights definition; likewise, he must (and does) assert that equity and law courts apply the same rules, for if they didn't, those entrusted with dispute-resolution authority could impose their own values. Obviously, this commitment to legalistically limited state power persists in our odes to judicial review of extraconstitutional action and in the legal economist's model of the state administrator as technical preference aggregator.[86]

I do not find any of these descriptive claims unhelpful, at least insofar as they all express social theoretical attitudes toward which we are more or less drawn, and which might more or less dominate mainstream or judicial or educated elite opinion at particular times. But the historiographic insights of the Critical scholars should make us dubious about the descriptive power of these very broad claims. Here are some examples of problems.

For one, timeless antihistorians were justly accused of conflating legal norms with legal practice; it may well be the case that in contrasting the preliberal regime's commitment to just prices with the liberal state's commitment to subjectively defined value, the CLS historians overstated the full-blown practical sway of doctrine. Critics of Horwitz's work on contract law have argued, not unpersuasively, that few preliberal courts actually struck down unfair bargains.[87] At the same time, the liberal regime's nominal commitment to completely free contract has been limited not just by relatively recent welfare state reforms (such as nondisclaimable warranties) but by the long-standing imposition of public utility regulation on a host of service providers or by particular price and subject matter controls (for example, antiusury laws, antiprostitution laws).

Similarly, the notion that the expectation damages sanctified in liberal *treatises* either fully dominate capitalist legal *regimes* or are absent in preliberal contract law is both empirically suspect and theoretically unlikely, at least insofar as it rests on the notion that the theoretical impetus behind the supposed growing dominance of expectation damages is the need for predictability and planning that capitalist commercial ventures ostensibly require. One of the primary theoretical insights of Realists and Realist-influenced CLS writers is that expansions of one party's rights contract a correlative party's privilege. Thus, even if "capitalists" both needed certainty and could drive the legal system to serve their ends, the idea that they would gain certainty by getting a property right in more extensive damages is surely suspect, since the gain in security for the promisee is undoubtedly offset by the loss in security for the promisor.[88] Empirically, the "reform" of contract law—in which expanded excuses for total nonperformance and/or liberalization of the treatment of imperfect tender may well partly, in practice, and surely, in doctrinal theory, undercut the certainty of the promisee's expectancy—has proved perfectly compatible with liberal capitalist enterprise; it may simply create different risk allocations *between* entrepreneurs.

Likewise, the idea that the state in liberal society becomes the sole legitimate mediator in civil society, the sole repository of the rights-enforcing power, is doubtless a juridical or doctrinal abstraction rather than a lived reality. Not only do we know that many disputes (for example, contracts between parties with ongoing business relations) are settled without any recourse to formal legal procedure or extensive reference to formal law;[89] we also know that nongovernmental institutions (from corporate managers to Mafia bosses) still often exercise fairly explicit local authority.[90]

For a second example, CLS adherents rightly accused both timeless antihistorians and nostalgic sentimentalists of misunderstanding concepts that had a particular meaning in the past, and of simply mistranslating nominally similar concepts into today's cultural milieu. The limited CLS descriptions of the preliberal mediation of the Fundamental Contradiction seem to suffer from the identical problem, though. While one could imagine, in some sense, that the Fundamental Contradiction was mediated through role, it seems more precise to say that its modern terms—self and other—were distinct enough in preliberal culture to make the notion of "mediation" (making a painful problem appear readily solved) quite inappropriate. The odd sense of timelessness in the CLS account of the preliberal vision of role-oriented behavior can be partly captured by considering how difficult it is to integrate the strong religious consciousness of feudal society into the picture of role-mediated contradiction. Clearly, some of the status hierarchy of roles can be tied to religion both directly (religious functionaries have a place in the hierarchy) and indirectly or metaphorically (the relation between roles on earth corresponded to imagined relations between God and Man). But a highly religious, medieval Catholic "self" whose primary goal is a selfless integration of a transcendent God's commands, a "self" who feels enjoined to love "others" not for their particularities but simply because they are ensouled, God's creatures, a "self" who may well feel that his sojourn on earth is relatively trivial, is hardly the prototypical modern self, concerned above all else with false submissiveness to authority and convention.[91]

For a third example, the typical CLS histories almost surely understate the significance of disputes in both vision and program among people with parallel grandiose commitments and overstate, in a sense, the significance of high-order theory in producing daily practice. It may certainly be important, for example, to see what actual beliefs people have about concrete state practice when they are broadly committed to the idea that the state mediates conflicts in civil society and yet must be restrained. For instance, Horwitz, while not *directly* criticizing the traditional CLS picture of liberalism, notes that it might be possible to understand at least some late nineteenth-century laissez-faire attitudes not in terms of the strength of the proponents' commitment to the desirability of private ordering within an established rights framework, but in terms of their suspicion that state action would inevitably favor certain particular private interests they especially mistrusted.[92] Likewise, the impetus for regulation can be seen in part as a "postliberal" attack on the restricted state, in part as a corporatist response to the breakdown of a small-scale producer-dominated economy, in part as a statement of faith in the incorruptibility of the state actors.[93] Similarly, the ostensible liberal commitment to free exchange may mean quite different things to people who see information problems and impediments to bargaining everywhere they look, and those who constantly see the ideal conditions of contract either present or readily producible if properly encouraged.[94]

Fourth, the most significant and general point, it seems to me, is that the best-developed understanding that the CLS movement gained of liberal culture was one that took it less completely on its own inevitably problematic libertarian terms. While the initial historical pictures assumed, as misled adaptationists so often had done in falsely discerning trends, that uncontradictory practice and theory dominated the legal field, the better-developed CLS views focus not only on the core optimistic libertarian self-presentation of liberal legalism but on its basic irrepressible contradictions as well. The commitment to "free exchange" may be constitutive of *idealized* liberalism, but liberalism must also be seen as that regime that simultaneously embraces and decries "free exchange," because it cannot fully repress altruism, notions of objective value, visions of the problem of the potential power of nominally "private" institutions. Likewise, the division of that world into contract and tort, a world of voluntary relations and rights-respecting strangers, may dominate our rhetoric, and may indeed be powerfully important to recognize in understanding how we're likely to focus, initially, on a legal or social problem. But to understand liberalism as a regime actually committed to a strong dichotomy between the fields is both descriptively preposterous (tort law has long been invaded by contractual and relational concepts, like assumption of risk, and subject matter domains, like products liability, while contract law is imbued with torts concepts, like failure to bargain in good faith, quasicontract, implied contract)[95] and theoretically implausible, given the obvious difficulty of drawing the line between voluntary or intentionally created relationships and those that we are "forced" into. It would be incomplete to present liberalism *just* as it pretends to be, just as it would be incomplete to forget that it is partly constituted by its pretenses. The earlier CLS histories seemed to miss both these points. They not only failed to see how implausible neat historical schematizations would be once one recognized that practice both was and is complex, not uniform, but also, because they confused pretenses with reality, they failed to develop a theory of the importance of pretenses, their significance *as ideals*. What the Critics now see is that ideals are not just more or less accurate *descriptions* of a fixed social life outside of us but accounts that alter social life in unpredictable and complex ways as we try to live as we think we ought or must, given the world picture we've come to believe in.

CHAPTER EIGHT

Critical Views of the Role of Law

It would be far easier to discern a variety of hypotheses on the "role of law" in most mainstream visions than it is in the emerging Critical tradition. For those in the mainstream, there are two distinct spheres, "society" and "law." In his "Critical Legal Histories," by far the best-developed and most elegantly argued account of CLS attitudes about the nature and role of law, Robert Gordon notes that in the main-stream picture, " 'society' is the primary realm of social experi-ence . . . [W]hat's immediately and truly important to people, like de-sire and its fulfillment or frustration, goes on there . . . the realm of production, commerce, the market, the family." Law, by contrast, is handmaiden to society in this picture: it is seen as a "specialized realm of state and professional activity that is called into being by the primary social world . . . an excrescence on social life."[1]

Mainstream theorists obviously differ in their conception of how law serves society. The various visions of the "role of law" are, in a sense, simply distinct hypotheses about the extent to which law is invariably functional or at least occasionally dysfunctional, relatively autonomous or fully superstructural, a servant of unified social needs or of more particular interests.

In the most Pollyannaish functionalist adaptationist views, societies as a whole have needs, which evolve over time as the society progresses, and the law adapts, more or less rapidly, to these changing needs.[2] At times, some mainstream writers may criticize various aspects of this pure, adaptive social functionalism. Some may believe that particular people or groups have wants or interests, to which the law responds, but that no meaningful organic society has either needs or wants.[3] Others believe that law is more responsive to certain interests than others (for example those of men rather than women,[4] of economic elites,[5] of law-yers and bureaucrats[6]). Still others believe that a variety of legal responses will satisfy certain social requirements or the desires of individuals or subgroups equally well,[7] while some emphasize the ambiguity of defining the "society" that may or may not have requirements.[8] One can concede that the law seemingly responds differently to the "same needs"; or one can expand the list of needs until we no longer have any distinct definition of a society's nature and requirements from an actual detailed description of its practices.

At times, in the traditional picture, law is seen *solely* as the exercise of explicit behavioral *control*. At other times, the language and rituals of law are significant as well.[9] One "need" that an "elite" may have is to minimize the necessity for confrontational force by convincing the "masses" that the existing distribution of perquisites and power is reasonably just, and legal rhetoric may help do that.

At times, too, the inevitably "progressive" character of legal and historical development may be called into question.[10] Both of the traditional progressive visions—the "Scottish Enlightenment" vision of freeholders unbound from feudal shackles and superstitions,[11] and the late nineteenth-century vision of a world of rapid technological advance, rationalized production, and expanded opportunities for the immigrants and underclass[12]—can be partly supplanted. "Progressivism" may be undercut by the view that legal change simply reflects the dominance of whichever pernicious elite has grabbed a greater degree of control, the view that "modernization" is predominantly gloomy, destroys communal bonds, decent work, faith, and family, and/or that development has generally moved us from a society of independent, civic-minded, and public-spirited citizens to a bunch of atomistic profit grabbers.

The evolving Critical analysis of law seems to me to achieve several quite distinct objectives. First, it reiterates and sharpens most of the traditional attacks on progressive or adaptationist functionalism. Second, it reconceives the relationship between law and society, at least as that relationship is understood in the materially developed, heavily legalized cultures that the Critics are interested in when they discuss the "role of law," by denying the possibility that one could imagine any advanced, heavily legalized society or the individuals within it independently from the legal structure. We can no longer speak coherently of law *responding* to distinct prelegal interests once we see how much these interests are defined by law. Third, it develops a more refined and general theoretical picture of why no materially advanced social system could possibly either require or hope to put in place any discrete and stable legal features to meet its needs, since it sees any "stage" of "modern" law as no more than a particular set of internally contradictory beliefs and practices. Fourth, it focuses rather little on the behavior control aspects of law, while obviously not utterly denigrating their importance, and focuses instead, to a growing degree, on the ways in which law is one of many cultural institutions that are constitutive of consciousness, that help delimit the world, make only certain thoughts sensible, thus "legitimating" existing social relations.

While I will not explore this point much further, I believe that it is important to note that an aspect of the first point (the reemphasis on legal sociologists' insistence on looking at whether abstract law governs actual practice), the second point (noting how law is inextricable from "private" life), and the fourth (deemphasizing behavior control), when analyzed in combination, support the usual Critical insistence that traditional lines between the public legal sphere and private civil society can readily be overestimated. There may well be no specialized group of legal or bureaucratic actors who actually possess the characteristics of the Weberian state, no public actors with the thoroughgoing capacity to direct others in the face of "private" resistance. In this sense, the public sphere of law seems to shrink. At the same time, law *expands* once one sees that "private" desire and power are both heavily influenced by formal legalistic decisions. Furthermore—and here I think the emerging Critical argument is even more discontinuous with the Law and Society tradition—in resolving controversies that no formal legal agent may referee, we may still engage in "law-speak," make arguments, both to ourselves and others, that have the virtues associated with acceptable legal argument. To the extent that the "law" is both a locus of explicit coercive power and a rhetoric, "private" life is further legalized to the extent that law's rhetorical tropes are generally either admired or simply used unself-consciously.

The Critique of Adaptationist Functionalism

Much of the CLS critique of the "adaptationist" side of adaptationist functionalism was already presented in Chapter 7. The notion that there is some uniform evolutionary path toward which societies tend to move (either as a descriptive or prescriptive matter) is highly dubious. To reiterate critiques of some of the most common adaptationist notions, status relationships need not be displaced by contractual ones; formal equality may or may not increasingly take hold; a concern with economic growth and industry subsidization may or may not be displaced by solicitude for unknowledgeable consumers or accidental victims of industry.

The CLS restatement of the traditional critique of functionalism—the claim that one could both understand what social needs exist and predict certain necessary legal responses to them—is probably more important to understanding the developing CLS view of law. The relevant traditional critiques of functionalism seem to be the ones that emphasize (1) indeterminacy of legal response, (2) social conflict over the appropriate legal agenda, and (3) legal system autonomy.

Indeterminacy of Response

The claim of legal indeterminacy emphasizes not so much the degree to which any set of legal practices is so inexorably internally contradictory that one would be hard pressed even to state an accurate *summary* of prevailing practice, but rather the degree to which we would find it impossible to match up prevailing practices (to the extent that we can discern them) with particular social conditions. The claim is largely skeptical or negative. It might conceivably be that we simply have not yet gathered enough *data* to generate general laws about both the legal responses certain social conditions give rise to and the feedback of law to society—that is, the changes in society produced by those legal moves. But the Critics, echoing traditional antifunctionalists, certainly imply that the search for lawlike regularities is likely to be perennially quixotic. Gordon notes two distinct ways in which the indeterminacy argument is made.

The more obvious and perhaps more powerful studies simply demonstrate that apparently similar social conditions have generated disparate legal responses, both cross-culturally and within the same culture. In other words, two different cultures with ostensibly parallel needs may adopt opposite legal rules, and a single society may seemingly adopt contradictory responses to the same need. Thus, for instance, while functionalists frequently hypothesize that the development of infant industries requires the use of a negligence rule that permits these industries to externalize the costs of the risks they impose, it is not so apparent either that the negligence rule, when actually in force, arose in response to industrialization in the United States or that many American industries in fact benefited by it.[13] The even more powerful Weberian claim that developing capitalism requires a high degree of rule-bound formality to increase certainty in planning is undercut by Weber's own comparative observations (England, for instance, industrialized without a highly predictable legal code).[14] More interesting, perhaps, it is undercut by the recognition that not all arenas within a society supposedly begging for increased certainty will become more settled and predictable. Gordon notes that even as contract law was becoming more stable and predictable in nineteenth-century America, the legal system was simultaneously destabilizing many other expectations (for example, by increasing state takings and regulatory powers, by divesting prior vested monopoly or antidevelopment rights).[15] Similarly, James Kainen notes that the typical elite theorist's argument that late nineteenth-century judges were particularly responsive to protecting emerging capitalists' interests is simply inconsistent with their refusal to protect many "vested rights" that had been protected under the contract clause earlier in the century. Corporations could no longer inevitably retain tax exemptions placed in their charters or receive compensation for more stringent safety regulations, nor was their traditional freedom to combine and contract protected against antitrust legislation.[16]

A second sort of skeptical view is to question the extent to which a generalized legal response to a perceived need in fact actually governs the whole social field, given ambiguities in interpretation of formal pronouncement and diferent degrees of enthusiasm for enforcement by both low-level officials and private parties who must often set the legal machinery in motion.[17] Thus, for instance, Gordon notes that if we are testing the proposition that ascending capitalism requires certainty, and if we know that formal rules of contract law became more mechanical during the nineteenth century, we may still have learned only that the *treatises* were becoming more predictable, not that the rules governing actual commercial bargaining were.[18] Likewise, when Alfred Konefsky notes that a local federal judge in early nineteenth-century Kentucky effectively precluded enforcement of the federal whiskey tax, thus preserving local customary expectations about whiskey production, through merciless invocation of traditional English technical rules, he sees that any functional theory that tried either to explain the importance of the assertion of central government taxing authority in the early nineteenth century or to theorize generally about when hypertechnicality comes into play in the legal system should be very careful to consider how institutions actually function. The case demonstrates both that taxing *statutes* do not always result in taxes and that the centralizing rationalizer's beliefs in hypertechnicality can at times be put to use by local antilegalists.[19]

Conflict

The second familiar critique of *social* functionalism—that societies are often arenas of conflict, not unity—is one that has been embraced, in only mildly different forms, by left- and right-wing critics alike. While those on the right may be more eager than those on the left to include professional do-gooders, anxious for welfare state employment, on the list of special-interest groups seeking governmental largesse,[20] the idea that state power is often exercised on behalf of those who capture influence in battle certainly seems to be the common wisdom of the 1980s, just as unified social functionalist views seemingly dominated the 1950s. Obviously, the Critics distance themselves from the liberal pluralist vision of this model. For the Critics, just as for left-liberal historians before them, like Willard Hurst or Lawrence Friedman, not every interest group has the same capacity to become state capturer of the day; Parker's critique of Ely and Choper's faith in pluralism typifies the Critical attitude that some people have far more access to power than others.[21]

While it is surely easy enough to find work in the Critical literature that emphasizes either the notion of elite state capture or a more structural view in which elites benefit more indirectly from decisions to preserve or create a particular productive structure, my sense is that the trend in CLS is toward skepticism of the sorts of claims I shall now review. There is, though, certainly both original CLS writing expanding the stories of the use of state force to advance both particular elite interests (economic elites, men, bosses),[22] and occasionally nonelite ones,[23] and a good deal of frequently cited writing from outside the CLS movement. Typical observations from outsiders are that particular influential eighteenth-century English country squires initiated the central government's concern with deer poaching,[24] and certain upper-class victims of particular crimes often influenced both the Parliament to expand the list of capital crimes and the courts to interpret the statutes loosely.[25] Likewise, unpunished physical terror and manipulation of the legal and political process, as well as of the local media, might well have been a significant aspect of mine-owners' efforts to suppress egalitarian movements in the Clear Fork Valley in Appalachia, particularly during a critical strike in the early 1930s;[26] abortion liberalization may have been reponsive primarily to the demands not of disempowered women but of men who wanted to strip women of a major socially functional barrier (fear of pregnancy) to men's demands for sexual access.[27]

At times, too, the pieces cited or written by CLS theorists are traditionally Marxist, in the sense that they view the law not so much as responding to particular interests of particular relatively powerful people, as responding to what should be thought of as materially constitutive interests; that is, decisions are seen as necessary to define historically developing class relations. In this sense there is obviously a relatively thin line between traditional generalized functionalism and a partial critique grounded in recognition of social division. The main difference would seem to be that the Marxists see "social" needs not just as historically specific and historically shifting (as more centrist functionalists may too) but as a history of the unfolding of particular forms of domination, of distinct exercises of class power. There is also a significant distinction between the more Marxist works and the "elite-responsive" work, highlighted initially in Mark Tushnet's critical review of Lawrence Friedman's explicit elite domination theories. The Marxists often distinguished between society-defining "epochal" legal rules (those that in theory define the basic social roles that supposedly shift as, say, capitalism emerges from feudalism) and the host of intrasystemic legal battles. Tushnet, and the Critics generally, seem to find it far harder to believe that elites dominate each decision that is made, whether because the legal system may be relatively autonomous, because ideological consistency imperatives may overcome result orientation, or simply because less is at stake materially in each intrasystemic dispute than the elite dominance theorists at least sometimes imply.[28]

E. P. Thompson's writings are typical of work with recourse to both elite dominance and Marxist traditions. Not only does he describe the elaborate patronage system of eighteenth-century English life, in which state-granted powers (for example to tax) were an important source of power differentiation that the initially privileged successfully used to expand their relative privilege; he also describes the degree to which the most basic disputes over land, battles between formal owners and those with traditional use claims, inexorably had to go the owners' way, not just because owners were more politically influential but because the transformation of land into an alienable productive factor (ostensibly) required it.[29] Similarly, Douglas Hay presents an elite theorist's picture of an eighteenth-century England where significant power-enhancing patronage (for example the prerogative of mercy or pardon) was one of the chief benefits a select subclass could grab from the state.[30] But at the same time, he also presents a more Marxist view. The focus on particular privileges is replaced by a look at the much broader fabric of social practice. The congruence of the absence of a police force, weak enforcement of all offenses against property (except for forgery, which threatened commercial paper, the one form of ruling-class property that was not, as a practical matter, unstealable), and a majestic legalism that preserved the image of authority, represented the triumph of the emerging superelite against middle-class artisans and small landholders, which was part of the (supposedly) historically necessary process of sharpening the class divisions between working class and owner.[31] Alan Freeman's arguments on the development of antidiscrimination law can be given a reasonably traditional Marxist interpretation as well. Antidiscrimination remedies (like busing) have paid great heed to norms of privacy and autonomy, so that only the elite is shielded from undesired participation in integration (a vision consistent with standard elite influence theory). Obviously, though, the elite would not have to participate in undesired remedies if there were no antidiscrimination law at all; but a significant fight against racism serves to stabilize the existing *regime,* by staving off both literal black revolt and the sort of pressure from the international community that would undermine America's vital imperialist prerogatives.[32] Likewise, Klare's emphasis on the degree to which the Supreme Court suppressed facially plausible accounts of congressional intent in passing the Wagner Act in order to ensure that the managerial command structure of the workplace was unthreatened by efforts to extend the domain of workers' control can also be given a traditional Marxist interpretation.[33] Though Klare himself is decidedly nondeterminist in his own approach, the piece can be readily, if incorrectly, viewed as an argument that a posture opposed to workers' control is so constitutive of fundamental capitalist social relations that the judicial misreading of the political impetus behind the act was inevitable.

Relative Autonomy

The third way in which the Critics embrace and extend traditional antifunctionalist positions is by arguing that the legal system is "relatively autonomous," that it is hardly inevitable that legal practices change with shifts in productive relations or the balance of political power because the practices often are derived largely from prior practice and the understanding of the legal subculture. Not only is the law not simply poorly understood as a *dependent* variable—that is, not only is it a mistake to believe that legal practice can always be explained by external factors—but also it is often the case that the supposedly external factors should be partly understood as dependent variables, altered by the internal

peculiarities of legal practice. The "world" will be different depending
on how people sort out their experience, what they think of as just or
inevitable, and the law helps define those expectations.

Critics have surely emphasized the noninstrumental significance of
law, the difficulty of seeing law as purely responsive to the material
world, and the impact of legal consciousness on decisions that undoubtedly have significant material consequences. Tushnet, for instance, notes
that employers often sought legal justification for their use of force,
even when they had access to and were permitted to use identical private
force without court certification.[34] If, as the functionalists imply, the
powerful seek law because the state has unique powers, it is hard to
comprehend why employers sought formal injunctions against concerted
labor activity before hiring private armies to break strikes. Gordon
points out that explaining the Constitution solely in terms of the material
interests of the adopters is inadequate. Reference to the prevailing political and legal ideologies of the day are needed if we are to make sense
of the content of the document.[35] Klare's study of judicial deradicalization of the Wagner Act[36] and Frug's study of the disempowerment of
cities[37] both emphasize the extent to which vital sociopolitical decisions
(the dampening of both intrafactory and local governmental collective
political power) have been not simply a response to the opposition of
the powerful to local collectivism but a function of the available limited
legal understandings of the issues at stake. Obviously, too, CLS writers
often call on Hay's and Thompson's works to validate their suppositions
both that law has a life of its own and that its having a life of its own
permits it to have an important impact on the greater society. Hay is
particularly adept at detailing the degree to which law's pompous rituals—what he calls its majestic aspect—convey a general respect for
order and authority, even when (perhaps especially when) legal authorities are meting out not the sort of behavior controlling punishment
that instrumentalists tend to think is all that matters, but a mercy supposedly grounded in hypertechnically vigilant protection of the rights
of the accused (for example, when throwing out death penalty charges
for trivially defective indictments).[38] Thompson even believes that the
legal system's commitment to universalistic decision making, to refusing
to act at the direct, detailed instrumental behest of the powerful, is so
strong as to make legality a genuine universal good.[39] While that position
is controversial within CLS,[40] the descriptive proposition—that legal
decision makers do feel constrained even in times of disorder to follow
exacting procedures, even at the cost of some loss of control—is a

recurring and widely accepted theme, not just in accounts of eighteenth-century England but in, say, Isaac Balbus's picture of the handling of American ghetto riots in the late 1960s[41] and Tushnet's vision of the application of the early nineteenth-century slave codes.[42]

CLS Attacks on Traditional Antifunctionalist Stances

It is important to note that while people within the CLS movement have in part embraced these traditional antifunctionalist stances, they have criticized them as well, in ways that helped to clarify and form the vision of law's significance that seems to me to be growing in dominance in the Critical literature.

First, while it may in some senses represent an advance over traditional functionalist thinking to recognize that there is *conflict* in society rather than a bland unity of interests, the idea that we can see law wholly as responsive to particular desires, whether of those persons whose will generally dominates or of more random winners in the pluralist sweepstakes, is certainly suspect. The Critical revisionists were undoubtedly correct in perceiving conflict and in focusing attention on the distributive consequences of both broad legal regimes and more narrow legal decisions, but they may have been quite wrong in completely abstracting political actors from their social roles, in assuming that the direction of causality is wholly from private desire to public response. Gordon, elegant as always, perhaps put the point best:

> For all its problems, the functionalist persepctive recognizes that societies have to be understood as systems and structures, not just as a series of collisions among the preferences and strategies of their constituent members . . . the more reductionist ["instrumentalists"] . . . seem to think that one is puncturing all the vagueness involved in reifying "society" into a thing with "needs" by getting down to the nitty-gritty reality of concrete individuals and groups. But the "interest groups" of pluralist theory and the "individuals" of economic theory are no less reified and no more real entities than the "society" of functionalists.[43]

Second, to the extent that mainstream antifunctionalists often use observations of the indeterminacy of legal response and the relative autonomy of the legal system as a pretext for a kind of disengagement, the Critics have been as harsh toward the antifunctionalists as they have been toward their functionalist forebears.[44] The disengaged response, typified by pieces by Charles Fried[45] and Richard Epstein,[46] is that law has *no* interesting relationship with society, that what happens within a legal culture has little external significance and that the precise occurrences within the system can be explained only by reference to its own peculiar, insular professional history.

The Critical response in part simply reiterates two positions most often associated with the Law and Society movement. First, to the extent that the disengaged *appear* to have a valid point, it is only because they focus their attention on aspects of the legal system that matter least (case law), even though lawyers spend the bulk of their time attending to less peripheral, less ignored (and hence, in a sense, autonomous by inattention) institutional regulations, whether statutes, administrative rulings and regulations, or local ordinances.[47] Second, to the extent that lawyers are charged with the task of settling significant social disputes—whether over property ownership, marriage, corporate governance, and so on—it is unlikely that they could fulfill this function if their positions were wholly the notions of an isolated subculture whose ideas did not resonate among the disputants.

The Critics also question the disengaged posture in two less traditional ways. First, they note the degree to which the disengaged have confused a valid methodological insight with an incorrect substantive conclusion. It is indeed often helpful in understanding *any* practice, including statute drafting or judicial opinion writing, to begin by looking at the task as it appears to its practitioners, by emphasizing the particular phenomenology of the activity; but the phenomenological approach hardly *precludes* a more structural understanding of the task. One of the Critics' main general methodological insights—that we waver between intentionalist and determinist accounts of actors—should make us wary of believing that a picture of the free, autonomous legal actor with her own projects *precludes* a picture of her as the handmaiden of forces she neither sees nor self-consciously serves. Obviously, the determinist account could be consistent with the idea of legal system autonomy; a particular actor could be the object solely of internal legal system conventions that frame her understandings. But, ordinarily, the claim of systemic autonomy and phenomenological method are blurred; the judge's overarching palpable concern with justice and technique is thought to disprove, by itself, accounts that see him largely as responsive.[48]

Second, and perhaps more important, the disengaged response often seems to confuse distinct points at different levels of generality. Particular legal decisions may be either undeniably peripheral or, even when they seem more significant, compatible with the realization of different private programs, given the flexibility that actors have in responding to a given legal environment. Still, it may well be that law as a whole is not the least bit insignificant, indeed that we could not even imagine a society separate from its legally defined relationships. As Gordon notes, Epstein's claim that alterations of any particular nineteenth-century private law rule would have had little consequence is utterly plausible, but to imagine the society without *any* of its rules of contract law, property, tort, debt collection, slave codes, and fugitive slave law is to imagine a radically different society.[49]

The Interpenetration of "Law" and "Society"

In a sense, the chief break the Critics have made with traditional legal sociology has been to refuse to accept the ordinary distinction between epiphenomenal law and "real" society. Many of the partial critiques of adaptationist functionalism, as well as the reaction to these partial critiques, partake of this Critical hostility to positing a dividing wall between "social" and "legal" spheres. Law, in a sense, significantly *defines* the actors who are frequently pictured as the social base that influences law. At least in the relatively legalized advanced economies, it is often impossible to conceive of the social cast of characters without reference to the legal attributes inhering in each person or "interest group." While this point is bolstered once one defines *law* in terms of both state control over conduct and rhetorical understandings of the world, for now I want only to reiterate Gordon's argument that "private relationships" are incomprehensible even if we disregard all but the narrower traditional, coercive state rules.[50]

The point is often seen most readily in historical writings. Thompson, for instance, notes that the underlying economic activities that traditional Marxists think of as the "base" would surely look different if legal rules were altered. Neither eighteenth-century farming nor quarrying would have been carried out in the same way but for prevailing legal ideas about what property is held commonly; the cast of characters with "interests" in the eighteenth-century forest is named, to a significant degree, by reference to their first-line *legal* interests in the forest.[51] Similarly, Gordon favorably cites Robert Brenner's work on preindustrial Europe,[52] which differentiates between Western and Eastern European responses to late medieval population declines. In Western Europe, labor terms by and large became more favorable, while in Eastern Europe, serfdom intensified. In some significant part, labor's gains in Western Europe were a result of the partly legally constituted vision of the peasantry, which had wrested enough legalistic concessions over the years that attempts to withdraw traditional prerogatives caused chaotic resistance. The law did not simply *respond* to variously powerful peasantries; it created significant differences. Finally, in Kennedy's view, Marx believed that the fetishism of commodities, the belief that the choice of both productive activities and exchange relations are determined by the objective characteristics of natural objects rather than by human choice, characterized capitalist but not pre- or postcapitalist cultures, not because of prelegal facts about capitalist technology but because the juridical relations in and/or shared legalized consciousness of actors in capitalist economies blind people to social choice. Fetishized commodity consciousness is not derivative of a definable prelegal base. Tbe determining structural base *includes* vital legal elements (for example, a competitive market, "free" labor). In the same fashion, non-fetishized feudal consciousness, in which serfs recognize that their activities are directed not by natural forces but by the discrete decisions of those with hierarchical authority over them, is a function of a highly legalized base with a certain pattern of accepted authority.[53]

Gordon notes that it is usually quite easy to make people recognize the fundamentally constitutive character of legal relations when describing bygone feudal or slaveholding societies. It seems obvious that one can't imagine how to either marginalize law's role or declare law to be in the interests of slaveholders without recognizing that slavery is fundamentally a legal relationship, that such a society cannot be described without reference to its basic legal relations.[54]

The more interesting task, Gordon realizes, is to make people understand that the law is significantly constitutive in modern, liberal societies, which formally define themselves as being free of ascriptive status relations, which define themselves as facilitating the realization of desire, given wholly *pre*legal policies and preferences. (It would, of course, also be interesting to see if the Critics believe that societies with less intrusive legal structures than Western capitalist ones would be far more readily definable without regard to either legal force or legal thinking, but I don't think that the Critics have really engaged the traditional domain of legal anthropology.) Gordon's effort to destabilize the notion that modern liberal societies are extralegal is essentially a two-step one. In the first step, he notes that any initial observation of a milieu requires noting the legal statuses of the actors; in the second, he notes that the labeled statuses may in part be a function of arguably prelegal facts, but will inevitably be partly legalized too.[55]

Thus, Gordon notes that the routine ways in which we would look at the people in a typical office makes implicit reference to their presumed powers and privileges. "An owner," "an office temp," "a senior associate," "a contractor in to do repairs" are not just random labels we attach to people; they are decidedly legal labels. Lots of people are working, but we know that we have given a needlessly incomplete picture of their job relations unless we know whether a particular employee is an employee at will, a major shareholder in the business that formally hires him, an illegal immigrant, married to the employer, protected against being fired for organizing concerted activity, and so on. Obviously, some of the powers each of these people has and doesn't have are a function of things we would hardly find it helpful to call predominantly legal: a person may, as Gordon notes, be indispensable to the office, stupendously physically attractive or intimidating, readily employable elsewhere. Even in ostensibly nonlegal descriptions, though, legal practices may well intrude. For instance, the degree to which anyone can be physically intimidating may in part be a function of the extent of public response to private physical violence. One's job options are a function of rules that help or hinder the creation of expansive job markets, a fact that, say, baseball players, who have faced many different legal regimes in the past decade, surely know.

It is perhaps even more clearly the case that pluralist interest groups are created and defined in part by legal decisions. As Gordon notes, regional pressure groups are surely defined in part by wholly legal jurisdictional definitions (undoubtedly some of what unifies the interests of people in the Berkshires and Boston is that they are represented by the same senators). Similarly, I might add, it would seem that the concept of local property owners with an interest in the level of the property tax may not be comprehensible without seeing that the existing property tax systems and alternatives on the political agenda define the class; races may be defined in America in some significant part by their relationship to antidiscrimination law in addition to constituting an independent influence on that body of law. Gordon even provides an example in which the absence of a clear consensus legal theory renders pluralist group definition problematic: it is hard to define particular corporations as interest groups precisely because we don't have a clear legal theory of how the corporation is ideally constituted out of its innumerable subparts.

There seem to be three common attacks on the Critical notion that it would be fruitless, even in a formally liberal society, to think of autonomous individuals and groups as "influencing" or demanding responsive law.

The first attack, in a sense, reiterates the Critics' position that many distinct laws are compatible with identical social relations. The position seems to imply that there is a reality to social relations separate from law, "real stuff" unaffected by particular legal form. But the implication is certainly as misleading as the "disengaged" vision of legal system autonomy that it quite obviously echoes. It confuses the marginality of particular decisions with the marginality of basic legal concepts. It is surely a far cry from the obvious insight that fairly parallel wealth transmission schemes could occur under more and less lax interpretations of the Rule against Perpetuities to an (obviously wrong) belief that the world would unquestionably be the same without any notion of either explicit inheritance or family "privacy" that permitted giving advantages to the children of the wealthy. It is not surprising that lawyers tend to forget the most centrally constitutive legal categories because they work on issues (whether as litigators, draftsmen, or mainstream academics) that are likely to be peripheral or marginal, since dealt with by institutions designed to accommodate marginal change. It is an easy (if misleading) step from experiencing one's legal work as relatively trivial to believing that law is trivial.[56]

Second, opponents of the Critical view that law and society cannot be meaningfully unbound bring up yet another insight the Critics endorse—that formal law often has limited impact on social practice—to denigrate the notion that society is strongly influenced by law. Once again, while the legal sociologists were undoubtedly correct to note that the Formalist was mistaken in his supposition that abstract rules announced by central institutions instantly governed all conduct, this hardly resuscitated the concept of a meaningful prelegal world.[57] The formal enactment of alcoholic prohibition may not "take" not solely because law does not matter in the face of raging desire (though that's unquestionably part of the story) but in part because "other" law does. Legalistic respect for privacy and nonintrusive criminal law enforcement are only the *obvious* surface legal components of the legal regime's more particular failure. In a more general sense, partly legalized "deep" notions of taste and value subjectivity and of the appropriate role of the collective in shaping individual activity play a significant role, too, in sustaining resistance to the particular formal law.[58]

Third, and surely most important, this Critical position arguably fails to account adequately for the existence of legal transformation. Legal rules *change* at the initiative of actors; it seems, at least at first blush, that if actors were not decidedly separate from their legal roles, they could not demand such change. Surely it is *possible,* then, to imagine each existing legal relationship as simply an affirmation of alegal power, shifting as soon as power shifts. But the fact that shifts in power and desire can precede a legal shift hardly goes to show that either power or desire can be understood alegally. As Gordon notes, one is likely to find the conditions of such ostensibly law-free Hobbesian power wars only in instances where the law has rather explicitly left actors to settle their own scores (for example the formal marital rape exception, the nonformal marital battery exception). Whether one can describe such accommodations as alegal is obviously problematic at best: the choice of zones of Hohfeldian privilege is surely often an explicit, significant legal choice in a heavily legalized culture.[59] More generally, when people struggle to shift entitlements to their advantage, we can hardly know if they will succeed without knowing what *initial* entitlements they took into the fray.[60] Whether, for instance, the marital rape exception will in fact effectively dissolve is a function not of some utterly prelegally constituted "power" that women have gained and will continue to gain but of a power that is built in some part on everything from obviously empowering decisions (from abolition of the common law's fictional unity of spouses to laws prohibiting discrimination in employment) to more subtly empowering ones (for example, the growth of tort and civil rights actions against sexually harassing employers may help change general social expectations about sexual ground rules, may even change women's conceptions of what their social meaning is).

Contradiction

Traditional functionalist accounts of law generally assume that we can always discover some fairly uniform legal practice, then match it up with either the interests of some powerful subgroup or some broader "social needs." Both Legal Realists and legal sociologists were mildly skeptical of the claim that uniform practice could readily be discerned, noting, in ways the Critics certainly endorsed, that what Formalists *perceived* as "the law," textbook pronouncements, might be irrelevant, ignored, effective only in certain places if local custom opposed it, and so on. But one could still have a functionalist *attitude* once one pierced the Formalist myth of legal uniformity; in fact, perfectly ordinary functionalist arguments could explain why the locally powerful "needed" exemptions from formal Mandarin rules.

The Omnipresence of Contradiction

The Critics' account of legal indeterminacy is far harder to square with *any* functionalist picture, although it is not logically incompatible with a form of functionalist explanation, to which I shall return, that has not yet, to my knowledge, been advanced. The Critics do not simply claim that contradictory practices persist in the face of efforts to unify practice by incomplete, hegemonic central legal institutions; they claim that it is impossible to imagine any central *or* local legal institutions advocating a coherent, noncontradictory body of basic rules. *All* rules will contain within them, deeply embedded, structural premises that clearly enable decision makers to resolve particular controversies in opposite ways. Local practice needn't fully *rebel* against the demands of law; all law seems simultaneously either to demand or at least to allow internally contradictory steps.

Obviously, the Critics have most fully detailed the way in which all practices within liberal capitalist legal systems can be interpreted so as to emphasize either the core privileged liberal values (rule-bounded legality, individualism, value subjectivity, intentionalism, nonpaternalism) or the dissident ones (situation-sensitive standards, altruism, value objectivity, determinism, paternalism). They have detailed the impossibility of suppressing the contradictions in theory and practice both by analyzing all existing doctrine (Chapters 1 through 3 attempt, essentially, to summarize those extensive efforts) and by looking, historically, at the particular path of American legal development as an unsuccessful effort to suppress these contradictions.

It is vital to reiterate that the internal contradictions detailed in Chapters 1 through 3 do not render daily outcomes wholly unpredictable or random, but simply that commitments to principles that undermine that practice are invariably available. Inertia is powerful; much practice is extremely predictable in the short run because we know that proposed decisions that would greatly change the world will be considered either wrong or too political for lawyers to accomplish. At the same time, practice is invariably eroding. An explicitly redistributive income taxation scheme comes to fruition at the same time that the constitutionalization of substantive due process appears to freeze the distributive shares generated by the common law rules; either the presence or absence of a heavy superfund tax on polluters seems simultaneously to regulate and to deregulate or privatize, given the absence of an acceptable theory of when conduct is solely self-regarding; the will theory of contract seems to require both limited and expansive duress rules, given the difficulty we have defining the degree of control over her circumstances that a truly "free" person must have.

Essentially, the historical picture is that in the emergence of liberal legalism from Blackstone's part-feudal, part-liberal construct, producers of legal thought attempted to purge their product of ambivalence and contradiction. Realms of freedom and necessity could ideally be readily distinguished; the world was neatly divided into the private sphere of contract and the collectively coercive but carefully delimited state.[61] It may well have been that late nineteenth-century judges subjectively *believed* that they had done a reasonably thorough job of purifying law of both preliberal elements and postliberal redistributive fervor, but even then the enterprise was fundamentally collapsing, because the contradictory commitments could never be purged. "Free" contract could never be defined without an implicit vision of the boundaries of duress and fraud. The *early* nineteenth-century use of the contract clause may have partly limited the state, but it protected only an arbitrary handful of similarly "harmed" private citizens, depending on whether they had already acquired vested rights before legislation altered the value of their holdings, a position inconsistent with the emerging late-century recognition that expectancy and property interests could not be meaningfully distinguished, just as interests in physical objects could no longer be distinguished from interests in other objects of value. When vested rights consciousness gave way to late nineteenth-century substantive due process law, judges felt forced to constitutionalize particular common law contract rules, declaring *that* regulatory regime to be one that people were entitled to act under, but the common law itself was rife with exceptions, and problems of fraud, duress, and externalities (the police power) could never long be held at bay. Thus neither contracts clause nor due process doctrine could truly protect against the collective desire to frame distributive outcomes that is always part of liberal consciousness.[62]

As the protection of property was extended during the century from the protection of a person's dominion over things to the protection of interests in value, it became clearer that property was simply a social creation, that since ownership was a "conclusion" rather than a premise to ground further argument, the distinction between (legitimate) distributive and (illegitimate) redistributive law was unsustainable. It may sound at least vaguely tenable to speak of protecting one's ownership of a thing without regard to the distributive consequences of that decision; but to speak of "protecting" some interest in a particular distributive share without acknowledging that as a distributive decision came to look infinitely harder.[63] Likewise, the insuperable difficulty of defending the distinction between the domain of tort and the domain of *damnum absque injuria* (injury without remedy),[64] as well as the difficulty of sustaining a belief that we had solved the causation problem[65] (that is, that we knew with scientific objectivity when and how much ostensible tortfeasors harmed victims), called into serious question the ideal of a nondistributive legal system in which all transfers were a function of private-sphere volition, either in mutual gain seeking (contract) or rectification of wrongdoing (tort). If we readily expand or contract the area of uncompensated damage causing within a formally identical system, in accord with our ever-shifting commitments to either self-reliance or sharing, and/or our shifting beliefs about encouraging each of us to protect himself versus the need to induce people to avoid damaging others, we have hardly *routinized* legal practice.[66]

Contradiction and Functionalism

It is, of course, theoretically possible that the existence of the particular pattern of contradictions in theory and practice is itself functional, either in the traditional sense (*responsive* to social needs or particular interests) or, in a more critical sense, constitutive of the sort of society we live in. Naturally, though, this is a very different claim from one that functionalists typically make. In the usual picture, some actors either want or need either caveat emptor *or* consumer protection, want or need formal rules *or* informal standards; they do not want or need complete and convincing arguments available for each position.

One could, though, imagine generating a theory that a society committed to interest-group liberalism requires that everyone have not just formal access to ongoing legislative power but factual access to culturally acceptable arguments for their political positions. Dissensus and conflict are avoided because no one's position ever really loses; all interests can see victories in the mush of self-contradictory practice. It is clear, too, that traditional elite theorists could conceivably argue that contradictory practices exist largely in the cosmetic domain of highly formal legal ideology; that if one analyzed cases with economic bite, practice would be clearer. I am deeply skeptical of both of these possible accounts, though.

The possible pluralist account, as I have sketched it, needs to be bolstered in a number of ways that seem infeasible. Why is it important that no one ever be fully defeated? Why will people treat the ideological availability of arguments compatible with their interests as a victory? What is most troubling about this vision, though, is the notion that the legal system is unsettled because distinct interest groups contribute separate irreconcilable visions. One of the main insights of the Critics seems to me to be that each of us, and each "pluralist interest group," *simultaneously* embraces both contradictory poles. Contradiction is not the summary outcome of conflict; it is instead embedded in each of us.

The most logical elite theorist's account, focusing on the insignificance of the issues decided according to "nondominant" norms, seems even less plausible. Why one would marginalize practices like redistributive taxation, protective orders against abusive husbands, and desegregatory busing while centralizing the occasional protection of property against takings or the marital rape exception is simply beyond me. Some paternalist practice undoubtedly protects the elite from improvidence (the Securities Acts, spendthrift trust rules), but other practice seems to protect the improvident from some elite (auto safety legislation, anti-harassment laws defining some sexual activity that is not induced by traditional force as nonetheless unduly coerced). The occasional recognition that determined, coerced action occurs in the traditional "private" sphere may sometimes benefit those already relatively advantaged (for example, in the protection of privacy rights in homeowners' or condominium associations), but the recognition is just as likely to be used by workers demanding speech rights at the plant.

It is possible to argue that while *practice* is muddled and contradictory, the privileged ideology is relatively consistent. Functionalists less concerned with the regulative force role of law than with its symbolic, ideological side might then argue that law serves either subgroup or social needs to generate a particular privileged world view, while suppressing the frequent practical departures from the privileged norms. It seems better to defer this argument until I discuss the ways in which CLS has dealt with the "symbolic" and "legitimating" roles of law.

In short, then, the Critical vision of structurally contradictory practice sees it as unlikely that law serves any discrete needs for particular predictable outcomes, for such outcomes are simply unavailable. Whether the structure of ideological contradictions—in which contradictions both exist and are suppressed—can be thought to serve a traditional social function remains to be discussed. It appears highly unlikely that traditional social functions are served either by contradictory practice itself or by an insidiously patterned set of contradictory practices in which the appearance of contradiction is an artifact of focusing on both unimportant and important clashes between elite and nonelite alike.

The Problem of Legitimation

The few outsiders who acknowledge that the CLS movement has generally rejected crude elite theory instrumentalism—the belief that lawmakers are lackeys of the dominant forces, unconstrained by legal traditions or understanding in their steadfast pursuit of their taskmasters' material advantage—believe that CLS theorists have adopted an almost equally crude instrumental legitimation theory. In the most prevalent form of this view, crude material instrumentalism is the dominant trope, legitimation theory the supplement. The constant is that the "ruling class" somehow always wins, either by getting what it wants at a particular material level or by deliberately losing a few controversies here and there so that disempowered people will believe that they have more power than they really do, and become generally quiescent.[67] Since this vision ignores, I think, all of the antifunctionalist aspects of CLS that I have discussed generally, most particularly insights about both the relative autonomy of law and the compatibility of a variety of legal decisions with closely parallel social structures, I shall simply dismiss this as a particularly implausible parody of the Critical position, even if, as with all straw men, there is a germ of truth in its description of the position it misstates.

In the more subtle (but still wrong) outsider's view, Critics are said to acknowledge that the legal system is relatively autonomous, that particular cases are governed not so much by the pursuit of material advantage for the dominant as by the existing legal norms. The disempowered aren't just tossed a crumb now and then; the system is quite constrained, internally "fair." The *primary* purpose of rule obedience in this view, however, is to convince the masses that they live in an unbiased, wholly just world; the fact that both the content of the impersonally applied norms and the very existence of a system committed to impersonal norms (rules) rather than situationally sensitive standards favor the privileged simply gets lost. The "legitimating" function of law in this view is, I take it, a threefold process: first, neutrality and impersonality in *application* are themselves confused with systematic fairness; second, legal norms that represent particular distributive and moral decisions are not scrutinized closely enough because law has the appearance of a technical science whose conclusions are beyond reproach; and third, "legalism" itself, understood as any system with a set of fixed entitlements, is essentially compatible only with greedy individualism, since it always permits people to treat others as objects, as long as one doesn't violate their legalistic rights.[68] While I don't believe that this description of the CLS vision of legitimation is nearly as off base as the vision that sees gains of legitimacy as the *residual* instrumental gain for the powerful, I think it too misses the mark in significant ways. The appearance of neutrality and objectivity (both impersonality and "scientific rationality") *does* mislead people; legalism itself may well be understood as a historically significant form of misleading reification. Still, I think that the Critics have implied, and I shall more explicitly embrace, a form of legitimation theory that is significantly distinct from either of the ones I've just sketched. It is not so much that legal thinking or norms *persuade* us that the world is just; it is that law creates and reinforces ideology that makes it difficult, in a cognitive sense, to perceive both its injustices and its mutability. I hope, now, to develop some of these distinctions.

When one says that a system has been "legitimated" in the eyes of its populace, whether by law, religion, schooling, or Saturday morning cartoons, one seems to mean at a minimum that members of the population almost invariably acquiesce in the existing distribution of perquisites and power, even when the distribution doesn't seem inevitably to redound to each obedient person's benefit. *Acquiescence* is contrasted sharply with *obedience,* which could presumably be grounded in a purely self-interested fear of the force of those who both control and get the benefits of the state's exercise of power.

Alan Hyde, quite skeptical that "legitimation" theories describe actual lived experience, posits three ways in which legitimation might hypothetically be observed in daily life. His claim is that the implausibility of each of the three accounts of "legitimation" renders the concept so incoherent that it should be purged from the critical vocabulary.[69]

First, it is possible that people come to believe in particular legal norms they would otherwise reject at least in significant part because the norms are properly justified either *formally* (through a kind of reasoning process they respect, most probably one that seems highly technical) or *substantively* (because legal reasoners are able to cast decisions in terms that appeal to actual shared values and hide or repress the ways in which a decision is dissonant with these values). Hyde suggests that it is highly implausible that one could sustain this vision if one looked at this abstract proposition as a testable empirical hypothesis—for example, by testing whether more people favor desegregatory busing once a Supreme Court opinion is written mandating the practice. The opinion, Hyde notes, would be likely to have little effect, because people have next to no awareness of the details of the decision and no great respect for the Supreme Court as an institution. Even if legal reasoning were capable of persuading people, polls show that they never see it; once people learn all that they ever seem to learn about a decision—the bottom-line result—they don't presume that it was inevitably right, since, as polls show, they don't have an especially high regard for the decision maker.[70]

While I don't think that this view of legitimation—specific norm legitimation—is particularly crucial to the Critical picture, I think that Hyde's attack on its plausibility is itself misleading. He gives no evidence that unpopular Court opinions are *less* unpopular than the parallel decisions would be without the imprimatur of the judiciary. And, more important, he does not address the fact that people may experience unpopular opinions, such as the busing decisions, as both ones they are morally bound to obey *and*, more significantly, as decisions that are relatively fixed and difficult to alter precisely because they respect the legitimacy of the judicial process. Even if the norm is not utterly embraced, it is rendered serious, worthy of a certain respect until it is overhauled in a rather elaborate way. Surely, however, no serious Critical legitimation theorist could believe that when mainstream legal norms are available to back up opposing positions, as they will inevitably be whenever anything is perceived as a legally cognizable controversy, the resolution of the case in favor of one of two acceptable legal positions will have an enormous impact on beliefs. It might be interesting to test the force of specific norm legitimation in the context of disputes between customary interests that can no longer readily defend themselves in mainstream legal language and the newer prevailing legal norms,[71] but in typical intrasystemic disputes, we should certainly expect people generally to cling to their losing, but utterly enunciable, positions.

Second, Hyde posits that legitimation theory may simply imply that a person is more likely to *obey* or follow a concrete legal order because it is legal, even without regard to his selfish interests, without concern for the practical consequences of disobeying legal commands. Hyde asks whether people are any less likely to run a red light when no one is nearby because to do so is to violate a legal norm, or to ration gas when the President urges them to because they believe in his authority. His claim is that it would be impossible in describing why someone stops at the light to sort out allegiance to law (a legitimation claim) from both custom and a self-interested decision to use a rule of thumb that it is simply never worth the possible cost of disobeying the law rather than to calculate each time if disobedience is selfishly desirable. To exemplify his approach, he claims that there is no evidence that the decision whether to ration gas in the face of presidential exhortations is affected by *any* beliefs at all rather than selfish calculation.[72] The point seems reasonably well taken if it serves to correct a prevalent mistake among those obsessed with legitimation. One certainly oughtn't to forget that explicit state force often backs up legal norms, and that someone may not tarry on her employer's property making speeches not because she has introjected norms of private property but because the police will jail her if she doesn't leave.

Hyde's point once more, though, is surely overstated. It fails to account for the desire to legalize decisions when resort to law does not affect whether force will be utilized. His account surely has trouble with both unenforced "symbolic" moralistic laws (on consensual sex, for instance) that legal sociologists have long paid attention to[73] and, more important, a variety of legalized norms that would probably be too costly to enforce purely legally (for example, the ordinances requiring fencing of cattle in Shasta County, California, that Robert Ellickson studied seem to be more or less obeyed, although violations are rarely formally acted upon).[74] Hyde also seems to assume that a person's vision of his self-interest is basically comprehensible without regard to law, that the internal perception of the number of situations in which self-interest clashes with legal demands is unaltered by law. That claim is surely inherently less plausible than the opposite; part of the negative experience of violating a law may be not simply the fear of explicit costs but the fear of shame, guilt, feeling strange, or whatever sensation is brought on by violating a legal norm. Hyde simply assumes that the would-be traffic light runner balances only the desire to get someplace faster against the expected fines plus the information-processing costs of case-by-case decision making, yet he gives no reason at all to reject the possibility that actors selfishly dislike violating laws. It seems bizarre to think that we can explain the "desire" to box or play football rather than batter, to be a rough cop rather than a rough thug, to ski rather than to drag race, as if all these desires either existed independent of legal relations or remained unaltered as desire from a "natural" state whose *expression* is changed only by fear of consequences. The social and symbolic meanings of all these practices is a function of their general legal status, not just the consequences any particular person faces. That there is no drag racing team at the local high school both responds to the existence of coercive law and creates a new set of desires about the activity, which are not themselves simply manipulated and directed by ongoing coercive force. Hyde *says* that he recognizes that "desires" are themselves a product of ideology, false consciousness, and social practice,[75] but he is never able to connect this awareness to his account of the peripheral nature of noncoercive law.

The relationship between law and selfish feelings may, of course, sometimes be less straightforward, but law could still be *important*. People may sometimes learn to think that something they would otherwise be happy to do is an unpleasant obligation because the law requires it, and their attention might go toward avoiding conduct (if they can get away with it) that they might, in the absence of law, desire. (Posner's notion that altruism is repressed by legal requirements to behave as if one were an altruist is somewhat related to this claim, although, as always, Posner translates traditionally noble urgings into more traditionally mean-spritied ones, in this case largely the desire to gain the selfishly beneficial special *reputation* of being an altruist.)[76] If the noncoercive impact of law is to make behavior less selfishly desirable than it would otherwise be, then adherence to a norm will not be *increased* because of law, but the *methodological* criticism of Hyde's point remains potent. His notion that we can coherently discuss the conflict between some prelegal selfish desire and a desire to accomplish ends the law prohibits either to avoid the explicit negative legal consequences attaching to violation or to obey law for its own sake is misleading. The "selfish desires" may well already introject the legal material.

Before turning to Hyde's third point, that of "order legitimation," I should further note that Hyde seems to follow the mainstream economistic tradition, though undoubtedly he consciously rejects it generally, in assuming that "legitimation" issues of both obedience and specific norm adherence are posed largely in the context of clashes between other-regarding law and selfish desire. Implicitly, Hyde's model of citizenship is economistic-pluralistic: people's opinions of and attitudes toward public decisions (specific norms) are simply a restatement of their selfish wishes; when their selfish wishes are defeated, they are faced with a secondary issue (of obedience) of whether to go along with the victors' will, even when the selfish costs of disobedience seem low. But if one believes, as I do, that the economistic-pluralistic model is often descriptively inaccurate in the first place—that is, that people's views of public issues are often other regarding in the first instance—then the most immediately relevant question in terms of both obedience to and opinion of a norm is how one comes to view the social world as one does. Obviously, the question of whether people vote or think explicitly selfishly on public issues cannot be definitively answered. But some work in political science suggests the importance of selfless opinions (for example, work by Donald Kinder and D. Roderick Kiewiet[77] and David Sears[78] suggests that there is far higher correlation between impersonal ideology and one's opinions on economic matters such as national health insurance, government-guaranteed jobs, or the performance of the macroeconomic policy of an existing regime than there is between voting behavior or beliefs and one's own direct economic interest in the different proposals). This work is clearly germane to the question of whether Hyde's focus is not simply completely off target in significant ways, given that people's norms on social relations may not intersect with their self-regarding "desires" at all on some occasions.

Still, even this second broad vision of legitimation—that people are more prone to obey particular commands when they are somehow legalized than they would be likely to alter their behavior in response to an otherwise precisely parallel nonlegal coercive threat—is not particularly vital to the CLS picture of legitimation. It is almost surely the case that the Critics are most interested in Hyde's third idea, that of "order" legitimation, the spreading of the perception that the system is generally just because each of a series of legal decisions that, when taken together, represent the sociopolitical order is itself affirmatively justified. Hyde seems to believe that this sort of order legitimation *may* occur to a limited extent but apparently finds it too difficult to give the term empirical or operative meaning for us to know whether he believes it exists.[79] More important, I think, he seems to find it distracting to argue about whether a false cluster of beliefs about an order has been inculcated by law, rather than to address the issue of whether the beliefs are wrong. In a sense, I think Hyde is chastizing the left for cavalierly dismissing the notion that people are acquiescent because they *should* be, for jumping ahead to look to the roots of false consciousness before establishing its falseness.[80] Certainly, the Critics, far more than the sociologists of the traditional left to whom they are often compared, have engaged in ongoing debate about norms, doing a great deal to resuscitate "left" pole values in liberal discourse.[81] But sympathetic as I am to the idea that one should not simply assume that prevailing politics are wrong, I think that Hyde is too cavalier in failing to see that "arguments" about the justice of particular institutions go on in a confined, biased world of linguistic justificatory practices, influenced by existing law. To engage in a study of how legal ideology frames value discourse is to open up the discourse as well.

CHAPTER NINE

Toward a Cognitive Theory
of Legitimation

In this chapter, I shall look at how the Critics have attempted to expand our discourse by detailing and structuring the legitimating strategies of mainstream thought.

Influenced by existing Critical thought, I believe I have begun to develop, in the same unself-conscious way in which the Critics have generally developed a picture of liberalism as an ideology beset by characteristic contradictions and modes of resolving them, a fairly short list of ways in which legal thinking is prone to be an effective justificatory ideology. Basically, the claim is quite *cognitive:* to the extent that people are "afflicted" by legal thinking (of either the intricate Mandarin sort or its more commonplace variants), counterhegemonic thoughts will simply make less sense, simply be harder to think. There seem to me to be six principal ways in which legal thinking blocks critical stances: (1) reification; (2) conflation of the potential legal solubility of a problem with the existence of a problem; (3) synthetic individualism (a belief that social relations can be understood only as the sum of readily comprehensible individual relations); (4) "take and give" (giving the appearance that the system is less harshly oppressive or biased than it could readily be); (5) denial of political stress through the use of technical thought; and (6) privileging of the libertarian poles in the face of contradictory political pulls. Let's look at each in turn.

Reification

The Critics certainly do *not* believe that the world around us can be perceived in some untainted, unmediated, direct, and "accurate" form. All our thoughts are, and seemingly must be, language mediated, and as soon as we name, we invariably reify in the sense of ascribing identical traits to objects or situations we could otherwise imagine differentiating

270 Critical Legal Studies

simply because we have given them the same name. We treat the external world as if it determines our ideas, ascribing false concreteness to the categories we have in fact invented.

The claim, then, that "legalism" blocks transformative, counter-hegemonic thought can only mean that the *particular* substantive reifying practices associated with our legal culture have a particular capacity to block thought of specific transformative programs and/or that the usual legal technique or procedure of reification itself solidifies politically conservative practice.

Some of the substantively conservative reifications are rather easy to see, and the case that any legal system should be understood predominantly by the particular categories it uses to sort the world is both obvious and powerful at the same time. In Robert Gordon's essay "New Developments in Legal Theory,"[1] he notes what is almost certainly the most politically significant reification within liberal legalist culture. The "right" of a homeowner to toss an unwelcome speaker from his living room and the "right" of an employer to expel a worker speaking in ways he disapproves of can most readily be seen, given prevailing legal practice, simply as *instances* of the exercise of rights to privacy on one's *private property*, even though any serious substantive account of why each "right" should be protected would have little in common. Even the right of "owners" to move or close a factory is most readily seen as the exercise of control over private property, and the validity of the power to kick out the unwanted guest would thus be seen to bolster the case for granting a power to close the plant. Even sophisticated purposive legal thinkers will almost invariably react to the issue of whether the employer can expel an unwanted speaker as an issue of whether there should be a *limit* on the presumptive private property right. But categorizing these situations as instances of disputes over the scope of private property rights, implying that what we have created (a parallel name) is an objective thing with a life of its own, determining our responses, so alters our ability to deal imaginatively and transformatively with the issue that it is almost impossible to *say* anything more than that it alters our ability to imagine greater shifts away from the traditional private property rights.

Gordon's point was bolstered in a significant historical context by E. P. Thompson, who notes that the acceptability of the widespread use of the death sanction in the eighteenth century was increased by the universalization of the reified property category.[2] As a variety of offenses (from forging to poaching) came to be understood as attacks on this newly integrated "thing," the notion spread that "crimes" of stealth or violence or disputes about the force of customary rights could obviously be dealt with in the same way. One can readily bolster the point further by recognizing the degree to which important consequences turn on *not* characterizing a situation as one involving private property. Even in a jurisdiction that *both* permits people to use force to protect their property *and* forbids discharge from employment without just cause as an enjoinable violation (thus, in a technical sense, making it a right protected just like some property rights), it is hard to imagine a worker defending an assault charge against an employer about to discharge him wrongfully by claiming that he was defending his property. I am sure that the right is not so protected against discharge not only because we *substantively* wish to avoid violence where interests can be vindicated without it (in theory, and sometimes in practice, stolen tangible property can be recovered through actions parallel to common law replevin; moreover, fully insured property holders have no fewer rights to use defensive force) but also because it has not taken on the coloration of "property," is simply conventionally or legally categorized differently.

Certainly, a parallel point on the impact of category choice can be made about another set of vital reified concepts in our legal system, the concepts of public and private. Again, the point, which I discussed at length in Chapters 3 through 5, is reasonably obvious, but it is quite important nonetheless. The notion that "private owners" are powerless to impose unwanted conditions and contractual arrangements while any governmental body, no matter how local, can readily be invested with the monopolistic coercive powers of a totalitarian state may dramatically affect our conception of the restricted role of community organizations and mislead us in assessing the degree of disempowerment we actually face in the routine workings of a privatized economy. Presumptions against formal worker control mechanisms seem to make more sense because we simply assume that workers are protected by the "exit" option, that they contract in the domain of freedom.

A more subtle, and difficult, point about the limits of transformative vision that arise from legal reification is seen in Frances Olsen's study of the limits placed on our conception of feminist politics by some similar reified categories.[3] While her piece is, in a sense, both too rich to summarize fully here and in some other senses so skew to the point I am making that I will have to mistranslate to some extent, several of her points seem quite relevant in looking at the impact of reification. The historical treatment and understanding of the family is a function of two distinct constructions of the place of the family, each one constructed by unanalyzed associations with arguably nongermane, overbroad linguistic categories. In one sense, the family is put on the side of the "private," along with the market, in the standard "public-private" division between the (coercive) state and (free) civil society. It is thus assumed, in this light, to be a domain of freedom and noncoercion, even when we dimly recall that it is a place in which quite explicit violent coercion frequently occurs. At the same time, it is distinguished from the market in terms of a distinct reified public-private division. In this second reified distinction, the market is public, like the state, in that it is the domain of competition, cold selfishness, impersonal relations in which others are objects. It is both degraded (it is "earthly," it is "mean") and glorified (it is rational, important, powerful). The family is private in that it is the domain of the personal and emotional, of altruism, caring, intimacy, ego fusion, self-expression without worry about and regard to appearances. It is glorified ("transcendent," "where all strong feelings go") and debased ("trivial" and "powerless").[4]

Traditionally, what followed from this dually reified picture of the family was an extreme form of hands-off nonregulation. Because it was "private" (part of civil society), the norm was laissez-faire. Utterly inapplicable arguments for the nonregulation of competitive markets implicitly colored our sense that family life should be left unfettered, even violence unpunished, because "chosen."[5] (Both Catharine MacKinnon[6] and Andrea Dworkin[7] have made parallel points about the assumption that family life is noncoercive because private.) At the same time, because it was "private" (emotional and altruistic), the legal norm was not one of active facilitation but utter neglect. In the market, the legal system had to enforce contracts, protect people against crimes and torts; at home, "love" protected victims (hence, tort immunity, the marital rape exception), mutual gain could be ensured by care, not bargain (hence, no enforceable contracts). Obviously, there was some regulation (even beyond the tautological observation that all legal regimes are forms of regulation), but the regulation was designed simply to ensure compliance with the ideal form of family life: fixed-obligation marriage dominated contractual relations.[8]

It is clear that we have overcome unbending traditional strictures against intervention in both family and market, in part because we recognize that our idealized descriptions of each were to some extent inaccurate (we see some violence and force in both family and market; we see self-seeking and economic gain as issues in family life).[9] But

Olsen notes, quite convincingly, that reform efforts remain premised on the idea that there are only two meaningful domains, the reified emotional family and the market, though reformers recognize that practices within the *actual* family should not assume that it is the *ideal* family, nor should practices in the market ignore the ways in which it fails to realize its ideal nature. Reforms, though, either try to protect women from nonaltruistic behavior at home (for example antiabuse protective orders) or give them actual access to the ideally impersonal traditional market (for example, by demanding formal equality of treatment or concessions to their special needs). The "liberated" woman, though, still bounces from the emotive to the impersonal domain; "liberated" men learn to *share* traditional power and, it is to be hoped, to love better those equal enough to them to be respected. Some women glorify their separateness, ignore the connection of their historical traits with their impotence; others disclaim all that was historically female. But fundamental notions of appropriate public behavior (selfish, instrumental, nonexpressive) remain unaltered; androgyny becomes no more than the incorporation in one person of traditional male and traditional female traits, with no transcendent resolution of the divisions. Basic suppositions about the features of private life (in both the civil and emotional sense) help block our perceptions of what genders have been and could become, restrict our understanding of the ways in which women have historically been shaped by the socially tolerated force they have been accustomed to and taught to seek a limited form of power equality as their sole salvation. Because we tended to look indirectly at issues of gender, through a prism of suppositions about the nature of the private and the public, we were blind to suffering and oblivious to the way in which we tried only to smooth over the imperfections of falsely idealized pictures rather than questioning the pictures altogether.[10]

It is fairly clear that particular reified categories contribute to the solidification of support for conservative practices.[11] What is less clear is whether a belief in universalization itself, the affirmative endorsement of reification, tends today, if not at all prior times, to bolster conservative cultural practices.[12] The claim can be made in two distinct ways. First, the presence of an occasionally operative universalization supposedly blinds people to the biased distribution of legally imposed benefits and sanctions. The Rule of Law—the impersonal, universalized application of categories to facts, ignoring particularities—is identified with justice, without regard to impact. Douglas Hay, for instance, notes the enormous amount of attention paid in eighteenth-century England to the occasional hanging of a rich thief, the degree to which it affirmed a false sense that executions were distributed in accord with an external category, not with regard to person.[13] But I am skeptical whether "universalization" is really the suspect practice here rather than the spectacle of the particular exemplary execution. One can, as Hay notes the eighteenth-century English in fact *did,* tailor a perfectly universal norm to work out in an explicitly biased manner: if mercy is granted to defendants whose families would be tremendously dishonored by hanging, only those from (rich) families with honors at stake will be spared.[14] (If today's judges were to commute sentences for those who are least capable of coping with prison, the rich would surely be spared.) Friedrich Hayek's claim that a commitment to impersonal law is a commitment to fairness[15] is not just wrong but, to my mind, too transparently wrong to serve as a bulwark of factual inequality; the *practice* of *actual* (even if only occasional) instances of class-random distribution of punishment would seem to have far more punch than the *ideal* of universalized judgment, at least when the practice is seen to exemplify an ideal that is celebrated as long as it is not practiced so often that it is able to alter actual social life.

Second, the norm of universalization is a key norm in our ordinary conception of rights-bounded interpersonal relations. A strong claim can be made that none of our notions of individual rights can ever be fully articulated without reference to reified, universalizing practice. In some sense, as we generally use the term, a *right* is that sort of claim that trumps particularistic dialogue about the purpose of allowing or disallowing a claim or (falsely) presupposes that some general purpose is in fact met in each case covered by the right.[16] The "right" to be paid one's marginal product may conceivably be justified in the run of cases by the general need to allocate labor efficiently, but no one need explain whether he would actually change jobs (reallocate his labor) if his wage were lowered in order to preserve his protected right to receive his market pay. The historical "right" to have sexual intercourse with one's wife in the face of resistance might have been justified by reference either to the supposition of continual consent or the fear of disrupting a functioning family through legal intervention in a dispute, but it could be exercised as a right without ever advancing explicit claims (let alone convincing ones) that consent existed or that the marriage was salvageable. The question, in a sense, is whether it is the particular practices that are suspect here, the reactionary *content* of these particular rights, or whether "rights consciousness" itself is suspect.

Epistemologically, it seems inevitable that even purposive explanations of one's entitlements will be mediated through *some* set of reified categories. Ideas we may come to express about when a wife has "really" consented will be no less language mediated and reified than historical ideas that consent can be conclusively inferred from marrying; the future category we imagine seems direct, particularized, and situation sensitive only *relative* to an existing practice that misses distinctions we now readily see as important. In this sense, the CLS scholars distance themselves from the Realist critics of traditional Formalism, from critics who imagined that they would be able to examine and judge the consequences of alternative legal rules without any mediating conceptual blinders. Still, the spirit of the antirights, antilegalist approach is to abandon *known* distorting categories, to leap ahead, not fully aware how one will reconstruct the world; that is surely a move toward transformation.

Conflating Legal Solubility with the Existence of a Problem

Kennedy believes that when Blackstone first observed that every right has a remedy, he meant the point to be *descriptive,* to extol the virtues of the actual functioning of the writ system by noting that it served, in fact, to vindicate all *preexisting* rights.[17] As dominant legal ideology became increasingly self-consciously positivistic, the phrase became circular. Since the presence of a right could be discerned only by reference to the remedies that vindicate it, since the list of rights was nothing but a summary of the interests that were in fact legally vindicated, every right had to have a remedy since rights had no existence independent of remedy. Though the modern, positivist definition formally governs sophisticated understanding, there is a sense in which the older usage still has considerable bite, a sense in which there is an unreasoned supposition that existing remedies do indeed vindicate all legitimate concerns. We are surer than ever that each right has a remedy (since we are always most confident in tautologies); we half forget that we ascribe a nontautological meaning to a phrase whose validity is bolstered by its tautological interpretation.

The key impact of the ongoing confusion between purely positivist, hence tautological, visions of the "completeness" of the remedy system and the slightly atavistic but vital, descriptive, natural rights visions is that we may blind ourselves to the presence of a social problem by focusing on the absence of a meaningful legal remedy for it. Because

there is no remedy, of course there is no right (at one level, tautologically). But the fact that there is no right suggests or means that there
is no significant interest to vindicate (at least in the lingering premodern,
natural law view of rights). The absence of a ready legal solution becomes confused with the absence of a significant social problem; the
world appears perfect (or at least as tolerable as we can make it) because
our tools for further perfecting it are so dull.

Perhaps the most counterintuitive and interesting instance of this
problem can be seen best when we discuss the ways in which the related
"synthetic individualist tradition" (a subject to which I shall return)
enormously bolsters otherwise unfathomably weak libertarian traditions
when it is combined with standard reifying practice and the conflation
of legal solubility with the existence of a problem, but the Critics have
raised the conflation issue in a variety of other contexts as well.

Feminist critics, like MacKinnon, stress the degree to which the routine force and coercion present in ordinary heterosexual sex becomes
invisible, in part because of the *legal* problems of identifying force that
is exceptional enough to demand state action, to create a right in victims
(either to compensation or to implicit protection through the criminal
law).[18] The point is obvious, but hardly trivial, in dealing with marital
rape. Even if we abolish the formal marital rape exception and crimi-
nalize the most overtly forcible marital rapes, it might conceivably be
a poor idea for a variety of reasons to jail all those husbands who use
what women perceive as excessive force or power to induce their wives
to have unwanted sexual relations with them. Within a culture in which
the relationship between protected rights and perceived wrongs is so
close, though, this may lead us to ignore both the frequent presence of
that intolerable force and our capacity to respond to it. The confusion
is intensified because, as both William Clune[19] and William Simon[20] have
so perceptively noted, we frequently assume that what we can readily
alter collectively is reactive "policies," while culture is immutable; the
strength of the reified public-private distinction bolsters the false conclusion that what we are dealing with in the political sphere is the "public
law," not "culture."

More counterintuitive, perhaps, is that the perceived harmfulness of
sexual harassment and of traditional rape may generally be *inverted*
because incidental rape is so much more readily legally cognizable (a
temporally discrete act and mental state allow us to measure defendant
culpability reasonably readily). In a world in which we never confused
the ready protection of legal remedy with increasingly serious problems,

though, it would not be obvious that rape is categorically the more despicable crime. Certainly, there are some rapes (but surely not all) in which the potential for nonsexual violence as well as sexual violence makes the crime doubly despicable, while by hypothesis the harasser is only sexually violative. Still, it is surely plausible that traditional rape may *less* damage one's general self esteem as a worker or student, may seem more exceptional and isolated, thus less frightening because less likely to recur, and, to the extent that it is important to a particular heterosexual woman to form future erotic bonds, may be easier to differentiate from sexual encounters one wants and thus less destructive of the capacity to enjoy heterosexuality.

The point here, though, is not to *grade* these offenses once and for all; it is rather to note that a grading scheme that is radical and transformative in a variety of ways (by severely condemning the behavior of higher-status men, by questioning the generalization of the use of authority to gain personal power and deference) is simply less thinkable once we allow, as we must, given prevailing cultural practices, our difficulty in imagining a full-blown criminal version of a harassment trial to color our view of the underlying wrong that such unimaginable trials would vindicate. If one thinks about how long it took the legal system even to become *cognizant* of harassment (its status as either a tort or the basis of a civil rights action is essentially only a decade old)[21] one sees not *just* nonresponsiveness to the voices of the disempowered but this distortion of perception. Women had not visibly raised demands for protection that were explicitly rejected; the problem stayed, in a sense, unperceived, although the "practice" has undoubtedly long occurred, in some part, I would claim, because the harm was so poorly comprehended by a legal system that routinely focuses on discrete incidents rather than patterns of behavior, observable force rather than ongoing manipulation. I should also note that yet another semilegal reified practice, the tendency to treat sexual demands as an *instance* of the category of (legally acceptable if unpleasant) demands that go along with "working for somebody," undoubtedly reinforces the tendency to block the recognition of the harm of harassment, at the same time as the unexceptionability of harassment furthers our acceptance of even exceptionally degrading employment.

Likewise, many of the dismissals of determinist insights into criminality are bolstered by this confused focus on legal remedy. Because we have no obvious intrasystemic way of dealing *legally* with the relationship between backdrop environment and antisocial behavior, we may learn to deny the significance of the determinist observation,[22] simply *invent* zones of freedom and merit and blame that influence both our treatment of criminals and our more general attitudes on meritocracy in ways that entrench existing conditions against both transformative critique and shifting practice.

In a parallel though decidedly more complex fashion, one fundamental misunderstanding of the concept of wealth maximization or cost-benefit analysis on the part of legal economists[23] is strongly bolstered by our tendency to conflate factual and legal interests. Assume that we are dealing with a problem discussed in Chapter 4: whether "wealth is maximized" or entitlements assigned in accord with proper cost-benefit analysis when a kidney dialysis machine is either given to the poor but medically needy by right or assigned to the highest bidder. We *assume,* in deciding whether or not to assign it to the needy, that transaction costs might prevent third-party moralists, interested in the needy person's receiving the good, from actively offering money to assign the machine as they wish, so that we will have to assign the dialysis machines as they would be assigned in a hypothetical market. The vital question is whether we should *measure* the moralists' desires to assign the machines to the poor but needy in terms of what they would pay (offer price) to purchase the use for them or what they would have to be paid (asking price) to let the machines be reassigned. The significant point for now is that legal economists often confuse the fact that we would not want to create an actual legal right in the moralists to block transfer with the wholly separate point of whether we should account for or measure their interests by looking at hypothetical asking prices in performing the cost-benefit analysis that must go on in assigning the actual right.

There are valid reasons why the moralist should not have a *right* to enforce the allocation of the machine (if nothing else, giving moralists such a right would inevitably preclude transfer), but unless we conflate the existence of a legal interest with a factual interest, this tells us nothing at all about whether to *value* the moralist's interests as if he were a rights holder—that is, at his asking price.[24]

Once more, the reactionary impact of the confusion could not be more obvious. It is possible, but difficult in our culture, to give independent justifications for the Posnerian principle that only those with money from other sources ought to have their ethical preferences really count, so that only offering prices should ever be used,[25] but it is far easier to accept that same operative principle surreptitiously if we falsely focus on the need to imagine ordinary legal vindication for an interest before we accept that the interest even *exists*.

The Synthetic Individualist Tradition

Unger notes the degree to which liberalism is both epistemologically and politically committed to the notion that groups are artificial, that they can be understood or analyzed only by reference to the individuals who compose them.[26] This is true in regarding general normative liberal rhetoric: the common refrain that society has no interests separate from the interests of the people who compose it seems unexceptionably tautological, given the common understanding of society as the aggregation of meaningfully separable individuals. It is true, too, in looking at methodologically acceptable description within our culture: groups move because many particular persons move; group "character" is just the norm of individual characters.

What is particularly important to gather from this insight is that liberal legalists reconstruct all socially acceptable claims in terms that break claims against groups back into claims against particular others. Wesley Hohfeld was (tautologically) correct that each right creates a correlative duty in some other parties;[27] the synthetic individualist tradition that liberal legalism both reflects and recreates helps to fool us into believing that we ought always to be able to imagine concrete individual *diads,* particular paired persons, one burdened party owing a duty to the other rights holder, a hypothetical plaintiff and a defendant in a lawsuit. When we combine the legal liberal tendency to think that all social obligations and claims should be understood as amalgamations of individualistic relations with the previously discussed habitual belief that in the absence of a vindicable legal claim no real problem can exist, our transformative imaginations may be deeply limited.

I want to use this insight to deal with one of the most instinctively powerful cultural artifacts of individualistic liberalism: the strong instinct that our duties to refrain from harm are enormously more extensive than our duties to render aid, which are either extremely restricted (either to persons in particular diadically comprehensible status relations, like our children or parties we have agreed to care for or perhaps strangers in extreme peril whom we can readily help) or nonexistent.[28] My primary claim is that this key reactionary "principle" is in fact sensible and appealing in large part *because* the synthetic individualist tradition makes it hard to see its limits, not because it is especially rationally powerful in all conceivable cognitive or social-meaning frameworks. A secondary claim that underlies this discussion is that it *is* indeed powerful in our culture—so powerful that efforts by even the most intellectually acute left-liberal legalists to justify affirmative rights to welfare support generally seem amazingly labored because it is so hard to confront directly the origins of our cultural blinders. The secondary claim can perhaps best be vindicated for legal academics by rereading Frank Michelman's three key pieces on welfare rights.[29] Despite his indisputably strong intellect, the first two seem both assertive and vacant; it took him more than a decade to see that he had to justify collectively enforced welfare rights without reference to individual duties to particular others in order to make his case plausible.

Here is the problem: libertarians faced with the dilemma of how to establish basic rights have a limited number of options. Say we are trying to establish that a child has a right not to be molested (a right protected by criminal and/or tort law). One obviously does not want, as a libertarian, to ground this right in the proposition that a desire to be free from molestation is legitimate while the desire to molest is an illegitimate desire, a pleasure that should be overruled because it poorly expresses the molester's long-term interests as a person. Such a rhetorical move would require disclaiming the libertarian's fundamental belief in the subjectivity and arbitrariness of values, require a paternalist interference premised on a belief that some knowable universal human nature exists and that the desire to see it manifest should guide public policy. Instead, quite obviously, the focus is on the *child,* and his or her protection.

But the argument also cannot be that we are simply factually aware that molestation *really harms* children and that we are trying to minimize harm to them, to make their lives better. A principle that one derives rights to maximize satisfaction is obviously the essence of nonlibertarian thinking. One can then either become religious (rights are declared by a God whose precepts are knowable) or abstract or metaphysical, or, most powerfully, resort to defending the granted right in substantive harm-reducing terms while *distinguishing* the right from nongranted "affirmative" ones that would also improve welfare. The religious arguments are, not surprisingly, not really arguments but statements of faith;[30] even if they were generally accepted, the strong Anglo-American tradition against establishing particular religious views as secular dogma makes it unlikely that we would argue that basic legal or secular rights are set by religious interpretation. The metaphysical arguments usually make reference to concepts like autonomy or personhood.[31] These generally have no discernible content. (Why is it inconsistent with a person's autonomy to be harmed at some times but not others? Why isn't molesting expressive of the molester's autonomy and capacity to define himself?) Worse, they seem to bear no relationship to one's actual concerns. It may well be intuitively obvious to me that I don't want my child molested, but it's no less obvious that I don't want him to starve to death, and the reasons for both positions are basically the same. Even if intentionally inflicted harm sometimes bothers me *more* (even a dog can distinguish between being kicked and fallen over), the harm in the two cases is surely paramount. Why, then, does my child have a right not to be molested but no right to be fed?

The key rhetorical move at this critical juncture is to assume, because of our traditional diadic legal practice, that my child's rights must be linked to particular correlative duties. Obviously, in fact, one can imagine perfectly rational nondiadic correlates: my child's right could be vindicated by your obligation to pay taxes used to pay for a food bank, not by his right to sue you for support. But our legal traditions make that a hard step to imagine; instead, we import all sorts of arguments that are applicable to the case against a *particular* person's having a duty to any particular child to a wholly different sphere, an argument about why no generalized *social duty* exists. Thus, for instance, you may have no duty to feed starving children because you can't fully realize that duty to all similarly situated children.[32] It is not at all obviously true, though, that the collective cannot realize its duty to feed all children if it imposes a general duty to pay taxes to finance a food bank. The argument of nonrealizability *falsely* influences our perception of whether my child should have a right to be fed, both because we assume that particular people must have obviously correlative duties to create rights *and* because we get used to certain reified legal categories (arguments against particular sorts of affirmative duties can be used to criticize the imposition of affirmative duties in all cases, whether or not they are applicable to each case).

Actually, if we look at the *collective* capacity to realize a duty to avoid starvation or to avoid molesting, it is not the least bit clear which is more readily fully realized. Even if the society criminally sanctions those molesters whom it is able to apprehend (who are not nonculpable according to some separate criteria, for example, as insane), it may do little actually to reduce the incidence of molestation, while rich countries may readily be able to prevent domestic starvation. Obviously, too, many of the other commonplace arguments against requiring particular individuals to be responsible for alleviating certain instances of suffering have little relevance to a social duty met through taxation. For instance, arguments about the perils of instrusiveness, the considerable constant moral burden of looking out for suffering,[33] or arguments about horizontal inequality (that otherwise indistinguishable people are unfairly burdened when they happen to encounter alleviable suffering)[34] both seem inapplicable to duties discharged through broader social mechanisms.

It is, of course, the case that the pure libertarian position does not govern existing social practice: we have a Food Stamp program, so we obviously were able to imagine it. But my claim is that it remains exceptional, hard to justify, deeply counterintuitive, and that recipients are still treated in significant ways as *charity* recipients rather than needs-based "rights holders" because the opposite social construction of their relationship to us is cognitively difficult. As Simon so cogently notes, we seem able to conceive of transfer-payment recipients as rights holders only by imagining either that they have gained a contractual right, analogous to simply receiving an insurance pay-out (as in social security and unemployment programs), or by supposing that people gain a vested interest in existing government largesse,[35] in part because we fear that if we don't consider the interests *vested,* they may be withdrawn by an overly intrusive state for bad reasons (Charles Reich's New Property view of welfare).[36] In neither case; though, do we treat mutable claims of need as justifying a strong claim of right.

It is by no means infrequent that a plausible, commonsensical mainstream argument rests, ultimately, on coupling the synthetic individualist notion that the web of legal relations can ultimately be understood by looking at the rights, duties, privileges, and immunities particular people hold with the confusion between the existence of a (simplified Hohfeldian) legal solution to a problem and its existence. Take Posner's defense of legal economics against Robin West's critique. West had attacked the presupposition that Pareto-optimal shifts are invariably morally acceptable on the ground that people may not, as economists assume, seek either utility or the enhancement of their autonomy but may rather be masochistic and self-destructive or freedom fleeing and authoritarian.[37] Two aspects of Posner's response[38] are interesting from the Critical vantage points I have been exploring.

First, Posner inexplicably translates the norm that canonizes Pareto-superior transactions into a norm of political theory ("The function of Pareto superiority when conceived as a principle of political philosophy, is not to provide the ultimate standard for ethical choice but merely to delimit the proper role of the state").[39] This translation is extremely quirky: issues about whether people will invariably be benefited by their choices (in utilitarian terms) or lead more autonomous lives (in libertarian terms) if allowed to proceed without interference surely arise even in what traditional liberals think of as the wholly private sphere. One could, of course, reject both Paretianism and the capacity of the state to remedy the defects West points to, but Posner clearly believes that his arguments and assertions against state capacity[40] resuscitate the Paretian position. That is simply wrong: it ought to have *no* effect on me at all in deciding whether to (attempt to) stop (with force, persuasion, or manipulative guilt peddling) a friend engaging in certain risky financial transactions or unwise sexual liaisons if I find out that no state actor can competently judge or intervene in my friend's life, though it clearly *would* have an effect on my behavior to find out that his choices were in fact beneficial and substantively autonomy enhancing. Posner has simply confused the legal unavailability of a solution with the absence of a problem.

Second, and far more interesting, Posner is able to picture only the simplest Hohfeldian relations when he imagines the domain of state action, so that he even further truncates his vision of the limits of Paretianism. The relevant passage is worth quoting at length because it so ideally illustrates the problems in everyday, commonsensical, legalized thought:

> In the first group [of voluntary transactions that make people worse off] are West's bulimic tomato consumer and Kafka's hunger artist, who (at the literal plane to which West confines Kafka) is anorexic. *Bulimia and anorexia are serious psychiatric conditions. A bulimic or anorexic person cannot be presumed to be making choices that maximize his . . . satisfactions . . .* Economists do not presume that choices made by mentally incompetent people are value-maximizing. *But let us not be too quick to pronounce people who make odd or even self-destructive choices incompetent.* Who among us would like to be ruled by people who thought that the administration of an insane asylum provided a mode for governing the United States? We know what the Soviet Union has done with an expansive definition of mental illness. The impersonality of market transactions protects privacy and freedom. *Professor West and I do not have to undergo a psychiatric examination before we can buy a tomato.*[41]

If one sets aside the unconscionable redbaiting in the passage and looks instead at its more mainstream content, one sees at least two fascinating rhetorical moves. First, Posner attempts to defend the core of economics by positing a wholly undefended (and indefensible) vacuum boundary between intentionalist and determinist discourse,[42] between utility-maximizing, healthy, intentionalistically described subjects and the sick, the medically determined, the nonsubject. While there is no doubt that bulimics are often in tremendous pain as a result of their powerful obsession with food and control over eating and body, there is also little doubt that few could be categorized as delusional or without ordinary rational capacities or as automatons. In fact, most function so well that even family members are generally unaware of their suffering.

But second, and far more interesting for our current purposes, Posner implies that the only choice we have, when thinking of state intervention, is between the bulimic's maintaining the Hohfeldian privilege to choose her own consumption goods and the surrendering of the privilege to another identifiable individual actor (the psychiatric examiner in this text). Posner, wholly consistent with the synthetic individualist tradition, imagines that the privilege to choose her consumption products must ultimately inhere in a discrete individual person and that the role of the state is simply to identify that person. If one steps back from the mistranslated Hohfeldian tradition, though, it should become obvious that the state might, for instance, decide simply to subsidize psychiatric counseling for bulimics if it believed bulimic "choices" self-destructive while not providing such subsidized counseling for those who made "better" choices. But Posner believes that our only recourse is to delude ourselves into thinking that the choices are fine, to make a real problem vanish from consciousness (don't be too hasty to pronounce the self-destructive incompetent, he warns), for he falsely believes that it is impossible to acknowledge the existence of a problem without seeing its legal solution, and worse, that the only legal solutions he can see involve state redefinitions of the individuals who hold particular privileges and duties.[43]

"Take and Give"

Legal system behavior and thought may also partly mislead us into believing that dominative "power" does not exist, because if it did, it would certainly be exercised more harshly. Dominative power is seized ("taken") in establishing basic ground rules; but it is then never fully exercised (is thus "given" back). The appropriate message *could* be that the basic ground rules are unjust, but the effect of not fully exercising all seemingly formally warranted dominative power may well be that the ostensible rulers appear limited, obviously less powerful than radical critics claim. While I don't believe that this is one of the more powerful or interesting cognitive blocking mechanisms, I do think it worth mentioning.

Hay's account of eighteenth-century criminal practice best illuminates this vision. An *overexpansive* criminal code is enacted, providing the death penalty for a staggering array of "offenses," some of them no more than the continuation of customary property law uses. At the same time, in practice, decision makers exercise both informal mercy (frequent pardon) and strict legalist protection (dismissing indictments that seem substantively correct but technically deficient).[44] The legal system both "takes" (in its basic definitions) and "gives" (in its restricted application). This may make it hard to believe that the rich are *really* pulling the strings when, quite visibly, they are getting less than they seem even to be entitled to under existing law, let alone successfully pressing for laws even more favorable to their interests.

MacKinnon and Dworkin, I believe, implicitly make a parallel point about the social role of rape laws. It may well partly blind women to the degree to which forced sexual access by men is the social norm to have been "given" back a domain of some autonomy, to be partly protected by laws against rape.[45] (MacKinnon also notes the degree to which rape laws could be interpreted as *entirely* male centered, as protecting against the jealous or possessive feelings of mainstream husbands and fathers, an interpretation consistent with, if not made necessary by, the nonenforcement of rape laws when fully "unpossessed" prostitutes are attacked, although this interpretation is hard to square with their enforcement in cases where other "unpossessed" women are victimized.) The implicit message of rape laws, in this view, is that men are not as dominative as oppressed women might otherwise suspect, that they obviously are not exercising all the power to "take" or "expropriate" women's sexuality that they might, and that rape laws prove that. The "right" to rape (in marriage) might otherwise be the significant *norm*, antirape laws the *exception;* the fact that we by and large *call* spousal immunity an *exception* (though most adult women are married) is reflective of the confusion engendered by the legal practice of "taking and giving," a confusion that produces an illusion of power and autonomy in an oppressed group.[46]

Staughton Lynd's analysis of the stripping of workers' rights in plant closing cases arguably has a similar structure.[47] In a collective bargaining agreement, management and labor are *both* ostensibly restrained: workers lose the privilege to strike, management its ordinary privilege to operate the business exactly as it pleases. In theory there is a quid pro quo, but since management "gives" back only some prerogatives (agrees to arbitrate only those grievances effectively covered by the contract), it is unclear why workers generally entirely lose the privilege to strike even over contractually *uncovered* entrepreneurial decisions. I suppose that the commonplace acceptability of what Lynd calls the "quid pro quo myth" is reinforced by the standard "take and give" structure. We start with the supposition that managers control, then accept it as extraordinarily empowering that some part of that control is waived when a collective bargaining agreement is in force, forgetting or blinding ourselves to the idea that the managers' enormously *disruptive* power to close or relocate is now even less restrained than in the prebargaining world.

Denial through Technical Thought

Critical Legal Studies may well most clearly emphasize the role of "legal" thinking in the suppression of the recognition of the powerful ambivalence we feel about basic existential stances. In this view the role of law is not so much to exalt a privileged pole in a battle of self-consciously acknowledged contradictory postures as to block the perception of the omnipresence of the contradictory. While this surely plays a part in expanding the domain that the privileged pole governs (because we see less frequently that it is challenged), I think that an equally vital, direct role is played by denial: to the extent that the acknowledgement of the presence of the contradictions is painful, the law is anesthetic. Complacency may well be the response to painlessness, transformative vision the response to an ongoing sense that the existing world is too hard to deal with. I feel more confident, though, that law can be seen as a technique of denial, rather than that denial has a particular political spin, even a particular historically relative spin.

My article "Interpretive Construction in the Substantive Criminal Law"[48] was perhaps the CLS piece most explicitly organized around the theme of denial. In order to construct a morally sensible criminal jurisprudence, one must constantly face insoluble issues of determinism and intentionalism if one premises moral guilt on individual self-control, and one must deal with equally insoluble questions of whether it is appropriate to use rigid rules or ad hoc standards. Since the issues are so tough, it is simply *easier,* less stressful, if we disguise their presence. My claim was that their presence is indeed hidden, again and again, by a variety of legal interpretive constructions of the "stuff" to be analyzed, interpretations in which we either extend or narrow a time frame, treat the material within an extended time frame as one or more than one incident, treat the objects of a defendant's intentions either in a narrow, act-focused way or as instances of increasingly broad categories, and, finally, ascribe to particular people traits of groups of which they are members, all the way up to "people generally."

Here is an example from the piece. In Chapter 3 I discussed the degree to which the case of Martin v. State raises two hidden issues in the conflict between intentionalism and determinism. First, since no statute was violated unless the defendant was *both* drunk in public and boisterous once there, did the holding that one could not convict a party involuntarily drunk in public (because carried there by the police) adequately *deal* with the tricky issue of whether boisterousness is itself sufficiently "intentional" for drunks that one should say that the defendant had an adequate chance to avoid violating the law by refraining from boisterousness?[49] Second, since we sometimes claim to believe that an actor has acted voluntarily (or intentionally or culpably) if he takes deliberate actions that cause him to act involuntarily at some later point, why don't we ask what Martin did in the first place to get himself arrested (and forced into public)? When do we adequately control conditions that then seem to determine us?[50] In both cases, these extremely thorny problems were evaded by standard legalistic technique: being drunk in public and boisterous once there were simply temporally unified into a single incident, and the "incident" was treated as voluntary or not (in comparison with, say, an instance in which a person dragged into public exposes himself once there, in which case the incidents are disjoined, and we see the second one as voluntary). Moreover, the arrest is dissociated from the precipitating grounds for arrest—the courts frame time narrowly, not broadly—and the tricky question of responsibility is obliterated because the germane material is simply gone.

The basic methodology whereby we look to see how the rhetorical techniques used by sophisticated legal thinkers manage to suppress awareness of the presence of one of the key insoluble philosophical dilemmas was extended in the article to innumerable examples. The actual propriety of strict liability raises issues of rules and standards (see the discussion in Chapter 1), but its impropriety is made to look obvious

because we frame time so as to make strictly liable defendants appear
utterly choiceless and helpless, ignore their assumption of positions in
which they risk harming others.[51]

The law of impossible attempts also raises painful issues of rules and
standards: in essence, the question is whether we can allow a fact-finder
to infer from ambiguous behavior that a particular defendant took substantial steps to violate an in-force legal norm or whether we must
categorically assert that whenever a defendant makes particular ("legal"
not "factual") sorts of mistakes, we can never pretend to *know* that the
defendant intended to violate a law. But the issue is invariably fancifully
"solved" by unconsciously defining some actors as intending to do only
the precise deeds they did (which are legal) while perfectly parallel
others are asserted to intend a broader category of deeds (which are
illegal) that effectuate the actor's goals.[52] Thus, competent traditional
commentators like Wayne Lafave and Austin Scott can readily say,
perfectly commonsensically, with no apparent sense of irony, that a
defendant should be guilty of attempting to receive stolen goods when
the precise deed we observe is that he received particular goods which
were no longer stolen but recovered, while a defendant who alters the
numbers, not the words, on a check did not intend forgery, did not
intend a material alteration of an instrument, because the numbers are
not material.[53] Of course, the second defendant could easily be seen as
intending the category of end-fulfilling action into which we would place
altering numbers as an instance: getting the bank to pay out more money
than the check initially indicated. The first, of course, could readily be
seen as intending only to receive the actual recovered goods. What
disappears is a conflict over the jury discretion inherent in announcing
as a vague standard that the jury can convict whichever one (or both)
it feels certain would have committed an existing crime if circumstances
out of his control hadn't prevented it; what disappears is the discomfort
over whether legality can really have full sway.

Similarly, the rule-bound legalist's ostensible commitment to the notion that the conditions for criminal punishment can be analyzed by
looking at whether a blameworthy act concurred with a blameworthy
mental state is only *unconsciously* undercut, never confronted at the
painful general level. The insistence on "concurrence" (and perhaps
strict legality) remains theoretically intact, but if one unconsciously defines defendants who have committed untoward acts as unjustified in
risking *separate* proscribed harms, subconsciously narrowing the "circumstances" in which they have taken the risk, the practice simply shreds

the theory.[54] In Regina v. Cunningham, we are told that a jury should not find a defendant who stole change from a gas meter guilty of poisoning his neighbor unless he was culpable in taking an unreasonable risk that he would do so when he tampered with the meter.[55] If, though, we *evaluate* whether the risk he took was even vaguely reasonable by reference to the costs and benefits of the *very particular,* utterly unbeneficial activity he was engaged in (stealing), his conduct will always seem to have posed an *undue* risk that the other harm would occur. Only if we compare the benefits of the activity looked at more generally (dealing with meters) will we believe that the risks the defendant took might have been justified. Perhaps concurrence doctrine is stupid; perhaps criminals *ought* to be atypically responsible for all harms they cause; perhaps it is insufficient to be bound by legalist stricture to judge the culpability of each act that is tied to harm without regard to the context of actions. But we need never face the challenge to the legalist ideal of contextless decision making if we can get contextual results simply by altering our focus in looking at the "situation" a defendant is in when he causes harm.

Legal discourse, then, need not *bring out* underlying policy or philosophical dilemmas; it may well suppress their presence through unconscious manipulation of material that allows us to believe that we are "solving" a case by applying settled or noncontroversial decision norms to "facts" that are found without reference either to norms or to a subconscious urge to avoid thorny issues.

In a parallel but grander vein, Kennedy's analysis of the role of rights in mediating the Fundamental Contradiction also emphasizes the importance of *denial.*[56] What is too painful to face is that we both need and abhor others, for they both form and destroy us; give us all meaningful power and subject us to their domination; help us form individual personalities and demand that we suppress them in the name of conformist demands. What "rights consciousness" allows is for us to believe that we have *solved* this problem. We will fuse with people as long as they respect our rights; we will insist on that separateness guaranteed us by our rights. That rights are in some deep sense so indeterminate as to be illusory—that the problems of fusion and separateness inevitably recur in *defining* rights, which may demand in an oscillating contradictory fashion more or less concern for others, more or less capacity to call on others to be concerned for us—never fully negates their fundamental mediating role. The legalist *ideal* that there are fixed and determinate boundaries that cannot be crossed, that define the realm within which

others can be warded off or ignored, promises a domain for the antisocial
self; the idea that interaction occurs within a framework where illicit
domination is prohibited fortifies the fantasy that the world of others is
no threat.

Privileged Positions

Finally, transformative thought may well be blocked by the utopian
imagery of ordinary life that legal discourse generates, a discourse in
which we are repeatedly allowed to imagine a lovely world of self-
determined subjects, expressing consistent, unambivalent, and unexceptionable desires, seeking their ends in a private world of voluntary
transactions freed from force or nonnatural necessity by a state that
imposes only clear rules against illicit force, using rules both because it
fears becoming forceful itself and because people should know precisely
what is expected of them.

The ideal picture, though, is ideal only if its preconditions are real.
If people really are never mistaken, antipaternalism seems unexceptionable; if there is no room for power or domination once formal fraud
and force are excluded, there is, tautologically, no remaining problem
of powerlessness and illegitimate hierarchy to strike at. How do the gaps
between the utopian fantasy and a shared, lived, complex reality become
obliterated? The ideal picture is confused with the real not solely because
the real is overtly *misdescribed;* the misdescription is bolstered by a
system of (largely legal) thought that portrays the ideal as nothing more
than the *summary* of routine rhetorical starting places, of normal practices, ordinary ways of dealing with and apprehending the world. All
the *privileged* poles in the contradictory world pictures need not actually
describe the bulk of existing legal practices (the strictest rule pole in
contract law formally governs few relationships; actual contracting practice may be even less rule bound) or normatively desirable ones (the
case for rules is surely no better than equivocal), as long as they remain
starting points.

Substantive positions may be covertly normatively privileged in several significant ways. We can structure our discourse so that the privileged position is the (normative) *rule* and the departures are the *exception;*
this is just one significant technique by which we obscure from ourselves
the degree to which we actually violate a supposed rule. Moreover, if
we view certain positions as necessary correlates of a hyperprivileged
position, they may themselves become both normatively and descrip-

tively privileged. Finally, once any position is covertly normatively privileged, it *becomes* descriptively privileged because we regularly conflate the ideal and the actual in legal thought, treat legal principles both as *imposed* on the social order and as *observed,* as derivative from or immanent in the order.[57] Once we decide, for instance, that we *should* ordinarily bolster a private sphere of free action, pursuit of arbitrarily chosen plans, we come to believe that we will find such a sphere out in the world. This is true both because of reifications of the sort I discussed earlier (ascribing traits true of some "private" transactions to all transactions called "private") *and* because we believe that law is not just "directive" but "reflective." The linguistic ambiguity is familiar: a *scientific* law does not direct nature but reflects it, and we are often covertly ambiguous about whether a state's *coercive* laws simply follow preexisting practice or are integral to it. The ambiguity leads us to believe that if we have established a normative rule against killing, it must reflect the factual deviance of the prohibited practice; if we normatively *extol* a particular private sphere, it must be because it is factually the norm, nondeviant.

The process of making one position seem to be a "rule" and the other an "exception" must go beyond counting instances where one should govern and comparing how often the other does. Rhetorically, it is much more critical that the exemplary cases chosen to support our intuitions when we defend an exception be extreme and excessive. Thus, for instance, a mainstream liberal contracts scholar like Melvin Eisenberg asks when we might overturn bargains because contracting parties overpay—that is, pay more than available market prices. The rhetorically typical examples he gives are extreme, obviously out of the ordinary. He tells us that tourists traveling cross-country, stopping in a town they've never been to before and won't be back to, so they know little of prevailing prices and no one cares about their repeat business, might be appropriate subjects for protection against the privileged bargain principle—privileged because it embodies ideals of rule form, subjective value, and presumption of intentionality in the private sphere.[58] But, of course, most buyers, most of the time, purchase in markets where prices are dispersed, where some pay higher prices than are available.[59] Similarly, Guido Calabresi supports the legitimacy of paternalist motives not by reference to our ordinary relations, in which we constantly try to nudge and influence and change the settings in which all the people we know choose, but by reference to children and those who would sell themselves into slavery.[60] How do we deal with the actual pervasiveness of nonneutrality toward value choices? Antiutilitarians traditionally wonder whether we ought to respect, categorically, overtly immoral choices, like the taking of pleasure in others' needless pain;[61] there is little mainstream literature questioning what to make of the way in which we evaluate all the goods we surround ourselves with when we can picture ourselves as shallow, status-oriented goods junkies.[62]

Rule-exception relations may also be communicated by undefended *ordering* practices. Kennedy notes that the law school curriculum is ordered in a way that surreptitiously communicates the idea that what is primary (first year, required) is the laissez-faire common law core (tort, property, contract); what is secondary (upper level, elective) is the administrative state that responds to the partial but more open acceptance of the unprivileged positions.[63] A commonly used contracts text (Fuller and Eisenberg) introduces nearly every section with a case expressing the privileged position, *then* poses limiting cases.[64]

Rule-exception relations are also communicated by subtle linguistic hints. We say that regulation *corrects* for market *failure,* not that we regulate social interactions through "free" markets when conditions allow us to. We focus on the "problem of discretion," accept it perhaps as inevitable, but it is still the *problem* that arises since the Fall of the legalist Utopia. Particular attacks on nondiscretionary systems (for example determinate sentencing) surely get written,[65] surely abound in fact, but they have no stock buzz words to rely on; there simply is no "problem of rules." (If there is a rough equivalent phrase to attack rule boundedness, it is probably the "discontents of legalism,"[66] a phrase that reeks of bored upper-class ennui, not quite serious stuff.) Discretion is what we're forced to live with because we can't get the rules just right; rules are not what we are forced to live with because we can't quite trust all exercises of discretion. The Stanford Law Library lists fifty-seven books organized around the theme of the "problem of discretion" (and, when you come to those on "administrative discretion," you are asked to "see also" books on the "abuse of administrative power"!). Of the twenty-odd books organized around the issue of legality and the Rule of Law, over half are pleas to organize international relations around a Rule of Law model that will sustain peace; far and away the next largest group affirm the traditionally asserted relationship between human rights and legality.

It is also the case that the unprivileged positions often govern only when we somehow become unaware that the battle between contradictory ideals has been joined. The uniform support for requiring negligence to predicate criminal conviction is, underlyingly, support for a standard, not a rule; the material gets constructed through legal rhetorical moves so that literally no writer attacking strict liability has had to affirm his support for the unprivileged position.[67] Epstein, quite typically of modern natural rights theorists, argues that rights are established on the basis of causation, not on the basis of a judgment that certain substantive subjective tastes are preferred to others.[68] The argument is utterly unconvincing in dealing with the standard Coasean paradigm cases, in which two parties simply want to use the same resource for their own benefit (whether recreational or manufacturing users of water; solar heating system users or neighbors looking for a tan), but it does obviate the need to acknowledge that one does not really believe that tastes should be treated as arbitrary, equally valid whims. Impure determinisms indeed show up in criminal law. Abandonment defenses are denied because too many defendants would have abandoned in parallel settings; boisterous public drunks can't be convicted if they've been forced into public, since boisterousness seems inadequately within their control. They remain unacknowledged, though.[69] Once more the most vapid formalism applied to facts conveniently ordered for the desired formal analysis most regularly rears its ugly head when the alternative might have been to face the departure from a privileged pole.

Further, if one takes it as a given, at least for the moment, that the commitment to rules and legality is *the* paramount privileged position, then it may be that we try to construct the world so that the commitment to rules is left relatively unshaken. The support for a rule-bound system, though, is most unexceptionable on the supposition that the other privileged positions are themselves either descriptively or normatively privileged: that is, that paternalism is unnecessary, that most conduct in the private sphere is voluntary, that force can readily be distinguished from nonforce, that the life plans people pursue are simply matters of arbitrary taste. The claim may simply be a coherence claim: one can construct a reasonably complete picture of the ideal, *starting* with the premise that social relations will be governed by rules, only if one buys into a lot of other positions (that there is no need for situational altruism or ad hoc paternalism, that the choice of rights simply facilitates realization of any life plan rather than the substantive imposition of particular plans by those who govern). Then, the newly privileged positions *bolster* the intitially privileged one; the "case" for rules is strengthened by the assumptions we make about the world, which we make in part because we covertly assumed that we must support the case for rules.

The initial privileging may itself be a function of covert manipulations of the sort I have mentioned (ignoring departures, giving a false rule-exception pattern), but might even simply be taken as the core article of system-defining faith, at an abstract, overly reified level. The contrast we typically learned to draw back in civics class is between a regime of impersonal rules and a regime of personal domination; a world of known duties and a world of surprise demands made by unreadable bureaucrats; formal equality against feudal status; formal equality and autonomy against Stalinist terror.[70] At that level, the choice of the Rule of Law seems unexceptionable; but how do we get from *that* to a privileged rule pole most compatible with right-wing libertarianism? If *that* Rule of Law (the one that separates us from the medievals and the maniacs) required *rules,* though, we would, as some say, all be speaking Church Latin or Russian. Certain forms of impersonality in administration may indeed both restrain madmen *and* be a virtue that can be attained by following rules; it is an easy enough error to make, though, that the trait is logically or actually inseparable from rules because it is a conceivable virtue of rules. "Killers are expressive; I like expressive people; therefore I like killers" demonstrates the logical problem. The practical connection is harder to assess, but examples suggest that this case for rules is hyperbolically overstated: for all its other flaws, the discretionary death penalty seems to be administered without much regard to ordinary prejudices, such as racial prejudice, about defendants.[71] Likewise, to say that the old discretionary welfare system was prejudiced against sexually active women is hardly to say that it was not fundamentally *impersonal;* the new system is systematically "prejudiced" against disorganized people unable to produce adequate documentation of needs.[72]

We think in prepackaged categories, clusters, reified systems. We forget the degree to which we invent the social world. We come to think that rules make us act impersonally; we often forget that we must continually choose to act impersonally, whether in applying a classic standard or a classic rule. A policeman may tell you that it is the Rule of Law that prevents him from stopping just the blacks who drive 30 miles per hour in a 25 mile an hour zone; that must be wrong, since there really *is* no rule that tells him which of the myriad speeding drivers to stop. Utterly racist immigration laws could be grounded in ostensibly neutral rules through which we sought to allow increases in only the population of peoples already here; formally unexceptionably prospective tax laws are frequently tailored for particular parties. If we don't firmly act on the injunction to administer impersonally, we won't. The lies we tell ourselves weave together, though, until the dream appears neat and concrete, reality a chaotic jumble (hence recalled like a dream). An abstract tribute to rules seemingly necessitates a blind commitment to a series of normative and descriptive propositions that won't undermine the supposedly necessary general commitment. The general commitment is bolstered by one's new-found faith in its ability to order beneficially a world of actors one has imagined to help sustain the preliminary commitment. The paramount nature of the initial general commitment itself is partly grounded in the illusion that the commitment alone sustains decent practice because it is obviously formally consistent with it, so soon we think that the rules make us do good rather than that we sometimes collectively choose to do the good things we do when applying rules or even when we don't. That, I think, is precisely the sort of confusion legalist practice engenders; it makes us passive by making us confused. The Critics try to retrace, hoping to see where we first got lost.

Notes

Introduction

1. The initial outreach letter, a January 17, 1977, "proposal for a gathering of colleagues who are pursuing a critical approach toward the study of law in society" tried to "describe in a general way two sorts of work that we [the organizing committee of Abel, Heller, Horwitz, Kennedy, Macaulay, Rosenblatt, Trubek, Tushnet, and Unger] would classify as critical" without making "an attempt to define in advance or even to influence the character of our meeting, should it occur." One sort of work was said to be in the tradition of Max Weber, and was said to be premised on the ideas that "all legal action must be assessed in terms of extra-legal categories and purposes" and that the "law-in-action" is radically different from the "law-in-books." "Scholars in this tradition often emphasized the failure of the real system to meet its professed ideals." The second sort of work (which is in fact the dominant subject of this book) had "a much less developed general approach"; but "if there is a single theme, it is that law is an instrument of social, economic and political domination, both in the sense of furthering the concrete interests of the dominators *and* in that of legitimating the existing order. This approach emphasizes the ideological character of legal doctrine, and is therefore more concerned with its internal structure than the approach that focuses on latent social functions."

2. For a good brief discussion of both substantive areas of inquiry that have occupied participants in the Law and Society movement and their methodology, see Richard Abel, "Redirecting Social Studies of Law," 14 *Law and Society Review* 805 (1980); and Lawrence Friedman, "The Law and Society Movement," 38 *Stanford Law Review* 763 (1986). For a good introduction to substantive themes, see also Lawrence Friedman, *Law and Society: An Introduction* (1977), and Lawrence Friedman and Stewart Macaulay, *Law and the Behavioral Sciences* (1977) (two texts reflecting the Law and Society movement's approach). Of the nine people on the organizing committee of the Conference on Critical Legal Studies, three (Abel, Macaulay, and Trubek) had been strongly associated with the Law and Society movement.

3. *The Politics of Law* (David Kairys ed. 1982).

4. See Duncan Kennedy and Karl Klare, "A Bibliography of Critical Legal Studies," 94 *Yale Law Journal* 461 (1984).

5. Critical Legal Studies Symposium, 36 *Stanford Law Review* 1 (1984). See also the Symposium on Critical Legal Studies, 6 *Cardozo Law Review* 691 (1985); "Perspectives on Critical Legal Studies," 52 *George Washington Law Review* 239 (1984); "A Symposium on Critical Legal Studies," 34 *American University Law Review* 939 (1985).

6. Roberto Unger, *Knowledge and Politics* 1–144 (1975).

7. See, e.g., Duncan Kennedy, "Cost-Benefit Analysis of Entitlement Problems: A Critique," 33 *Stanford Law Review* 387 (1981) (claiming to criticize only the "liberal" Law and Ecnomics school though nearly all his critiques apply to conservative Chicago school spokesmen as well).

8. Roberto Unger, *The Critical Legal Studies Movement* (1986).

9. See, e.g., Calvin Trillin, "A Reporter at Large (Harvard Law School)," *New Yorker,* March 26, 1984, at 53.

10. See Duncan Kennedy, "The Structure of Blackstone's *Commentaries,*" 28 *Buffalo Law Review* 205, 211–218, 258–261 (1979).

11. See Karl Klare, "Judicial Deradicalization of the Wagner Act and the Origins of Modern Legal Consciousness, 1937–1941," 62 *Minnesota Law Review* 265 (1978). A typical attack is found in Matthew Finkin, "Revisionism in Labor Law," 43 *Maryland Law Review* 23 (1984). See also Karl Klare, "Traditional Labor Law Scholarship and the Crisis of Collective Bargaining: A Reply to Professor Finkin," 44 *Maryland Law Review* 731 (1985); Matthew Finkin, "Does Karl Klare Protest Too Much?" 44 *Maryland Law Review* 1100 (1985); Karl Klare, "Lost Opportunity: Concluding Thoughts on the Finkin Critique," 44 *Maryland Law Review* 1111 (1985).

12. The furor of the battle may conceivably arise from an *aspect* of CLS academic writing: its general tone and posture, its removal from the usual debates over resolving cases or policy issues that preoccupy lawyers. The fury the "others" feel may come from what amounts to psychologistic dismissal of their lifework. Law professors are used to hearing their colleagues call their arguments *wrong,* but are quite unused to having their arguments *typologized, anthropologized,* treated as unself-conscious *instances* of characteristic modes of "liberal" thought. Adolescents are rarely happy when their elders not only fail to answer their furious accusations but begin instead to explain sagely *why* they are making them, given, say, their tender age and impotent social position. One suspects that the typical law teacher is even less thrilled than the typical adolescent at having what he thinks of as arguments treated as symptoms, as objects of study to help understand him and his ilk.

It strikes me as even more likely, though, that CLS is often loathed by mainstream law professors not for its academic work at all, whether its content or tone, but for its institutional role. The CLS movement may be perceived by hostile "others" predominantly as something of a fringe political party with conspiratorial ambitions to seize local power through manipulative coups. At best it may be viewed as a dissident voting bloc at faculty meetings that attempts to prey on insecure and guilty liberal colleagues to build coalitions that will hire only unqualified "politically correct" hacks; undo "meritocratic" (test-based) admissions programs; force students into serving the poor at storefront clinics without any respect for those who believe that they better serve the poor by greasing the wheels of commerce or simply feel that serving the poor is just not what they had in mind. Or it may be perceived as a kind of gloomy, nay-saying, strength-sapping parasite, so bent on challenging the intellectual and social vitality of the traditional work the "others" do, as both academics and "policy advisers," that nothing at all gets done.

In a sense, from these points of view—the perspectives of those who see themselves as victims of CLS madness—the movement is basically about the chilling (if no doubt ludicrously exaggerated) possibility that teaching at the Harvard Law School may lose much of its glamour and prestige. This is most obviously a concern for those at Harvard itself; but to the extent that Harvard remains the most visible symbol of legal education generally, status degradation at the (self-proclaimed) pinnacle threatens all those whose status is measured always, in their minds, as a sort of constant fraction of the maximum available status. First, the fear is that the "party platform" of the CLS wing (or is it cell?) may call for steps (like lottery admissions) that might drive away the elite employers who continually recertify the school's status by courting its graduates with a no-frills-barred furor that one would generally expect only in a sexually obsessed suitor. Second, the fear is that the observer-anthropologist stance threatens to open a chasm between the Law School and one elite vision of the "real world." Even if CLS helps *close* the gap between Harvard and some of the impoverished, legally underserved, disempowered residents of the real world (and many of the politically liberal CLS opponents deny that), it may be a recurring nightmare that no one in a CLS-dominated school would shuffle off to help run the government, Bar committees, Law Reform Commissions. Third, the Critical attacks on the notion that one can readily evaluate academic work apolitically, that "smartness" will invariably shine through regardless of how compelling or banal one finds an appointment candidate's agenda, seems an attack on the most powerful basis of intellectual status: if no one is uncontroversially "qualified," it is always possibe that one has been certified not for one's brilliance but for one's conventionality, for saying well what we all already know. Finally, the very fact that the mainstream faculty has "allowed" so many of the young assistant professors to join the CLS camp may in itself cause a loss of prestige. Duncan Kennedy has likened the position of his mainstream colleagues to the attitude of prep school graduates in the State Department in the early 1950s, embarrassed in front of their blue-blooded friends to have "lost China."

13. Paul Carrington, "Of Law and the River," 34 *Journal of Legal Education* 222, 227 (1984).

14. See Perry Anderson, *Considerations on Western Marxism* (1976), for a particularly lucid exposition of these disputes. See Alan Hunt, "The Theory of Critical Legal Studies," 6 *Oxford Journal of Legal Studies* 1 (1986), and Christine A. Desan Hussan, "Note: Expanding the Legal Vocabulary: The Challenge Posed by the Deconstruction and Defense of Law," 95 *Yale Law Journal* 969 (1986), for two reasonably illuminating efforts to describe the CLS movement in these terms.

15. See, for representative instances, Isaac Balbus, "Commodity Form and Legal Form: An Essay on the 'Relative Autonomy' of the Law," 11 *Law*

and Society Review 571 (1977); Robert Gordon, "New Developments in Legal Theory," in David Kairys, note 3 above at 281; Edward Greer, "Antonio Gramsci and 'Legal Hegemony,' " in David Kairys, note 3 above at 304; Thomas Heller, "Structuralism and Critique," 36 *Stanford Law Review* 127, 165–192 (1984); Elizabeth Mensch, "The Colonial Origins of Liberal Property Rights," 31 *Buffalo Law Review* 635 (1982).

    16. See, e.g., Ed Sparer, "Fundamental Human Rights, Legal Entitlements, and the Social Struggle: A Friendly Critique of the Critical Legal Studies Movement," 36 *Stanford Law Review* 509, 555–574 (1984); Frank Munger and Carrol Seron, "Critical Legal Studies vs. Critical Legal Theory: A Comment on Method," 6 *Law and Policy* 257 (1984).

    17. There are at least two reasons worth mentioning for the growing left focus on ideology. First, while it is possible to attribute the striking absence of radical movements in the advanced capitalist states to pure repressive force, many have preferred to see that these regimes have gained at least the superficial consent and support of the populations. Obviously it could well be the case that the regimes are *deservedly* stable, that acquiescence shows supreme good judgment; but those on the critical left are obviously more prone to believe that the stability is unwarranted. Theories of unwarranted stability need not involve the production of legitimating ideologies (like legal doctrine that seems to justify everyone's distributive scheme as flowing from the neutral application of unexceptionable rules to readily discernible factual settings). They might instead involve the coercive implantation of needs and desires that, once engendered, can be satisfied only by the existing social structure. See, e.g., Herbert Marcuse, *One-Dimensional Man* (1964). Or they might involve not ideologies that convince people that the world is just but those that teach it is immutable. Still, it is not surprising that those on the left would study the more self-congratulatory and complacent socializing institutions, whether mainstream religion, schools that both create and confirm the validity of class structure through implicit or explicit tracking systems, legal systems that both resolve controversies over the distribution of certain disputed goods and rule out certain potential controversies as beyond the pale of rational dispute. CLS might then simply be seen as that typical modernist-Marxist group that, because it is composed of lawyers most familiar with the legal system, *emphasizes* that particular system's pacifying role as socializer, while perhaps retaining the revisionist's usual fond nostalgia for starker Leninist statements about the state serving as executive committee for the ruling class so that one still tries to point out that brute state force may come into play in clashes over control of the workplace or the state itself.

    Second, the general revisionist focus on ideology that CLS surely shares may arise not just from the absence of revolutionary movements but from a loss of intellectual faith in Marx's teleological determinism, his sense that there were objective laws of historical motion that would result in a particular transformation of social roles, even in the absence of self-conscious political action. Just as traditional liberal theory was fundamentally one-sided in its account of human experience, emphasizing an untrammeled phenomenological perspective, dwelling on subjectivity and intentionality to the exclusion of determinist accounts that repress the subject, so traditional Marxism lacks a cogent theory of politics, of intentionality, of will, emphasizing only the ways in which classes play predetermined objective roles. See Thomas Heller, note 15 above at 167–172.

Ideology fits in two distinct ways in a world picture where the free political subject must be resuscitated. First, for revisionist social scientists the question "Why no revolutions?" may recur as a question of the lack of *will* to revolt. Historical materialists indeed tried to revise Marx's precise answer to the question of *when* capitalism would unravel without altering the materialist methodological focus. The *objective* crisis of capitalism that Marx foresaw—the crisis that would arise from the falling profit rate—was still seen as the *root* of social transformation; earlier revisionists simply claimed to have discovered objective reasons why the crisis did not come as soon as Marx implied it would. But many leftists have lost faith in these more "objective" and determinist explanations of the hitch in the coming of inevitable revolution offered by the earlier revisionists, explanations (like those offered by Baran and Sweezey) that imperialism, monopoly consolidation through finance capital, or Keynesian business-cycle management have simply *delayed* the inexorable final crisis of capitalism, a crisis that would still come without *politics* as a central causative factor. See Paul Baran and Paul Sweezey, *Monopoly Capital: An Essay on the American Economic and Social Order* (1966). There are, of course, expositions that bridge traditional Marxist determinisms and politics-focused accounts. One may, for instance, try to explain the lack of a politically cohesive class-conscious proletariat by reference to the development of a mode of production where workers' objective interests appear to divide. See, e.g., Michael Reich and David Gordon, *Segmented Work, Divided Workers* (1982) (a history of the appearance of segmented labor markets in twentieth-century America, which is precisely such a narrative). But some have looked to politics without treating politics itself as a symptom of material life. Second, insofar as the revisionists see themselves as political *organizers* as well as society's *students,* active debate over ideology becomes potentially transformative; undermining the hegemony of ruling ideals becomes a necessary project.

The revisionists' seeming idealism, particularly their obvious concern with their own ideology, may also be seen to result from yet another break with traditional Marxism. In a sense, the appropriate ideological posture of the left-bourgeois academic was theoreticlly *set* by an understanding of the laws of historical motion. While recognizing the true political program of the proletariat may well have been difficult given the problem of false consciousness, there was little question but that one's aim was to align oneself with that one class whose self-interest was universalistic—the workers. As innumerable postwar leftists lost faith that there was even much descriptive meaning to the traditional picture of a society stratified into the proletariat, bourgeoisie, petit-bourgeoisie, and so on, let alone much reason to believe that the ever-shrinking industrial work force was in fact politically privileged, the articulation of ideals separate from those either held by actual factory workers or ascribed to them became critical. I suspect that the preoccupation of the Frankfurt school with the metaethical question, the problem of discerning moral truth (e.g. through competent communication in Habermas), in some part arises from the sense that the *appropriate* political stance is far more open to issue. For a brief discussion of Habermas's method, see Thomas McCarthy, "Translator's Introduction," in Jürgen Habermas, *Communication and the Evolution of Society* (1979). See also Jürgen Habermas, id. at 26–29, and *Knowledge and Human Interests* 43–63, 301–317 (1971). This preoccupation is clearly echoed in the most influential of early CLS works, Roberto Unger's *Knowledge and Politics* (1975), which talks at length of the need to create a nondominative context in which one could *trust* the morality one discerned, knowing it was neither Platonically objective nor individual and subjective, the simple preference assertions or tastes of wholly autonomous subjects that liberal skeptics assert morality must be. See Roberto Unger, note 6 above at 238–253. Critical theorists (and some in CLS) are preoccupied, then, with both a metaidealism (How does one get ideals? What are the social conditions under which one can trust one's ideals?) and more routine everyday philosophizing—the debate over the ideals one ought to hold—of a sort that traditional Marxists generally abhorred. (It was once practically a *de rigueur* sign of Marxist "toughness" to swear that both you and Marx found the "ethical" question of whether income distribution in capitalist societies was fair or just to be utterly uninteresting and silly; it was simply historically appropriate that surplus value be seized, not right or wrong. See, e.g., Allen Wood, "The Marxian Critique of Justice," 1 *Philosophy and Public Affairs* 246 [1972], and Robert C. Tucker, *The Marxian Revolutionary Idea* 37–53 [1969]. For a critique of this reading of Marx, see, e.g., Allen E. Buchanan, *Marx and Justice: The Radical Critique of Liberalism* [1982].)

18. Of course, many Realists have tended to doubt that one could do much of a job distinguishing courts from other loci of state power, while one branch of neoformalists, the so-called Legal Process school, has labored mightily to revitalize separation-of-powers arguments as not only convincing but constitutive of the proper way to resolve many substantive disputes.

19. The best account of Formalism, critical yet adequately sympathetic to make the position *imaginable,* is in Thomas Grey, "Langdell's Orthodoxy," 45 *University of Pittsburgh Law Review* 1 (1983). See also Duncan Kennedy, "Toward an Historical Understanding of Legal Consciousness: The Case of Classical Legal Thought in America," 3 *Research in Law and Sociology* 3 (1980).

20. See Felix Cohen, "Transcendental Nonsense and the Functional Approach," 35 *Columbia Law Review* 809, 812 (1935).

21. See the discussion in Charles Clark, *Real Covenants and Other Interests Which Run with Land* (2d ed. 1947) (arguing that traditional Formalist judicial decisions allowed assignees to be bound in cases that appear random from the vantage point of policy).

22. See Felix Cohen, note 20 above.

23. See James Krier, book review, 122 *University of Pennsylvania Law Review* 1664, 1678–1681, 1697 (1974) (reviewing R. Posner, *Economic Analysis of Law*). See also Uriel Reichman, "Judicial Supervision of Servitudes," 7 *Journal of Legal Studies* 139 (1978).

24. George Fletcher, *Rethinking Criminal Law* 160–166 (1978).

25. Mark Kelman, "Interpretive Construction in the Substantive Criminal Law," 33 *Stanford Law Review* 591, 620–624 (1981).

26. See, e.g., Morton Horwitz, "Law and Economics: Science or Politics?" 8 *Hofstra Law Review* 905 (1980); Elizabeth Mensch, "The History of Mainstream Legal Thought," in David Kairys, note 3 above at 18, 36–37.

27. See James Boyle, "The Politics of Reason: Critical Legal Theory and Local Social Thought," 133 *University of Pennsylvania Law Review* 685, 708–714 (1985); David Kairys, "Law and Politics," 52 *George Washington Law Review* 243–257 (1984); Mark Tushnet, "Critical Legal Studies and Constitutional Law: An Essay in Deconstruction," 36 *Stanford Law Review* 623 (1984). The incorrect belief that CLS commentators think that case results are invariably unpredictable is probably most widespread among commentators who then attack it. See, e.g., Kenney Hegland, "Goodbye to Deconstruction," 58 *Southern California Law Review* 1023 (1985). The position I ascribe in the text to CLS more generally is gleaned in part from Boyle, id. especially at 756–761, 766–778; Joseph Singer, "The Player and the Cards: Nihilism and Legal Theory," 94 *Yale Law Journal* 1, 19–25 (1984); Gary Peller, "The Metaphysics of American Law," 73 *California Law Review* 1151, 1221–1259, 1272–1289 (1985). The account of CLS views on indeterminacy most consistent with my own views is Andrew Altman, "Legal Realism, Critical Legal Studies, and Dworkin," 15 *Philosophy and Public Affairs* 205 (1986).

28. The major critical works on the *indeterminacy* of the legal economist's proscriptions are Thomas Heller, "The Importance of Normative Decisionmaking: The Limitations of Legal Eonomics as a Basis for Liberal Jurisprudence as Illuminated by the Regulation of Second Home Development," 1976 *Wisconsin Law Review* 385; Thomas Heller, "Is the Charitable Exemption from Property Taxation an Easy Case? General Concerns about Legal Economics and Jurisprudence," in *Essays on the Law and Economics of Local Governments* (Daniel Rubinfeld ed. 1979); Mark Kelman, "Consumption Theory, Production Theory, and Ideology in the Coase Theorem," 52 *Southern California Law Review* 669 (1979); Mark Kelman, "Misunderstanding Social Life: A Critique of the Core Premises of Law and Economics," 33 *Journal of Legal Education* 274 (1983); Mark Kelman, "Trashing," 36 *Stanford Law Review* 293, 306–318 (1984); Duncan Kennedy, "Cost-Benefit Analysis of Entitlement Problems: A Critique," 33 *Stanford Law Review* 387 (1981); Duncan Kennedy and Frank Michelman, "Are Property and Contract Efficient?" 8 *Hofstra Law Review* 711 (1980).

29. Owen Fiss, "Objectivity and Interpretation," 34 *Stanford Law Review* 739 (1982).

30. Paul Brest, "Interpretation and Interest," 34 *Stanford Law Review* 765 (1982).

1. Rules and Standards

1. Duncan Kennedy, "Form and Substance in Private Law Adjudication," 89 *Harvard Law Review* 1685 (1976).

2. Al Katz and Lee Teitelbaum, "PINS Jurisdiction, the Vagueness Doctrine, and the Rule of Law," 53 *Indiana Law Journal* 1 (1978).

3. William H. Simon, "Legality, Bureaucracy, and Class in the Welfare

System," 92 *Yale Law Journal* 1198 (1983). Other works in the CLS literature that helped me especially in dealing with the issue of the choice between rules and standards include Roberto Unger, *Law in Modern Society* 203–216 (1976); William H. Simon, "The Ideology of Advocacy: Procedural Justice and Professional Ethics," 1978 *Wisconsin Law Review* 29; William H. Simon, "Legal Informality and Redistributive Politics," 19 *Clearinghouse Review* 384 (1985); Duncan Kennedy, "Legal Formality," 2 *Journal of Legal Studies* 351 (1973); Peter Gabel, "Reification in Legal Reasoning," 3 *Research in Law and Sociology* 25 (1980); Robert Gordon, "New Developments in Legal Theory," in *The Politics of Law* 281 (David Kairys ed. 1982); Kenneth J. Vandevelde, "The New Property of the Nineteenth Century: The Development of the Modern Concept of Property," 29 *Buffalo Law Review* 325 (1980); Richard Abel, "The Contradictions of Informal Justice," in *The Politics of Informal Justice* 267 (Richard Abel ed. 1982); Marc Galanter, "Why the 'Haves' Come Out Ahead: Speculation on the Limits of Legal Change," 9 *Law and Society Review* 95 (1974).

4. The virtues and flaws have been discussed by both major social theorists and legal academics. See, e.g., 6 *The Works of Jeremy Bentham* 60–86, 508–585 (Sir John Bowring ed. 1839); 2 Max Weber, *Economy and Society* 656–667, 880–888 (Gunther Roth and Claus Wittich eds. 1969); Ronald Dworkin, "The Model of Rules," 35 *University of Chicago Law Review* 14 (1967); Lon Fuller, "Consideration and Form," 41 *Columbia Law Review* 799 (1941); Lawrence Friedman, "Law, Rules, and the Interpretation of Written Documents," 59 *Northwestern University Law Review* 751 (1965); Roscoe Pound, "The Theory of Judicial Decision, III," 36 *Harvard Law Review* 940 (1923).

5. See Duncan Kennedy, "The Structure of Blackstone's *Commentaries,*" 28 *Buffalo Law Review* 205, 211–213 (1979).

6. See, e.g., William W. Bratton, Jr., "Manners, Metaprinciples, Metapolitics, and Kennedy's *Form and Substance,*" 6 *Cardozo Law Review* 871, 892–898 (1986); Louis Schwartz, "With Gun and Camera Through Darkest CLS-land," 36 *Stanford Law Review* 413, 418 (1984); Paul M. Shupack, "Rules and Standards in Kennedy's *Form and Substance,*" 6 *Cardozo Law Review* 947 (1986); Pierre Schlag, "Rules and Standards," 33 *U.C.L.A. Law Review* 379, 418–422 (1985).

7. See, e.g., Shepard v. Carpenter, 54 Minn. 153, 55 N.W. 906 (1893) (breach of an agreement to negotiate a contract cannot itself be the basis of a cause of action). Samuel Williston, "Mutual Assent in the Formation of Contracts," 14 *Illinois Law Review* 85 (1919).

8. See Restatement (Second) of Contracts §205 (1979). The obligation is described with case law referents, in more depth, in Robert Summers, " 'Good Faith' in General Contract Law and the Sales Provisions of the UCC," 54 *Virginia Law Review* 195 (1968). A serviceable critique of positing an obligation to bargain in good faith, focusing on the usual problems of implementing a formally nonrealizable standard, can be found in Clayton Gillette, "Limitations on the Obligation of Good Faith," 1981 *Duke Law Journal* 619.

9. See UCC §2–204 (formation in general) and UCC §2–305 (open price term can be filled in unless parties intend not to be bound unless price is settled).

10. See Restatement (Second) of Contracts §90 (1979) (charitable subscription enforceable even in the absence of proof that the promise induced action or forbearance; other promises that promisor should know alter promisee conduct will be enforced only if injustice can be avoided only by enforcement of the promise, demanding either full or part performance as justice dictates). See especially Illustration 1 (A, knowing that B is going to college, promises him $5,000 on completion; A notifies B of intention to revoke before performance is completed, but A's promise is deemed binding).

11. See, e.g., Batsakis v. Demotsis, 226 S.W. 2d 673 (1949); Buckner v. McIlroy, 31 Ark. 631 (1877). The "principle" traces back at least to Hobbes. See Thomas Hobbes, *Leviathan* 75 (1651): "The value of all things contracted for is measured by the appetite of the contractors; and therefore the just value, is that which they be contracted to give."

12. See, e.g., Campbell Soup Co. v. Wentz, 172 F. 2d 80 (3d Cir. 1948); American Home Improvement Co. v. MacIver, 105 N.H. 435, 201 A. 2d 886 (1964); UCC §2–302, especially Official Code Comments 2–302–1: "The basic test is whether . . . the clauses involved are so one-sided as to be unconscionable . . . The principle is one of the prevention of oppression . . . and not of disturbance of allocation of risks because of superior bargaining power."

13. See Duncan Kennedy, "Distributive and Paternalist Motives in Contract and Tort Law, with Special Reference to Compulsory Terms and Unequal Bargaining Power," 41 *Maryland Law Review* 563, 614–624 (1982).

14. See, e.g., Arthur Leff, "Unconscionability and the Code: The Emperor's New Clause," 115 *University of Pennsylvania Law Review* 485, 487–488, 532–537 (1967).

15. See, e.g., Restatement of Contract §492 (1932), Silsbee v. Webster, 171 Mass. 378, 50 N.E. 555 (1898). For standard Realist critiques of this view of duress, see John Dawson, "Economic Duress: An Essay in Perspective," 45 *Michigan Law Review* 253 (1947); John Dalzell, "Duress by Economic Pressure I," 20 *North Carolina Law Review* 237 (1942); "Note: Economic Duress after the Demise of Free Will Theory: A Proposed Tort Analysis," 53 *Iowa Law Review* 892 (1968).

16. See, e.g., Anthony Kronman and Richard Posner, *The Economics of Contract Law* 3–5 (1979); A. Mitchell Polinsky, *An Introduction to Law and Economics,* 25–36, 57–63 (1983); John Barton, "The Economic Basis of Damages for Breach of Contract," 1 *Journal of Legal Studies* 277 (1972); Charles Goetz and Robert Scott, "Liquidated Damages, Penalties, and the Just Compensation Principle: Some Notes on an Enforcement Model and a Theory of Efficient Breach," 77 *Columbia Law Review* 554 (1977); Steven Shavell, "Damage Measures for Breach of Contract," 11 *Bell Journal of Economics* 466 (1980).

17. See Armen Alchian and William Allen, *Exchange and Production: Theory in Use* 50 (1969): "The trader may find that his new chosen position is not as nice as he imagined it would be. Information before the exchange is sometimes inaccurate and inadequate; the assumption that the trader preferred to get what he actually did get is then open to doubt." See also Alan Schwartz and Louis Wilde, "Intervening in Markets on the Basis of Imperfect Information: A Legal and Economic Analysis," 127 *University of Pennsylvania Law Review*

630 (1979); Charles Stuart, "Consumer Protection in Markets with Informationally Weak Buyers," 12 *Bell Journal of Economics* 562 (1981).

18. See Anthony Kronman, "Mistake, Disclosure, Information, and the Law of Contracts," 7 *Journal of Legal Studies* 1 (1978). See also, for more particular applications, Frank Easterbrook, "Insider Trading, Secret Agents, Evidentiary Privileges, and the Production of Information," 1981 *Supreme Court Review* 309; Daniel Fischel, "Efficient Capital Theory, the Market for Corporate Control, and the Regulation of Cash Tender Offers," 57 *Texas Law Review* 1 (1978); Sanford Grossman, "The Informational Role of Warranties and Private Disclosure about Product Quality," 24 *Journal of Law and Economics* 461 (1981).

19. See John Pratt, David Wise, and Richard Zeckhauser, "Price Differences in Almost Competitive Markets," 93 *Quarterly Journal of Economics* 189, 205–210 (1979); John Dunlop, "The Task of Contemporary Wage Theory," in *New Concepts in Wage Determination* 117 (George Taylor and Frank Pierson eds. 1957) for empirical evidence. A reasonable model of why one would expect price dispersion can be found in Steven Salop and Joseph Stiglitz, "Bargains and Ripoffs: A Model of Monopolistically Competitive Price Dispersion," 44 *Review of Economic Studies* 493 (1977).

20. Melvin Eisenberg, "The Bargain Principle and Its Limits," 95 *Harvard Law Review* 741, 755, 782–785 (1982).

21. See especially Robert Hale, "Bargaining, Duress, and Economic Liberty," 43 *Columbia Law Review* 603 (1943); Robert Hale, "Coercion and Distribution in a Supposedly Non-Coercive State," 38 *Political Science Review* 470 (1923).

22. See Anthony Kronman, note 18 above.

23. See Robert Nozick, "Coercion," in *Philosophy, Science, and Method* (Sidney Morgenbesser, Patrick Suppes, and Morton White eds. 1969).

24. See, e.g., Richard Epstein, *Takings: Private Property and the Power of Eminent Domain,* 112–125, 318–324 (1985); Richard Epstein, "A Theory of Strict Liability," 2 *Journal of Legal Studies* 131, 189–204 (1973); Judith Jarvis Thompson, "The Trolley Problem," 94 *Yale Law Journal* 1395 (1985).

25. See Ronald Coase, "The Problem of Social Cost," 3 *Journal of Law and Economics* 1 (1960). For a more detailed discussion, see Mark Kelman, "Taking *Takings* Seriously: An Essay for Centrists," 74 *California Law Review* 601 (1986).

26. See Richard Epstein, "A Theory of Strict Liability," note 24 above. For a discussion of the ways in which the view is psychologically primitive at the personal level, as well as resonating in premodern ideas of objective cause, see Donald Gjerdingen, "The Coase Theorem and the Psychology of Common-Law Thought," 56 *Southern California Law Review* 711, 729–740 (1985).

27. See Richard Epstein, "Nuisance Law: Corrective Justice and Its Utilitarian Constraints," 8 *Journal of Legal Studies,* 49, 60–65 (1979); Richard Epstein, *Takings,* note 24 above at 118, makes similar distinctions between "invasive" and "noninvasive" harms.

28. Clare Dalton, "An Essay in the Deconstruction of Contract Law," 94 *Yale Law Journal* 997 (1985).

29. See Herbert Packer, *The Limits of the Criminal Sanction* 79–102 (1968). "The principle [that conduct may not be treated as criminal unless it has been explicitly so defined by an authority] may be essentially sound, and the all-but-universal compliance with it that characterizes the administration of the criminal law in this country . . . may be the loftiest of tributes to the civilized state we have achieved." Id. at 80.

30. Jerome Hall, *General Principles of Criminal Law* 27–69 (2d ed. 1960). "The principle of legality is in some ways the most fundamental of all the principles . . . the principle means that no conduct may be held criminal unless it is precisely described in a penal law." Id. at 25, 28.

31. George Fletcher, *Rethinking Criminal Law,* 157–159, 170–174 (1978). "The premise underlying objectivist theory is a general proposition about the nature of legal liability, particularly criminal liability. The proposition is that no liability should attach unless . . . the defendant's conduct objectively conforms to criteria specified in advance." Id. at 157.

32. Rex v. Eagleton, 169 Eng. Rep. 766 (1855).

33. Model Penal Code §5.01.

34. The King v. Barker, [1924] N.Z.L.R. 865 (Ct. App.).

35. Hyde v. United States, 225 U.S. 347, 387 (1912) (dangerous proximity test); Commonwealth v. Peaslee, 177 Mass. 267, 59 N.E. 55 (1901) (attempt if harm would have occurred but for unforeseen interruption.)

36. Wis. Stat. Ann. §939.72 (West 1958).

37. Callanan v. United States, 364 U.S. 587, 593 (1961).

38. Model Penal Code §1.07(1)(b). See also §5.03, Comment at 99 (Ten. Draft No. 10, 1960).

39. For an illuminating discussion of the tension, see Robert Weisberg, "Deregulating Death," 1983 *Supreme Court Review* 305.

40. Furman v. Georgia, 408 U.S. 238 (1972).

41. The Supreme Court approved such statutes in Gregg v. Georgia, 42 U.S. 153 (1976).

42. The Supreme Court invalidated such statutes in Woodson v. North Carolina, 428 U.S. 280 (1976), and Roberts v. Louisiana, 428 U.S. 325 (1976).

43. Lockett v. Ohio, 438 U.S. 586 (1978).

44. See Samuel Gross and Robert Mauro, "Patterns of Death," 37 *Stanford Law Review* 27 (1984) (defendants more likely to be executed when victims are white).

45. See Mark Kelman, "Interpretive Construction in the Substantive Criminal Law," 33 *Stanford Law Review* 591, 660–662 (1981), and Anthony Amsterdam, "Note: The Void-for-Vagueness Doctrine in the Supreme Court," 109 *University of Pennsylvania Law Review* 67 (1960).

46. See, e.g., United States v. Balint, 258 U.S. 250 (1922); N.D. Cent. Code §12.1–02–02(2), (3)(e) (1976).

47. See, e.g., Joel Feinberg, *Doing and Deserving* 111–112 (1970); H. L. A. Hart, *Punishment and Responsibility* 152 (1968); George Fletcher, note 31 above at 717–736; Jerome Hall, note 30 above at 342–359; Herbert Packer, note 29 above at 121–131.

48. See Model Penal Code §2.05. See also Paul Robinson, *Criminal Law*

Defenses, 219 (1984): "Strict liability is permitted in modern codes in very limited instances, generally only for the least serious offenses, such as traffic violations."

49. For instance, in Commonwealth v. Koczwara, 397 Pa. 575, 155 A. 2d 825 (1959), the court decided that it is unconstitutional to imprison a bar owner for selling liquor to minors in the absence of proof of culpability, unconstitutional to convict him even if "he had been meticulously careful"; §494(a) of the Pennsylvania Criminal Code had made prison mandatory on a *second offense,* and it is this conclusive presumption that the defendant must be imprisoned if he violates the statute twice that the court in fact condemns, though no attention is paid to this aspect of the case.

50. "Consider the following case: A liquor store license holder faces a $100 fine [representing the social cost of violation] for each violation of the sale-to-minors proscription. In a strict liability regime, he would adopt System A, which costs $400 to implement and would result in five violations. His net private and social cost is $900. In a negligence regime, he might adopt System B—the one preordained as nonnegligent by the legislature—though it costs $600 to implement and results in 10 violations. If he is certain to be found nonnegligent using System B, and he is fairly certain that System A, though better in his circumstances at avoiding the socially feared result, will lead to his being judged negligent, then given a preordained description of reasonable care, he will adopt B. Its private cost will be only $600, while System A will cost him $900, though its social cost is $1,600 rather than $900." Mark Kelman, note 45 above at 609–610.

51. See, e.g., Allison v. State, 74 Ark. 444, 86 S.W. 409 (1905).

52. See, e.g., Herbert Packer, note 29 above at 107.

53. See, e.g., State v. Woods, 107 Vt. 354, 179 A. 1 (1935); Model Penal Code §2.02.

54. See, e.g., McQuirk v. State, 84 Ala. 435, 4 So. 775 (1887).

55. See United States v. Short, 4 C.M.A. 437, 16 C.M.R. 11 (1954).

56. While it is obviously linguistically less natural to think of intention, a seemingly forward-looking concept, in *ex post* terms, it is hardly unusual for us to believe that we will *name* the objects of an actor's intentions to serve our own purposes. If a boy jumps into the water saying, "Watch me do the butterfly," and he proceeds to do the breast stroke, few of us would think there is a single answer to the question of what he actually intended. If we thought the boy was eager to impress us with his manliness, we might believe he intended the butterfly; if he intended only to imitate a stroke he had seen, he might have intended the breast stroke. If someone says she intends to go to bed late and then goes to bed at nine o'clock, just as she intended, do *we* say she intended to go to bed late or not? For *punishment* purposes, the ones relevant to the example in the text, a complicated, nonlegal analogy might help. Assume you're a general manager of a baseball team (in the equivalent position to the judge in the attempted rape case) and you're deciding whether to fire the manager (convict the defendant). The consummated "crime" is "letting opponent get a hit by not playing the percentages," and the unconsummated attempt version is "not playing percentages but opponent makes an out anyway." If we assume the "crime" can be committed negligently—we expect that managers do not *try* to hurt the

team, that they would make a mistake such as bringing in a lefty screwball pitcher to face a lefty batter only inadvertently—you'd probably as readily fire the manager for making the negligent error when the batter makes an out as when he gets the hit, or certainly that the absence of the intent to harm would hardly provide an excuse in the case in which harm is unconsummated if it didn't in the case where the batter got a hit. I tried to make this same point in Mark Kelman, note 45 above at 625–627, but expand it now because the more cryptic version seems to have been unduly hard to comprehend.

57. William Simon, "Legality, Bureaucracy, and Class in the Welfare System," 92 *Yale Law Journal* 1198 (1983).

58. For a fuller discussion of the professional social work vision, see William Simon, "The Invention and Reinvention of Welfare Rights," 44 *Maryland Law Review* 1 (1985).

59. See Steven Kelman, *Regulating America, Regulating Sweden: A Comparative Study of Occupational Safety and Health Policy* (1980).

60. See James Krier, "The Pollution Problem and Legal Institutions: A Conceptual Overview," 18 *UCLA Law Review* 429 (1971).

61. Compare Robert Bork, "The Rule of Reason and the Per Se Concept: Price Fixing and Market Division," 74 *Yale Law Journal* 775 (1965), with Donald Turner, "The Principles of American Antitrust Law," in *Comparative Aspects of Antitrust Law in the United States, the United Kingdom, and the European Economic Community* 9–12 (6 *International and Comparative Law Quarterly Supplement* 1963).

62. See John Coffee, "Regulating the Market for Corporate Control: A Critical Assessment of the Tender Offer's Role in Corporate Governance," 86 *Columbia Law Review* 1195 (1986) (arguing that any general theoretical argument about whether transfer of control improves corporate performance will invariably be wrong in particular cases, that efficiency effects will vary).

63. See George Cooper, "The Avoidance Dynamic: A Tale of Tax Planning, Tax Ethics, and Tax Reform," 80 *Columbia Law Review* 1553 (1980).

64. Gregory v. Helvering, 69 F. 2d 809, 810 (2d Cir. 1934) aff'd. 293 U.S. 465 (1935).

65. Gilbert v. Commissioner, 248 F. 2d 399, 411 (2d Cir. 1957).

66. See Al Katz and Lee Teitelbaum, note 2 above.

67. See, e.g., Richard Posner, *Economic Analysis of Law* 122 (2d ed. 1977).

68. See William Prosser and W. Page Keeton, *The Law of Torts* 694–696, 699 (5th ed. W. Page Keeton, Dan Dobbs, Robert Keeton, David Owen eds. 1984). See also Turner v. General Motors, 584 S.W. 2d 844 (Tex. 1979); Azzarello v. Black Brothers Co. 480 Pa. 547, 391 A. 2d 1020 (1978).

69. See William Prosser and W. Page Keeton, note 68 above at 687. See also Sawyer v. Pine O. I. Sales Co., 155 F. 2d 855 (5th Cir. 1946).

70. See William Prosser and W. Page Keeton, note 68 above at 545–559; see also Restatement (Second) of Torts §520 (1979).

71. See William Prosser and W. Page Keeton, note 68 above at 229–231. See also Martin v. Herzog, 228 N.Y. 164, 126 N.E. F. 14 (1920).

72. See William Prosser and W. Page Keeton, note 68 above at 242–262. See also Restatement (Second) of Torts §328D (1979).

73. See H. Richard Smith, "An Independent Tort Action for Mental Suffering and Emotional Distress," 7 *Drake Law Review* 53 (1957) (nervously hoping that the outrageousness standard of the Restatement of Torts §46 will restrain discretion so that the cause of action will not "be of real concern to individuals who . . . tend to disregard the feelings of other fellow men").

The developing tort was defended by one of its initial leading proponents against the accusation that it might be unduly unadministrable. See Calvert Magruder, "Mental and Emotional Disturbance in the Law of Torts," 49 *Harvard Law Review* 1033, 1058 (1936): "We would expect . . . the gradual emergence of a broad principle . . . that one who . . . beyond all bounds of decency, purposely causes a disturbance . . . is [liable] . . . [S]uch a formula would not decide concrete cases; but it is as practicable to apply as the standard of reasonable care in ordinary negligence cases."

74. See Fadgen v. Lenker, 469 Pa. 277, 365 A. 2d 147 (1976) (majority first derides absence of defenses in the traditional tort, then abolishes tort outright without seriously addressing claim of J. Roberts, dissenting, that "our legal system is capable of ascertaining . . . defenses . . . worthy of judicial recognition"). See also Bearbower v. Merry, 266 N.W. 2d 128 (Iowa 1978).

75. See John Langbein, "Substantial Compliance with the Wills Act," 88 *Harvard Law Review* 489 (1975), for a good discussion of requisite formalities.

76. See, e.g., Green v. Richmond, 369 Mass. 47, 337 N.E. 2d 691 (1975).

77. See, e.g., Farkas v. Williams, 5 Ill. 2d 417, 125 N.E. 2d 600 (1955).

78. See, e.g., Nelson v. American Tel. and Tel. Co., 270 Mass. 471, 170 N.E. 416 (1930).

79. See, e.g., Holbrook v. Taylor, 532 S.W. 2d 763 (Ky. 1976); Shepard v. Purvine, 196 Or. 348, P. 2d 352 (1952).

80. See, e.g., Jee v. Audley, 1 Cox 324, 29 Eng. Rep. 1186 (Ch. 1787).

81. See, e.g., Merchants Bank v. Curtis, 98 N.H. 225, 97 A. 2d 207 (1953); Ronald Maudsley, "Perpetuities: Reforming the Common-Law Rule—How to Wait and See," 60 *Cornell Law Review* 355 (1975).

82. This discussion is predominantly derived from Gregory Alexander, "The Dead Hand and the Law of Trusts in the Nineteenth Century," 37 *Stanford Law Review* 1189, 1195–1208, 1210–1219, 1250–1254 (1985).

83. See, e.g., Broadway Bank v. Adams, 133 Mass. 170 (1882).

84. Claflin v. Claflin, 149 Mass. 19, 20 N.E. 454 (1889).

85. For instance, trusts can be terminated prematurely only when all beneficiaries give consent to termination (and are competent to do so) and when premature termination would not jeopardize a "material purpose" of the trustor. See Restatement (Second) of the Law of Trusts §337 (1959).

86. See Amalgamated Food Employees Union v. Logan Valley Plaza, 391 U.S. 308 (1968); Lloyd Corp. v. Tanner, 407 U.S. 551 (1972); Hudgens v. NLRB, 424 U.S. 507 (1976); Pruneyard Shopping Center v. Robins, 447 U.S. 74 (1980).

87. See, e.g., J. Reed (dissenting) in Marsh v. Alabama 326 U.S. 501 (1946) at 511. Richard Epstein, *Takings,* note 24 above at 65–66.

88. See J. Marshall (dissenting) in Hudgens v. NLRB, note 86 above at 525.

89. For an excellent general discussion of the relationship between "rules" and this sort of reification, see Robert Gordon, note 3 above.

90. The last-possible-step rule seems arguably overinclusive if it inculpates people who have taken the last possible step in a plan so inapt that some may find the actor foolish, not dangerous. Believing that a contract is inevitably formed once a party has accepted an offer in mirror-image terms is overinclusive if, for instance, there is a mistake.

91. See Samuel Gross and Robert Mauro, note 44 above.

92. See Donald Partington, "The Incidence of the Death Penalty for Rape in Virginia," 22 *Washington and Lee Law Review* 43 (1965); Marvin Wolfgang and Marc Riedel, "Race, Judicial Discretion, and the Death Penalty," 407 *Annals* 119 (1973). The death penalty can no longer be applied, as a constitutional matter, in rape cases. See Coker v. Georgia, 433 U.S. 584 (1977).

93. See Treas. Reg. §1.471–6(a) (1958). "Incorrect" accounting methods for farmers were allowed shortly after the enactment of the Sixteenth Amendment. See T.D. 2153, 17 Treas. Dec. Int. Rev. 101 (1915) as amended T.D. 2665, 20 Treas. Dec. Int. Rev. 45 (1918). For a fuller discussion of problems in this area, see Larry Ward, "Tax Postponement and the Cash Method Farmer: Analysis of Revenue Ruling 75–152," 53 *Texas Law Review* 1119 (1975), and Charles Davenport, "A Bountiful Tax Harvest," 48 *Texas Law Review* 1 (1969).

94. See Rev. Rul. 75–152, 1975–17 I.R.B. 15 (responding to deduction abuse by allowing deductibility of prepaid feed expenses only as long as prepayment is for reasons of business, not tax avoidance). See also I.R.C. §447 (attempting to restrict benefits of cash accounting to "smaller" farmers), and I.R.C. §278 and 464 (attempting to restrict use of benefits of cash accounting by "farming syndicates").

95. See William Simon, "The Ideology of Advocacy," note 3 above.

96. See, e.g., Roscoe Pound, note 4 above at 940. The complexity of Weber's actual position is discussed in Anthony Kronman, *Max Weber,* 118–137 (1983). See also Roberto Unger, note 3 above at 73–76, 189, and David Trubek, "Max Weber on Law and the Rise of Capitalism," 1972 *Wisconsin Law Review* 720.

97. See, e.g., Mark Tushnet, "Critical Legal Studies and Constitutional Law: An Essay in Deconstruction," 36 *Stanford Law Review* 623 (1984); David Kairys, "Law and Politics," 52 *George Washington Law Review* 243–257 (1984).

98. See, e.g., 12 Code of Ala. 1975, Title 13A §13A–5–40(a)(7), §13A–5–40(a)(14); Nebraska Code §29–2529(1)(b)–(d).

99. See, e.g., Ex Parte Johnson, 399 So. 2d 873 (Ala. 1979) (aggravating statutory circumstance that defendant committed the crime for purpose of preventing arrest or effecting an escape does not apply to getting rid of a victim so that he could not identify the defendant but only to killing those effectuating arrests or to deaths occurring during escapes). The solution in some states is considerably less rulelike: if and only if defendant is found to have been *motivated* to kill the victim by fear of identification will he be deemed to have killed a witness or in order to avoid arrest. See, e.g., State v. Goodman, 298 N.C. 1,

257 S.E. 2d 569 (1979); Demps v. State, 395 So. 2d 19 (Fla. 1979). Likewise, while all killings committed in the course of robberies might be thought to be motivated by pecuniary gain, which is frequently defined by statute as an aggravated form of homicide, courts may decide that the section applies only to cases of murder for hire or murder to obtain insurance proceeds or bequests. See, e.g., State v. Simants, 197 Neb. 549, 250 N.W. 2d 881 (1977).

100. See Wisconsin Cheeseman, Inc. v. United States, 388 F. 2d 420 (7th Cir. 1968); Revenue Procedure 72–18, 72–1, C.B. 740.

101. See Calvert Magruder, note 73 above; Robert Rabin, "Tort Recovery for Negligently Inflicted Economic Loss: A Reassessment," 37 *Stanford Law Review* 1513 (1985). Rabin argues that the cases are relatively readily harmonized by looking to the courts' fear of "widespread liability," but the distinction he draws, in terms of our fear of "disproportionate punishment" given a certain level of defendant blameworthiness, between defendants who *are* liable for *mass* torts and those immune from paying for "remote" economic damage seems quite tenuous; moreover, the economic account—that defendants won't be deterred from misconduct by a low probability of high damages—can at best be only roughly true for only certain defendants (those who both rarely risk causing widespread harm *and* those who cognitively underestimate the expected value of low probability–high damage events rather than overestimating it because of the salience of the occasional dramatic verdict).

102. See Friedrich Kessler and Grant Gilmore, *Contracts: Cases and Materials* (2d ed. 1970), cases and comments collected at 478–508. For typical case law, compare Stilk v. Myrik, 2 Camp. 317, 170 Eng. Rep. 1168 (K.B. 1809) (midterm reformation void for want of consideration) with Watkins & Son v. Carrig, 91 N.H. 459, 21 A. 2d 591 (1941) (parties may rescind and form new contract; threat of breach of first contract need not constitute duress).

103. See Restatement (Second) of Contracts, §209–218 (1979). See also Hurst v. Lake & Co. 141 Or. 306, 16 P. 2d 627 (1930); Gordon State Plaza Corp. v. S. S. Kresge Co. 78 N.J. Super 485, 189 A. 2d 448 (1963).

104. For a somewhat fuller discussion of this problem, see Mark Kelman, "Trashing," 36 *Stanford Law Review* 293, 311–312 (1984).

105. William Simon, "Legality, Bureaucracy, and Class in the Welfare System," note 3 above at 1228–1230.

106. Robert Weisberg, note 39 above at 386–388.

107. Al Katz and Lee Teitelbaum, note 2 above at 31–33.

108. Id. at 17–27.

109. William Simon, "Legality, Bureaucracy, and Class in the Welfare System," note 3 above at 1227.

110. Id. at 1235–1238.

111. Duncan Kennedy, note 1 above at 1766–1774.

112. "My purpose is the rational vindication of two common intuitions . . . The first is that altruist views on substantive private law issues lead to a willingness to resort to standards . . . while individualism seems to harmonize with an insistence on rigid rules rigidly applied." Id. at 1685. See also id. at 1686–1687. Even outside the introduction, Kennedy can certainly be read

to make claims of fairly strong correspondence between the positions. See, e.g., id. at 1737–1751.

113. Id. at 1702–1710, 1722–1724, 1738, 1746.

114. See sources cited in note 6 above.

115. See Duncan Kennedy, note 1 above at 1738, 1746, 1748–1749.

116. See, e.g., Model Penal Code §210.6(3)(h). But see Godfrey v. Georgia, 446 U.S. 420 (1980) (such a provision may be, on its face, unconstitutionally vague in the absence of limiting interpretations by state courts).

117. Libertarian opposition to the negligence standard is premised precisely on this sense that it requires sharing. See, e.g., Richard Epstein, *Takings,* note 24 above at 40.

118. Duncan Kennedy, note 1 above at 1728–1731.

119. See UCCC §2.502 (buyer may revoke a home solicitation sale until midnight of the third business day after sale agreement signed except when buyer requests goods without delay owing to emergency).

120. See, e.g., Javins v. First National Realty Corp. 428 F. 2d 1071 (D.C. Cir. 1970).

121. See Stewart Macaulay, "Non-Contractual Relations in Business: A Preliminary Study," 28 *American Sociological Review* 55 (1963); Macaulay, "Elegant Models, Empirical Pictures, and the Complexities of Contract," 11 *Law and Society Review* 507 (1977).

122. See, e.g., Thomas Nagel, *The Possibility of Altruism* (1970).

123. Duncan Kennedy, note 1 above at 1717–1722.

124. Feminist legal literature has made far greater inroads than the early Critics made in revealing the psychocultural suppositions behind rule boundedness. Many of the feminists have been particularly interested in the claim of psychologists such as Carol Gilligan that rule orientation, generalization, and nonaccommodating egotism are linked male traits, and that women speak in "a different (moral) voice," one that seeks accommodation among affected parties based on norms of situation-specific fairness rather than conflict resolution in accordance with general rules. For a particularly good discussion of some of these issues, see "Feminist Discourse, Moral Values, and the Law—A Conversation," 34 *Buffalo Law Review* 11 (1985). See also generally Carol Gilligan, *In a Different Voice* (1982).

125. See Duncan Kennedy, note 5 above at 211–212.

126. Id. at 258–261.

2. The Subjectivity of Value

1. Roberto Unger, *Knowledge and Politics* (1975).

2. For instance, Hume said, "Whenever we depart from . . . equality we rob the poor of more satisfaction than we add to the rich . . . the gratification of a frivolous vanity in one individual costs more than bread to many families." See David Hume, "An Enquiry Concerning the Principles of Morals," in *Hume's Moral and Political Philosophy* 173, 193 (Henry Aiken ed. 1948).

3. See, e.g., Anthony Kronman, "Paternalism and the Law of Contracts,"

92 *Yale Law Review* 763, 766–774, 786–797 (1983) (defects may be either general and ontological or situation specific, i.e., a result of a party's being misinformed in particular cases).

4. Ronald Coase, "The Problem of Social Cost," 3 *Journal of Law and Economics* 1 (1960).

5. See, e.g., Richard Epstein, "The Social Consequences of Common Law Rules," 95 *Harvard Law Review* 1717, 1726–1727 (1982). For general discussions of the notion that we can plausibly treat parties as compensated *ex ante* by changes in rules that hurt them in particular cases, see A. Mitchell Polinsky, "Probabilistic Compensation Criteria," 86 *Quarterly Journal of Economics* 407 (1972); Frank Michelman, "Constitutions, Statutes, and the Theory of Efficient Adjudication," 9 *Journal of Legal Studies* 431 (1980).

6. See Guido Calabresi, *The Costs of Accidents: A Legal and Economic Analysis* 150–152 (1970); Harold Demsetz, "When Does the Rule of Liability Matter?" 1 *Journal of Legal Studies* 13, 25–28 (1972).

7. See, e.g., Gary Schwartz, "Economics, Wealth Distribution, and Justice," 1979 *Wisconsin Law Review* 799, 804–808.

8. See Richard Epstein, "A Theory of Strict Liability," 2 *Journal of Legal Studies* 151 (1973).

9. For a fuller discussion of the defects of Epstein's focus on cause see Mark Kelman, "Taking *Takings* Seriously: An Essay for Centrists," 74 *California Law Review* 601 (1986).

10. See, e.g., Model Penal Code §5.01(4).

11. See especially Friederich Hayek, *The Constitution of Liberty* 205–233 (1960); Friederich Hayek, *The Road to Serfdom* 72–88 (1944).

12. Lee Sheppard, "Metzenbaum Wages War on Finance Bill's Transition Rules," 31 *Tax Notes* 1155 (June 23, 1986).

13. See, e.g., Alexander Bickel, *The Least Dangerous Branch* (1962); John Ely, *Democracy and Distrust* (1980); James Thayer, "The Origin and Scope of the American Doctrine of Constitutional Law," 7 *Harvard Law Review* 129 (1893), Robert Bork, "Neutral Principles and Some First Amendment Problems," 47 *Indiana Law Journal* 1 (1971).

14. See, e.g., Richard Epstein, *Takings: Private Property and the Power of Eminent Domain* (1985).

15. See, e.g., Laurent B. Frantz, "The First Amendment in the Balance," 71 *Yale Law Journal* 1424 (1962); Robert Bork, "The Impossibility of Finding Welfare Rights in the Constitution," 1979 *Washington University Law Quarterly* 695.

16. See Raoul Berger, *Government by Judiciary* (1977); William Rehnquist, "The Notion of a Living Constitution," 54 *Texas Law Review* 693 (1976). For a good critique of such efforts generally, see Paul Brest, "The Misconceived Quest for the Original Understanding," 60 *Boston University Law Review* 204 (1980).

17. See John Ely, note 13 above. Jesse Choper, *Judicial Review and the National Political Process* (1980). For criticism, see Richard Parker, "The Past of Constitutional Theory—and Its Future," 42 *Ohio State Law Journal* 223

(1981); Paul Brest, "The Substance of Process," 42 *Ohio State Law Journal* 131 (1981).

18. See Gerald Gunther, "Foreword: In Search of Evolving Doctrine on a Changing Court: A Model for a Newer Equal Protection," 86 *Harvard Law Review* 1 (1972).

19. See, e.g., Owen Fiss, "Objectivity and Interpretation," 34 *Stanford Law Review* 739 (1982); Alexander Bickel, note 13 above at 143–272. For a telling critique, see Roberto Unger, note 1 above at 100–103.

20. See Thomas Heller, "Is the Charitable Exemption from Property Taxation an Easy Case? General Concerns about Legal Economics and Jurisprudence," in *Essays on the Law and Economics of Local Governments* 183 (Daniel Rubinfeld ed. 1979); Thomas Heller, "Structuralism and Critique," 36 *Stanford Law Review* 127, 172–181 (1984).

21. See Duncan Kennedy, "Cost-Benefit Analysis of Entitlement Problems: A Critique," 33 *Stanford Law Review* 387 (1981); Mario Rizzo, "The Mirage of Efficiency," 8 *Hofstra Law Review* 641 (1980). Posner's supposed "counterexample," that someone initially formally entitled to enslave others might still prefer workers to own their own labor if he could capture some of the surplus produced when they were freed, depends on the unwanted entitlement at issue being one that has dynamic effects on production, rather than simply being borne as a consumption loss. Thus, even if his example is true, it is not especially generalizable. See Richard Posner, "The Ethical and Political Basis of the Efficiency Norm in Common Law Adjudication," 8 *Hofstra Law Review* 487, 501–502 (1980). He does incidentally argue, by using an artificial numerical example in which the numbers happen to support his point, that we can imagine the consumption disutility of an unwanted entitlement being sufficiently low that the disfavored party *could,* by working more, hypothetically pay to have it removed, but since we could readily imagine that *not* being the case, the point of Posner's discussion of nonpecuniary losses is obscure.

22. See Clare Dalton, "An Essay in the Deconstruction of Contract Law," 94 *Yale Law Journal* 997, 1036–1038 (1985), for a brief discussion of the tension between procedural and substantive accounts of unconscionability. The procedural interpretation is more favored by the Restatement (Second) of Contracts §208 (1979) than by UCC §2–302.

23. See Duncan Kennedy, "Distributive and Paternalist Motives in Contract and Tort Law, with Special Reference to Compulsory Terms and Unequal Bargaining Power," 41 *Maryland Law Review* 563, 614–624 (1982).

24. See Standard Oil Co. of N.J. v. United States, 221 U.S. 1 (1911); United States v. American Tobacco Co., 221 U.S. 106 (1911); United States v. Grinnell Corp., 384 U.S. 563 (1966) (monopolization, *not* monopoly, is violative of the Sherman Act).

25. See, e.g., Anthony Kronman, "Mistake, Disclosure, Information, and the Law of Contracts," 7 *Journal of Legal Studies* 1 (1978).

26. See Duncan Kennedy, note 23 above at 642–644. I criticize Kennedy's views in Chapter 4, though.

27. See, e.g., Wisconsin & Michigan Railway v. Powers, 191 U.S. 379

(1903) (purely formal interpretation of consideration, in which nothing serves as consideration unless declared to be so); Maughs v. Porter, 157 Va. 415, 161 S.E. 242 (Sup. Ct. App. 1931) (consideration present if party objectively benefited from other party's conduct). See also Restatement (Second) of Contracts, §71, §81 (1979).

28. The discussion borrows heavily from Clare Dalton, note 22 above at 1066–1095.

29. Roberto Unger, note 1 above at 79–81.

30. William Simon, "The Ideology of Advocacy: Procedural Justice and Professional Ethics," 1978 *Wisconsin Law Review* 29. While I criticize the Simon-Unger position in the text, their insight is surely not without some merit. It helps explain, for instance, some of the "discontents" of the law of criminal attempts. Punishing attempts inevitably requires, to a degree, shifting from the privileged intentionalist discourse (see Chapter 3), in which a party is presumed to control her own conduct, to a determinist one, in which cause follows inexorably from effect, precisely because we are unable to know another's will without recourse to determinism. When we punish an attempter, we claim to *know* her desires, what she will ultimately "choose" to do—to infer her goals without ever *seeing* them fully realized, objectively, and our knowledge, in the absence of confession, must come from general (determinist) theories of what a person who takes certain steps must ultimately want. Thus, attempt law is unprivileged in liberal discourse, and hence staggeringly troublesome, along all three critical dimensions. First, it generally requires us to use relatively vague standards; second, it covertly adopts a determinist discourse in which an ultimate desire or aim is treated not so much as a privately-held, inaccessible whim but as an obvious, general feature of a socially observable course of conduct; and third, it treats the actor's imputed end as something other than individual, arbitrary, and whimsical. Though the presumed end is by no means objectively *"valid"* it *is* the end inevitably attributed to a group (similar criminals) rather than to the particular person, and it is imagined to be the end because it "makes (objective) sense" of a course of conduct.

Impossible attempts are particularly problematic, in this view, because the ordinary intentionalist, subjective-value assumptions again hold sway in the absence of the availability of a hypothetical counterfactual determinist account of conduct rather than desire. If the defendant did a particular deed, the value subjectivist must believe it is always plausible that he intended *just* that deed, inane or atypical though it may be. We are most reluctant to make a straightforward, determinist account of *ends,* to say that the defendant must have desired something more rationally, objectively sensible; such a move poses the most straightforward attack on value skepticism and pluralism. Only when attempts are temporally incomplete can a determinism of objective *action* permit us to introduce, surreptitiously, a determinism of objective values: we claim that we are only trying to infer what defendant would inexorably have done, not what he would inexorably have wanted, though, if pressed, we would see that we know what would have been done only by knowing what was desired.

31. See Anthony Amsterdam, "Note: The Void-for-Vagueness Doctrine in the Supreme Court," 109 *University of Pennsylvania Law Review* 67 (1960);

Mark Kelman, "Interpretive Construction in the Substantive Criminal Law," 33 *Stanford Law Review* 591, 660–662 (1981).

32. See Roberto Unger, note 1 above, especially at 55–62. See also Roberto Unger, *Passion: An Essay on Personality* 53–64, 95–100 (1984).

33. See generally Margaret Mahler, Fred Pine, and Anni Bergman, *The Psychological Birth of the Human Infant* (1975).

3. Intentionalism and Determinism

1. See Thomas Heller, "Is the Charitable Exemption from Local Property Taxation an Easy Case? General Concerns about Legal Economics and Jurisprudence," in *Essays on the Law and Economics of Local Governments* 183 (Daniel Rubinfeld ed. 1979); Thomas Heller, "Structuralism and Critique," 36 *Stanford Law Review* 127 (1984) Mark Kelman, "Interpretive Construction in the Substantive Criminal Law," 33 *Stanford Law Review* 591 (1981).

2. See Mark Kelman, "The Origins of Crime and Criminal Justice" 214, 215–216, 219–220, in *The Politics of Law* (David Kairys ed. 1982).

3. See H. L. A. Hart, *Punishment and Responsibility* 1–28 (1968); John Rawls, "Two Concepts of Rules," 64 *Philosophical Review* 3 (1955).

4. See, e.g., Herbert Packer, *The Limits of the Criminal Sanction* 77–78, 97–100 (1968); Laurence Tribe, "An Ounce of Detention: Preventive Justice in the World of John Mitchell," 56 *Virginia Law Review* 371, 379–380, 392–396 (1970).

5. See, e.g., David Gordon, "Capitalism, Class, and Crime in America," 19 *Crime and Delinquency* 163 (1973); Marvin Krohn, "Inequality, Unemployment, and Crime: A Cross-National Analysis," 17 *Sociological Quarterly* 303 (1976); John Braithwaite, *Inequality, Crime, and Public Policy* (1979).

6. For examples of how vaguely the connections are drawn between self-control and responsibility in mainstream writing, see, e.g., Herbert Packer, note 4 above at 74, 132–135; George Fletcher, *Rethinking Criminal Law* 799–807 (1978); H. L. A. Hart, note 3 above at 46–53, 173–177.

7. See, e.g., David Bazelon, "The Morality of the Criminal Law," 49 *Southern California Law Review* 385, 388–396, 403 (1976).

8. The puppet-puppeteer relationship is most openly asserted in traditional cases of duress, in which the defendant's will is said to be overborne and another's operative. See, e.g., Regina v. Hudson [1971] 2 All E.R. 244. See also Richard Delgado, "Ascription of Criminal States of Mind: Toward a Defense Theory for the Coercively Persuaded ('Brainwashed') Defendant," 63 *Minnesota Law Review* 1 (1978).

9. See Norval Morris, *Madness and the Criminal Law* 151–152, 156 (1982). See also Richard Delgado, " 'Rotten Social Background': Should the Criminal Law Recognize a Defense of Severe Environmental Deprivation?" 3 *Journal of Law and Inequality* 9, 81–89 (1985).

10. See Paul Hollander, "Sociology, Selective Determinism, and the Rise of Expectations," 8 *American Sociologist* 147, 148 (1973), for an unsympathetic description of this view.

11. See Michael Moore, "Causation and the Excuses," 73 *California Law*

Review 1091, 1128–1139 (1985); Michael Moore, *Law and Psychiatry: Rethinking the Relationship* 9–112 (1984).

12. The most fully developed account of Moore's position is in "Causation and the Excuses," note 11 above. The three-part argument, in essence, is as follows: First, behavior can be considered an action even if caused (see 1132–1137). The argument is undoubtedly true, but completely uninteresting unless we believe that because we don't blame nonacts, we are even minimally compelled to blame acts. Second, existing excuses can be adequately accounted for without making reference to causation (see 1128–1131). This is true only if one believes each of Moore's three dubious and unsupported assertions: (1) The people we characterize as criminally insane invariably lack a kind of rational agency rather than adequate volitional control. (2) Traditional duress and addiction "constrain an actor's choice in a way that other kinds of causes do not" (see 1131); that is, not only should one be, as some sort of normative matter, freer to avoid criminal urges that arise from psychologically rooted blood lust than to be heroic and hence noncriminal in the face of threats, but also the rage-filled person is, as a descriptive matter, less compelled to act badly, is less an agent than a person under duress or an addict. (3) Moore's failure to deal with provocation, the partial excuse that fits his already strained theory most poorly (since provoked conduct is the act of the very sort of rational agent he believes culpable but is nonetheless differentiated from less clearly causally explained conduct), damages the claim that one can account for existing practice without admitting that we are drawn to the idea that determinist accounts disturb our capacity to blame comfortably. Thus, even if one believes that it is especially damaging to determinists to see that one could adequately explain existing practice without reference to determinism, though one could clearly explain the excuses as instances of determinist discourse as well, Moore has simply failed to account in a satisfactory fashion for all of the excuses. Third, no one's praising and blaming practices are consistent with a view that causation negates responsibility. This is telling only on the seriously wrongheaded assumption that the most appropriate characterization of the practice of blame and praise emphasizes its logical consistency rather than its deeply felt contradictory nature. The view that such practices are contradictory, though, is far more consistent with Moore's own complete account of our practices in assigning responsibility (see 1140–1147). He must explain away parts of our practices of negating blame or responsibility as resulting from guilt, suppressed resentment, or elitist condescension (see 1146–1147) while, for no good nonrhetorical reason, failing to give parallel explanations, like egotism, suppressed smugness, and self-satisfaction or elitist contempt for the blame-*assigning* positions he favors.

13. See Thomas Szasz, *Law, Liberty, and Psychiatry* (1963); Thomas Szasz, *The Therapeutic State* (1984).

14. See Michael Moore, "Causation and the Excuses," note 11 above at 1118–1119.

15. See, e.g., Herbert Packer, note 4 above at 74–75.

16. See id. at 131–135. See also George Fletcher, note 6 above at 835–846.

17. Martin v. State, 31 Ala. App. 334, 17 So. 2d 427 (1944).

18. People v. Decina, 2 N.Y. 2d 133, 138 N.E. 2d 799 (1956).

19. See, e.g., Robinson v. California, 370 U.S. 660, 668 (1962). (J. Douglas concurring); United States v. Moore, 486 F. 2d 1139, 1242–1244 (D.C. Cir. 1973) (J. Wright dissenting.)

20. One assumes that Wright suppresses the intentionalistic interpretation of an addict's initial "decision" to use drugs because he actually believes such "choices" are themselves determined by "social background." Perfectly aware that, as a matter of predictable practice, one cannot make such general determinist arguments in our legal culture, his best bet, rhetorically, is to cut off the midrange intentionalist argument, to narrow the time frame to such an extent that the intentionalist interpretation is unavailing.

21. See H. L. A. Hart, note 3 above at 152.

22. See Joel Feinberg, *Doing and Deserving* 111–112 (1970).

23. Phil Johnson's rather off-the-mark set of responses to my article on strict liability seems entirely to miss, among many other things, this rather obvious distinction. See Phillip Johnson, "Strict Liability," 4 *Encyclopedia of Crime and Justice* 1518, 1521 (Sanford Kadish ed. 1983).

24. See, e.g., H. L. A. Hart, note 3 above at 136–157; George Fletcher, "The Theory of Criminal Negligence: A Comparative Analysis," 119 *University of Pennsylvania Law Review* 401 (1971).

25. See, e.g., Jerome Hall, "Negligent Behavior Should Be Excluded from Penal Liability," 63 *Columbia Law Review* 632 (1963); Glanville Williams, *Criminal Law: The General Part* §43 (2d ed. 1961).

26. Glanville Williams, note 25 above at 122–123. Even if a negligence standard were framed in such a way that it required all actors to behave in a way that some were simply incapable of (for example, requiring drivers to react more quickly than a particular driver is able to), one could still interpret an incapable negligent actor's behavior intentionalistically if he chose to engage in a category of behavior he was incapable of performing responsibly. Only in a society that criminalized unavoidably inadequate performance of unavoidable behavior could we squeeze out socially plausible intentionalistic interpretations and condemn the legislation without hesitation as criminalizing wholly uncontrollable, determined conduct.

27. See Wayne LaFave and Austin Scott, *Handbook on Criminal Law* §76 (1972).

28. Model Penal Code §210.3. See also Jerome Michael and Herbert Wechsler, "A Rationale of the Law of Homicide II" 37 *Columbia Law Review* 1261, 1280–1282 (1937), for an explanation of the theory behind the Model Penal Code approach.

29. See Richard Delgado, note 8 above.

30. See, e.g., United States v. Russell, 411 U.S. 423 (1973).

31. This "objective" view is set out in cases like State v. Mullen, 216 N.W. 2d 375 (Iowa 1974). It was well defended by Justice Roberts, concurring in Sorrells v. United States, 287 U.S. 435, 457 (1932), a case in which the majority adopted the view that defendants could be acquitted only if they lacked the predisposition to commit the crimes they were accused of committing.

32. See, e.g., Henderson v. United States, 237 F. 2d 169, 175 (5th Cir.

1956) ("Well settled, of course, it is that the doctrine of entrapment does not extend to acts of inducement on the part of a private citizen who is not an officer of the law").

33. See Martin v. State, note 17 above.

34. LeBarron v. State, 32 Wis. 2d 294, 145 N.W. 2d 79 (1966).

35. 32 Wis. 2d at 300, 145 N.W. 2d at 82, citing State v. Danns, 9 Wis. 2d 183, 100 N.W. 2d 592 (1960).

36. See, e.g., Wesley United Methodist Church v. Harvard College, 366 Mass. 247, 316 N.E. 2d 260 (1974).

37. See, e.g., William Andrews, "Personal Deductions in an Ideal Income Tax," 86 *Harvard Law Review* 309 (1972).

38. See, e.g., Mark Kelman, "Personal Deductions Revisited: Why They Fit Poorly in an 'Ideal' Income Tax and Why They Fit Worse in a Far from Ideal World," 31 *Stanford Law Review* 831 (1979).

39. See Charles Tiebout, "A Pure Theory of Local Expenditures," 64 *Journal of Political Economy* 416 (1956). For a legal application, see Robert Ellickson, "Cities and Homeowners Associations," 130 *University of Pennsylvania Law Review* 1519, 1547–1554 (1982) (tenants might reasonably be disenfranchised for lacking sufficient stake in local elections, given the hypothesis that each owner's property values will shift with shifts in local government policies).

40. See, e.g., Harvey Rosen and Richard Quandt, "Estimation of a Disequilibrium Aggregate Labor Market," 60 *Review of Economics and Statistics* 371 (1978); Kim Clark and Lawrence Summers, "Labor Market Dynamics and Unemployment: A Reconsideration" 1979(1) *Brookings Papers on Economic Activity* 13.

41. See, e.g., Robert Lucas and Leonard Rapping, "Real Wages, Employment, and Inflation," in *Microeconomic Foundations of Employment and Inflation Theory* (Edmund Phelps ed. 1970); Stephen Salant, "Search Theory and Duration Data: A Theory of Sorts," 91 *Quarterly Journal of Economics* 39 (1977); Costas Azariadis, "Implicit Contracts and Underemployment Equilibria," 83 *Journal of Political Economy* 1183 (1975).

42. See, e.g., Peter Linneman, "The Economic Impact of Minimum Wage Law: A New Look at an Old Question," 90 *Journal of Political Economy* 443 (1982); Charles Brown, Curtis Gilroy, and Andrew Kohen, "The Effect of the Minimum Wage on Employment and Unemployment," 20 *Journal of Economic Literature* 487 (1982).

43. See, e.g., Milton Friedman and L. J. Savage, "The Utility Analysis of Choices Involving Risk," 56 *Journal of Political Economy* 279 (1948); Richard Posner, *Economic Analysis of Law* 432–434 (3d ed. 1986).

44. See Robert Hale, "Bargaining, Duress, and Economic Liberty," 43 *Columbia Law Review* 603 (1943); Robert Hale, "Coercion and Distribution in a Supposedly Non-Coercive State," 38 *Political Science Quarterly* 470 (1923).

45. Robert Hale, "Bargaining, Duress, and Economic Liberty," note 44 above at 609–610 (accumulating checks to draw down reserves of a bank is illicit owing to impermissible motive) and 610–611 (damages not measured at monopoly price that might have been available had plaintiff been permitted to

withhold services and bargain to provide them). The key cases Hale cites are American Bank & Trust Co. v. Federal Reserve Bank of Atlanta, 256 U.S. 350 (1921), Vincent v. Lake Erie Transportation Co., 109 Minn. 456 (1910), Smith v. Staso Milling Co., 18 F. 2d 736 (2d Cir. 1927).

46. John Dawson, "Economic Duress: An Essay in Perspective," 45 *Michigan Law Review* 253 (1947).

47. Clare Dalton, "An Essay on the Deconstruction of Contract Law," 94 *Yale Law Journal* 997, 1014–1024, 1097–1104 (1985).

48. Morton Horwitz, "The Doctrine of Objective Causation," in *The Politics of Law* 201 (David Kairys ed. 1982).

49. See Albert Hirschman, *Exit, Voice, and Loyalty* (1970).

50. Id. at 26–29.

51. See, generally, Charles Clark, *Real Covenants and Other Interests Which Run with Land* (2d ed. 1947).

52. See, e.g., James Krier, book review, 122 *University of Pennsylvania Law Review* 1664, 1679–1680 (1974) (reviewing R. Posner, *Economic Analysis of Law*).

53. Posner, at least, is fairly consistent in his commitment to private ordering, opposing the touch-and-concern requirement that negated certain covenants that were intended to run. See Richard Posner, *Economic Analysis of Law* 50 (2d ed. 1977). Whether this is consistent with his more general belief that the common law is efficient, as a descriptive matter, is dubious.

54. The decline is traced in William Prosser, *Handbook of the Law of Torts* §68, 439–457 (4th ed. 1971). The classic defense of the notion that risk is assumed in the "private domain" in the absence of fraud or duress is in Francis Bohlen, "Voluntary Assumption of Risk," 20 *Harvard Law Review* 14 (1906). See also St. Louis Cordage v. Miller, 126 F. 495 (8th Cir. 1903), for a standard classical application in the employment context.

55. See Gerald Frug, "Cities and Homeowners Associations: A Reply," 130 *University of Pennsylvania Law Review* 1589 (1983).

56. See Thomas Heller, "Is the Charitable Exemption from Property Taxation an Easy Case?" note 1 above.

57. See Mark Kelman, "Choice and Utility," 1979 *Wisconsin Law Review* 769.

58. See Thomas Heller, "Is the Charitable Exemption from Property Taxation an Easy Case?" note 1 above; Mark Kelman, "Spitzer and Hoffman on Coase: A Brief Rejoinder," 53 *Southern California Law Review* 1215 (1980).

59. See, e.g., Max Horkheimer, *Eclipse of Reason* (1974).

60. Gary Peller argues that the Realists were engaged in a parallel radical deconstruction of the self, that they viewed the legal classicist's free individual as a pernicious myth. See Gary Peller, "The Metaphysics of American Law," 73 *California Law Review* 1151, 1154, 1224–1226, 1246–1259 (1985). I find his summary account of the Realists, particularly Robert Hale, essentially unpersuasive and off the mark, though his more concrete descriptions often seem more apt. See id. at 1222–1224, 1232–1234. Hale was predominantly a *political* theorist, interested in demonstrating that individuals are no less subject to state

power in ostensibly nonregulatory, laissez-faire regimes than in openly regulatory ones; he did not have much to say about whether the concept of individuality loses its meaning if we are invariably subject to some variety or other of collective force. In fact, Hale's writing seems to me to *assume* that all individuals have meaningful, particular, self-defining individual projects, and the state's inevitable role is to mediate the unavoidable clashes between those projects. Hale simply corrects the classical assumption that the collective can *avoid* favoring one or another party's demands in these inexorable clashes, can maintain a wholly detached *distributional* neutrality.

4. *Legal Economists and Normative Social Theory*

1. See Thomas Heller, "Is the Charitable Exemption from Property Taxation an Easy Case? General Concerns about Legal Economics and Jurisprudence," in *Essays on the Law and Economics of Local Governments* 183 (Daniel Rubinfeld ed. 1979); Thomas Heller, "The Importance of Normative Decision-Making: The Limitations of Legal Economics as a Basis for Liberal Jurisprudence—As Illustrated by the Regulation of Vacation Home Development," 1976 *Wisconsin Law Review* 385; Mark Kelman, "Choice and Utility," 1979 *Wisconsin Law Review* 769; Mark Kelman, "Consumption Theory, Production Theory, and Ideology in the Coase Theorem," 52 *Southern California Law Review* 669 (1979); Mark Kelman, "Spitzer and Hoffman on Coase: A Brief Rejoinder," 53 *Southern California Law Review* 1215 (1980); Mark Kelman, "Misunderstanding Social Life: A Critique of the Core Premises of Law and Economics," 33 *Journal of Legal Education* 274 (1983); Mark Kelman, "Trashing," 36 *Stanford Law Review* 293, 306–318 (1984); Mark Kelman, "Comment on Hoffman and Spitzer's Experimental Law and Economics," 85 *Columbia Law Review* 1037 (1985); Duncan Kennedy, "Cost-Benefit Analysis of Entitlement Problems: A Critique," 33 *Stanford Law Review* 387 (1981); Duncan Kennedy, "Distributive and Paternalist Motives in Contract and Tort Law, with Special Reference to Compulsory Terms and Unequal Bargaining Power," 41 *Maryland Law Review* 563 (1982); Duncan Kennedy, "The Role of Law in Economic Thought: Essays on the Fetishism of Commodities," 34 *American University Law Review* 939 (1986); Duncan Kennedy and Frank Michelman, "Are Property and Contract Efficient?" 8 *Hofstra Law Review* 711 (1980); C. Edwin Baker, "The Ideology of the Economic Analysis of Law," 5 *Journal of Philosophy and Public Affairs* 3 (1975); C. Edwin Baker, "Starting Points in the Economic Analysis of Law," 8 *Hofstra Law Review* 939 (1980).

2. See, e.g., Morton Horwitz, "Law and Economics: Science or Politics?" 8 *Hofstra Law Review* 905 (1980); Elizabeth Mensch, "The History of Mainstream Legal Thought," in *The Politics of Law* 18, 36–37 (David Kairys ed. 1982).

3. See, e.g., Richard Posner, "A Reply to Some Recent Criticisms of the Efficiency Theory of the Common Law," 9 *Hofstra Law Review* 775 (1981); Richard Posner, "Some Uses and Abuses of Economics in Law," 46 *University of Chicago Law Review* 281 (1979).

4. See, e.g., Richard Posner, *Economic Analysis of Law* 495–499 (3d

ed. 1986); Richard Posner, "Theories of Economic Regulation," 5 *Bell Journal of Economics and Management Science* 335 (1974).

5. See George Stigler, "The Theory of Economic Regulation," 2 *Bell Journal of Economics and Management Science* 3 (1971); Sam Peltzman, "Toward a More General Theory of Regulation," 19 *Journal of Law and Economics* 211 (1976); Gary Becker, "A Theory of Competition among Pressure Groups for Political Influence," 98 *Quarterly Journal of Economics* 371 (1983).

6. See, e.g., George Priest, "The Common Law Process and the Selection of Efficient Rules," 6 *Journal of Legal Studies* 65 (1977); Paul Rubin, "Why Is the Common Law Efficient?" 6 *Journal of Legal Studies* 51 (1977); John Goodman, "An Economic Theory of the Evolution of the Common Law," 7 *Journal of Legal Studies* 393 (1978). These theories are criticized in Lewis Kornhauser, "A Guide to the Perplexed Claims of Efficiency in the Law," 8 *Hofstra Law Review* 591, 627–633 (1980).

7. Richard Posner, "A Theory of Negligence," 1 *Journal of Legal Studies* 29 (1972).

8. Gary Schwartz, "Tort Law and the Economy in Nineteenth-Century America: A Reinterpretation," 90 *Yale Law Journal* 1717 (1981).

9. Robert Rabin, "The Historical Development of the Fault Principle: A Reinterpretation," 15 *Georgia Law Review* 925 (1981).

10. Richard Posner, *Economic Analysis of Law* 46 (3d ed. 1986).

11. See Stephen Williams, "Solar Access and Property Rights: A Maverick Analysis," 11 *Connecticut Law Review* 430, 442–443, 451–452 (1979).

12. See Richard Posner, note 10 above at 46, n. 2, and Richard Posner, *Economic Analysis of Law, Teachers' Manual* 4 (3d ed. 1986).

13. See, e.g., William Whitford, "The Function of Disclosure Regulation in Consumer Transactions," 1973 *Wisconsin Law Review* 400; William Whitford and Harold Laufer, "The Impact of Denying Self-Help Repossession of Automobiles: A Case Study of the Wisconsin Consumer Act," 1975 *Wisconsin Law Review* 607; James White, "The Abolition of Self-Help Repossession: The Poor Pay Even More," 1973 *Wisconsin Law Review* 503.

14. Compare, e.g., Frank Michelman, "Property, Utility, and Fairness: Comments on the Ethical Foundations of 'Just Compensation' Law," 80 *Harvard Law Review* 1165 (1967) (sophisticated traditional policy analysis), with Lawrence Blume and Daniel Rubinfeld, "Compensation for Takings: An Economic Analysis," 72 *California Law Review* 569 (1984), or Guido Calabresi, "Concerning Cause and the Law of Torts," 43 *University of Chicago Law Review* 69 (1975) (traditional policy analysis), with Steven Shavell, "An Analysis of Causation and the Scope of Liability in the Law of Torts," 9 *Journal of Legal Studies* 463 (1980) (formalized but highly similar analysis).

15. Richard Posner, note 10 above.

16. Guido Calabresi, *The Costs of Accidents: A Legal and Economic Analysis* (1970).

17. See, e.g., Richard Posner, note 10 above at 260–261.

18. Richard Posner, "Utilitarianism, Economics, and Legal Theory," 8 *Journal of Legal Studies* 103 (1979).

19. Id. Lewis Kornhauser does a fine job summarizing the ways in which

Posner's wealth-maximization principle is subject to almost all standard anti-utilitarian claims. See Lewis Kornhauser, note 6 above at 591, 599–604.

20. Richard Posner, note 10 above at 219.

21. Guido Calabresi and Philip Bobbitt, *Tragic Choices* (1978).

22. See, e.g., Richard Posner, note 10 above at 45.

23. See Richard Posner, "The Ethical and Political Basis of the Efficiency Norm in Common Law Adjudication," 8 *Hofstra Law Review* 487, 492–497 (1980).

24. See Richard Posner, *The Economics of Justice* 88–89, 94–99 (1981).

25. See, e.g., Richard Posner note 10 above at 512–514. Isaac Ehrlich and Richard Posner, "An Economic Analysis of Legal Rulemaking," 3 *Journal of Legal Studies* 257 (1974).

26. See Richard Posner, note 10 above at 129.

27. Id. at 137–138.

28. See, e.g., Guido Calabresi, "Optimal Deterrence of Accidents," 84 *Yale Law Journal* 656 (1975); Guido Calabresi, "Torts: The Law of the Mixed Society," 56 *Texas Law Review* 519 (1971); Posner, note 10 above at 148.

29. See the discussion in Lewis Kornhauser, "The Great Image of Authority," 36 *Stanford Law Review* 344, 353–354 (1984). See also Richard Posner, note 10 above at 205–210.

30. For a discussion of this distinction, see Mark Kelman, "The Origins of Crime and Criminal Violence," in *The Politics of Law* 214, 215–216, 219–220 (David Kairys ed. 1982).

31. See, e.g., Posner's discussion of why abused wives "consent" to abuse, given the availability of lax divorce laws (legally "privileging" separation), in Posner, "The Ethical Significance of Free Choice: A Reply to Professor West," 99 *Harvard Law Review* 1431, 1444 (1986). See also W. Kip Viscusi, *Risk by Choice: Regulating Health and Safety in the Workplace* (1983) (worker job choice creates optimal safety levels, given demand for safety and safety costs).

32. Richard Posner, note 23 above at 492–497.

33. See, e.g., discussion of implicit in-kind compensation in Richard Epstein, *Takings: Private Property and the Power of Eminent Domain* 195–215 (1985), or Richard Epstein, "Nuisance Law: Corrective Justice and Its Utilitarian Constraints," 8 *Journal of Legal Studies* 49, 77–78 (1979).

34. See the discussion in Lucien Bebchuk, "The Pursuit of a Bigger Pie: Can Everyone Expect a Bigger Slice?" 8 *Hofstra Law Review* 671, 692–709 (1980) (on restricting the domain of the wealth-maximizing test to account for distributive entitlements). See also Tibor Scitovsky, "A Note on Welfare Propositions in Economics," 9 *Review of Economic Studies* 77 (1941) (Kaldor-Hicks efficient decisions desirable only if they don't maldistribute gains). See also Guido Calabresi and Douglas Melamed, "Property Rules, Liability Rules, and Inalienability: One View of the Cathedral," 85 *Harvard Law Review* 1089, 1098–1105 (1972); Richard Markovits, "The Distributive Impact, Allocative Efficiency, and Overall Desirability of Ideal Housing Codes: Some Theoretical Clarifications," 89 *Harvard Law Review* 1815 (1976).

35. See Richard Markovits, "Duncan's Do Nots: Cost-Benefit Analysis

and the Determination of Legal Entitlements," 36 *Stanford Law Review* 1170 (1984).

36. See, e.g., Anthony Kronman and Richard Posner, *The Economics of Contract Law* 1–4 (1979).

37. See, e.g., Charles Meyers, "The Covenant of Habitability and the American Law Institute," 27 *Stanford Law Review* 879 (1975).

38. See, e.g., W. Kip Viscusi, note 31 above. Robert Smith, *The Occupational Safety and Health Act: Its Goals and Its Achievements* (1976).

39. See, e.g., Richard Epstein, "Unconscionability: A Critical Reappraisal," 18 *Journal of Law and Economics* 293 (1975).

40. See, e.g., Richard Posner, note 10 above at 139–143, 308–310, 346–347. See also Steven Crafton, "An Empirical Test on the Effect of Usury Laws," 23 *Journal of Law and Economics* 135 (1980); Richard Posner, "An Economic Theory of the Criminal Law," 85 *Columbia Law Review* 1193, 1200 (1985) ("It is hard for an economist to understand why the voluntary exchange of valuable goods [like prostitution, baby sales, narcotic sales] should be criminal").

41. Compare, e.g., Michael Darby and Edi Karni, "Free Competition and the Optimal Amount of Fraud," 16 *Journal of Law and Economics* 67 (1973), with Howard Beales, Richard Craswell, and Steven Salop, "The Efficient Regulation of Consumer Information," 10 *Journal of Law and Economics* 491 (1981), or Victor Goldberg, "Institutional Change and the Quasi-Invisible Hand," 17 *Journal of Law and Economics* 461 (1974).

42. Compare, e.g., Richard Posner, note 10 above at 101–105, with Anthony Kronman, "Contract Law and Distributive Justice," 89 *Yale Law Journal* 472, 477–483 (1980); Melvin Eisenberg, "The Bargain Principle and Its Limits," 95 *Harvard Law Review* 741 (1982).

43. See, especially, Melvin Eisenberg, note 42 above, for an example of this starting point–exception structure.

44. See, e.g., Guido Calabresi, note 16 above at 150–152.

45. See, e.g., Richard Posner, note 10 above at 45.

46. See, e.g., Richard Posner, note 10 above at 76 (Question 7), and Richard Posner, *Teacher's Manual,* note 12 above at 9–10.

47. See Richard Epstein, "A Theory of Strict Liability," 2 *Journal of Legal Studies* 151 (1973).

48. See, e.g., Richard Posner, note 10 above at 45–46.

49. For a good general discussion, see Robert Cooter and Lewis Kornhauser, "Can Litigation Improve the Law without the Help of Judges?" 9 *Journal of Legal Studies* 139 (1980).

50. See Thomas Heller, "Is the Charitable Exemption from Property Taxation an Easy Case?" note 1 above.

51. See Mark Kelman, "Choice and Utility," note 1 above.

52. Robin West, "Authority, Autonomy, and Choice: The Role of Consent in the Moral and Political Visions of Franz Kafka and Richard Posner," 99 *Harvard Law Review* 384 (1985).

53. The "metataste" imagery is invoked by Amartya Sen. See A. K. Sen, "Rational Fools: A Critique of the Behavioral Foundations of Economic

Theory," 6 *Philosophy and Public Affairs* 317, 336–341 (1977). See also Jon Elster, *Ulysses and the Sirens* (1979).

54. The predominant strategy employed by the neoclassical economists who dealt with issues of dynamic instability of taste was to posit such a "governor." See, e.g., Robert Strotz, "Myopia and Inconsistency in Dynamic Utility Maximization," 23 *Review of Economic Studies* 165 (1956); Richard Thaler, "Toward a Positive Theory of Consumer Choice," 1 *Journal of Economic Behavior and Organization* 39 (1980).

55. Mark Kelman, "Choice and Utility," note 1 above at 787.

56. See, e.g., John Kenneth Galbraith, *The Affluent Society* (4th ed. 1984).

57. See Herbert Gintis, "Consumer Behavior and the Concept of Sovereignty: Explanations of Social Decay," 61 *American Economic Review* 267 (1972).

58. In a similar vein, Richard Posner, note 31 above at 1439–1440, posits that bulimics are either "sick" (determined) or free, intentionalist actors whose choices are presumptively satisfying.

59. See Mark Kelman, "Choice and Utility," note 1 above at 772–773, for a brief summary of some work on "goods addiction."

60. See, e.g., the statute invalidated by the Supreme Court in City of Akron v. Akron Center for Reproductive Health, 462 U.S. 416 (1983).

61. See, e.g., U.C.C.C. §2.502 (buyers may ordinarily revoke home solicitation purchases until midnight of the third business day following sale).

62. See, e.g., California Health and Safety Code §7191(b) (West Supp. 1985) ("living will" providing that patient will refuse "extraordinary care" must be reexecuted at least fourteen days *after* diagnosis of terminal disease to have more than advisory force); California Health and Safety Code §7189.5 (West Supp. 1985) ("living will" must be reexecuted every five years); California Health and Safety Code §7189 ("living will" is revocable at any time).

63. See, e.g., statutes validated in Planned Parenthood of Kansas City, Mo., Inc. v. Ashcroft, 462 U.S. 476 (1983), and Belotti v. Baird, 443 U.S. 622 (1979).

64. See, e.g., Robert Crain, Rita Mahard, and Ruth Narot, *Making Desegregation Work* (1982); Elizabeth Cohen, "The Effects of Desegregation on Race Relations," 39 *Law and Contemporary Problems* 271 (1975).

65. See discussions of offer-asking problems in Mark Kelman, "Production Theory, Consumption Theory, and Ideology in the Coase Theorem," note 1 above, and Duncan Kennedy, "Cost-Benefit Analysis of Entitlement Problems," note 1 above, for insight into why people might be unwilling to *give* a sum of money to "charity," while being perfectly willing not to demand that same sum from the "charity" that has prior constructive possession of it, because the money has already been taxed from the person and transferred to the charity.

66. See Robert Crandall, Howard Gruenspecht, Theodore Keeler, and Lester Lave, *Regulating the Automobile* 3, 33–34, 48 (1986) (of fifty federal safety regulations, only one, the seatbelt interlock, has generated political or consumer opposition).

67. See generally, e.g., Vidya Dutt, *Problems of Collectivization of Soviet*

Agricultural Farms 1929–38 (1949); Stephen Osofsky, *Soviet Agricultural Policy: Toward the Abolition of Collective Farms* (1974); Moshe Lewin, *Russian Peasants and Soviet Power* (1975).

68. See William Simon, "Visions of Practice in Legal Thought," 36 *Stanford Law Review* 469, 474–489 (1984).

69. See Duncan Kennedy, "Distributive and Paternalist Motives," note 1 above at 646–649.

70. Id. at 641–642.

71. For a lucid discussion of these criteria, see Jules Coleman, "Efficiency, Utility, and Wealth Maximization," 8 *Hofstra Law Review* 509 (1980).

72. See Executive Order No. 12291 (1981) (requiring that all regulations be subject to cost-benefit analysis before being acted upon). For a good discussion of the deregulatory bias in the implementation of the order, see W. Norton Grubb, Dale Whittington, and Michael Humphries, "The Ambiguities of Benefit-Cost Analysis: An Evaluation of Regulatory Impact Analyses Under Executive Order 12291," in *Environmental Policy under Reagan's Executive Order 12291* (V. Kerry Smith ed. 1984).

73. See, e.g., Richard Posner, note 10 above at 15, 44.

74. See Duncan Kennedy, "Cost-Benefit Analysis of Entitlement Problems," note 1 above at 433–438; Mario Rizzo, "The Mirage of Efficiency," 8 *Hofstra Law Review* 641, 648–654 (1980).

75. See Duncan Kennedy, "Cost-Benefit Analysis of Entitlement Problems," note 1 above at 401–421.

76. See Richard Posner, "The Ethical and Political Basis of the Efficiency Norm in Common Law Adjudication," 8 *Hofstra Law Review* 487, 498–499 (1980).

77. See Richard Markovits, note 35 above. Markovits "solves" one technical problem in cost-benefit analysis by demanding that participants value an end state by reference to the wealth they would have should the end state be adopted, thus precluding them from stating a value for the end state that will prove inaccurate if the system in question is adopted. But this "solution" does nothing to eliminate asymmetries that arise when a rule and its opposite both appear efficient, given the chosen measurement method. Thus, Markovits's article largely misses Kennedy's main point.

78. See Duncan Kennedy, "Cost-Benefit Analysis of Entitlement Problems," note 1 above; Mark Kelman, "Production Theory, Consumption Theory, and Ideology in the Coase Theorem," note 1 above.

79. Mark Kelman, "Production Theory, Consumption Theory, and Ideology in the Coase Theorem," note 1 above.

80. Id. at 682–685. See also Mark Kelman, "Spitzer and Hoffman on Coase," note 1 above at 1215–1218.

81. See, e.g., Richard Posner, note 3 above (both articles), and Richard Posner, note 18 above.

82. See Jules Coleman, note 71 above.

83. See Mario Rizzo, note 74 above.

84. See Lewis Kornhauser, note 19 above.

85. See, e.g., Mark Kelman, "Trashing," note 1 above at 307.

86. See Paul Samuelson, "Evaluation of Real National Income," 2 *Oxford Economic Papers* 1, 2–3, 10–13 (1950).

87. A traditional argument within the utilitarian tradition might be of some help to Posnerians here. It is at least plausible that the utility I derive from others' enjoyment oughtn't to be counted when we endeavor to maximize utility. The argument is that it would be "double counting" to allow such derivative utility to matter. The argument *cannot* be that my pleasure at another's pleasure (for example my child's) *never* counts, since such pleasure is impossible to distinguish from routine private subjective pleasures. (A utilitarian would surely choose to give an ice cream cone to a child with an observing, doting parent nearby rather than one standing all alone if the two children themselves got equal utility from the cone.) Perhaps the more convincing argument is that *if* my desire is simply to maximize *everyone else's* utility, and if we have already agreed to follow a procedure whereby utility is maximized, I ought to be interested only in summing "primary" consumption utilities. It is possible, of course, that this double-counting critique renders the Critical position suspect insofar as our hypothetical moralists' desires for "nongoods" may be met if we simply agree to follow a social procedure (wealth maximizing or utility maximizing) that they approve of.

I think, though, that the critique of the CLS position is unavailing for three significant reasons. First, even if I decide to discount my *own* utility through seeing utility maximized on the condition that the utility of others be maximized, there is no reason to think that other utility maximizers should ignore that utility or that I should ignore parallel enjoyment in others. If people are indeed happier when a particular decision rule is used, or unhappier when it isn't, that is simply a fact about preferences to be reckoned with. The point is even more obvious if we're dealing with a wealth-maximizing principle: such principles do not readily admit scrutiny of motivation for the decision to buy or not buy an end state. Second, it is simply a *hypothesis* that the moralist would pay for (or have to be paid to lose) the end state that maximizes direct consumer utility or "social wealth"; it is seemingly the case that *if* that were his true goal, the moralist would simply get no additional utility from (nor pay for nor have to be paid to lose) any particular assignment of goods, but would rather be generally indifferent to assignments, as long as he believed that proper procedures were in use. We have no strong reason to believe that this is the case; but if it were, the aggregate utility calculations would simply be *unaltered,* as a matter of fact, by factoring in the desires of the moralists, but there would be no reason not to do the accounting. Third, and most significant, if wealth maximization is invariably based on ability to pay, as Posner asserts, it is implausible that egalitarian moralists will be satisifed that if the Posnerian procedure is adopted, their own subjective ends will be met, in such a way that they could presume to be uninterested in distributive issues. One can safely surrender one's rights to have one's own preferences counted only as long as others are following a procedure one approves of that promises to match one's own preference. For good discussions of some of these issues, see C. Edwin Baker, "Counting Preferences in Collective Choice Situations," 25 *UCLA Law Review* 381 (1976);

Ronald Dworkin, *Taking Rights Seriously* 222–239 (1977); Harold Hochman and James Rodgers, "Pareto Optimal Redistribution," 59 *American Economic Review* 542 (1969).

5. Legal Economists and Conservative Preferences

1. See Duncan Kennedy and Frank Michelman, "Are Property and Contract Efficient?" 8 *Hofstra Law Review* 711, 715, 757–769 (1980) (an excellent effort to define in technical legal detail what participants in our legal culture generally mean when they refer to a regime as a private property regime).

2. Not atypical of the problem of confusing Western regimes with private property regimes, particularly for rhetorical effect, is Richard Epstein's remark that "private property, in a word, nourishes freedom of speech, just as freedom of speech nourishes private property. Can anyone find a society in which freedom of speech flourishes where the institution of private property is not tolerated?" Richard Epstein, *Takings: Private Property and the Power of Eminent Domain* 138 (1985). But, of course, if free speech flourishes anywhere, it flourishes *only* in regimes that, by Epstein's own lights, consistently violate private property rights since they not only tolerate but politically *centralize* innumerable illegitimate uncompensated takings, from redistributive taxation to price controls to environmental controls stricter than common law nuisance regulation.

3. Duncan Kennedy and Frank Michelman, note 1 above.

4. The argument Kennedy and Michelman attack is made, for instance, in Richard Posner, *Economic Analysis of Law* 30–31 (3d ed. 1986). Posner attempts, to no apparent effect, to defend and supplement the obviously naive assertion he had made in earlier editions of *Economic Analysis* that substitution effects will inexorably dominate income effects. He now "adds" one of the other false general arguments for private property that Kennedy and Michelman have dealt with, that it avoids wasteful precautionary expenditures (including investment in activities with a rapid, easily consumed payoff), and the truly bizarre (and not clearly relevant) factual assertion that because a growing *proportion* of a producer's goods will supposedly be taken if he produces more (by thieves in a state of nature), the producer will despair and not bother to produce more. Id. at 30–31, n. 1.

5. See, e.g., Glen Cain and Harold Watts, "Towards a Summary and Synthesis of the Evidence," in *Income Maintenance and Labor Supply* 328 (Glen Cain and H. Watts ed. 1973); Don Fullerton, "On the Possibility of an Inverse Relationship between Tax Rates and Government Revenues," 19 *Journal of Public Economics* 3 (1982); Barry Bosworth, *Tax Incentives and Economic Growth* 172–176.

6. Compare, e.g., Jerry Hausman, "Labor Supply," in *How Taxes Affect Economic Behavior* (Henry Aaron and Joseph Pechman eds. 1981) (high substitution *and* income effects), with Barry Bosworth, note 5 above at 143 (both income and substitution effects are small, elasticities ranging from 0 to 0.3 or −0.3 in the studies).

7. See Michael Piore, "Fragments of a 'Sociological' Theory of Wages," in *Unemployment and Inflation* 134 (Michael Piore ed. 1979).

8. See John Witte, *The Politics and Development of the Federal Income Tax* 71 (1985); Congressional Record, 63d Cong., 1st sess., vol. 50, 3837, 3839 (1913) (remarks of Sens. Crawford and Lodge).

9. The initial statute levied a 1 percent tax with an exemption of $3,000 for a single taxpayer and $4,000 for a married taxpayer. A surtax, graduated from 1 percent to 6 percent was applied to net income in excess of $20,000. Act of Oct. 3, 1913, ch. 16, §11, 38 Stat. 166. The bottom rate today is 11 percent for income above $3,400. See I.R.C. §1.

10. See, e.g., Robert Hall and Alvin Rabushka, *Low Tax, Simple Tax, Flat Tax* (1983).

11. See, e.g., John Dunlop, "Wage Contours," in *New Concepts of Wage Determination* 127 (George Taylor and Frank Pierson eds. 1957).

12. See, e.g., Hugh Aitken, *Did Slavery Pay?* (1971); Robert Fogel, *Time on the Cross* (1974); Alfred Conrad, *The Economics of Slavery and Other Studies in Econometric History* (1964).

13. Problems of agency are central to the control of corporate managers. See, e.g., Michael Jensen and William Meckling, "Theory of the Firm: Managerial Behavior, Agency Costs, and Ownership Structure," 3 *Journal of Financial Economics* 305 (1976); Alison Anderson, "Conflicts of Interest: Efficiency, Fairness, and Corporate Structure," 25 *UCLA Law Review* 738 (1978); Steven Shavell, "Risk Sharing and Incentives in the Principal and Agent Relationship," 10 *Bell Journal of Economics* 55 (1979).

14. For discussions favorable to the assumption that worker ownership may alleviate problems of inefficiency that result from the inability of pure capitalist managers to monitor work performance, see Masahoki Aoki, "A Model of the Firm as a Stockholder-Employee Cooperative Game," 70 *American Economic Review* 600 (1980); Jan Svejnar, "On the Theory of the Participatory Firm," 27 *Journal of Economic Theory* 313 (1982). For supportive, if radically incomplete and unconvincing empirical support, see Corey Rosen and Katherine Klein, "Job Creating Performance of Employee-Owned Firms," 106 *Monthly Labor Review,* no. 8, August 1983 at 15. But see Michael Jensen and William Meckling, "Rights and Production Functions: An Application to Labor-Managed Firms and Codetermination," 52 *Journal of Business* 479 (1979) (asserting that labor-managed firms will maximize short-term cash flow, not value).

15. Obviously it remains a live issue whether such efforts will be worthwhile, given, say, problems consumers may have processing information, or problems of inducing adequate information production when there are not only few incentives to know more but some disincentives. These themes are explored in much of the antiregulatory literature. See, e.g., George Stigler, "The Economics of Information," in *The Organization of Industry* 171 (1968); Jeffrey Davis, "Protecting Consumers from Overdisclosure and Gobbledygook: An Empirical Look at the Simplification of Consumer-Credit Contracts," 63 *Virginia Law Review* 841 (1977) (both focusing on informational overload). But see Alan Schwartz and Louis Wilde, "Intervening in Markets on the Basis of Imperfect Information: A Legal and Economic Analysis," 127 *University of Pennsylvania Law Review* 630, 675–676 (1979) (denying that information overload is a prob-

lem). See also Anthony Kronman, "Mistake, Disclosure, Information, and the Law of Contracts," 7 *Journal of Legal Studies* 1 (1978) (need to protect incentives to produce information).

16. See Richard Freeman and James Medoff, *What Do Unions Do?* (1984).

17. See Richard Posner, "A Theory of Negligence," 1 *Journal of Legal Studies* 29 (1972). For an account of the necessary consistency between strict liability and private property, see Richard Epstein, note 2 above at 39–41. See also Richard Epstein, "A Theory of Strict Liability," 2 *Journal of Legal Studies* 151 (1973). Obviously, Posner does not present a negligence regime as inconsistent with ideas of private property, and, given the difficulty of defining private property exactly, it is hard to claim that negligence is inconsistent with private property rules. In a sense, there is a definition of private property rights that make *all* legal regimes seem like private property regimes: that is, a regime of private property simply enforces whatever rights the state declares inhere in particular people. But strict liability, unlike negligence, is consistent with traditional private property ideology in its pursuit of *generality,* of insensitivity to situation. Protections of interest do not vary with the contingency of others' needs in a strict liability regime, while expectations are inevitably socially relative in a negligence regime.

18. See E. P. Thompson, *Whigs and Hunters: The Origin of the Black Act* e.g. 31–33, 57–61 (1975).

19. See, e.g., Richard Posner, note 4 above at 30–31.

20. See, e.g., Robert Hall and Alvin Rabushka, note 10 above at 15–16, 58–60.

21. See, e.g., Richard Posner, note 4 above at 30. See also Garrett Hardin, "The Tragedy of the Commons," 162 *Science* 1243 (1968).

22. See, e.g., the analysis suggested by the structure of Richard Stewart and James Krier, *Environmental Law and Policy* 255–324 (2d ed. 1978) (arguing that environmental regulation supplants private law or private property remedies, given transaction-cost problems). See also Steven Shavell, "Liability for Harm versus Regulation of Safety," 13 *Journal of Legal Studies* 357 (1984).

23. See Carl Dahlman, *The Open Field System and Beyond: A Property Rights Analysis* (1980).

24. See, e.g., Charles Meyers, "The Covenant of Habitability and the American Law Institute," 27 *Stanford Law Review* 879 (1975).

25. See, e.g., Richard Posner, note 4 above at 234–235, 311–312; W. Kip Viscusi, "Wealth Effects and Earnings Premiums for Job Hazards," 60 *Review of Economics and Statistics* 408 (1978).

26. See, e.g., *Rent Control Myths and Realities: International Evidence of the Effects of Rent Control in Six Countries* (Walter Block and Edgar Olsen eds. 1981); Richard Posner, note 4 above at 546–547; Peter Linneman, "The Economic Impacts of Minimum Wage Laws: A New Look at an Old Question," 90 *Journal of Political Economy* 443 (1982); Theodore Keeler, "Airline Regulation and Market Performance," 3 *Bell Journal of Economics* 399 (1972).

27. See, e.g., Charles Stuart, "Consumer Protection in Markets with Informationally Weak Buyers," 12 *Bell Journal of Economics* 562 (1981).

28. See, e.g., Richard Arnould and Henry Grabowski, "Auto Safety Reg-

ulation: An Analysis of Market Failure," 12 *Bell Journal of Economics* 27 (1981); Michael Spence, "Consumer Misperceptions, Product Failure, and Product Liability," 44 *Review of Economic Studies* 561 (1977).

29. Mark Kelman, "Trashing," 36 *Stanford Law Review* 293 (1984).

30. See, e.g., Steven Salop and Joseph Stiglitz, "Bargains and Ripoffs: A Model of Monopolistically Competitive Price Dispersion," 44 *Review of Economic Studies* 493 (1977).

31. See, e.g., Hal Varian, "A Model of Sales," 70 *American Economic Review* 651 (1980).

32. See, e.g., Mark Kelman, note 29 above at 316. John Pratt, David Wise, and Richard Zeckhauser, "Price Differences in Almost Competitive Markets," 93 *Quarterly Journal of Eonomics* 189 (1979).

33. Lester Thurow, *Dangerous Currents: The State of Economics* 11–19 (1983).

34. See Dunlop, note 11 above.

35. In early April 1986, when wholesale gas prices dropped dramatically, the full-service term for regular gas at the station labelled Shell I in the initial "Trashing" piece had risen to a whopping 70 cents per gallon, compared to an average of 35 cents per gallon and 16 cents per gallon for premium unleaded when "Trashing" was published. The aggregate full-service price did not drop *at all* at two of the four stations that still offered both kinds of service during a two-week period when self-service prices dropped by roughly 30 cents a gallon; it dropped by less than 15 cents a gallon at the other two stations.

36. See W. Kip Viscusi, note 25 above.

37. See Steven Crafton, "An Empirical Test on the Effect of Usury Laws," 23 *Journal of Law and Economics* 135 (1980).

38. See, e.g., Richard Bird, *Tax Incentives for Investment: The State of the Art* (Canadian Tax Paper no. 64) (1980).

39. See Richard Posner, note 17 above, and Richard Posner, "Strict Liability: A Comment" (emphasizing those conditions that make negligence more likely to work and strict liability to be inefficient), and Guido Calabresi and Jon Hirschoff, "Toward a Test for Strict Liability in Torts," 81 *Yale Law Journal* 1055 (1972) (emphasizing departures from ideal conditions that might render negligence systems inefficient).

40. Duncan Kennedy, "Two Phases of the Fetishism of Commodities" (unpublished manuscript, 1979).

41. Steven Shavell, "Strict Liability versus Negligence," 9 *Journal of Legal Studies* 1 (1980).

42. See A. Mitchell Polinsky, *An Introduction to Law and Economics* 44–48 (1983).

43. For a fuller explication, see Mark Kelman, "Misunderstanding Social Life: A Critique of the Core Premises of 'Law and Economics,' " 33 *Journal of Legal Education* 274, 278–283 (1983).

44. Jerry Green, "On the Optimal Structure of Liability Laws," 7 *Bell Journal of Economics* 553 (1976).

45. See, e.g., Mark Kelman, note 29 above at 310–312. See also Palma Strand, "Note: The Inapplicability of Traditional Tort Analysis to Environ-

mental Risks: The Example of Toxic Waste Pollution Victim Compensation," 35 *Stanford Law Review* 575, 582–584 (1983).

46. See Mario Rizzo, "The Imputation Theory of Proximate Cause: An Economic Framework," 15 *Georgia Law Review* 1007 (1981).

47. See Steven Shavell, "An Analysis of Causation and the Scope of Liability in the Law of Torts," 9 *Journal of Legal Studies* 463 (1980). But see Steven Shavell, "Uncertainty over Causation and the Determination of Civil Liability," 28 *Journal of Law and Economics* 587 (1985) (seemingly more worried about the problem of underdeterrence if there is a threshold level of increase in probability of harm before defendants are held liable).

48. See, e.g., Kallenberg v. Beth Israel Hospital, 45 App. Div. 2d 177, 357 N.Y.S. 2d 508 (1974), affirmed without opinion, 37 N.Y. 2d 719, 337 N.E. 2d 128, 374 N.Y.S. 2d 615 (1975) (defendants liable for failure to administer an antihypertensive, though plaintiff would have had but a 20 to 40 percent chance of surviving the surgery that administration of the antihypertensive would have permitted). See also Hicks v. United States, 368 F. 2d 626 (4th Cir. 1966).

49. See, e.g., A. Mitchell Polinsky, note 42 above at 107–110; Harold Demsetz, "Wealth Distribution and the Ownership of Rights," 1 *Journal of Legal Studies* 223 (1972).

50. See, e.g., A. Mitchell Polinsky, note 42 above at 110–112. See also Steven Shavell, "A Note on Efficiency vs. Distributional Equity in Legal Rulemaking: Should Distributional Equity Matter Given Optimal Income Taxation?" 71 *American Economic Review Papers and Proceedings* 414 (1981).

51. See, e.g., Anthony Kronman, "Contract Law and Distributive Justice," 89 *Yale Law Journal* 472 (1980).

52. See, e.g., Richard Markovits, "Duncan's Do Nots: Cost-Benefit Analysis and the Determination of Legal Entitlements," 36 *Stanford Law Review* 1170 (1984).

53. See, e.g., Duncan Kennedy and Frank Michelman, note 1 above at 729–735.

54. Duncan Kennedy, "Distributive and Paternalist Motives in Contract and Tort Law, with Special Reference to Compulsory Terms and Unequal Bargaining Power," 41 *Maryland Law Review* 563, 609–614, 655–656 (1982).

55. Bruce Ackerman, "Regulating Slum Housing Markets on Behalf of the Poor: Of Housing Codes, Housing Subsidies, and Income Redistribution Policy," 80 *Yale Law Journal* 1093 (1971).

56. See, e.g., Robert Crandall, Howard Gruenspecht, Theodore Keeler, Lester Lave, *Regulating the Automobile* 6, 34–36 (1986) (costs of complying with automobile safety regulations have declined substantially over time).

6. The Deification of Process

1. For typical explications of these problems in utilitarianism, see, e.g., Ilmar Waldner, "The Empirical Meaningfulness of Interpersonal Utility Comparisons," 69 *Journal of Philosophy* 87 (1972); Alan Donagan, "Is There a Credible Form of Utilitarianism?" in *Contemporary Utilitarianism* 187 (Michael Bayles ed. 1968); Bernard Williams, "A Critique of Utilitarianism," in *Utili-*

tarianism; For and Against 77 (J. J. C. Smart and Bernard Williams eds. 1967).

2. See, e.g., Henry Hart and Albert Sacks, *The Legal Process: Basic Problems in the Making and Application of Law* e.g. 882–888, 979–980 (Tentative Edition 1958).

3. This point is made most clearly in the works of economists, not lawyers. See, e.g., Wallace Oates, *Fiscal Federalism* 3–20 (1972); Charles Tiebout, "A Pure Theory of Local Expenditures," 64 *Journal of Political Economy* 416 (1956); James Buchanan and Gordon Tullock, *The Calculus of Consent* 113–115 (1969). But it is echoed to some extent in the lawyers' paeans to state rights. See, e.g., Robert Ellickson, "Cities and Homeowners Associations," 130 *University of Pennsylvania Law Review* 1519, 1547–1548 (1982); Jesse Choper, *Judicial Review and the National Political Process* 247 (1980); David Rudenstine, "Judicially Ordered Social Reform: Neofederalism and Neonationalism and the Debate over Political Structure," 59 *Southern California Law Review* 449, 467 (1986) (emphasizing diversity of supply and cost conditions, rather than demand for collective goods, to a slightly greater degree); Lewis Kaden, "Politics, Money, and State Sovereignty: The Judicial Role," 79 *Columbia Law Review* 847, 851–855 (1979); Ralph Winter, "State Law, Shareholder Protection, and the Theory of the Corporation," 6 *Journal of Legal Studies* 251, 289–292 (1977). Much of the most famous Process school legal literature praising local institutions is so devoid of substantive content, however, that it is extremely difficult to discern why the author is wedded to local institutions. See, e.g., Henry Hart, "The Relations between Federal and State Law," 54 *Columbia Law Review* 489 (1954).

4. See, e.g., discussion in Robert Dahl, "The City in the Future of Democracy," 61 *American Political Science Review* 953 (1967); Richard Posner, *Economic Analysis of Law* 599–600 (3d ed. 1986).

5. See Charles Tiebout, note 3 above.

6. The phrase was first used, apparently, by Justice Brandeis. See New State Ice Co. v. Liebmann, 285 U.S. 262, 311 (1931) (J. Brandeis dissenting). Certainly it remains a common theme in deciding whether federal action was meant to preempt local initiative to look at whether Congress would have wanted diverse experiments. See, e.g., Pacific Gas & Electric v. State Energy Resources Conservation & Development Commission, 461 U.S. 190, 205–208 (1982). For commentary on this sort of reasoning, see Charles Wiggins, "Federalism, Balancing, and the Burger Court: California's Nuclear Law as a Preemption Case Study," 13 *U.C. Davis Law Review* 3, 60–69 (1979). See also David Rudenstine, note 3 above, and Lewis Kaden, note 3 above.

7. See, generally, Laurence Tribe, *American Constitutional Law* 328–330, 332–335 (1978). The landmark cases declaring a preference for open borders include Gibbons v. Ogden, 22 U.S. (9 Wheat.) 1 (1824); Brown v. Maryland, 25 U.S. (12 Wheat.) 419 (1827). See comments in Mark Tushnet, "Rethinking the Dormant Commerce Clause," 1979 *Wisconsin Law Review* 125, 130–141 (on whether the theory has been implemented coherently). See also Stephen Williams, "Severance Taxes and Federalism: The Role of the Supreme Court in Preserving a National Market for Energy Supplies," 53 *Colorado Law Review* 281 (1982), for an analysis of how difficult it is to assess, when, in traditional

terms, a state's efforts to appropriate quasirents from its own resources disintegrate a national market.

8. See Thomas Heller, "Legal Theory and the Political Economy of American Federalism," in *Integration through Law: Europe and the American Federal Experience* 270–274, 254, 306 (Mauro Cappelletti, Monica Seccombe, Joseph Weiler eds. 1986); Richard Stewart, "Pyramids of Sacrifice? Problems of Federalism in Mandating State Implementation of National Environmental Policy," 86 *Yale Law Journal* 1196, 1211–1212 (1979); William Cary, "Federalism and Corporate Law: Reflections upon Delaware," 83 *Yale Law Journal* 663 (1974).

9. In fact, of course, our welfare systems are partly federalized, partly localized, and partly joint efforts, rather than wholly "centralized." See, e.g., the discussion in Frank Bloch, "Cooperative Federalism and the Role of Litigation in the Development of Federal AFDC Eligibility Policy," 1979 *Wisconsin Law Review* 1. But the case for federalization has frequently been voiced. See, e.g., Richard Musgrave and Peggy Musgrave, *Public Finance in Theory and Practice* 623 (2d ed. 1976); Wallace Oates, note 3 above at 7–8, 148.

10. See, e.g., Jesse Choper, note 3 above at 252–254; Loren Beth, "The Supreme Court and American Federalism," 10 *St. Louis University Law Journal* 376 (1966).

11. See, e.g., Laurence Tribe, note 7 above at 326–327.

12. John Ely, *Democracy and Distrust: A Theory of Judicial Review* (1980).

13. See Henry Hart and Albert Sacks, note 2 above.

14. See, e.g., Robert Dahl, *Who Governs?* (1961). For even cheerier postwar views, see Wilfred Binkley and Malcolm Moos, *A Grammar of American Politics* (3d ed. 1958); David Truman, *The Governmental Process* (2d ed. 1971). For a recent, even more optimistic assessment in the constitutional law context, see Jesse Choper, note 3 above at 12–45.

15. See Laurence Tribe, note 7 above at 886–990. See also David Richards, "Sexual Autonomy and the Constitutional Right to Privacy: A Case Study in Human Rights and the Unwritten Constitution," 30 *Hastings Law Journal* 957 (1979).

16. See, e.g., Michael Perry, "Substantive Due Process Revisited: Reflections on (and beyond) Recent Cases," 71 *Northwestern University Law Review* 417 (1977); Michael Perry, *The Constitution, the Courts, and Human Rights: An Inquiry into the Legitimacy of Constitutional Policymaking by the Judiciary* (1982).

17. See, e.g., Kenneth Karst, "The Freedom of Intimate Association," 89 *Yale Law Journal* 624 (1980).

18. See, e.g., Owen Fiss, "The Supreme Court, 1978 Term—Foreword: The Forms of Justice," 93 *Harvard Law Review* 1 (1979).

19. See Richard Epstein, *Takings: Private Property and the Power of Eminent Domain* (1985).

20. See Harry Wellington, "Common Law Rules and Constitutional Double Standards: Some Notes on Adjudication," 83 *Yale Law Journal* 221 (1973), and Michael Perry, "Abortion, the Public Morals, and the Police Power: The

Ethical Function of Substantive Due Process," 23 *UCLA Law Review* 689 (1976).

21. See Frank Michelman, "In Pursuit of Constitutional Welfare Rights: One View of Rawls' Theory of Justice," 121 *University of Pennsylvania Law Review* 962 (1973); Frank Michelman, "Foreword: On Protecting the Poor through the Fourteenth Amendment," 83 *Harvard Law Review* 7 (1969).

22. Epstein to some extent disclaims reliance on libertarians like Nozick. See, e.g., Richard Epstein, note 19 above at 334–338. He declares that he can derive his "natural rights" framework through the sort of utilitarian reasoning Nozick (and most libertarians) deplore as paying inadequate attention to the separateness of persons. Epstein's efforts to defend his libertarian rights as a utilitarian, though, are such transparent failures that it is best to account for his principles in more traditional libertarian terms. For a fuller discussion of the difficulties with Epstein's utilitarian arguments, see Mark Kelman, "Taking *Takings* Seriously: An Essay for Centrists," 74 *California Law Review* 601 (1986).

23. Duncan Kennedy, "Distributive and Paternalist Motives in Contract and Tort Law, with Special Reference to Compulsory Terms and Unequal Bargaining Power," 41 *Maryland Law Review* 563, 564–565 (1982).

24. Roberto Unger, *Knowledge and Politics* (1975).

25. Richard Parker, "The Past of Constitutional Theory and Its Future," 42 *Ohio State Law Journal* 223 (1981).

26. See, e.g., Mark Tushnet, "Dia-Tribe," 78 *Michigan Law Review* 694, 702–703 (1980).

27. See Roberto Unger, note 24 above at 83–88, 100–104.

28. Ely's utilitarianism is made most explicit in his work prior to *Democracy and Distrust,* which essentially assumes the desirability of democracy, or treats its desirability as a shared value or starting point. See John Ely, "Constitutional Interpretivism: Its Allure and Impossibility," 53 *Indiana Law Journal* 399 (1978). For a parallel defense of democracy in the constitutional law context, see Robert Bork, "Neutral Principles and Some First Amendment Problems," 47 *Indiana Law Journal* 1 (1971).

29. See, e.g., Cass Sunstein, "Interest Groups in American Public Law," 38 *Stanford Law Review* 29 (1985). See also Cass Sunstein, "Naked Preferences and the Constitution," 84 *Columbia Law Review* 1689 (1984); Frank Michelman, "Political Markets and Community Self-Determination: Competing Judicial Models of Local Government Legitimacy," 53 *Indiana Law Journal* 145 (1977); Frank Michelman, "Politics and Values, or What's Really Wrong with Rationality Review?" 13 *Creighton Law Review* 487 (1980); Richard Stewart, "Regulation in a Liberal State: The Role of Non-Commodity Values," 92 *Yale Law Journal* 1537 (1983).

30. See Jesse Choper, note 3 above, and John Ely, note 12 above.

31. Alexander Bickel, *The Least Dangerous Branch* 111–198 (1962).

32. See Richard Parker, note 25 above. Views like his are explored more fully in the political science literature. See, e.g., William Connolly, *The Bias of Pluralism* (1969); Henry Kariel, *The Decline of American Pluralism* (1961); Charles Lindblom, *Politics and Markets* (1977).

33. See, for instance, Samuel Bowles, "The Production Process in a Com-

petitive Economy: Walrasian, Neo-Hobbesian, and Marxian Models," 75 *American Economic Review* 16 (1985); Samuel Bowles and Herbert Gintis, "The Invisible Fist: Have Capitalism and Democracy Reached a Parting of the Ways?" 68 *American Economic Review* 358 (1978).

34. See Diana Russell, *Sexual Exploitation* 34–37 (1984) (56 percent of women reported that they had been forced to have sexual intercourse as a result of threats at some point in their lives), and Diana Russell and Nancy Howell, "The Prevalence of Rape in the United States Revisited," 8 *Signs* 688 (1983) (22 percent of women reported that they had been "raped," forced to have intercourse in a way they surmised the criminal law would condemn). See also Neil Malamuth, "Rape Proclivity Among Males," 37 *Journal of Social Issues* (Fall 1981) at 138, 152 (over half of female college students reported experiencing offensive male sexual aggression during the previous year). See also discussions in Robin West, "The Difference in Women's Hedonic Lives: A Phenomenological Critique of Liberal and Radical Feminist Legal Theory" (unpublished manuscript prepared for University of Wisconsin feminist theory workshop, 1986); Susan Estrich, "Rape," 95 *Yale Law Journal* 1087 (1986).

35. See, e.g., Wallach Loh, "The Impact of Common Law and Reform Rape Statutes on Prosecution: An Empirical Study," 55 *Washington Law Review* 543 (1980) (suggesting that reform efforts have had little impact), and Jeanne Marsh, Alison Geist, and Nathan Caplan, *Rape and the Limits of Law Reform* (1982) (only shift was on conviction rates, and even on this score, finding of change is debatable). But see Susan Estrich, note 34 above at 1161, noting that disposition rate shifts underestimate the impact of law reform.

36. See Roberto Unger, note 24 above at 88–100.

37. Duncan Kennedy, "Utopian Rationalism in American Legal Thought" (unpublished manuscript, June 1970).

38. See Harry Wellington, note 20 above, and Ronald Dworkin, *Taking Rights Seriously* (1977).

39. Mark Tushnet, "Truth, Justice, and the American Way: An Interpretation of Public Law Scholarship in the Seventies," 57 *Texas Law Review* 1307, 1311–1313 (1979).

40. Paul Brest, "Interpretation and Interest," 34 *Stanford Law Review* 765, 770–773 (1982).

41. John Ely, note 12 above at 63–69.

42. Roberto Unger, note 24 above at 68, 78–79.

43. Id. at 71.

44. Id. at 86–88.

45. Mark Tushnet, note 39 above at 1316–1321 (on Rawls), and Mark Tushnet, note 26 above at 700–701, 707–709 (Rawlsians and libertarians).

46. Unger's hastily sketched attack on Rawls is, I believe, a pale precursor of the far more developed political theoretical critique developed by Sandel. See Michael Sandel, *Liberalism and the Limits of Justice* (1982). Sandel better develops, for instance, the argument that the search for "just" principles itself cannot be universally validated without regard to whether particular persons view "justice" (social division of scarce rights and claims between persons assumed to be potentially antagonistic) as a central problem. Only if a sense of

community is seen as an *attribute* of particular selves, rather than constitutive of a well-ordered society, will Rawlsian principles of justice be sought. More powerfully, Sandel recognizes that the individuals behind the veil of ignorance must be stripped of all significant particular attributes of liberal personhood to reach Rawls's hypothetical liberal agreement. The Rawlsian contractor must enter the implicit social contracting process without owning or deserving his unique talents; he must accept contracting as a just procedure although the particular contract he is being asked to affirm has none of the ordinary selfish advantages of a mutually advantageous accommodation between diverse agents. (In this regard, see also Ronald Dworkin, "The Original Position," in *Reading Rawls* [Norman Daniels ed. 1975]). Moreover, his "contractual" choices do not ultimately respond to the give and take of diverse individuals but are rather the beliefs at which a *single* decision maker constrained to solve a problem in maximizing his own utility under radical conditions of uncertainty over his ends might arrive. Moreover, the "person" who contracts behind the veil of ignorance is not ideally free and rational but is without character and depth, because character and depth arise out of an effort to locate oneself within a given history, to come to terms with the gap between one's independent authenticity and one's determined social character.

47. Richard Parker, note 25 above at 233–235. Paul Brest, "The Substance of Process," 42 *Ohio State Law Journal* 131, 140 (1980); Mark Tushnet, "Darkess on the Edge of Town: The Contributions of John Hart Ely to Constitutional Theory," 89 *Yale Law Journal* 1037, 1045–1051 (1980).

48. Paul Brest, note 47 above at 134–147; Richard Parker, note 25 above at 236–237.

49. Laurence Tribe, "The Puzzling Persistence of Process-Based Constitutional Theories," 89 *Yale Law Journal* 1063, 1072–1077 (1980).

50. Paul Brest, note 47 above at 138–139. Brest's point can perhaps be better understood by reference to one of the most often cited philosophical works on abortion, Judith Jarvis Thomson's. See Judith Jarvis Thomson, "A Defense of Abortion," 1 *Philosophy and Public Affairs* 47 (1971). Her most telling point is that abortion may not be morally or legally wrong, even if we consider a fetus a person, if we recognize that a pregnant woman may be asked to take extraordinarily burdensome affirmative steps to sustain a person's life if she is legally required to carry a fetus to term, compared to the steps we generally require people to take to save a life. (Thomson notes that one is not obliged to stay strapped to a famous violinist for nine months to sustain his life.) The point is *not* whether one is convinced by Thomson's analysis or not; it is that a male-dominated legislature is unlikely to compare the affirmative life-saving duties citizens generally owe one another to the duties demanded of pregnant women.

51. Mark Tushnet, note 39 above at 1314–1315, and, generally, Mark Tushnet, note 47 above. See also Paul Brest, note 47 above at 140–141 (individual rights of great significance can be trampled in a democracy), and Paul Brest, "The Fundamental Rights Controversy: The Essential Contradictions of Normative Constitutional Scholarship," 90 *Yale Law Journal* 1063, 1096–1109 (1981) (the Madisonian tradition under which we live is rightly ambivalent about

the virtues of democratic outcomes, particularly where democracy is of the preference-registering rather than the republican variety).

52. Richard Parker, note 25 above at 236–237.

53. Laurence Tribe, note 49 above at 1067–1072.

54. Mark Tushnet, note 39 above at 1314–1315.

55. Richard Parker, note 25 above at 249–252. See also Mark Tushnet, note 39 above at 1319, who notes in a parallel fashion that justice-oriented theories, like Tribe's, fail to account for the poor fit between the dominant distributive concerns of moral theorists like Rawls and the court's actual agenda.

56. Al Katz, "Studies in Boundary Theory: Three Essays in Adjudication and Politics," 28 *Buffalo Law Review* 383 (1979).

57. Mark Tushnet, note 39 above at 1330–1334.

58. Gerald Frug, "The City as a Legal Concept," 93 *Harvard Law Review* 1057 (1980).

59. Thomas Heller, note 8 above.

60. Duncan Kennedy, "The Stages of Decline of the Public/Private Distinction," 130 *University of Pennsylvania Law Review* 1349 (1982).

61. The point is suggested by Thomas Heller, "Structuralism and Critique," 36 *Stanford Law Review* 127, 184–192, 194–197 (1984).

62. Alexis de Tocqueville, 1 *Democracy in America* 242–251, and 2, 129–146 (H. Reeve trans. 1898).

63. See Mark Tushnet, note 39 above at 1332–1334. See also Mark Tushnet, "Critical Legal Studies and Constitutional Law: An Essay in Deconstruction," 36 *Stanford Law Review* 623, 636–637 (1984).

64. See Thomas Heller, note 8 above.

65. See, e.g., Karl Klare, "Judicial Deradicalization of the Wagner Act and the Origins of Modern Legal Consciousness, 1934–1941," 62 *Minnesota Law Review* 265 (1978).

66. Katharine Stone, "The Post-War Paradigm in American Labor Law," 90 *Yale Law Journal* 1509 (1981).

7. Visions of History

1. See, e.g., J. G. A. Pocock, *The Ancient Constitution and the Feudal Law* (1967) (early seventeenth-century common law is the source of the deepest principles to which we return in politically healthy times); Richard Epstein, *Takings: Private Property and the Power of Eminent Domain* 95, 101, 113–114 (1985) (common law rights are naturalized, assumed normatively desirable).

2. Paul Brest, "The Misconceived Quest for the Original Understanding," 60 *Boston University Law Review* 204 (1980). Brest's main purpose in attacking interpretivism may well have been to debunk a rhetorically powerful traditional argument against the sort of judicial activism he favors, not to analyze one of the standard modes of interpreting history. Nonetheless, I believe that the piece contributes a great deal to the Critical understanding of the typical rhetorical uses of history, regardless of its design.

3. The classical works include Max Weber, *Economy and Society* (Guenther Roth and Claus Wittich eds. 1968); Henry Maine, *Ancient Law* (1861); Adam

Smith, *Lectures in Jurisprudence* 13–76, 200–292 (Ronald Meck, David Raphael, and Peter Stein eds. 1978). See, for a more modern legal example, Benjamin Cardozo, *The Growth of the Law* (1924).

4. See Robert Gordon, "Historicism in Legal Scholarship," 90 *Yale Law Journal* 1017 (1981) (hereafter cited as "Historicism"), and Robert Gordon, "Critical Legal Histories," 36 *Stanford Law Review* 57 (1984) (hereafter cited as "Critical Histories").

5. See, e.g., Richard Epstein, "The Static Conception of the Common Law," 9 *Journal of Legal Studies* 253 (1980).

6. See Robert Gordon, "Historicism," note 4 above at 1025–1028.

7. See, e.g., Duncan Kennedy, "The Structure of Blackstone's Commentaries," 28 *Buffalo Law Review* 205, 237, 244–249 (1979) (discussion of Blackstone's belief that the soon-to-be defunct writ system was critical to the preservation of liberty in England).

8. See Robert Gordon, "Critical Histories," note 4 above; see also my discussion in Chapter 8.

9. See discussion in Paul Brest, note 2 above at 225–226, 234–237. See also, e.g., Richard Wasserstrom, *The Judicial Decision* 25–30 (1961).

10. See, e.g., John Ely, *Democracy and Distrust: A Theory of Judicial Review* 13–14, 28, 30, 34 (1980).

11. See Paul Brest, note 2 above at 209–217.

12. See Paul Brest, note 2 above at 220–222. For a parallel discussion, see John Ely, note 10 above at 11–41, 45.

13. See Ronald Dworkin, *Taking Rights Seriously* 134–135 (1977). See discussion in Paul Brest, note 2 above at 216–217.

14. See Paul Brest, note 2 above at 225–226, 234–237. See also Joseph Tussman, *Obligation and the Body Politic* (1960); Hanna Pitkin, "Obligation and Consent," 59 *American Political Science Review* 990 (1965), and 60 *American Political Science Review* 39 (1966), for general political theoretical statements of the problems of premising obligation on nonemigration from a polity.

15. See Paul Brest, note 2 above at 223–224, 231.

16. Id. at 225.

17. Id. at 235–236.

18. Id. at 229–231.

19. Id. at 231–234, 237.

20. See, generally, Henry Maine, note 3 above; Ferdinand Tönnies, *Community and Society* (Charles P. Loomis trans. and ed. 1957).

21. See, e.g., Lucy Mair, *An Introduction to Social Anthropology* 10–11, 69 (1972).

22. Alexis de Tocqueville, 1 *Democracy in America* 242–251, 2, 129–146 (Henry Reeve trans. 1898).

23. See, e.g., Mary Ann Glendon, *The New Family and the New Property* 97, 219 (1981); Roscoe Pound, "Public Law and Private Law," 24 *Cornell Law Quarterly* 469 (1939); Roscoe Pound, "The New Feudal System," 19 *Kentucky Law Journal* 1 (1930); Lawrence Friedman and Jack Ladinsky, "Social Change and the Law of Industrial Accidents," 67 *Columbia Law Review* 50, 73–74 (1967).

24. See Karl Marx, *Critique of the Gotha Program* 6–11 (C. P. Dutt ed. 1938); Karl Marx, *The Economic and Philosophical Manuscripts of 1844* 132–146 (Dirk Struik ed. 1964); Karl Mark, *The German Ideology* 9–18, 23–27, 43–78 (Roy Pascal ed. 1947).

25. See, e.g., J. Wright in Javins v. First National Realty Corp., 428 F. 2d 1071 (D.C. Cir. 1970).

26. See, e.g., Mary Ann Glendon, note 23 above at 176–185; Jesse Dukeminier and James Krier, teacher's manual for *Property* 3–1 (1981).

27. See discussion in Mary Ann Glendon, note 23 above at 143–175, 192–205.

28. See, e.g., William Rehnquist, "We Are Family, Lawyers Stay Away," *National Law Journal* 15 (July 28, 1980); John Whitehead, "Judicial Schizophrenia: The Family and Education in a Secular Society," 1982 *Journal of Christian Jurisprudence* 49, 76–99 (1982); Matthew Hilton, "Comment: An Analytical Model to Assure Consideration of Parental and Familial Interests When Defining the Constitutional Rights of Minors: An Examination of In Re Scott K.," 1980 *Brigham Young University Law Review* 598.

29. See, e.g., Mary Ann Glendon, note 23 above at 11–96.

30. Sec, e.g., Derrick Bell, "In Defense of Minority Admissions Programs: A Response to Professor Graglia," 119 *University of Pennsylvania Law Review* 364 (1970); Randall Kennedy, "Persuasion and Distrust: A Comment on the Affirmative Action Debate," 99 *Harvard Law Review* 1327 (1986).

31. See, e.g., *Report of the Platform Committee to the 1984 Democratic National Convention* 32; Alfred Blumrosen, "Wage Discrimination, Job Segregation, and Title VII of the Civl Rights Act of 1964," 12 *University of Michigan Journal of Law Reform* 397 (1979); Winn Newman and Jeanne Vonhof, " 'Separate but Equal': Job Segregation and Pay Equity in the Wake of Gunther," 1981 *University of Illinois Law Forum* 269.

32. See Doug Ireland, "Open Season on Gays," *The Nation* 207 (Sept. 15, 1979); Connie de Boer, "The Polls: Attitudes toward Homosexuality," 42 *Public Opinion Quarterly* 265, 272 (58 percent of Americans polled in 1977 thought gays should not be school principals; 77 percent polled in 1970 thought a gay man should not be a judge).

33. Whether conservative economists have convincingly made the case that the welfare state displaces private philanthropy on a dollar-for-dollar basis, there is little doubt that many private charities have become less viable. For a typical account of the conservative economist's position, see Russell Roberts, "A Positive Model of Private Charity and Public Transfers," 92 *Journal of Political Economy* 136 (1984).

34. See Robert Gordon, "Critical Histories," note 4 above at 64–65; Robert Gordon, "Historicism," note 4 above at 1043.

35. Betty Mensch, book review, 33 *Stanford Law Review* 752 (1981) (reviewing P. Atiyah, *The Rise and Fall of Freedom of Contract*).

36. See Robert Crandall, Howard Gruenspecht, Theodore Keeler, Lester Lave, *Regulating the Automobile* 45–49, 80–84 (1986). See also 49 Fed. Reg. 28962 (1984) (no passive restraints will be mandated if two-thirds of the states put laws on the books that mandate seat belt use).

37. For instance, social welfare expenditures were 9.2 percent of GNP (gross national product) in 1939–40 but only 8.6 percent in 1954–55. *Social Security Bulletin Annual Statistical Supplement* 44 (1976). Total *nominal dollar* public aid expenditures dropped from $82.4 billion to $80.7 billion from 1981 to 1982; expenditures on child nutrition programs dropped by more than 10 percent and food stamp spending by nearly 4 percent. *Social Security Bulletin Annual Statistical Supplement* 60 (1983).

38. It is far easier to find unsubtle versions of these evolutionary homilies in the Legal Process literature of the 1950s. See, e.g., Stanley Reed, "The Living Law," in *Legal Institutions, Today and Tomorrow* 310 (Monrad Paulsen ed. 1959); Harry Jones, "The Rule of Law and the Welfare State," 58 *Columbia Law Review* 143–144, 154 (1958).

39. Roscoe Pound, "The End of Law as Developed in Legal Rules and Doctrines," 27 *Harvard Law Review* 195, 196–198, 209–213, 225–234 (1914); Harry Jones, note 38 above at 153–154. Once again, the "purer" versions of these evolutionist statements seem to have appeared in print a while back; I suspect that they are now transmitted primarily through the oral tradition.

40. See Robert Hale, "Bargaining, Duress, and Economic Liberty," 43 *Columbia Law Review* 603 (1943); John Dalzell, "Duress by Economic Pressure," 20 *North Carolina Law Review* 237 (1942).

41. Roberto Unger, *Law in Modern Society* 66 (1976). Unger's general discussion of the emergence of the legal order can be found at 66–86.

42. See Morton Horwitz, *The Transformation of American Law, 1780–1860* 79, 162–169, 251 (1977).

43. See Roberto Unger, note 41 above at 94, 96, 229.

44. See, e.g., Karl Klare, "Law-Making as Praxis," *Telos* 123 (Summer 1979); James Atleson, *Values and Assumptions in American Labor Law* 66, 205 (1983).

45. E. P. Thompson, *The Making of the English Working Class* (1968); E. P. Thompson, "Time, Work-Discipline, and Industrial Capitalism," 38 *Past and Present* 72 (1967).

46. Karl Marx, "The Future Results of British Rule in India," in *Karl Marx: Selected Writings* 332 (David McLellan ed. 1977).

47. See, e.g., Jürgen Habermas, *Communication and the Evolution of Society* 69–94 (Thomas McCarthy trans. 1979).

48. Carol Gilligan, *In a Different Voice* (1982). See also Owen Flanagan, Jr., "Virtue, Sex, and Gender: Some Philosophical Reflections on the Moral Psychology Debate," 92 *Ethics* 499 (1982). Some Critics have certainly embraced the idea that women's moral methodology may be both different from and superior to men's in precisely the way Gilligan explores. See, e.g., "Feminist Discourse, Moral Values, and the Law," 34 *Buffalo Law Review* 11, 49–60 (1985) (Menkel-Meadow's remarks); Carrie Menkel-Meadow, "Portia in a Different Voice: Speculations on a Woman's Lawyering Process," 1 *Berkeley Women's Law Journal* 39 (1985); Janet Rifkin, "Mediation from a Feminist Perspective: Promise and Problems," 2 *Journal of Law and Inequality* 21, 23–25 (1984). Others, though, have emphasized the degree to which Gilligan's "accommodating" girls, with their elaborate, altruistic attention to maintaining everyone's

satisfaction in a complex social network, are simply doing the best they can to circumvent violence, that their position is less an affirmative moral stance than a self-defense strategy. See, e.g., "Feminist Discourse, Moral Values, and the Law," 34 *Buffalo Law Review* 11, 27–29, 73–75 (1985) (MacKinnon's remarks).

49. Mark Kelman, "Choice and Utility," 1979 *Wisconsin Law Review* 769, 772–773.

50. Richard Parker, "The Past of Constitutional Theory—And Its Future," 42 *Ohio State Law Journal* 223, 245–246 (1981).

51. Duncan Kennedy, *Legal Education and the Reproduction of Hierarchy* 1–2, 33–35, 73–77 (1983).

52. See, e.g., Catharine MacKinnon, "Toward Feminist Jurisprudence," 34 *Stanford Law Review* 703, 705 (1982).

53. Robert Gordon, "Historicism," note 4 above at 1021.

54. Id. at 1026–1028.

55. Id. at 1021, 1042.

56. Id. at 1023, 1027. Robert Gordon, "Critical Histories," note 4 above at 107–108. See also Stewart Macaulay, "Elegant Models, Empirical Pictures, and the Complexity of Contract," 11 *Law and Society Review* 507 (1977); John Griffiths, "Is Law Important?" 54 *New York University Law Review* 339 (1979); Pauline Maier, "Popular Uprising and Civil Authority in Eighteenth-Century America," 27 *William and Mary Quarterly* 3 (1970).

57. Robert Gordon, "Historicism," note 4 above at 1023. See also Murray Edelman, *The Symbolic Uses of Politics* 37–38, 47–49 (1964); Joseph Gusfield, *Symbolic Crusade* 166–171 (1963).

58. See especially Stewart Macaulay, "Non-Contractual Relations in Business: A Preliminary Study," 28 *American Sociological Review* 55 (1963), and Stewart Macaulay, note 56 above.

59. See, e.g., Stephen Jay Gould, *The Mismeasure of Man* 108–112 (1981) (his critique of historical traditions of craniology is described at 73–108). See also Ysabel Rennie, *The Search for Criminal Man: A Conceptual History of the Dangerous Offender* (1978).

60. See Duncan Kennedy, note 7 above.

61. Id. at 342–346.

62. Morton Horwitz, "The Historical Contingency of the Role of History," 90 *Yale Law Journal* 1057 (1981).

63. See, e.g., Patrick Atiyah, *The Rise and Fall of Freedom of Contract* 420–424 (1979). Scholars within CLS, particularly in their more traditionally Marxist mode, are likely to share this belief that competitive capitalists require rules. See, e.g., Peter Gabel and Jay Feinman, "Contract Law as Ideology," in *The Politics of Law* 172 (David Kairys ed. 1982).

64. Betty Mensch, note 35 above at 765–767. See also Duncan Kennedy, "Form and Substance in Private Law Adjudication," 89 *Harvard Law Review* 1685, 1702–1705 (1976); Robert Gordon, "Critical Histories," note 4 above at 114–116.

65. Duncan Kennedy, note 64 above at 1703–1704.

66. See, generally, Robert Gordon, "Historicism," note 4 above at 1025–1028, 1037–1050; Robert Gordon, "Critical Histories," note 4 above at 88–93.

67. See Michael Moore, "Moral Reality," 1982 *Wisconsin Law Review* 1061, and, for a better-developed view, Michael Moore, "A Natural Law Theory of Interpretation," 54 *Southern California Law Review* 277 (1985).

68. See, e.g., Robin West, "Authority, Autonomy, and Choice: The Role of Consent in the Moral and Political Visions of Franz Kafka and Richard Posner," 99 *Harvard Law Review* 384 (1985); Mark Kelman, note 49 above.

69. See Robert Gordon, "Historicism," note 4 above at 1025–1026. See also Betty Mensch, note 35 above, who makes a parallel point.

70. Robert Gordon, "Historicism," note 4 above at 1026–1028.

71. See Duncan Kennedy, note 7 above at 213.

72. See Betty Mensch, note 35 above at 759–761, 796.

73. See Duncan Kennedy, note 7 above at 213.

74. See Roberto Unger, note 41 above at 214–231.

75. See Morton Horwitz, note 42 above at 162–169.

76. See, e.g., Morton Horwitz, "The Historical Foundations of Modern Contract Law," 87 *Harvard Law Review* 917, 919–936 (1974); Roberto Unger, *Knowledge and Politics* 76–77, 119–121 (1975).

77. Morton Horwitz, note 76 above at 925, 930–932, 936–941. See also Duncan Kennedy, note 7 above at 320–326; Betty Mensch, note 35 above at 756.

78. See Duncan Kennedy, note 7 above at 258–261 (describing "rights" as mediating contradictions in liberal thought). Kennedy is not especially explicit in defining *preliberal* modes of mediation. I derive my conception of Kennedy's views of preliberal modes of mediation from his descriptions of Blackstone's preliberal beliefs, at 264–272, 280–294, 300–303, 332–337, 342–346.

79. See Duncan Kennedy, note 7 above at 231–232, 238–246.

80. Id. at 266–268, 280–286.

81. Id. at 258–266, 363–368.

82. See, generally, Thomas Heller, "Is the Charitable Exemption from Local Property Taxation an Easy Case? General Concerns about Legal Economics and Jurisprudence," in *Essays on the Law and Economics of Local Governments* 183 (Daniel Rubinfeld ed. 1979).

83. See Mark Kelman, note 49 above; Morton Horwitz, note 76 above.

84. See Duncan Kennedy, "Distributive and Paternalist Motives in Contract and Tort Law, with Special Reference to Compulsory Terms and Unequal Bargaining Power," 41 *Maryland Law Review* 563, 576–583 (1982); Duncan Kennedy, note 7 above at 358–360; Duncan Kennedy, note 64 above at 1728–1737.

85. Morton Horwitz, note 76 above; Betty Mensch, note 35 above.

86. See Duncan Kennedy, note 7 above at 258–261, 360–362, 366–368.

87. See A. W. B. Simpson, "The Horwitz Thesis and the History of Contracts," 46 *University of Chicago Law Review* 533 (1979).

88. Betty Mensch, note 35 above at 759–763, 769–770, particularly emphasizes this point.

89. See, e.g., Stewart Macaulay, note 58 above; Robert Ellickson, "Of Coase and Cattle: Dispute Resolution among Neighbors in Shasta County," 38 *Stanford Law Review* 623 (1986).

90. See, e.g., Arthur Jacobson, "The Private Use of Public Authority: Sovereignty and Associations in the Common Law," 29 *Buffalo Law Review* 599 (1981) (corporate managers often exercise quasisovereign authority over workers, shareholders); Michael Burawoy, *Manufacturing Consent: Changes in the Labor Process under Monopoly Capitalism* (1978) (extensive participant-observer's description of the "internal state" inside a modern industrial factory); Peter Reuter, *Disorganized Crime: The Economics of the Visible Hand* 151–173 (1984) (the Mafia as dispute settler for a variety of illicit business contexts).

91. See, generally, Marc Bloch, *Feudal Society* 81–88 (L. A. Manyon trans. 1961); and C. Warren Hollister, *Medieval Europe: A Short History* 58–62, 197–203 (5th ed. 1982).

92. Morton Horwitz, "Progressive Legal Historiography," 63 *Oregon Law Review* 679, 683–685 (1984).

93. See, generally, Thomas Heller, "Legal Theory and the Political Economy of American Federalism," in *Integration through Law: Europe and the American Federal Experience* 254, 257–260, 262–267, 277–279 (Mauro Cappelletti, Monica Seccombe, Joseph Weiler eds. 1986).

94. Compare, e.g., Charles Stuart, "Consumer Protection in Markets with Informationally Weak Buyers," 12 *Bell Journal of Economics* 562 (1981), with W. Kip Viscusi, "Wealth Effects and Earning Premiums for Job Hazards," 60 *Review of Economics and Statistics* 408 (1978).

95. See, generally, Grant Gilmore, *The Death of Contract* (1974).

8. Critical Views of the Role of Law

1. Robert Gordon, "Critical Legal Histories," 36 *Stanford Law Review* 57, 60 (1984).

2. See, e.g., Talcott Parsons and Neil Smelser, *Economy and Society: A Study in the Integration of Economic and Social Theory* 284–294 (1956); Robert Clark, "The Interdisciplinary Study of Legal Evolution," 90 *Yale Law Journal* 1238 (1981).

3. See, e.g., Gabriel Kolko, *The Triumph of Conservatism: A Reinterpretation of American History, 1900–1916* (1963); George Stigler, "The Theory of Economic Regulation," 2 *Bell Journal of Economics and Management Science* 3 (1971). Unger believes that it is a constitutive feature of liberal thought that societies are artificial, only individuals real. See Roberto Unger, *Knowledge and Politics* 75, 81–83, 121–124 (1975).

4. See, e.g., Susan Estrich, "Rape," 95 *Yale Law Journal* 1087 (1986).

5. See, e.g., Lawrence Friedman, *A History of American Law* (1973); Harry Scheiber, "Property Law, Expropriation, and Resource Allocation by Government," 33 *Journal of Economic History* 232 (1973); Gabriel Kolko, note 3 above.

6. See, e.g., B. Peter Pashigian, "Regulation, Preventive Law, and the Duties of Attorneys," in *The Changing Role of the Corporate Attorney* 3 (William Carney ed. 1982); Deborah Rhode, "Policing the Professional Monopoly: A Constitutional and Empirical Analysis of Unauthorized Practice Prohibitions," 34 *Stanford Law Review* 1 (1981).

7. See, e.g., Lawrence Friedman, note 5 above at 234; Gary Schwartz, "Tort Law and the Economy in Nineteenth-Century America: A Reinterpretation," 90 *Yale Law Journal* 1717 (1981).

8. See, e.g., Alfred Chandler, *The Visible Hand* (1977) (the "ordinary" evolutionary path toward managerial capitalism was blocked in Western Europe by social needs beyond the need for economic development).

9. See, e.g., Thurman Arnold, *The Folklore of Capitalism* (1938); Lawrence Friedman, *The Roots of Justice: Crime and Punishment in Alameda County, California, 1870–1910* 150–195 (1981); Arthur Leff, "Law and," 87 *Yale Law Journal* 989 (1978).

10. See, e.g., Willard Hurst, *Law and Economic Growth* (1964); William Nelson, *Americanization of the Common Law* (1975).

11. See the discussion of this tradition in J. W. Burrow, *A Liberal Descent: Victorian Historians and the English Past* 21–35 (1981).

12. See Robert Clark, note 2 above. See discussion in Joyce Appleby, "Modernization Theory and the Formation of Modern Social Theories in England and America," 20 *Comparative Studies in Society and History* 259 (1978).

13. See Gary Schwartz, note 7 above; Robert Rabin, "The Historical Development of the Fault Principle: A Reinterpretation," 15 *Georgia Law Review* 925 (1981).

14. See discussions in Anthony Kronman, *Max Weber* 118–125 (1983); David Trubek, "Max Weber and the Rise of Capitalism," 1972 *Wisconsin Law Review* 720.

15. Robert Gordon, note 1 above at 79–80. See also Harry Scheiber, "The Road to Munn: Eminent Domain and the Concept of Public Purpose in the State Courts," in 5 *Perspectives in American History* 329 (Donald Fleming and Bernard Bailyn eds. 1971).

16. James Kainen, "Nineteenth Century Interpretations of the Federal Contract Clause: The Transformation from Vested to Substantive Rights against the State," 31 *Buffalo Law Review* 381 (1982).

17. Difficulties of implementing centralized commands by local agencies are frequently studied by legal sociologists. See, for instance, Kenneth Dolbeare and Phillip Hammond, *The School Prayer Decisions: From Court Policy to Local Practice* (1971); Neal Milner, *The Court and Local Law Enforcement* (1971); Robert Birkby, "The Supreme Court and the Bible Belt: Tennessee Reaction to the 'Schempp' Decision," 10 *Midwest Journal of Political Science* 304 (1966).

18. Robert Gordon, note 1 above at 78–79.

19. Alfred Konefsky, "On the Early History of Lower Federal Courts, Judges, and the Rule of Law," 79 *Michigan Law Review* 645 (1981).

20. See, e.g., Richard Posner, *Economic Analysis of Law* 441 (3d ed. 1986); Sam Peltzman, "Toward a More General Theory of Regulation," 19 *Journal of Law and Economics* 211 (1976).

21. See Richard Parker, "The Past of Constitutional Theory—and Its Future," 42 *Ohio State Law Journal* 223 (1981).

22. See, e.g., William Chambliss, "Toward a Radical Criminology," in *The Politics of Law* 230 (David Kairys ed. 1982) (crime defined so as to protect harm-causing elites from liability); Nadine Taub and Elizabeth Schneider, "Per-

spectives on Women's Subordination and the Role of Law," in *The Politics of Law* 117 (David Kairys ed. 1982) (law relegates women to inferior status by explicitly excluding them from the public sphere and refusing to regulate the domestic sphere to which they are confined); Morton Horwitz, "The Historical Foundations of Modern Contract Law," 87 *Harvard Law Review* 917 (1974) (workers are disadvantaged by rules that treat them as having failed to perform at all if they quit prior to the end of contracted work period, though others, e.g., contractors, are entitled to payment for part performance); Staughton Lynd, "Investment Decisions and the Quid Prop Quo Myth," 29 *Case Western Reserve Law Review* 396 (1979) (workers lose valuable right to strike over relocation decisions in a collective bargaining regime).

23. See, e.g., David Kairys, "Freedom of Speech," in *The Politics of Law* 140 (David Kairys ed. 1982) (popular movements press the state to expand speech opportunity, against the interests of the elite); Catharine MacKinnon, "Symposium: Sexual Harassment: Introduction," 10 *Capital University Law Review* i (1981) (women's political work created recognition within the legal system of sexual harassment as an actionable form of sex discrimination).

24. See E. P. Thompson, *Whigs and Hunters* 27, 205–206 (1975).

25. Id. at 245–258. See also Douglas Hay, "Property, Authority, and the Criminal Law," in *Albion's Fatal Tree: Crime and Society in Eighteenth-Century England* 17, 20–21 (Douglas Hay, Peter Linebaugh, John Rule, and E. P. Thompson eds. 1975).

26. John Gaventa, *Power and Powerlessness* esp. 96–121 (1980).

27. Andrea Dworkin, *Right-Wing Women* 71–105 (1983).

28. Mark Tushnet, "Perspectives on the Development of American Law: A Critical Review of Friedman's 'A History of American Law,' " 1977 *Wisconsin Law Review* 81, 94–96, 105–106.

29. E. P. Thompson, note 24 above at 197–198, 239–241, 245.

30. Douglas Hay, note 25 above at 45–46.

31. Id. at 49–63.

32. See Alan Freeman, "Antidiscrimination Law: A Critical Review," in *The Politics of Law* 96 (David Kairys ed. 1982); Alan Freeman, "Race and Class: The Dilemma of Liberal Reform," 90 *Yale Law Journal* 1880 (1981).

33. Karl Klare, "Judicial Deradicalization of the Wagner Act and the Origins of Modern Legal Consciousness, 1937–1941," 62 *Minnesota Law Review* 265 (1978).

34. See Mark Tushnet, note 28 above at 99.

35. Robert Gordon, "Historicism in Legal Scholarship," 90 *Yale Law Journal* 1017, 1021 (1981).

36. Karl Klare, note 33 above.

37. Gerald Frug, "The City as a Legal Concept," 93 *Harvard Law Review* 1057 (1980).

38. Douglas Hay, note 25 above at 32–33.

39. E. P. Thompson, note 24 above at 258–269.

40. See, e.g., Morton Horwitz, "The Rule of Law: An Unqualified Human Good?" 86 *Yale Law Journal* 561 (1977).

41. Isaac Balbus, *The Dialectics of Legal Repression* (2d ed. 1977).

42. Mark Tushnet, *The American Law of Slavery: 1810–1860* (1981).

43. See Robert Gordon, note 1 above at 74. His general discussion of the problems of interest analysis is at 73–74.

44. Id. at 87–93.

45. Charles Fried, "The Artificial Reason of the Law: Or What Lawyers Know," 60 *Texas Law Review* 35 (1981).

46. Richard Epstein, "The Social Consequences of Common Law Rules," 95 *Harvard Law Review* 1717 (1982). It is worth noting, in passing, that Epstein's decision in this piece to argue that *variations* in common law rules are of little consequence clearly has a particular political agenda—probably to argue both with other right-wing legal economists about whether "moralistic" or deontological or utilitarian-consequentialist theories are more likely to account for legal practice, and to criticize those on the left who see law as instrumentally responsive to elite control. Epstein surely doesn't believe that the common law *system* as a whole is without consequences; he believes that its basic rules of property, contract, and tort define a just society and that departures from the rights established by the rules—for example through redistributive taxation—destroy free societies. See Richard Epstein, *Takings: Private Property and the Power of Eminent Domain* (1985).

47. This point is made especially clearly in Lawrence Friedman and Stewart Macaulay, "Contract Law and Contract Teaching: Past, Present, and Future," 1967 *Wisconsin Law Review* 805.

48. Robert Gordon, note 1 above at 91.

49. Id. at 91–92.

50. Id. at 102–109. See also William Simon, "Visions of Practice in Legal Thought," 36 *Stanford Law Review* 469, 490–501 (1984) (the distinction between "law," traditional politics, and politics imbued in "private" life is often vastly exaggerated in defining appropriate lawyers' roles).

51. See E. P. Thompson, note 24 above at 29, 45, 261.

52. Robert Brenner, "Agrarian Class Structure and Economic Development in Pre-Industrial Europe," *Past and Present* 30 (Feb. 1976), discussed in Robert Gordon, note 1 above at 106–107.

53. Duncan Kennedy, "The Role of Law in Economic Thought: Essays on the Fetishism of Commodities," 34 *American University Law Review* 939, 968–1001 (1985).

54. Robert Gordon, note 1 above at 104. See also M. I. Finley, "The Servile Statuses of Ancient Greece," in *Economy and Society in Ancient Greece* 133 (Brent Shaw and Richard Saller eds. 1981).

55. Robert Gordon, note 1 above at 104–107.

56. Id. at 108.

57. Id. at 107.

58. See discussions in David Kyvig, *Repealing National Prohibition* (1979); Larry Engelmann, *Intemperance: The Lost War against Liquor* (1979).

59. Robert Gordon, note 1 above at 105–106.

60. Id.

61. See, generally, Duncan Kennedy, "The Structure of Blackstone's Commentaries," 28 *Buffalo Law Review* 205 (1979); Duncan Kennedy, "Toward

an Historical Understanding of Legal Consciousness: The Case of Classical Legal Thought in America, 1850–1940," 3 *Research in Law and Sociology* 3 (1980).

62. See James Kainen, note 16 above.

63. See Kenneth Vandevelde, "The New Property of the Nineteenth Century: The Development of the Modern Concept of Property," 29 *Buffalo Law Review* 325 (1980).

64. See Joseph Singer, "The Legal Rights Debate in Analytical Jurisprudence from Bentham to Hohfeld," 1982 *Wisconsin Law Review* 1975.

65. See Morton Horwitz, "The Doctrine of Objective Causation," in *The Politics of Law* 201 (David Kairys ed. 1982).

66. See Robert Gordon, note 1 above at 114–116, for quite a different discussion of the centrality of contradiction in the CLS attack on functionalism.

67. See, e.g., John Langbein, "Albion's Fatal Flaws," *Past and Present* 96, 114–115 (Feb. 1983).

68. Lewis Kornhauser, "The Great Image of Authority," 36 *Stanford Law Review* 349, 371–379 (1984), makes an argument somewhat, though by no means precisely, like this one. See also Allan Hutchinson and Patrick Monahan, "Law, Politics, and the Critical Legal Scholars: The Unfolding Drama of American Legal Thought," 36 *Stanford Law Review* 199, 216–219 (1984).

69. See Alan Hyde, "The Concept of Legitimation in the Sociology of Law," 1983 *Wisconsin Law Review* 379.

70. Id. at 407–412.

71. See, e.g., E. P. Thompson, note 24 above at 225–227 (customary use rights in the forest are no longer defensible in purely legal terms; levels of violence and "general outlawry" increase as the *legally* repressed view loses legitimacy).

72. Alan Hyde, note 69 above at 386–389, 395–399.

73. See, e.g., Joseph Gusfield, *Symbolic Crusade* (1963).

74. See Robert Ellickson, "Of Coase and Cattle: Dispute Resolution among Neighbors in Shasta County," 38 *Stanford Law Review* 623, 671–685 (1986).

75. Alan Hyde, note 69 above at 423.

76. William Landes and Richard Posner, "Salvors, Finders, Good Samaritans, and Other Rescuers: An Economic Study of Law and Altruism," 7 *Journal of Legal Studies* 83 (1978).

77. Donald Kinder and D. Roderick Kiewiet, "Economic Grievances and Political Behavior: The Role of Personal Discontents and Collective Judgments in Congressional Voting," 23 *American Journal of Political Science* 495 (1979).

78. David Sears, Richard Lau, Tom Tyler, and Harris Allen, Jr., "Self-Interest vs. Symbolic Politics in Policy Attitudes and Presidential Voting," 74 *American Political Science Review* 670 (1980).

79. Alan Hyde, note 69 above at 412–415.

80. Id. at 419–420.

81. See, e.g., Roberto Unger, "The Critical Legal Studies Movement," 96 *Harvard Law Review* 561 (1983).

9. *Toward a Cognitive Theory of Legitimation*

1. Robert Gordon, "New Developments in Legal Theory," in *The Politics of Law* 281 (David Kairys ed. 1982).

2. E. P. Thompson, *Whigs and Hunters* 197, 206–207. See also Douglas Hay, "Property, Authority, and the Criminal Law," in *Albion's Fatal Tree: Crime and Society in Eighteenth-Century England* 17, 19 (Douglas Hay, Peter Linebaugh, John Rule, and Cal Winslow, eds. 1975).

3. Frances Olsen, "The Family and the Market: A Study of Ideology and Legal Reform," 96 *Harvard Law Review* 1497 (1983).

4. Id. at 1501–1507.

5. Id. at 1506–1507, 1509–1513.

6. Catharine MacKinnon, "Feminism, Marxism, Method, and the State: Toward Feminist Jurisprudence," 8 *Signs: Journal of Women in Culture and Society* 635 (1983).

7. Andrea Dworkin, *Right-Wing Women* 21, 26–29, 77–88, 212–213, 231–233 (1983). See also Nadine Taub and Elizabeth Schneider, "Perspectives on Women's Subordination and the Role of Law," in *The Politics of Law* 117 (David Kairys ed. 1982); Michael Freeman, "Violence against Women: Does the Legal System Provide Solutions or Itself Constitute the Problem?" 3 *Canadian Journal of Family Law* 377 (1980).

8. Frances Olsen, note 3 above at 1504–1507.

9. Id. at 1508–1513, 1522–1524.

10. Id. at 1560–1578.

11. It is certainly questionable, for instance, whether we would have the same affirmative-action debate if programs benefiting minority members were not frequently characterized as instances of race-conscious public policies, so that historical arguments associated with past instances of race consciousness, none of which involved advantaging groups suffering from generalized prejudice, would not simply be dismissed out of hand. For another good example of the conservative impact of familiar reifications raised in the Critical literature, see Gary Peller, "The Metaphysics of American Law," 73 *California Law Review* 1151, 1183–1186 (1985) (Henry Hart and Albert Sacks, in the Legal Process materials, typically associate order with nonviolence, and disorder and disobedience with violence, drawing on the class of cases where that association is germane to make arguments about, say, political protest where it is not at all clearly germane).

12. Universalization in reasoning is frequently identified with legality and morality, both in the German Rechtstaat tradition typified by Hayek and in the powerful "neutral principles" Legal Process school, typified by Herbert Wechsler. See, e.g., Friedrich Hayek, *The Road to Serfdom* 72–88 (1944); Friedrich Hayek, *The Constitution of Liberty* 205–233 (1960); Herbert Wechsler, "Toward Neutral Principles of Constitutional Law," 73 *Harvard Law Review* 1 (1959).

More interesting, perhaps, the liberal Kantian philosophical tradition that seemingly *demands* that norms be stated without regard to the particularities of claimants supposedly resonates with the ideal of general law. Since, however, any command to generalize is a command to draw only *relevant* distinctions, the force of the ideal is limited in the absence of a strongly stated sense of which differences between situations are relevant. Nonetheless, I suspect that I can illustrate the distinction between the Kantian universalizer's instincts and my own Critical ones by reference to the work of one of the most prominent neo-Kantians: John Rawls. See John Rawls, *A Theory of Justice* (1971). Rawls's difference principle—that only that degree of inequality that benefits the representative worst-off individual is just—seems to me easily denigrated, either if it is interpreted as a universalized *rule* or if it is believed to have been derived solely from universalistic reason. As a rule, it is subject to any number of familiar objections: for instance, it allows the possibility of trivial gains for the badly off to outweigh large gains for others; it may sacrifice morally pressing claims to have particular needs filled when members of the worst-off class generally have no such needs; it ignores the particular relational position of an actor or observer to a situation in evaluating his ethical conduct. See, for far fuller explications of such problems, R. M. Hare, "Rawls' Theory of Justice," and Frank Michelman, "Constitutional Welfare Rights and a Theory of Justice," both in *Reading Rawls* (Norman Daniels ed. 1975); Bruce Ackerman, *Social Justice in the Liberal State* §59.2 (1982); A. K. Sen, "Rights and Agency," 11 *Philosophy and Public Affairs* 3 (1982). Moreover, conceived of as the principle chosen by disinterested persons acting in their universalistic mode, it is easily critiqued as a factually implausible solution to the problem of maximizing choice under uncertainty. See, e.g., R. M. Hare, "Rawls' Theory of Justice," and Benjamin Barber, "Justifying Justice: Problems of Psychology, Politics, and Measurement in Rawls," both in *Reading Rawls*. Moreover, there are deep reasons to doubt that the "universalized" persons who adopt the difference principle are sufficiently full people to adopt any principles at all. See, e.g., Michael Sandel, *Liberalism and the Limits of Justice* (1982); Ronald Dworkin, "The Original Position," in *Reading Rawls*.

If, though, one reads the difference principle as an astute observation about appropriate distributive predilections in an advanced Western economy in which the rich already have to work hard to come up with things to consume, treat it as an *observation* that a growth in national income is of little policy interest except insofar as it effectively trickles down, it's a perfectly good consideration to keep in mind. The fact that one can readily construct a thought experiment that "falsifies" one's ostensible commitment to the concern (involving great gains to the rich and trivial losses to the poor) without adopting an alternative universalistic commitment (to, say, strict utilitarianism) seems a telling objection only if one believes for some peculiar reason that perfect-fit rules are plausible. Moreover, the idea that we could have a universalized sense of the *appropriateness* of concern for the worst off without situating ourselves explicitly in a context in which we have some idea about how both the relatively privileged and the worst off will be affected concretely by different levels of economic growth seems preposterous to me. It is self-deluding, I think, to try to capture that sense by imagining applying universal principles to different facts (for example, by claiming that one is simply comparing the "utility gains" to the rich in two different regimes) when in fact one's reactions undoubtedly encompass a far more richly textured series of judgments (for example, partial "objective value" judgments that the baubles of the rich are unworthy in complicated ways; ideas that their consumption habits are best unlearned, for they will soon become addictive rather than pleasure enhancing; ideas about the moral quality of communities and the moral choices of individuals in communities that become increasingly inegalitarian after going through egalitarian periods, and so on). Rawls undoubtedly believes that he *derived* the difference principle by reflecting about the conclusions those committed to acceptably abstract moral reasoning would come to; to the extent that it is sensible, I am quite sure that it was derived from observation of the inanity of concerning oneself a great deal with altering the economic lot of America's nonpoor.

13. Douglas Hay, note 2 above at 33–34, 38–39.

14. Id. at 44–45.

15. See Friedrich Hayek, note 12 above.

16. See Peter Gabel and Duncan Kennedy, "Roll Over Beethoven," 36 *Stanford Law Review* 1, 26–41 (1984); Peter Gabel, "The Phenomenology of Rights-Consciousness and the Pact of the Withdrawn Selves," 62 *Texas Law Review* 1563 (1984); Anthony Chase, "The Left on Rights: An Introduction," 62 *Texas Law Review* 1541, 1553–1561 (1984); Michael Davis, "Critical Jurisprudence: An Essay on the Legal Theory of Robert Burt's *Taking Care of Strangers,*" 1981 *Wisconsin Law Review* 419; Duncan Kennedy, "Critical Labor Law Theory: A Comment," 4 *Industrial Relations Law Journal* 503 (1981).

17. Duncan Kennedy, "The Structure of Blackstone's Commentaries," 28 *Buffalo Law Review* 205, 240 (1979).

18. Catharine MacKinnon, "Toward Feminist Jurisprudence," 34 *Stanford Law Review* 703, 705 (1982).

19. William Clune, "Unreasonableness and Alienation in the Continuing Relationship of Welfare State Bureaucracy: From Regulatory Complexity to Economic Democracy," 1985 *Wisconsin Law Review* 707.

20. William Simon, "Visions of Practice," 36 *Stanford Law Review* 469, 489–506 (1984).

21. See, generally, "Symposium: Sexual Harassment," 10 *Capital University Law Review* i (1981); Catharine MacKinnon, *Sexual Harassment of Working Women: A Case Study of Sex Discrimination* (1979).

22. See, particularly, Louis Schwartz, "With Gun and Camera through Darkest CLS-Land," 34 *Stanford Law Review* 413, 457 (1984). See also Philip Johnson, "Do You Sincerely Want to Be Radical?" 36 *Stanford Law Review* 247, 263–264 (1984); Herbert Packer, *The Limits of the Criminal Sanction* 74, 132–134 (1968).

23. See, e.g., Richard Posner, "The Ethical and Political Basis of the Efficiency Norm in Common Law Adjudication," 8 *Hofstra Law Review* 487 (1980).

24. Duncan Kennedy, "Cost-Benefit Analysis of Entitlement Problems: A Critique," 33 *Stanford Law Review* 387, 403 (1981), makes this point rather explicitly.

25. See Richard Posner, note 23 above at 498–499. For a critique, see Mark Kelman, "Trashing," 36 *Stanford Law Review* 293, 295 (1984).

26. Roberto Unger, *Knowledge and Politics* 81–83 (1975).

27. Wesley Hohfeld, "Some Fundamental Legal Conceptions as Applied in Judicial Reasoning," 23 *Yale Law Journal* 16 (1913); Wesley Hohfeld, "Fundamental Legal Conceptions as Applied in Judicial Reasoning," 26 *Yale Law Journal* 710 (1917). For lucid applications see Arthur Corbin, "Jural Relations and Their Classifications," 30 *Yale Law Journal* 226; Walter Wheeler Cook, "Privileges of Labor Unions in the Struggle for Life," 27 *Yale Law Journal* 779 (1918); Ellen Kelman, "American Labor Law and Legal Formalism: How 'Legal Logic' Shaped and Vitiated the Rights of American Workers," 58 *St. John's Law Review* 1 (1983).

28. See, e.g., Richard Epstein, *Takings: Private Property and the Power of Eminent Domain* 318–324 (1986); George Fletcher, *Rethinking Criminal Law* 588–593, 600–606, 611–625 (1978); Eric Mack, "Bad Samaritanism and the Causation of Harm," 9 *Philosophy and Public Affairs* 230 (1980).

29. Compare Frank Michelman, "Welfare Rights in a Constitutional Democracy," 1979 *Washington University Law Quarterly* 659, 680–685 (recognizing the need for nondiadic reasoning), with Frank Michelman, "Foreword: On Protecting the Poor through the Fourteenth Amendment," 83 *Harvard Law Review* 7 (1969); and Frank Michelman, "In Pursuit of Constitutional Welfare Rights: One View of Rawls' Theory of Justice," 121 *University of Pennsylvania Law Review* 692 (1973) (both unable to "legalize" the Rawlsian difference principle adequately because of problems of specifying duty holder). Even in the 1979 piece (at 659, 685), the Hohfeldian trap makes Michelman seemingly despair that a court could overrule a legislature that flatly abolished a redistributive tax program. Not all liberal legal theorists have had the difficulties Michelman had overcoming traditional libertarian diadic thought. See, for instance, Charles Fried, *Right and Wrong* 128–130 (1978), which offers arguments not enormously distinct from those I make in the text against opposing "positive rights" because no correlative duty holder clearly exists.

30. See, e.g., Richard Epstein, note 28 above at 5, 11, specifically disclaiming reliance on divine authority.

31. Id. at 335.

32. Id. at 319. See also Bruce Russell, "On the Relative Strictness of Positive and Negative Duties," in *Killing and Letting Die* 215 (Bonnie Steinbock ed. 1980).

33. See, e.g., Charles Fried, note 29 above at 37–38. Note, "The Failure to Rescue: A Comparative Study," 52 *Columbia Law Review* 631, 641–642 (1952); H. D. Minor, "Moral Obligation as a Basis of Liability," 9 *Virginia Law Review* 421 (1923); Francis Bohlen, "The Moral Duty to Aid Others as a Basis of Tort Liability," 56 *University of Pennsylvania Law Review* 217 (1908). See also the discussion in Robert Hale, "Prima Facie Torts, Combination, and Non-Feasance," 46 *Columbia Law Review* 196, 214–215 (1946).

34. See, e.g., George Fletcher, note 28 above at 604–606; T. B. Macauley, *A Penal Code Prepared by the Indian Law Commissioners* note M 53–56 (1837).

35. William Simon, "Rights and Redistribution in the Welfare System," 38 *Stanford Law Review* 1431 (1986).

36. Charles Reich, "The New Property," 73 *Yale Law Journal* 733 (1964).

37. Robin West, "Authority, Autonomy, and Choice: The Role of Con-

sent in the Moral and Political Visions of Franz Kafka and Richard Posner," 99 *Harvard Law Review* 384 (1985).

38. Richard Posner, "The Ethical Significance of Free Choice: A Reply to Professor West," 99 *Harvard Law Review* 1431 (1986).

39. Id. at 1431.

40. Id. at 1446–1447.

41. Id. at 1439–1440 (emphasis added).

42. See, generally, Chapter 3 for a discussion of the contradiction between intentionalism and determinism. Posner's argument is obviously an instance of the denial of contradiction in discourse, here through recourse to false vacuum boundaries. I discuss the denial of contradiction in the text accompanying notes 57–72 below.

43. It might be worthwhile to return to the example of marital rape here as well. In the synthetic individualist tradition, we may learn to deny that unwanted sex is a problem unless we can conceive of giving particular victims rightlike claims (in tort, or as implicit prosecutor-plaintiffs in a criminal case) against particular duty holders (men who have a duty not to induce women to engage in unwanted sex). There may be reasons not to treat all men who induce unwanted sex as violating an affirmative duty, particularly once one recognizes that unwanted sex may occur in the absence of explicit force; but these reasons say nothing about whether we should, collectively, try to educate men about the pain they cause in disregarding women's actual sexual desires or try to train women to be more verbally or physically assertive. A subsidy for a women's self-defense course may, for instance, help remedy a real problem; it does not alter the rights-duties relationship between particular identifiable parties (and it does not create a hypothetical individual plaintiff and defendant in a lawsuit).

44. Douglas Hay, note 2 above at 18–24, 32–33, 40–44.

45. Catharine MacKinnon, note 6 above at 638–639, 643–644. See also Catharine MacKinnon, "Feminism, Marxism, Method, and the State: An Agenda for Theory," 7 *Signs: Journal of Women in Culture and Society* 515 (1982); Andrea Dworkin, note 7 above at 77–80, 85–87.

46. Catharine MacKinnon, note 6 above at 647–651. The problem of marital rape is hardly marginal either: even using fairly restrictive legal definitions of rape, in which women accede to sexual advances as a result of the immediate presence of overwhelming force, 14 percent of married women have been raped. See Diana Russell, *Rape in Marriage* (1982). Obviously, if we believe that some wives accede because they fear male violence more generally, or because they have been beaten in a not explicitly sexual context before and fear what would occur if there were a direct confrontation over sex, or accede because of illegitimate but nonviolent pressure, we recognize that the 14 percent figure is almost certainly a very restricted, conservative one.

47. Staughton Lynd, "Investment Decisions and the Quid Pro Quo Myth," 29 *Case Western Reserve Law Review* 396 (1979).

48. Mark Kelman, "Interpretive Construction in the Substantive Criminal Law," 33 *Stanford Law Review* 591 (1981).

49. Id. at 618–620.

50. Id. at 603–605.

51. Id. at 605–611. See also, Mark Kelman, "Strict Liability," in 4 *Encyclopedia of Crime and Criminal Justice* 1516 (Sanford Kadish ed. 1983).

52. Mark Kelman, note 48 above at 620–624.

53. Wayne Lafave and Austin Scott, *Handbook on Criminal Law* 443 (1972).

54. Mark Kelman, note 48 above at 633–635.

55. Regina v. Cunningham, [1957] 2 Q.B. 396, 401.

56. Duncan Kennedy, note 17 above at 205, 214–217, 258–261 (1979).

57. This point was initially made in a powerful form within the CLS literature in Petèr Gabel, book review, 91 *Harvard Law Review* 302 (1977) (reviewing R. Dworkin, *Taking Rights Seriously*).

58. Melvin Eisenberg, "The Bargain Principle and Its Limits," 95 *Harvard Law Review* 741, 755, 782–785 (1982).

59. See Mark Kelman, note 25 above at 315–318; Steven Salop and Bruce Stiglitz, "Bargains and Ripoffs: A Model of Monopolistically Competitive Price Dispersion," 44 *Review of Economic Studies* 493 (1977).

60. Guido Calabresi and Douglas Melamed, "Property Rules, Liability Rules, and Inalienability: One View of the Cathedral," 85 *Harvard Law Review* 1089, 1113 (1972).

61. See R. M. Hare, "Ethical Theory and Utilitarianism," in *Utilitarianism and Beyond* 23, 30 (Amartaya Sen and Bernard Williams eds. 1982), and John Harsanyi, "Morality and the Theory of Rational Behavior," in *Utilitarianism and Beyond* 39, 56.

62. For a brief discussion of goods addiction, see Mark Kelman, "Choice and Utility," 1979 *Wisconsin Law Review* 769, 772–773.

63. Duncan Kennedy, "The Political Significance of the Structure of the Law School Curriculum," 14 *Seton Hall Law Review* 1 (1983).

64. See Lon Fuller and Melvin Eisenberg, *Basic Contract Law* (4th ed. 1981).

65. See, e.g., D. J. Galligan, "Guidelines and Just Deserts: A Critique of Recent Trends in Sentencing Reform," 1981 *Criminal Law Review* 297; Caleb Foote, "Deceptive Determinate Sentencing," in National Institute of Law Enforcement and Criminal Justice, *Determinate Sentencing: Reform or Regression* 133 (1978).

66. See, e.g., Richard Stewart, "The Discontents of Legalism: Interest Group Regulation in Administrative Regulation," 1985 *Wisconsin Law Review* 655.

67. See, especially, Philip Johnson, "Strict Liability," in 4 *Encyclopedia of Crime and Justice* 1519 (S. Kadish ed. 1983), which purportedly replies to my piece on strict liability without making any substantive comments on the problems of a negligence standard.

68. Richard Epstein, "A Theory of Strict Liability," 2 *Journal of Legal Studies* 151 (1973).

69. See discussion in Mark Kelman, note 48 above at 618–620, 649–651.

70. As usual, one can rely on Louis Schwartz to express what might otherwise be thought to be the "straw man's" position. His provocative notion that CLS, at convention, ought to debate, once and for all, whether "the rule

of law be abandoned" relies on just this sort of elementary school civics class understanding of legality. See Louis Schwartz, "With Gun and Camera through Darkest CLS-Land," 36 *Stanford Law Review* 413, 454 (1984).

71. See, e.g., Samuel Gross and Robert Mauro, "Patterns of Death," 37 *Stanford Law Review* 27, 66–67 (1984); Michael Radelet, "Racial Characteristics and the Imposition of the Death Penalty," 46 *American Sociological Review* 918 (1981); Joseph Jacoby and Raymond Paternoster, "Sentencing Disparity and Jury Packing: Further Challenges to the Death Penalty," 73 *Journal of Criminal Law and Criminology* 379 (1982). By contrast, some believe that the defendant's race matters in determining capital sentencing to a reasonably significant extent. See William Bowers and Glenn Pierce, "Arbitrariness and Discrimination under Post-Furman Capital Statutes," 26 *Crime and Delinquency* 563 (1980).

72. See, generally, William Simon, "Legality, Bureaucracy, and Class in the Welfare System," 92 *Yale Law Journal* 1198 (1983).

Index

Ackerman, Bruce, 14, 118, 182
Andrews, William, 101

Balbus, Isaac, 251
Bickel, Alexander, 190, 195
Blackstone, William, 231, 236, 237, 259, 275
Bobbitt, Philip, 118
Brenner, Robert, 253
Brest, Paul, 14, 203, 205, 206, 213–217, 219–221

Calabresi, Guido, 117, 118, 291
Carrington, Paul, 8–9
Causation, 24, 106–107, 175–176
Choper, Jesse, 190, 195, 196, 197, 247
Clune, William, 276
Coase Theorem, 67–69, 145–149, 160, 293
Coleman, Jules, 149
Commons, tragedy of, 165–167
Conference on Critical Legal Studies, 1, 2, 8–9, 297n1, 298–299n12
Constitutional law, 192, 203, 213–223, 229, 230, 234–235, 249–250, 350n11
Contract law, 104–106, 237–240, 246, 259, 260, 291, 292; and rules/standards analysis, 18–25, 233; duress and fraud, 20–25, 103–104, 178–180; and subjectivity of values, 76–78; state role, 103–109; redistribution of wealth through shifts in rules, 176–185; evolution from status relationships, 222–224, 235–236, 244
Criminal law, 12, 86, 286–288, 293; and rules/standards analysis, 25–32, 51–52, 231–232, 287; attempts, 26–27, 70–71,

74, 98–99, 288, 308–309n56, 316n30; conspiracy, 27; death penalty, 27–28, 41, 46–47, 49–50, 99, 217–218, 250, 270–271, 273–274, 285; strict liability, 28–29, 94–95, 287–288; self-defense, 29; mistakes, 29–31; rape, 30–31, 68–69, 75, 98–99, 276–277, 285, 354nn43, 46; theories of punishment, 88–99; defendant culpability, 90, 91, 318n12, 319n20; voluntary acts, 92–93, 97–98, 287; negligent crimes, 95, 319n26

Dahl, Robert, 191
Dalton, Clare, 25, 104, 105
Dawson, John, 104
Democratic theory, 189–199
Distribution of wealth, 155–161, 176–185, 259–260, 263, 279–282, 350n12
Douglas, Justice William, 93–94
Dworkin, Andrea, 285
Dworkin, Ronald, 202

Efficiency, 120–122, 124, 126, 141–150, 159, 172, 229, 282–284, 315n21, 327n87; claims for private property, 153–167; claims for competitive markets, 167–171; claims for tort rules, 171–176
Eisenberg, Melvin, 20–21, 291, 292
Ellickson, Robert, 109, 265
Ely, John, 189–191, 194–197, 203, 205, 228, 247
Epstein, Richard, 24, 192, 204, 251, 253, 293

Federalism, 6, 187, 188–190, 206–212, 235
Feinberg, Joel, 94